Capital Markets and Investments

Essential Insights and Concepts for Professionals

Siddhartha G. Dastidar

First Edition

Reading Light Publication
New York

First Edition

Copyright © 2017 by Siddhartha Ghosh Dastidar

Book/ Author Website: www.columbia.edu/~sgd2002

All rights reserved. This book or any portion thereof may not be reproduced or used in any manner whatsoever without the express written permission of the publisher, except for the use of brief quotations (not exceeding 50 words) in a book review or scholarly journal.

Although the author and publisher have made efforts to ensure that the information in this book was correct at press time, the author and publisher do not assume and hereby disclaim any liability to any party for any loss, damage, or disruption caused by errors or omissions, whether such errors or omissions result from negligence, accident, or any other cause.

First Printed in the United States of America in 2017

Paperback ISBN 978-0-9988145-0-6
Hardcover ISBN 978-0-9988145-1-3

Library of Congress Control Number: 2017913083

Reading Light Publications, New York
www.readinglightpubs.wordpress.com

Special discounts are available on quantity purchases by corporations, associations, educators, and others. For details, contact the author/publisher at the book website, or email at sid.readinglightpubs[AT]gmail.com.

To my *family* for support,
To my *friends* for encouragement,
To my *teachers* and generations of *authors* and websites for sharing their knowledge,
To my *professional colleagues* for emphasizing what matters in the real world,
To my *students* for refining my knowledge and keeping me on my toes
And
To the *readers* who will read, comment on and improve this effort

About the Author

Siddhartha G. Dastidar

Dr. Siddhartha Ghosh Dastidar is an Associate Professor (adjunct) at Columbia University, and has taught at the Graduate School of Business and the Department of Industrial Engineering & Operations Research. He teaches courses on capital markets and investments to full-time graduate and undergraduate students, and also in the executive education program.

Sid has nearly two decades of experience in the financial services industry, both buy-side and sell-side, across asset classes and regions. As part of the Quantitative Portfolio Strategy team at Lehman Brothers and Barclays Capital in New York, he has advised large institutional clients on portfolio construction, management and risk budgeting issues. He was also the chief US equity derivatives strategist at Newedge, part of Société Générale. He is currently a risk manager in Brigade Capital, a USD18 billion credit alternatives asset manager, where he has been responsible for coming up with portfolio construction, risk and quantitative frameworks. He has also worked in emerging market private equity for three years.

Sid received a Ph.D. in Finance & Economics from Columbia Business School in New York, a MBA from Indian Institute of Management Ahmedabad and an undergraduate degree in economics from Presidency College Kolkata (both in India). He holds the CFA charter and has published in top journals such as the Journal of Financial Economics and the Journal of Portfolio Management. He has presented at the National Bureau of Economic Research in Boston and at top universities globally. He is a member of the Economic Club of New York.

Acknowledgements

I would like to thank everyone involved in putting this together- family, colleagues and friends. The content is essentially a culmination of teaching notes over the last few years from my class on Global Capital Markets at the IEOR department Columbia University and at Columbia Business School. Most of the notes are borrowed from the Capital Markets & Investments class at the finance department at Columbia Business School, where I obtained my Ph.D. from and subsequently taught at. During my Ph.D., I have been either a student or a teaching assistant in many classes on related topics at Columbia; I adapted some of the material and examples from those classes too.

I have often referred to several textbooks during my teaching; some of the content here is influenced by/borrowed from those books. These books have been listed among the references at the end of every chapter; most readers who need more information and do not want to scour the Internet can refer to these authoritative sources.

Being self-published, I have been forced to be a jack-of-many-trades. But, participants at many online forums, such at Lulu.com and Textbook & Authors Association have helped me navigate this landscape.

My wife Sunanda has patiently tolerated my whims, and championed the publishing process. My one-year old son Shreyan takes credit for choosing the cover design and colors (and for a few typos). My parents and father-in-law (who know very little finance) read the first draft and gave me the first set of comments on readability and flow.

Several colleagues, instructors and friends have offered constructive suggestions and painstaking feedback, which helped make this book better. I am extremely grateful to their generosity, and their interest in wholeheartedly supporting this project. Some names that come to mind are Charles Jones, Garud Iyengar, David Weisbrod, Steven Kass, Bruce Phelps, Adam Krause, Michelle Behrend, Peeyush Misra, Thomas Philips, Darwin Choi, Fabio Moneta, Mikhail Chernov, John Kiff, Aaditya Iyer, Robert Whitelaw, Ranadeb Chaudhuri, Adri Guha, Ajit Agrawal, Aziz Lookman, Eugene Gaysinskiy, Dong Luo, Emilia Simeonova, Martin Lee, Jon Hilsenrath, Vidya Atal, Nandu Nayar, Andreas Stathopolous, Ravi Mattu, Emanuel Derman, Vikrant Vig, Binu Balachandran, Divya Anantharaman, Margarita Tsoutsoura, Andrew Dubinsky, Brijesh Gulati, Ruslan Bibkov, Philippe Mueller, Paul Tetlock, Michael Johannes, Xing Huang, Hayong Yun, Rosanna Pezzo-Brizio, Kenneth Wilson, Sumit Roy, Seth Blackman, Ramon Verastegui, Tarun Gupta, Madhur Ambastha, Shivam Ghosh, Glenn Hubbard, Rob Lefkowitz, Darshan Bansal, Mitch Rosen, Justin Pauley, Susanta Basu, Andrew Clerico, Zeeshan Arif, Jatin Bindal, Stephen Isaac, Bill Falloon, Mukul Chhabra and Joseph Stiglitz. I am also grateful to the staff at IEX, especially Sara Forster and Dan Aisen, for providing their input.

Finally, I would like to thank my employer Brigade Capital for supporting this project.

Reader Comments

Dastidar has put together a concise, very readable book covering the essentials of capital markets and investments. It nicely covers the big three – fixed income, equities, and options – at a mathematical level that is typically just short of using calculus. But what really stands out is the very current discussion of the institutional mechanics behind the markets. Automated trading markets and high-frequency traders get more than a passing mention, and Dastidar details the process of offering new securities and the role of sell-side investment banks. Well worth adding to your investments bookshelf!

- **Charles M. Jones, *Robert W. Lear Professor of Finance and Economics Chair, Finance Sub-division, Columbia Business School, New York***

This concise book provides a wide perspective on capital markets ranging from asset pricing, and the anatomy of buy and sell side firms, to financial statements and macro-economics. It is ideal for anyone needing a rapid introduction or re-introduction to finance and financial institutions -- students transitioning into a graduate program in financial engineering, or technologist exploring opportunities, or even finance professional transitioning areas.

- **Garud N. Iyengar, *Chair and Professor, Department of Industrial Engineering and Operations Research, Columbia University, New York***

An excellent survey of financial markets, explaining in concise language everything from the different asset classes to fixed income and equity markets and portfolio theory. A useful and very practical orientation for finance professionals and students alike.

- **David Weisbrod, *former CEO of LCH Clearnet LLC (one of the world's largest clearinghouses) and Vice Chairman of JPMorgan, New York***

Finally, a clear and concise book that uniquely marries sound theoretical constructs with close-up practical insights... an excellent body of knowledge for both students of finance and practitioners in the asset management industry.

- **Adri Guha, *Chief Investment Officer, Advanced Portfolio Management (institutional fund-of-funds/ advisory services)***

Siddhartha does an excellent job of mixing finance concepts with real life examples, thus helping build a good foundation.

- **Ajit Agrawal, *Managing Director, Investment Research, UBS Securities LLC***

This manuscript is an excellent supplement to the existing textbooks about Investments. It distinguishes itself by concise introduction of the key financial instruments and tools for analyzing them. Big-picture description of the financial system and the role of financial intermediaries is an invaluable feature.

- **Mikhail Chernov, *Professor of Finance, Anderson School of Management, UCLA***

This book is written with the student in mind. With clear language and sharp focus on essentials, it feels like learning from a personal tutor.

- **Hayong Yun, *Associate Professor of Finance, Eli Broad College of Business, Michigan State University***

Essential reading for anyone looking for a comprehensive introduction to investment management. This book makes quantitative finance accessible by succinctly blending various key aspects of investment management while also describing the pricing and mechanics of common financial instruments and important metrics and models most relevant in finance. Qualitative investors can use it to incorporate quantitative tools into their investment process, and it serves as a helpful refresher for experienced quantitative investors. The annexures contain relevant background including an overview of concepts in accounting, economics and statistics.

- **Tarun Gupta, Ph.D.,** *Managing Director at AQR Capital Management*

Dastidar's book provides a concise, readable and up-to-date coverage of key capital markets topics. It's perfect for introductory finance classes, and practitioners looking for quick refreshers.

- **John Kiff,** *Senior Financial Sector Expert, International Monetary Fund*

Capital Markets and Investments provides a comprehensive review of today's capital markets, financial industry structure and the latest theories underlying asset pricing and portfolio construction. Professor Dastidar, based on his experience in both industry and academia, clearly and succinctly explains important concepts without glossing over those essential details that every aspiring market professional must know. The book's logical and topical format lends itself to being used as a handy desk reference.

- **Bruce D. Phelps,** *Managing Director (Research), Barclays Capital*

Masterful rendering of a complex subject into an easily digested elixir of finance; students will love the rarely-seen practical perspective that Dastidar brings to the topics.

- **Nandu Nayar,** *Hans J. Baer Chair in International Finance and Chair of the Perella Department of Finance, Lehigh University, PA*

The textbook is like a bible for me.

- **Anonymous Student, Columbia University, New York**

Table of Contents

1. **THE FINANCIAL SYSTEM – INTRODUCTION** 16
   - **What is the Financial System? Why does it exist?** 16
   - **Key Players in the Financial System** 17
   - **Specialization within the financial system** 18
   - **Principles of pricing financial instruments** 19
   - **Are Financial Markets "Efficient"?** 22
     - Efficient Market Hypothesis 22
     - Counterclaims to Market Efficiency 23
   - **References** 25

2. **MAJOR ASSET CLASSES AND MARKETS** 26
   - **Major types of instruments** 26
     - Bonds (Fixed Income) 27
     - Loans 27
     - Stocks (Equities) 27
     - Hybrid Instruments 28
     - Derivatives/ Synthetic Instruments 28
   - **Major asset classes** 30
     - Fixed Income 30
     - Equities 34
     - Commodities 34
     - Currencies 34
     - Emerging Markets 35
   - **Connections between different markets** 35

3. **THE ANATOMY OF THE SELL SIDE** 36
   - **Structure of a Bulge Bracket Sell-side Firm** 36
     - Investment Banking Division 36
     - Capital Markets 37
     - Prime Brokerage 40
     - Support Functions 41
   - **Basic Market Microstructure** 42
     - How do instruments trade? 42
     - Exchange-Traded Markets 42
     - Over-the-Counter (OTC) Markets 44

  Trade Date and Settlement Date 46

Further thoughts 47

4. OVERVIEW OF BUY SIDE FIRMS 49

What do buy-side firms do? 49

Investment Styles 50

Investment Product Offerings 51
  Mutual Funds 52
  Exchange Traded Funds (ETFs) 52
  Alternative Investments 53
  Liquid Alts 55
  Separately Managed Accounts 55
  High-Frequency Algorithmic Trading Products 55
  Sell-side Index Swaps 55

Capital Owners 56
  Retail Investors 56
  Institutional allocators 57

Intermediation – Consultants, OCIO, Fund of Funds 58
  Process of picking an institutional manager 59

Working at a buy-side firm 59

5. INDICES, BENCHMARKING, RISK MODELS AND PERFORMANCE EVALUATION 62

Indices – What are they? Why do we need them? 62
  Criteria for a Good Index 62
  Index Rebalancing 63
  Examples of Popular Indices 63

Efficiency of index investing 63

Benchmark Indices vs Strategy Indices 64

Index Mechanics and Terminology 65

Measuring Risk – Risk Models 67
  Risk definition 67
  Risk factors – Factor-based Risk Models 67
  Risk Measures 69
  Role of Risk Models in Portfolio Construction 69

Performance Evaluation 70
  Performance Evaluation Measures 71
  Performance Attribution 71

| Portfolio Management Summary | 73 |
| References | 73 |

6. TOPICAL ISSUES IN CAPITAL MARKETS ... 74

Market Microstructure	74
Responsible Investing	75
Central Bank Policy	76
Regulation	77
FinTech	79
Big Data in Investment Management	79
Quantitative Investing	82
Factor-based investing	82
Crowdfunding	83
Marketplace Lending	83
Robo-advisors	83
Blockchaining	83
Payment Mechanisms and Cryptocurrencies	83
Compliance Software	84
References	85

7. INTRODUCTION TO BONDS – TREASURY PRICING AND INSTITUTIONAL DETAILS ... 87

Treasuries - The Basic Idea	87
What is a bond?	88
Our first example – a simple bond and its yield	88
U.S. Treasury Auction Mechanics ***	91
When-issued Market	92
Financing Treasury Purchases – the Repo Market ***	93
Microstructure of the US Treasury Market ***	94
Treasury quoting convention	94
Treasury Trading and Execution	94
The Simple Example Re-visited – Spot Curve and Accrued Interest	95
Different discount rates for different payment dates – the spot curve	95
Bootstrapping – from bond prices/ yields to spot rates	97
Bond prices on non-coupon payment dates – Accrued Interest	98
Forward curves	100
Expected patterns in bond price movements	101

Pull to par 101

Rolling down the yield curve 102

Summary 103

References 103

8. FACTORS AFFECTING TREASURY BOND PRICES 104

Reviewing Bond Price-Yield Relationship 104

Price-yield graph 104

Choosing between bonds 105

Quantifying Interest Rate Risk in Treasuries 107

Macaulay Duration – How long is a bond? 108

Price Sensitivity (Risk) of Bonds – Modified Duration 109

Price Sensitivity (Risk) of Bonds – DV01 109

Interest Rate Risk of Portfolios of Treasury bonds 111

Hedging Interest rate risk – Applications of Duration 112

Immunization 112

Yield curve movements – parallel versus non-parallel movements 113

Convexity 114

Further comments 116

References 116

9. FURTHER TOPICS IN INTEREST RATE MARKETS 118

Why do yields / interest rates move? 118

Central Bank Policy 118

Business Cycle 119

Economic Variables and News Releases 119

Inflation Expectations 120

Term Structure of Interest Rates – Theories of the Shapes of yield curve 120

Interest rate volatility and Interest Rate Models* 121

Interest Rate Volatility 121

Interest Rate Models 122

Investing in Treasury Markets - Expressing views using Treasuries * 122

Leverage 123

Carry Trades 123

Steepeners and Flatteners 123

Relative Value Trades 124

Other Instruments Based on the Risk-Free Rate* 124

Forward Rate Agreements	124
Treasury Futures	124
TIPS (Treasury Inflation Protected Securities)	127

LIBOR-based instruments **128**
What is LIBOR?	128
EuroDollar Futures	128
Interest Rate Swaps	129
ETFs related to Treasury Markets	131
Options on the above securities	132

Topical issues in the Treasury market **132**

Conclusion **134**

References **134**

10. OTHER FIXED INCOME MARKETS 135

US Mortgages **136**
Prepayments	137
The TBA Market	138
Valuing MBS	139
Mortgage Market Liquidity	140

Municipal Bonds **141**
Municipal Bond Classifications	141
High-Yield Munis	142
Primary and Secondary Muni Markets	142

Corporate Credit **143**
Capital Structure	143
Bankruptcy	144
Quantifying Default Risk	145
Credit Rating Agencies	145
Important Elements of Credit Analysis	146
Credit Instruments	147
Market Dynamics and Liquidity	151
Credit Analytics	153
Quantitative Credit	154
Investing in Credit	155

Securitization **157**
Securitization Overview and Motivations	157
Why does Securitization Work?	159
Different Types of Securitization Structures***	160

Concluding Comments on Fixed Income **166**

References **166**

11. EQUITIES - VALUATION 168

What is equity? **168**

Equities and the Capital Structure –Role of Leverage for a Corporation **168**

Capital structure theories - Tax Benefit of Debt **170**

Corporate Governance **170**

Valuing Equities **171**
    Setting the Stage 171
    Equity Valuation Models 172

Equity Valuation in Real Life **176**
    Role of Macro Analysis in Equity Valuation 176
    Fundamental versus Quantitative Investing 177
    Value Investing 178
    Non-traditional data sources 178
    Role of Algorithms 179
    Model Robustness 179
    Thematic Investing 179
    Shorting Equities 180

Equity Instruments **180**
    Forwards 181
    Futures 182

Equities as an Asset Class - Microstructure of Equities **183**
    Current Status 186

References **187**

12. PORTFOLIO THEORY, ASSET ALLOCATION AND FACTOR MODELS 188

Expected Return and Risk **188**

Investors' Risk-Return Tradeoffs – Utility Function and Indifference Curves **188**

Diversification – The Core Ideas **189**

Building on Diversification – Portfolio Theory and Efficient Frontiers **192**
    Case 1: Optimal Portfolio with One Risky Asset and the Risk Free Asset 192
    Case 2: Optimal Portfolio with Multiple Risky Assets and One Risk-Free Asset 195
    When does adding a new security improve a portfolio's risk characteristics? 197
    Market Frictions - Effect on the Optimal Portfolio 198

Capital Asset Pricing Model (CAPM) **199**
    Assumptions of the CAPM 199

Relevance of the CAPM 199
Interpreting the CAPM.. 199
Estimating Betas (and Alphas) in the CAPM 200

Introduction to Factor Models... 202
Arbitrage Pricing Theory Overview 202
Multi-Factor Models 203

Risk Management in Equity Portfolios 205

Portfolio Construction Techniques 207
Markowitz Mean-Variance Optimization 208
Black-Litterman Model 208
Risk Parity 209

References 209

13. INTRODUCTION TO OPTIONS 211

What is an Option? Basic Terminology 211

Some Simple Examples – Call and Put options 212

Options trading - Mechanics 213

Using Options in Trade Construction 214
Directional trades with Call and Put options 214
Volatility Trades with Straddles and Strangles 215
Covered call 216
Protective Puts.. 216
Call spread, Put spread, Calendar spread 217

Put-call parity 217

Exotic Options 218

References 219

14. OPTIONS VALUATION 220

Option Pricing Overview.. 220

Modeling Stock Prices – a Binomial Model 220
Call Option - Pricing mechanics 221
Further details 223
Multi-period models 226
.American Options 227

Black Scholes Formula 229
Graph of Call Option Prices before Expiration – some more Greeks... 230
Implied Volatility and Realized Volatility 232

    Drawbacks of Black-Scholes - Modifications 233

    Relevance of the Imperfect Black Scholes Formula 234

Volatility-based option trades **234**

    VIX 235

Summary **237**

References **237**

ANNEXURES **238**

I.   RETURN - CONCEPTS AND CALCULATIONS **239**

Types of return – simple, compound **239**

    Compounding single period returns 239

    Log-normal prices and normal returns 240

Time value of money **240**

Net Present Value **241**

Internal Rate of Return (IRR) **242**

    More details on the IRR methodology 243

II.   INTRODUCTION TO FINANCIAL STATEMENTS – CONCEPT OF CAPITAL STRUCTURE **244**

Balance Sheet **244**

    Capital Structure 245

Income Statement **246**

Cash Flow Statement **247**

Footnotes and disclosures **248**

Using the information in the Financial Statements **249**

    Metrics 249

    Modeling, Forecasting 249

    Ratio Analysis 249

    Management views 249

III.   MACROECONOMICS PRIMER **250**

What is Macroeconomics? **250**

Measuring Output (GDP) Growth **251**

    The Expenditure Approach to GDP– Drivers of Aggregate Demand 251

    Drawbacks of GDP as a Measure of Economic Activity 252

Macroeconomic Theory and Models **252**

Basic Premises of Economic Modeling 252
A Simple Aggregate Demand-based Macroeconomic Model of the Goods Market 254
Adding Interest Rates, Money and Financial Assets to this model 256
General Equilibrium, Full-Employment and Price Level Adjustments 258
The Role of Money and the Banking System 258
Modeling Summary 259
Beyond the Static Macro Models 260
The Bridgewater (Ray Dalio) Approach to Macroeconomics 261

Currency Markets 262

Practical Macroeconomic Considerations for Finance Professionals 263

Major US Macroeconomic Data Series 264
Data on Overall Economy – Employment and GDP 264
Consumer Data 265
Manufacturing/ Services Data 266
Housing Data 266
Federal Reserve Reports 267
Inflation 267

References 268

IV. BASIC STATISTICS AND DATA ANALYSIS 269

Summarizing Data 270
Central Tendency – Mean, Median and Mode 270
Dispersion – Standard Deviation 271

Probability – Distribution Types 272
Normal Distribution 273
Drawing inferences about the population from sample statistics 274

Some More Summary Statistics 275

Further Comments on Describing Data 276

Multi-variate Analysis 276
Regressions 277

V. INTRODUCTION TO THE BLOOMBERG SOFTWARE/ TERMINAL 281

Basic Orientation 281

Getting Started 282

Functions 282

Excel integration – FLDS, BDP, BDH, BDS, overrides, XLTP 283

About this Book

I have intentionally placed this section after the Table of Contents, because I hope readers will spend a few minutes reading this.

Who is this book for?

This book is meant to help practitioners and students understand the essentials of capital markets, *quickly*. It requires no specific prerequisites, except possibly some fluency in high school/ undergraduate math. Basic information on financial statements and statistics are included in self-contained annexures at the end. The annexures can help bridge any gaps in background that readers may have to understand the content in the body of the book thoroughly and build on it.

Over the years, more people need a rapid orientation in finance:

- Finance professionals need a quick refresher on a market that they do not deal with regularly.
- Professionals with qualifications in other disciplines continue to look to switch careers into finance.
- Students with prior background in another discipline often join a Masters degree program, specializing in finance (MBA, quantitative finance, etc.)
- Advanced undergraduate students want to decide whether finance is right for them.
- Mid-career professionals in another industry, serving financial services clients, need to understand the basics of financial markets better. For example, Fintech professionals with a technology background are looking to connect more with mainstream finance companies.
- Or, it may be a curious individual who simply wants to understand the financial periodicals better, and possibly make more sensible investment decisions!

Practitioners currently employed in the finance profession will find this book useful in refreshing basic concepts in a part of the market they do not deal with regularly. Students of finance will find the book useful in teaching them preliminary/ intermediate ideas, putting facts in context and "connecting the dots".

Because of the book's introductory nature, *it is heavy on principles, mechanics, details, etc. and light on perspective*. This book gives readers the tools to formulate opinions and evaluate the opinions of others, but it does not offer opinions on a platter. The best way to form opinions on the market is to read and assess commonly offered opinions, and assimilate them yourself. This book helps, but the hard work has to be yours.

What makes this book different?

This book scratches the surface of several potentially interesting areas within finance, allowing the reader an informed choice regarding which topics to go deeper. I would recommend most students read this book in its entirety (even if they only care about a few topics) as I consider most of this information essential knowledge for aspiring finance professionals. The first section, in particular, describes the operations of large financial organizations; this is less relevant for finance professionals but will help beginner students (even in interviews!).

As the emphasis is on quick learning, *the book aims to be concise, at the cost of being cryptic* at times. The book avoids detailed explanations and examples of concepts, expecting readers to look that up elsewhere if necessary (many people may not need it), once they have an idea what to look for. At the same time, the book delves into institutional detail not commonly found in textbooks, instead of being merely conceptual, because these details often drive the market dynamics. This book is heavy on jargon, as the biggest hurdles in finance are not the concepts but the vocabulary. Because of the emphasis on brevity, most concepts are introduced but not explained comprehensively.

I wrote this book because I wanted an inexpensive book to introduce motivated readers without a prior background quickly (in a one-semester course for students) to the essential elements of capital markets, while not skipping important (albeit dry) practical details. Finance (and most other fields, from my experience) is much more about gory details than lofty ideas, a perspective lost in most introductory books. Market plumbing matters a lot!

This book will be regularly updated, as the industry is in a state of constant flux. A necessary step in keeping the price low was to publish to book personally, without a large publisher. Hopefully, the content and price more than makes up for the lack of "features" and look-and-feel.

How, practically, to use the book

Readers need to be active participants in the reading and learning process. By itself, the book is unlikely to teach much, because it is cryptic and does not reinforce concepts (a fallout of brevity). This book will especially help participants get a quick overview of a topic before diving deep into it (using some other source). Alternatively, it will help synthesize concepts and reinforce the broad idea after having studied the painstaking details elsewhere.

So, introductory readers would do well to:

- Read unfamiliar material slowly and with deliberation – many sentences are dense and introduce multiple concepts. Re-read; subsequent readings will get easier.

- Take copious notes in the book or elsewhere (and jot down questions for later clarification) while reading the book.

- Have access to the Internet or other references (most concepts are common and easy to find examples and information on) to get more details on any topic that the student finds interesting or relevant. Many topics which the book covers in a sentence or a paragraph need a book to do justice, but that would defeat the objective of being concise and quick, and may be of marginal importance to many readers (and of primary importance to others).

- The index is detailed. If a term is unfamiliar, please consider looking it up at the back to check for another section of the book that explains it in more detail.

- The reference section at the end of every chapter have lists of sources with more details; this may be easier for readers who do not want to search the Internet continually for supplementary information.

Organization and Formatting

Most of the information in the different sections of the book – Institutional Overview, Bond Markets, Equity Markets, Options Markets and Annexures – is independent. I would suggest instructors (and students) sequence the sections whichever order they please, and refer liberally to the relevant Annexures for background detail. There are a few sections on institutional detail in most chapters; this can be skipped in an introductory class, or a first reading. The first section on Institutional Overview can also be treated like a (very large) annexure; while advanced readers can skip it and use it as a reference, introductory readers would do well to go through that material, to understand the building blocks.

I use the male pronoun "he" almost exclusively; I'm not biased against women capital markets professionals, but it's just easier to use one pronoun.

Within a chapter, the headers are organized in the following manner:

SECTION HEADING

Sub-Section Heading

Topic Heading within Sub-Section

Some words in the text are *italicized*, either for *emphasis* or to indicate (the first few times) that it is *financial market terminology*. They mean something precise and are used in a specific context, and may (or may not) be discussed in a later section in the book. Internet searches (or a different part of the book, navigated with the index) can help here to understand the concept better. Sometimes, words are in "quotes", when the meaning is markedly different from regular usage. *Keywords*, often discussed in nearby pages, are highlighted and italicized. Of course, the headings will also contain some keywords, which we will not format distinctively.

This book has a significant amount of material that can be skipped on a first reading or treated like the Appendix. Chapters 3, 4, 5, 6 and 10 are totally optional. Most chapters also have sections with details that can be glossed over initially. These optional chapters and sections have been marked with "***" in the relevant headers.

While the book is certainly suitable for a global audience, certain examples and details have taken on a more US-centric tone. Usually, these sections are fairly apparent and disjoint, like the discussion of the US bankruptcy code, and can be easily skipped.

Suggested Teaching Plan

The independent reader can pick and choose which chapters and sections he wants to read. I've made an effort to keep various parts of the book self-contained, while focusing on central themes. Since several professors and students will use this as a textbook, I am taking the liberty of proposing a tangible teaching plan for instructors who wish to cover most of this material in one semester.

This book can probably not replace an extensive textbook with many solved examples and exercises with lots of illustrations, so most instructors who have a workflow that they are happy with will find it easiest to assign this book as a supplementary text. But, for instructors using this as a primary text, here are some suggestions:

Instructors can either assign Chapter 1 and 2 (and Annexure I) as prior background reading, or cover them in an introductory session. Students should be required to go through the annexures on their own, at least to be familiar with the concepts so that they can return to the back when necessary. Classes with a more quantitative background can begin with fixed income (Chapters 7, 8 and parts of 9), where the concepts are more tangible, before transitioning to equities (Chapters 11 and 12) and ending with options (Chapters 13 and 14). Classes where the emphasis is predominantly on qualitative insights will find it more natural to cover the equities section first, before fixed income and finally options.

Chapters 3, 4, 5, 6 and 10 are completely optional; one can visualize them as an extension of the Appendix section. Further, many chapters (especially Chapter 9) have a few sections which can easily be skipped, adding to the "list" of optional topics. These sections have been marked with "***" in the respective headers.

Institutional Overview

1. The Financial System – Introduction

WHAT IS THE FINANCIAL SYSTEM? WHY DOES IT EXIST?

The financial system exists to "match the forces of thrift and productivity". Innovative entrepreneurs, growing companies, and other "producers" of goods and services need "capital" to achieve their goals (i.e. "projects"); these projects, if successful, will generate positive cash flows (i.e. revenues, net of costs) in future. The producers themselves sometimes invest part of this capital, but the vast majority of this capital is sourced from external sources – banks, equity markets, bond issuances, etc. This capital eventually comes from private savers (or, sometimes from government incentive schemes). These investors (i.e. savers) have more capital than they currently need and invest in the projects promoted by the producers, in the hope of achieving a return (hopefully large, and at least positive!). The investors are promised a portion of the project's future cash flows and get paid back if and when the project does well. In a broad sense, the "producers" are also investors; they invest primarily by providing their time, skills and effort, and they too share in the returns of the project. As we start thinking generically, these distinctions between external investors, the project sponsor, employees, etc. begin to blur, and we refer to all of them as stakeholders.

These projects have uncertain outcomes – some will succeed beyond their wildest expectation (think *Facebook* or *Google*), and others will fail. The returns that the investors *expect* (or demand) to earn depends critically on the risks that they perceive in the project or company that they are investing in. Of course, the return that investors end up earning can be very different, depending on how well the project performs; there is no absolute guarantee. What happens when there is too much capital for all the available projects/ investments? In that situation, the producers will be able to raise their target capital by promising a lower share of the project proceeds than they would normally need to, and external investors will be forced to accept a lower rate of return.

For the financial system to function, several agents have to play important roles, and act as facilitators. For example, the investors and the producers have to find each other. In a simple world, we can think of a massive database where they are all listed, and people find each other. In fact, in many ways, we are coming full circle, with platforms such as Kickstarter and LendingTree trying to do exactly that (or at least part of it, where projects are listed and investors scan them); in finance terminology, this is an example of *disintermediation* (regular middle-men/ firms are being eliminated because of market changes). But, it's apparent that this cannot be a one-size-fits-all solution, as many projects are complex, require large sums of money, significant amounts of fact checking, etc. This requires several intermediaries. Further, if different investors have cash flow needs at different times, certain other intermediaries facilitate transfer of the rights to the project cash flows to a new investor by paying out the earlier investor.

The Financial System comprises:
- ✓ Entrepreneurs/ Project Owners who have ideas but need capital to produce future cash flows
- ✓ Investors with capital to invest, who expect to earn returns (receive future cash flows)
- ✓ Intermediaries that help
  - investors and producers transact with one another (invest capital today for future cash flows)
  - transfer risk from one investor to another, after the initial transaction with the producer.

Capital Markets and Investments

KEY PLAYERS IN THE FINANCIAL SYSTEM

The most important part of the financial system is, arguably the commercial banks, who accept deposits from savers, and use these deposits to make loans to businesses and individuals. The fractional reserve system (banks need to hold only a small fraction of the money they raise through deposits, and can lend the remaining) allows banks to lend out many multiples of the deposits they receive, effectively increasing the money supply if there is demand for loans. With commercial banks, both the provider of capital (i.e. the saver) and the borrower of capital face the bank (and are exposed only to the risk of the bank not honoring its obligation). In many markets, especially the US, the capital markets supplement the role of banks as a distributor of capital, where investment banks serve mainly as a facilitator and the provider and user of capital face each other. We will not focus on commercial banks in this book.

The market for raising capital, where money flows to the producer from the investor, is referred to as the *primary market*. Some intermediaries are responsible for getting these projects/ ideas/ companies in front of the investor audience for the first time. These are the origination/ *investment banking*/ corporate finance/ M&A divisions of investment banks; they may be parts of large "bulge-bracket" houses or smaller "boutique" shops (part of the *sell-side*). We will discuss them (and all the other players we mention here) in later chapters, but it should be apparent that these divisions need to have deep relationships with both the producers (i.e. entrepreneurs and companies who engage them to raise money for their projects) and the investor community who rely on them to get opportunities to invest in these projects.

Along with the investment bankers, several other players play an important facilitating role. *Accounting firms* vet the books and records of the firms that are trying to raise capital, *regulators* check to make sure that appropriate information is disclosed to every party at the same time, all investors are treated fairly, etc. *Lawyers* are involved in drafting legal agreements between various parties (e.g. investors and entrepreneurs/ companies) and making sure that all documents are filed properly with regulators, etc. Of course, the specifics of the role of the investment banks and the other players depend crucially on the exact type of project, and the instrument for raising money/ paying back investors later – is it a start-up raising venture capital, a large company filing for its IPO, an organization doing a bond issuance for a M&A, whether the investment is open both to large investors and retail accounts, etc. *Rating agencies* assess the risk of the projects/ companies and express the risks on a scale relative to other available investment opportunities.

The *investors (i.e. the buy-side)* are responsible for investing capital judiciously by taking measured risks. At any time, they are expected to compare the risk-return tradeoffs of alternative investment prospects to choose the investments that appear most attractive in their investment universe. Most of the book deals with this issue and discusses some standard frameworks that investors follow, to map investment opportunities on the risk-reward spectrum. Given the plethora of opportunities, much of this analysis is often initially reduced to a set of metrics. For the potential opportunities that pass this initial screen, a deep-dive may be conducted, depending on the investment philosophy of the investing firm.

As alluded above, if too many investors show interest in a certain investment proposal, the project company has the luxury of changing the terms of the investment (of course, before money changes hands and terms are agreed to), to either part with a smaller proportion of future cash flows to external investors, or raise more money than originally planned for the same cash flow proportion as earlier. As a result, the original return (i.e. expected future cash flows, suitably adjusted for the delayed gratification of receiving money later, as a proportion of current investment) gets reduced, and some investors drop out of the bidding process, until the supply of capital to the project at the current terms matches what the producers want the raise at the same terms. But, on several occasions, the sponsors of a "hot" investment will change terms only slightly, allowing

The Financial System - Introduction

the deal to remain "oversubscribed", with only some of the interested investors eventually to get an "allocation" (i.e. "participate in the deal). This scarcity of the opportunity to invest in the proposal creates buzz, which also allows the secondary market (described below) in the name to do well.

The primary market facilitates the allocation of risk capital to (potentially) future cash flow generating projects. But, if this were the only market, then the investors would need to part with their capital for the duration/ time horizon of the project, or until all promised cash flows are paid back, which may take decades. Meanwhile, the risk characteristics of the project may change because of market conditions. Also, since most projects take several years to mature, investors with short-term capital (e.g. available for six months to three years) would find it difficult to invest.

The *secondary market* addresses this issue; in this market, risk is transferred from one investor to another; the producers or the project sponsors do not usually participate in this market. After an instrument is issued, current holders of the security who want to sell it are matched with prospective buyers in the secondary market. Depending on the trading mechanism of the particular instrument, brokers can play an active role here, by finding buyers and sellers, and providing a layer of anonymity. An active secondary market allows investors to have a flexible time horizon, and allows them to exit a position based on liquidity needs or current attractive valuations. It also allows speculators to participate, providing another source of liquidity.

- ✓ Investors and Corporations/Project Owners transact in the primary capital markets.
- ✓ Investors trade (i.e. exchange these claims to future uncertain cash flows for certain cash today) with other investors in the secondary market.

SPECIALIZATION WITHIN THE FINANCIAL SYSTEM

In case it hasn't been clear, the investment world is very specialized (we have an entire chapter on this). There are various kinds of contractual terms/ structures that project companies typically use to raise capital (most obviously debt and equity, but there are many sub-classifications too). Each of these financing structures requires different *risk appetite*, and different analytical skill-sets, even if the underlying project proposal is the same. Even for investment firms that want to invest across the risk spectrum, analyzing investments in different industry sectors or geography require domain knowledge in every sector or region, providing a natural reason to specialize. Since the investment banking world depends on relationships, this specialization effectively partitions the sell-side too.

Additionally, the risk appetite is often driven by the exact source of the investment firm's capital. For example, a fund that is capitalized by 401K money (i.e. individual retirement plan money) is likely to have a conservative mindset, but also have a long investment horizon. High-net-worth individuals often invest through Registered Investment Advisors (RIAs) and are very sensitive to tax rates. A pension fund of a state/ corporate has fairly well-defined future liabilities because of defined benefit pension plans of its employees, and needs to invest with that in mind. An insurance company has a long-horizon perspective, makes money primarily from its insurance underwriting business and has more of a "preservation of capital" mindset. A corporate treasury may have specific time-sensitive needs and invest accordingly. The source of capital drives investment philosophy, risk tolerance and defines the investment universe.

Within the buy-side too, there is a layer of intermediation. There are institutions and individuals that have capital to invest, and there are investment managers who are skilled in the profession of investing capital in the financial markets. A capital owner would ideally like the most capable investment manager to invest on his behalf. For most investment firms, it is easier to claim expertise in a focused niche, than broad-based superiority. Since capital owners can easily use multiple investors to invest in different markets, the best-of-breed specialization has become dominant among investment managers.

As we discuss specialization within the financial system, it is important to recognize that many of these businesses do not need massive investments in physical capital, decades to build, and armies of people. A handful of smart seasoned people, focused on the specific market, can play a meaningful role in this chain of value-creation. Formally, these specialized individuals may be a separate stand-alone firm, or work within the boundaries of a larger firm, so a larger broad-based firm will often have smaller dedicated teams, often working in silos (which could easily fit into another firm instead). The performance of these focused teams is relatively easy to isolate; both these issues lead to the apparently large compensation bonuses that the press reports.

The current financial system is a loosely connected set of silos. Sometimes these silos occur within a large organization, and sometimes they are stand-alone. Each of these set-ups has its own costs and benefits. While assessing these systems, it is important to understand how each of these agents gets compensated, because that ultimately points to the biases of these players.

> The financial system is extremely specialized:
> - ✓ Different contractual structures allocate risk differently between company and investor
> - ✓ Different capital owners have different risk tolerances
> - ✓ Investment managers specialize by skill sets and the part of the financial markets they focus on
> - ✓ Many financial services businesses have low capital intensity, and can be set up in a lean format
>   - Silos can be are often spun out as separate businesses

PRINCIPLES OF PRICING FINANCIAL INSTRUMENTS

This book is about the financial capital markets, which primarily deals with how instruments are traded and priced. We will get into lots of details, mechanics and conventions in the later chapters, but there are a few basic considerations that are worth introducing early.

- The *Time Value of Money* is based on the idea that the same dollar amount paid out at different times in the future has different values today, since money received earlier can be re-invested to earn interest for a longer period. More formally, cash flows to be received at different (future) points in time can be *discounted* to an equivalent present value (or discounted to any other future period), by applying the principles of compound interest. Algebraically, a cash flow of C dollars paid out after i periods from now is worth P today, where $P = \dfrac{C}{(1+r)^i}$, and r is the interest rate (per period) that an investor can earn by investing money today for i periods. P dollars can be invested today and compounded at $r\%$ per period (often a year) to result in C dollars at the end of i periods, so P dollars today is equivalent to C dollars i periods later, if the market interest rate is r. Importantly, in addition to the time valute of money, the rate r should also reflect the risk (uncertainty) of receiving the cash flow C; the greater the risk, the higher should be the interest rate used to discount the cash flows. *Net Present Value (NPV)* and *Internal Rate of Return (IRR)* are important concepts based on this idea; readers should refer to Annexure 1 for further information.

- Investors can either take long or short positions in securities. Buying a security is often referred to as going *long* the security. Investors get long a security when they expect its price to go up (i.e. feel "*bullish*"); a buyer's aim is often to buy the security at a low price, and sell it at higher price, while collecting any interim cash flows that the security pays while he owns the security. Conversely, an investor takes a *short* a position

The Financial System - Introduction

in a security when he feels that the security is likely to go down in price (i.e. feel "*bearish*"). This position has diametrically opposite risks to the long investor; the investor benefits from a short position when the price goes down, and loses when it goes up. This is mechanically achieved by selling a security without owning it first, by *borrowing* the security from a *securities lending program* and then selling it. The short "seller" receives cash flows from this initial sale (in reality, these proceeds effectively serve as *collateral* to the lender of the security, and may earn a small interest), and plans to buy back (i.e. *cover*) the security hopefully at a lower price, to earn the difference between the initial sale price and the later covering (i.e. purchase) price. During this time, the short seller needs to pay the security's original owner any cash flows that the security pays during this period, and also a per-period security borrowing cost (and receives a small interest payment on the collateral), so it is costly to be short for an extended period, since there is a recurring cost every day. If the security's price goes up after the short, it is terrible for the short since now the security has to be bought back at a higher price. Further, if the seller chooses to stay in the position, the earlier collateral is now inadequate and needs to be replenished, since a more expensive asset needs to be secured.[1]

As we will learn later, most of the world's financial assets are managed through *long-only* accounts such as mutual funds, so the concept of shorting securities is only directly relevant to a small investor base. But, it is an important mechanism to keep asset prices fair, as some (large) investors can definitely short if prices get too high. If no investor was allowed to short securities, prices could theoretically get higher from fair value and remain high, driven by either speculators betting on even higher prices, or by investors with different opinions about future prospects. We discuss shorting in more detail, in the section on prime brokerage in Chapter 3.

- The *principle of no-arbitrage* emphasizes that if a security A has the same cash flows as security B in every possible future period (or state), they will have the same price today. Otherwise, an investor could short the more expensive security (based on today's price) and buy the cheaper security simultaneously and lock in a profit upfront, with all subsequent cash-flows offsetting each other. This principle is also important in pricing securities – if a security's cash flows can be replicated using a portfolio of other securities with known prices, this security's fair price can be calculated using those known prices.

  More formally, an arbitrage is said to exist when an investor receives some (positive) cash inflow today, with zero probability of having to pay more than that amount (adjusted for time value of money) in future. Alternatively, the investor enters the position today at zero cost, with at least some probability of getting a positive cash inflow in future, and zero probability of a cash outflow in future.

  > To build on the topic about pricing securities using replication/ no arbitrage, let us consider the following *example*:
  >
  > Let us consider a world with three time periods – 0 (today), 1 and 2. The payoffs of instruments A, B and C are given below. The prices of B and C are known, the price of A is to be determined. Figure 1.1 shows these prices and payoffs.

---

[1] This *long/short* terminology gets more confusing for *unfunded* positions since no cash is exchanged upfront; the convention is to look at the direction of risk exposure to determine the long or the short side.

Capital Markets and Investments

Figure 1.1 Prices and Payoffs of Instruments A, B and C

Asset	Price Today	Payoff Period 1	Payoff Period 2
A	??	250	250
B	450	500	0
C	410	0	500

It is apparent, from the table above, that two units of instrument A will pay off exactly the same amount in each period as the total of one unit of B and one unit of C. So, two units of A should cost (today) the same as a portfolio comprising one unit of B and one unit of C (since they provide exactly the same cash flows in future), or one unit of A should cost 430 [i.e. 0.5*(450+410)] today. If the market price of A is anything else, there will be a potential arbitrage opportunity.

To elaborate, suppose, for example, the market price of A is 460 and the other values are as above. In this situation, an investor would sell (short) 2 units of A, receive 920 in sales proceeds and spend 860 of that to buy one unit of each of B and C. The investor collects 60 today, and his future liabilities (by selling A) are exactly matched by cash inflows from B and C[2]. This seems like a way to make money for free without taking any risk; such opportunities should not exist in an efficient market.

Such situations are rare in the real world. When they do occur, it usually either represents hidden (cash flow) risk or because transaction costs are high/ the security to be shorted is in limited supply, driving up the borrow cost, so the arbitrage may not be compelling after considering all costs fully.

- The example above discussed securities whose cash flows were known with certainty. To extend this principle to instruments with uncertain cash flows, we introduce the concept of *risk-adjusted returns*, which formalizes the notion that securities with higher risk (uncertainty of future return) should earn higher returns (as we discussed above). How exactly to measure the risk and how to translate the extra risk into additional expected return is more an art than a science; models/ frameworks can help with the initial steps. Investors should principally be keen to invest in the securities with high risk-adjusted returns (if they believe in the risk adjustment methodology), because that's where they are supposedly getting the best deal beyond being compensated for taking on the risk.

- Stated simply, the underlying goal of all investing is to buy securities that are likely to gain in value, and sell/ short securities that are more likely to lose value. Now, today's market valuation reflects the future outlook of securities, so it is often not enough to simply assess whether the underlying company's/ country's future prospects are positive or not. It is essential to form an opinion on the future outlook relative to the market's view of the same company/ country, so it is crucial to figure out *what outlook is priced into current market prices*. Often the outlook priced in is a (probability-weighted) average of the security prices in various scenarios; if the investor feels differently about the likelihood various scenarios that could possibly play out, that insight is sometimes adequate to put on a trade.

---

[2] In reality, the investor would need to borrow A from a securities lending program through his broker, pay a borrow cost, and put up collateral, maybe including the assets B and C that he purchased, reducing the profits from the trade. There is also usually a bid-offer spread which we will discuss later. There are some popular examples of such trades not working out, such as the Palm spin-off from 3Com in 2000 and the VW-Porsche deal in 2008.

The Financial System - Introduction

> Some Basic Principles and Terminology:
> - ✓ The Net Present Value (NPV) and Internal Rate of Return (IRR) concepts to evaluate investments are based on Time Value of Money, which requires project cash flows to be discounted to adjust cash flow dollars paid at different times to make them equivalent and comparable.
> - ✓ Investors who are optimistic go long (or buy) a security; pessimists go short (or sell). A short seller needs to locate a security to borrow and pay the borrow cost, and pay any intermediate cash flows (e.g. coupon or dividend). The short position is eventually closed out by covering.
> - ✓ No-arbitrage principles suggest that asset markets should be efficient and it should not be possible to make money without taking risk. Risk-adjusted returns indicate a security's performance after adjusting for the risk the investor takes to invest in it.

ARE FINANCIAL MARKETS "EFFICIENT"?

How well do the principles described in the last section (no arbitrage, short selling, risk-adjusting returns, etc.) apply in practice? How accurately do current market prices of financial securities reflect their future potential returns? The *Efficient Market Hypothesis* says that security prices immediately adjust to incorporate new information, which arrives randomly. To be clear, *this is merely a hypothesis*; staunch believers will feel that there is no point trying to pick securities in the market (because price movements are random); arbitrage opportunities will exist if the market is not efficient. Securities are all fairly valued, and holding the entire market index is the best bet. We discuss the Random Walk model in the section on option pricing, which is based on this fundamental idea. At the other end of the spectrum, non-believers insist that the market is inefficient because of various reasons (illiquidity, regulatory constraints, capital/ position-based limits to arbitrage, too much information and being able to sort it all out, behavioral biases, entry barriers in terms of deep domain knowledge, etc.), so price movements can be predicted with some degree of success. This fundamental question is not addressed in this book, but the truth is probably somewhere in between.

Efficient Market Hypothesis

There are a few "versions" of the Efficient Market Hypothesis, which we are touching on mainly to introduce terminology. It's a matter of choice what readers choose to believe; but be aware that believing in the strongest form of the statement is inconsistent with being an ardent bottom-up stock picker.

The *Weak Form Efficiency* is the weakest form of the hypothesis, which says that historical prices and volume data are not useful in predicting returns. The implication of this is that technical analysis should not work. Momentum has been one of the strongest predictors of returns over the past several decades (before it got too common and algorithmic over the last few years), so even the simplest form of efficiency has some evidence against it. Studies on serial correlation of securities have demonstrated some short term persistence, but transaction costs are too great to profit from it. Further, for every theory like momentum, there is an opposite theory like *Mean Reversion*. One of these is always going to be true, tautologically. Analysts often say that mean reversion is a longer term phenomenon, whereas momentum is shorter term, but the horizon is tricky to define. With the advent of technology, these time horizons are likely getting shorter and more random.

Semi-strong form Efficiency implies that prices incorporate all publicly available information, not just historical prices and volume. So, this implies that none of the fundamental and technical analysts add incremental value. It is possible that the same information may be interpreted differently by different analysts, or there may be some information that most analysts haven't chanced upon; this version of efficiency does not allow for that too. Most analysts will believe that this version of efficiency does not always hold.

Strong-form Efficiency insists that even with private information, it is not possible to predict security returns; this is probably a stretch.

The core argument justifying market efficiency is that there are millions of investors and analysts following financial markets, several hundred track any particular focus area. If a security's price were obviously wrong, capital would flow in / out of that security until the price reflects fair value. In particular, investors could put on arbitrage strategies and lock in profits if prices are not aligned with the economic reality.

Whichever version one chooses to believe in, it is indeed true that new public information is getting disseminated and incorporated in prices very rapidly, so the edge to analyzing information may be going down; in fact speed may even lead to misinterpretation and present an opportunity. Further, many pricing anomalies may appear to exist or investment opportunities appear lucrative, but they are either transient, or may not be thoroughly researched or may reflect (incorrectly assessed) investment risk. So, in a sense, recognizing that the market may plausibly be somewhat efficient overall should cause the investor to ask why the other person wants to sell when the investor wants to buy (or vice versa) and convince himself that he is not missing anything.

Counterclaims to Market Efficiency

Theories of Asymmetric Information - Agency Theories

Efficient market theories are based on frictionless markets, with all players having the same information (among other assumptions), consistent with perfect competition. In both the retail and the institutional investment world, professional investment managers manage most of the financial capital on behalf of their clients (who own the capital), as we elaborate in Chapter 4. In the real world, the entity owning the capital (principal) cannot precisely observe if the manager deploying the capital (agent) is doing an earnest job to create value, or doing "just enough" to maintain a good impression or taking excessive risk to get paid incentive fees[3]. So, the capital owner often decides on the performance of the agent based on returns over a certain pre-specified time horizon. This also motivates the creation of investment guidelines, which restricts the agent's investment universe to his stated expertise. This leads to the frictions discussed in the justification for limits to arbitrage, below.

Limits to Arbitrage

The first line of skepticism to market efficient arguments is that it is not easy to implement arbitrages as the textbooks will have readers believe. This is because of investor guidelines (limiting which assets investors can invest in), short selling constraints, lack of borrow availability/ cost of borrow, prices deviating even more from fundamentals in the short run, high transaction costs, short investment horizons aligned with investor performance evaluation cycles, etc. The counter to this argument is that, for arbitrage to disappear, not all investors need to be adept at implementing arbitrage trades; one large investor with the capital and flexibility should be able to drive out mispricing and profit from it. Said differently, if prices reflect a weighted-average of trader beliefs, an arbitrageur, because of reasons above, may not be in a position to build a large enough position to influence prices significantly, leading to the persistence of a potential arbitrage opportunity.

---

[3] This line of thinking was pioneered by Michael Spence, George Akerlof and Joseph Stiglitz in the early 1970s, for which they won the Nobel Prize for Economics in 2001. This (asymmetric information) problem can be mitigated by signaling (where the informed party takes a costly action to credibly disclose private information) or screening (where the uninformed party presents the informed party with a menu of choices; the pick from the menu reveals the private information).

The Financial System - Introduction

Further, most mispricings do not show up as textbook arbitrages (where one makes certain money, or has a zero probability of losing and a non-zero chance of making money) but show up as lucrative trades in an expected value framework (high positive expected values). So, while putting on such trades, there remains a non-zero chance of losing (potentially large amounts of) money; investors may be reluctant to allocate massive amounts of capital to such trades, and invest only in small size in a risk-controlled manner. And, if new capital flows to investors with views divergent from the arbitrageur, the arbitrageur will find himself on the wrong side of the trade, in the short term.

Principal-agent issues also make risk-control issues especially important. This is because the capital owner cannot precisely monitor the investment manager's actions, so needs to come up with a contract to create a suitable incentive structure. Now, such contracts can also lead to perverse incentives, so the contract usually also contains guidelines to restrict the manager's actions. Even in the absence of such contracts, the manager may choose to "play it safe" instead of putting on (potentially risky and contrarian) arbitrage trades, which may lead to large losses and stick out, leading to the capital owner firing the manager.

Behavioral Biases of Investors

All the arguments put forward in this chapter (and in most of the book) assume that investors behave rationally, based on the information at their disposal. Studies have shown that this is not always true[4]. Individual (and institutional) cognitive biases lead to non-rational judgments and decisions, which affect trading dynamics and market prices. These biases can broadly be classified as either related to overconfidence, or limited cognitive processing[5] (e.g. simplifying decision-making by using quick heuristics, feelings short-circuiting well thought-out decision frameworks).

Overconfidence leads to investors believing that their estimates are much more precise than reality, their ability is higher than that of their peers; they selectively pick facts to reinforce these biases. This causes investors to trade aggressively, invest actively instead of indexing (Chapters 4, 5). Overconfidence also leads to over-reaction in prices which eventually corrects, leading to short-term momentum but longer term mean-reversion (Chapter 12). This may also show up in large investment allocations to local assets or own-company stock.

Limited focus and mind space to absorb/ analyze information also causes people to ignore information for pricing financial assets. For example, investors overreact to salient or recent information, and de-emphasize less salient information. Investors' subjective probabilities of events are influenced by how easily they can think of examples. Investors often frame the decision problem narrowly, leading them to ignore relevant investment aspects such as employer 401k matches, tax implications or diversifying characteristics to overall portfolios. Investors have been shown to usually simply default to an equally weighted average of securities in their portfolio, without due consideration to risk. Reference points seem to matter to investors, be it the price at which they acquired a security in the past and their aversion to sell losers, their anchoring to initial ideas and premises, mentally compartmentalizing using quick heuristics to get to an answer rather than deliberating fully on the problem. These biases slow down the incorporation of information into market prices.

To summarize, it's probably fair to say that most of the market behaves in a (more or less) efficient manner most of the time. But, for the other times (and parts of the market), behavioral biases become important in determining/ explaining the final outcome. And, these effect of these biases may linger, because of agency effect and the resulting limits to arbitrage. Reinforcing behavioral actions by groups of investors (rather than

---

[4] While several researchers, beginning with Savage and Ellsberg have documented investor irrationality in various forms, Daniel Kahneman and Amos Tversky provided the Prospect Theory to explain some of these behavioral patterns, for which Kahneman shared the Nobel Prize in 2002

[5] A strand of academic literature in microeconomic theory refers to this phenomenon as *bounded rationality*.

individuals) can also affect prices. Some investors may be in a position to exploit these inefficiencies at the margin, at least temporarily.

> Are Markets Efficient?
> - ✓ *Yes*: Efficient Markets Hypothesis
>   - Many analysts continuously analyzing information, to find money-making opportunities
> - ✓ *No*: Limits to Arbitrage, Agency Theories and Behavioral Biases
>   - Delegating to outside managers, investment rules and risk budgets allow arbitrages to persist.
>   - Investors have common behavioral traits such as overconfidence and limited attention, which make them vulnerable to biases.

REFERENCES

- Akerlof, George A., O. Blanchard, D. Romer and J. E. Stiglitz (ed., 2014). *What Have We Learned?* MIT Press.
- Barberis, Nicholas & Thaler, Richard (2003). *A Survey of Behavioral Finance*, in: G.M. Constantinides & M. Harris & R. M. Stulz (ed.), Handbook of the Economics of Finance, edition 1, volume 1, chapter 18, pages 1053-1128 Elsevier.
- Hirshleifer, David A (Aug, 2014). *Behavioral Finance*. Retrieved from SSRN: http://ssrn.com/abstract=2480892
- Kahneman, Daniel (2011). *Thinking, Fast and Slow*. Farrar, Straus and Giroux.

2. Major Asset Classes and Markets

Chapter 1 talks about the relation between investments today, expected future returns and potential risks. At any time, several diverse investments opportunities exist, which compete with each other for the investor's capital. For example, governments may need money to fund projects or provide tax breaks; corporates may need capital for new investments or to acquire other companies, etc. Apart from the abilities of the project producer and the characteristics of the project itself, the specifics of the security and the consequent rights of the investor also defines the risk levels. Financial investors can also participate in markets such as commodities or currencies, and earn returns based on their future prices relative to their current levels, using *unfunded* instruments. This chapter will introduce simplified versions of some popular security types, and also touch on some key asset classes (the distinction between security types and asset classes is often blurry). This is not meant to be precise or comprehensive; we discuss this so that readers who are learning finance for the first time get some reference points to fix ideas, as we go through examples. This chapter is more like a glossary of a few relevant terms.

Most securities (except derivatives) that we discuss below (including bonds, stocks, loans, hybrids) are initially issued (directly by a firm) in their respective primary markets, where capital is transferred between investors and firms than require capital for business needs. These instruments are often referred to as *cash* instruments, and collectively form part of the issuing firm's *capital structure*; Annexure 2 has more details. They provide the firm with capital, and provide the investors with claims to the firm's future cash flows[6]. Depending on the type of security, the cash flow claims are different. Secondary markets for these assets also exist, and facilitate the transfer of securities, risk and capital between financial investors; the original issuing company is not involved in these subsequent (secondary) trades.

In contrast, a derivatives are usually simply a contract between two investors, with no issuing company being involved[7]. The value of a derivative is dependent on movements in a predefined *underlying*, which may be either the price of a cash security issued by a firm (or the average price of many securities issued by many such firms) or a macroeconomic variable (or anything, for that matter). On a pre-decided *expiration date*, depending on how the underlying has moved since the initiation of the contract, one party pays the other the dues under the derivative's terms. Depending on the exact type of derivative, there may be little or no initial payment at the time of entering the contract (relative to potential economic exposure), with possibly large payment obligations/ receipts at expiration.

MAJOR TYPES OF INSTRUMENTS

Financial Instruments have unique (but standardized) identifiers that are used in systems/ trading to identify them – *CUSIP* and *ISIN* are the two common identifiers, with SEDOL and NAICS being much less common. Loans use LX IDs, stocks use tickers (but they also have CUSIPs/ ISINs). CUSIPs have 9 digits – only 8 of them matter for identification; the 9th digit is a check digit. ISINs have 13 digits. For example the IBM stock

---

[6] The nature of these cash flow claims are different, based on the security. Regulators also treat different types of securities differently (both from tax and regulatory reporting perspective); these reasons also affect issuance/ investor participation.

[7] Derivative securities are said to be in "zero net supply" among the investors; for every buyer of a derivative there is a seller, and the total amount outstanding by adding holdings of all the investors. This is in contrast to cash instruments, where the amount outstanding equals the issuance by the firm, less any subsequent purchases the firm may have made (of its own security) in the secondary market.

ticker is IBM, and has CUSIP 459200101 and ISIN US4592001014[8]. While ISINs are globally used, CUSIPs are primarily used in the US.

Bonds (Fixed Income)

A (par) bond is a contract between the investor (lender) and the borrower, where the investor pays the borrower a lump sum of cash upfront (bond *issue price*), and is promised a periodic (semi-annually in the US, annually in Europe) cash flow (i.e. the *coupon* rate, specified as a percentage of the *par value*, a notional amount usually close to what the investor typically parts with initially. The investor is also paid back the par amount (*principal*), which in most cases is close to what he initially paid the borrower, at a specified final date (maturity). Several tweaks are often added to this base contract, which we will gloss over at this point. This initial interaction between the borrower and investor (when the bond is first issued) is referred to as the primary market.

Note that the cash flows from the borrower to the investor are mere promises at the time of investment; the borrower needs to be solvent when the payments come due. The investor gets more than the initial investment, usually in form of periodic cash flows, to compensate for the risk of borrower default, and also for the time value of money i.e. the opportunity cost of not being able to earn income elsewhere from this capital. If the issuer is unable (or unwilling) to pay the bondholder the contractual payments; the bondholder can pursue legal remedies such as forcing the issuer into *bankruptcy*, or other remedies that the *indenture* (contract) may allow. Bonds may be classified as *senior* or *subordinated*, *secured* or *unsecured*, depending on the type of collateral explicitly attached to the bond. While these bonds are often not secured by specific assets (sometimes they are), in a bankruptcy proceeding, bonds are paid out before the project sponsors (i.e. equity holders) get anything. The promised cash flows are the maximum that the investor can earn; there is no further upside.

In the secondary market, bonds change hands across investors (i.e. trade) at a market-determined dynamic price, but the contract terms stay exactly as they were at bond issuance. So, if that earlier contract has now become more desirable (for whatever reason), a new investor will pay more to get access to the existing bond's (already decided) cash flows. The expected return for this bond is lower now (than what it was earlier), because the new investor has to put up more money to get the same cash flows. To be clear, the previous investor gets to keep all coupons that he had received before he sold the bond to the new investor. Bonds are valued primarily based on *yield*, which is the discount rate that equates the future promised cash flows to today's price.

Loans

Loans are similar to bonds, but are usually secured by assets (so more senior than bonds in a bankruptcy), pay a floating rate coupon based off a reference rate (usually LIBOR) subject to a minimum floor, and are easy for the issuer to call back. Risky corporates are the largest issuers of loans. In the 1980s, the loans used to be a predominantly bank-dominated market, but over the past few decades, loan documentation has been (more) standardized are sold to institutional investors, especially in the US. This market is clunky, with very archaic settlement and trading practices. Loan funds and CLOs are large buyers of this asset, in addition to institutions.

Stocks (Equities)

A (equity) share/stock is a slice of the ownership of the firm, but with the shareholder's liability for losses usually limited to the value of the investment (*limited liability*). Technically, stockholders are entitled to what remains of the firm after all liabilities are paid off. So, the accounting value of the entire shareholding is the difference between the value of all the firm's assets and its liabilities; the market value of equity values these assets and liabilities on a forward-looking basis. When a firm issues shares, the value of these shares is driven by how much investors expect the firm to be able to earn in future, and the riskiness of the business. If the firm were to fail, shareholders have no recourse and stand at the end of the line, behind all other liabilities, i.e.

---

[8] Usually, the CUSIP comprises a part of the ISIN.

they can claim only the *residual value*. So, this is the most volatile of all the security types that a firm issues; any change in a solvent firm's value affects the equity value first, which gets divided pro-rata across all shareholders. In comparison, for minor changes in investor expectation of the firm's future prospects, bond prices may not move at all, especially if the cash flows due to bondholders are a small part of the firm's total cash flows.

Hybrid Instruments

The two types of securities described above are polar opposites – bonds have high priority when it comes to returning capital, but have no upside beyond the contractual payments, whereas equity shares have no contractual payments and a lot of downside because they have value only after the other securities are paid back in full, but have unlimited upside because they own all the residual value after the other securities are paid back. Aside from these securities, there are also several *hybrid instruments* that firms sometimes issue, with flavors of both debt and equity.

Convertible bonds

A convertible bond (i.e. a convert) is a bond issued by a corporate, with the additional provision that it can be converted into shares (at the investor's option; the issuer can force conversion under certain situations) at a fixed share price, usually well above the share price of the company's stock when the bond was issued. This bond also pays a coupon like a regular bond, but the coupon (more specifically, yield) on the bond is lower than a bond without the conversion feature. While regular bonds have no upside beyond the timely payment of interest and principal, the investor in the convert can benefit if the company does really well and the stock shoots up. If the stock goes down instead, this functions like a regular bond (albeit at a lower yield), so the downside is likely lower than the stock (i.e. the bond floor kicks in).

Preferred stock

Preferred stock is similar to a bond, with a stated coupon (usually higher than a regular bond), principal and maturity (sometimes perpetual, with a call feature). The coupons payments are optional for the company; non-payment does not constitute a default and preferred stock holders cannot initiate bankruptcy proceedings; this is why the coupons are higher. However, the coupons are cumulative, so if the company does not pay the preferred holders one period, it has to make good on multiple payments the next time it pays. Also, the company cannot declare a dividend to stockholders before paying off the preferred dividends. Analysts and regulators do not treat preferred stock as debt, since payments are optional, so the company appears less indebted on paper.

Companies, especially in the financial services industry, issue several other less common securities, such as Co-Cos (Contingent Convertible), AT1s and warrants, but we skip these for now.

Derivatives/ Synthetic Instruments

A derivative is a security whose cash flows are (explicitly) derived based on the value of an underlying security, which needs to be precisely specified. For example, different derivatives could pay off based on the value of an underlying such as an index (e.g. S&P 500), a single stock (e.g. IBM), the price of a commodity (e.g. Copper), a bond issued by US Treasury or anything else. The exact form of the payoff function can also vary, based on the derivative type. Derivatives are available purely as secondary market instruments. They are issued by an exchange or intermediary (the entity issuing the underlying is not involved), and both sides of the market contain either speculators betting on price movements, or investors hedging cash flow risk. Unlike the earlier examples, investment capital does not change hands initially, but risk exposures change (often similar to the underlying), so these instruments are also called synthetics. They are a mechanism to gain economic exposure without putting down large amounts of cash at trade inception. Such instruments include futures, swaps and options

Capital Markets and Investments

Futures/ Forwards

Futures is a contract that allows the investor to buy (or sell) a specified amount of the underlying on a future date (expiration), at a price that is decided today (today's futures price of the underlying, with settlement on the expiration date). No money is exchanged today (i.e. unfunded) when the investor enters into the futures contract, but the contract is binding, and the investor must follow through with the agreement on the future date decided today. When the price of the underlying goes up, the price of a future that delivers this underlying on a future date also goes up, one for one. On the expiration date, depending on the specifics of the contract, one of two things happens: the future either *settles physically* (i.e. the seller delivers to the buyer the specific underlying and receives the contracted futures price, regardless of the current underlying price), or there is *cash settlement* (i.e. if the underlying price at expiration is higher that the futures price on contract date, the investor who is supposed to buy the underlying gets paid the price difference between the current (*spot*) price and the contracted futures price; if the current price is lower the buyer pays the difference.). In cash-settled contracts, the underlying does not change hands.

It is easy to identify the buyer and seller of a funded instrument like a stock; the buyer pays cash to get the rights, and vice versa. For a futures, since there is no money changing hands at trade inception, there is no actual buyer or seller today; the corresponding terminology in the unfunded worlds is *long* versus *short*. The investor who is long the futures contract has to buy the underlying on the settlement date at the pre-decided price, and (currently) almost has the same economics as having bought the underlying already), vice versa for short. Forwards are similar to futures (as are total return swaps) but differ in technicalities; we will discuss later. We discuss these instruments in detail in Chapter 8.

Swaps

Swaps are another example of unfunded instruments, like futures, and provide exposure to an underlying by spending very little cash (upfront payments, zero in many markets) initially. There are three main types of swaps – interest rate swaps (discussed in Chapter 8), credit default swaps and index swaps. *Interest rates swaps* allow investors to make or lose money whether interest rates are going to go up or down in future, so they are economically similar to Treasuries and Treasury Futures (but there are differences!). *Credit Default Swaps* (CDS) are like bankruptcy insurance bought by an investor; they pay off when the issuer incurs a "credit event", often bankruptcy or failure to pay a coupon/ principal payment. *Index swaps* are essentially customized swaps where an investor can receive (or pay) the (uncertain) future gains or losses in a pre-decided underlying index (basket of securities) on certain future dates (say, quarterly or semi-annually) in exchange for a fee, thereby avoiding the hassle and the cash requirements to invest directly in that basket. The investor will pay or receive money in future, depending on whether the underlying securities moved in his favor or not. Swaps are governed by International Swap Dealers Association (ISDA), which standardizes the legal agreements and conventions based on which these instruments trade.

Options

Options give the buyer i.e. owner of the option the right but not necessarily the obligation to transact (i.e. buy or sell the underlying, as pre-decided in the contract, hence the term *option*) at the pre-decided (*strike*) price on the *expiration* date; every options contract specifies these details. Options to buy the underlying are referred to as *call options*; options to sell the underlying are called *put options*. So, if the underlying price is higher than the strike price on expiration date, a call option holder will *exercise* the call option and buy the underlying at the contracted strike price, which is below the current market; if the price is lower that strike, the option owner lets the option expire worthless (and, if necessary, buys the underlying from the market at a price lower than the strike). In contrast, put option owners own the right to sell the underlying at the strike price; they exercise only if the underlying price is below the strike price (and sell at an above-market price). To get this right, the option buyer has to pay the option *premium* to the seller, who sells this right to the buyer. The buyer

Major Asset Classes and Markets

of a call option benefits when the underlying price goes up, but it's not a dollar-for-dollar benefit. As a proportion of the premium, though, the change in the option value can be huge. We have separate chapters on options towards the end of the book.

> Major Instruments:
> - ✓ Bonds – Contractually fixed payments, with no upside if the company does really well.
> - ✓ Loans - Similar to bonds but with floating interest rate, flexible maturity and secured by collateral.
> - ✓ Stocks – residual ownership stake in company; gets paid after all other liabilities have been met.
> - ✓ Hybrids – Contain features of both bonds and stocks
>   - Convertible Bonds are have terms similar to bonds, but the investor has the option to convert these bonds into stock at a pre-decided price, often significantly higher than issue price.
>   - Preferred Stocks have bond-like terms, but the company can choose to defer payment. The company cannot pay shareholders until it has met current obligations on the preferred bonds.
> - ✓ Derivatives – Similar economic exposure as underlying, with minimal initial cash outlay.
>   - Futures – Instrument that changes into the underlying on a future date at a price fixed today.
>   - Swaps – Both parties exchange market-contingent periodic cash flows for a pre-decided time
>   - Options – The option owner has the right but not the obligation to fulfil the pre-decided transaction on the future date. For this choice, the option buyer pays a premium to the seller.

MAJOR ASSET CLASSES

We will not quibble about what constitutes an asset class; it is not precisely defined and is usually some combination of issuer-based market segments and security types. Asset classes are broadly classified into fixed income, equities (wait, weren't they security types?), commodities, currencies, emerging markets, etc.

Fixed Income

The major asset sub-classes within fixed income are Treasuries, Mortgages, Agencies, Municipals, Corporates, Securitized Products, Swaps. Many (not all) these products are special cases of bonds that we discussed earlier; we will delve into more details in later chapters.

Some professionals will refer only to Treasuries, Mortgages and maybe Agencies and Munis as Fixed Income, since the primary risk in these products is the market interest rate. To them, anything less liquid and/ or with meaningful credit risk is not fixed income. For example, in sell-side organizations, Credit is a separate business, less liquid than regular fixed income. In fact, currencies and commodity market reporting lines often blur with fixed income at senior levels, whereas the credit business is its own world.

Most of these asset classes have derivatives (i.e. futures/ options/ swaps), which trade based on the underlying asset class.

Treasuries/ Government Securities

Treasury Bonds are issued by the US Treasury, but each country has its own equivalent (UK Has Gilts, Germany has Bunds, etc.). These are bonds backed by the full faith of the government. The government regularly issues bonds of various maturities, starting with shorter term 3-6 month T-bills, to 2, 3, 5, 7, 10 and 30 year

Capital Markets and Investments

bonds. The yield on each of these bonds can be implied from market prices; bonds of different maturities generally have different yields. As there is virtually no default risk in these (local currency) bonds (since the government can always print money to satisfy obligations), the yield primarily compensates investors for the time value of money, and is a proxy for the risk-free rate at different maturities. The bond yield and the market interest rate are very closely linked; an increase in the market interest rate will increase the bond yield, thereby lowering prices and ex-post returns.

The Treasury also issues *TIPS* (or Treasury Inflation Protected Securities), where cash flow payments are adjusted for inflation. There is an active futures market based on Treasuries, which settle every quarter. Options are traded on these futures. A closely-related interest rate swaps market is also very active; we will discuss this in a subsequent chapter.

All other high quality (mortgages, agencies, investment-grade rated credit) bonds are quoted as a spread over similar maturity Treasuries (T + Spread). A common measure of spread is referred to as *Option-Adjusted Spread (OAS)*.

(Interest Rate) Swaps

As we mentioned above, the distinction between an asset class and an instrument can be blurry; we just talked about swaps as an instrument. Interest rate swaps are such a large market (probably the biggest unfunded market globally), with many derivatives referencing the swap rate, that they are referred to as an asset class. A fixed-for-floating interest rate swap is a transaction where one party agrees to receive a fixed interest rate on a notional principal amount for a specific time horizon (the *swap rate* for that maturity), and pays a floating interest rate (usually 3-month interest rate) in exchange; all these terms are agreed upon today. The swap rate is set so that this equals the expected average floating over the period of the swap, so that an investor would be indifferent taking either side of the transaction today; it is zero NPV. Derivatives on swap rates (swaptions) are common.

Mortgages

The residential mortgage universe is divided up into *Agency* and *non-Agency* mortgages; Agency mortgages refer to mortgages that conform to certain criteria, which qualify for a Government Agency (e.g. Fannie Mae / Freddie Mac) guarantee. Conforming homeowner mortgages are *pooled* together based on geography, which bank originated the mortgage (sometimes) and the coupon of the loan. Bonds (also called MBS or) are issued with this pool as a collateral, and the cash flows from the monthly mortgage repayments are used to pay interest and principal on these bonds. Because of the guarantee, investors are not concerned about the credit of the homeowners; if they default, the Agency makes up the difference. In the US, homeowners can prepay the mortgage anytime without penalty. While there are several variables affecting prepayments, the most important variable is the current interest rate i.e. can the homeowner refinance to a lower mortgage interest rate? Since mortgage rates follow Treasury yields closely, a lowering of interest rates will lead to easier refinancing at lower rates, causing more mortgages to be prepaid. From the perspective of the bondholder, this is treated as an early repayment of principal. Normally, a decline in interest rates would lead to an increase in bond value (more on this in the chapter on Treasuries), this upside is lower in mortgages because the bondholder is involuntarily saddled with cash (because of faster prepayments), exactly when rates are low. When rates are high, prepayments are slower than the norm, and the bond maturity *extends* (i.e. gets longer than expected), exactly when the investor would like more capital to invest at the higher rates. Commercial mortgage pools also exist; those mortgages have pre-payment penalties. . The idea of pooling single loans and issuing securities against the pool (often after *tranching*) is discussed further in the paragraph on securitized products.

Major Asset Classes and Markets

Agencies

The government agencies that guarantee mortgages (Fannie Mae, Freddie Mac, etc.) also issue bonds. This was a huge market historically as agencies used to issue large volumes of debt to buy mortgages from the market that they had guaranteed (they could issue cheaper paper than the MBS), but has become less active since the agencies have been under receivership, following the 2008 financial crisis.

Municipal Bonds

Municipalities also issue bonds to fund various programs. These bonds can either be *General Obligation* (GO, where the investor has recourse to the general tax revenue that the muni receives, or they could be *Revenue bonds*, which use only the proceeds of a particular project to pay down the debt. Some bonds are *Double Barreled*, which provide recourse to both sources of cash flows. The unique characteristic of Muni bonds is that the coupon income is typically exempt from US Federal Taxes. Many bonds are also exempt from state and local taxes, and some even from Alternate Minimum Tax (AMT). So, this asset class often attracts the retail investor in a high tax bracket. The bonds trade based on their yield, which is low because of the tax break. Usually Muni bonds are of high quality and low risk, though several high-profile risky muni investment opportunities (Detroit/ Puerto Rico) have become more common, as municipalities have struggled to collect taxes because of demographic shifts/ business closures.

Corporates

All non-equity issuance by companies is considered *corporate credit*. These may be in the form of bonds, loans or hybrid securities such as preferred stock, which have elements of both bonds and equity. Investors buy these securities either at original issuance or in the secondary markets, hoping to receive the promised coupon and principal payments or benefiting from interim price fluctuation, as the market reassesses its view of the creditworthiness of the issuer. Credit Default Swaps (CDS) also trades on several corporate names, and forms part of the sector.

The corporate credit universe is divided by credit quality (determined by credit rating/ market prices, fundamentally characterized by default likelihood) and sector. Ratings are broadly aggregated into *investment grade* and *high-yield* categories; the market dynamics of these two segments are very different. Credit Rating Agencies such as Moody's, S&P, and Fitch assign *ratings* (i.e. letter grades to reflect credit quality for the issuer (corporate family) or the specific bond/ loan issue), and *notch* these ratings with a +, - or no sign (similar to course grades, but have more layers)[9]; each rating also has an *outlook* (positive, negative or neutral). Like the other fixed income securities, credit risk is reflected in the spread (OAS) over Treasuries / Swaps (i.e. LIBOR), although high yield bonds are quoted and traded in price terms.

Securitized products

Securitized products come in all forms, depending on the underlying assets. In some sense, the mortgages described above are also securitized products, though not referred to as such. Generally, a *Special Purpose Vehicle* (SPV) issues bonds (and sometimes equity) to buy a pool of specific assets (any one of credit card receivables, auto loans, student debt, aircraft leases (collectively referred to as ABS), bank loans (CLOs), agency mortgages (CMOs), corporate debt (CDOs), credit default swap (synthetic CDOs), commercial mortgages (CMBS), etc.). The cash flows generated from these assets are then distributed to holders of the SPV's liabilities (e.g. bonds that the SPV has issued). Now, the SPV, like a corporate, doesn't issue only one kind of bond (supported by these asset cash flows), but several kinds, differing in credit quality rated AAA through B; rating agencies play

---

[9] For example, S&P ratings vary from AAA (highest/ best), AA, A, BBB, BB, B, CCC and D (defaulted). Except AAA and D, all the other ratings are further *notched* +,- or without a sign. Each rating also has an *outlook* (positive, negative or neutral) which i

Capital Markets and Investments

an especially important role. Many securitized product liabilities are *sequential pay*, meaning that the higher rated liabilities are paid before the lower rated liabilities. This idea of slicing the liabilities is called *tranching*; each slice is called a tranche. The higher tranche begins incurring losses only after the lower tranche is completely wiped out. Expected levels of losses are reflected in the pricing / yield of the tranche. These liabilities are priced relative to the market rate for bonds with similar rating, and any difference between the cash flow of the assets and the payouts to the liabilities is kept by the equity holders, who are junior to all the different bonds. The equity is also the "first-loss" piece, so when the assets incur losses (e.g. Payment default), the equity takes the hit before other parts of the capital structure. Since these securities also essentially involve taking credit risk, some investors consider this to be part of credit (i.e. *Structured Credit*). Chapter 10 has more details.

Money Markets

The money markets are short-dated markets, comprising exclusively of instruments that mature in one year or less. This market is considered extremely safe and less volatile; corporates and individuals invest in these instruments to park cash, either directly or through specific *money market funds* focused on money market instruments. The most common instrument is the Treasury Bill, a short-dated fixed income instrument issued by the US Treasury. High quality corporates and municipals also issue money market instruments (commercial paper) to fund themselves, and keep rolling over the exposure close to maturity. Some closed-end mutual funds also issue money market instruments to lever themselves (the 1940s Act permits this within limits). Risker companies used to issue Asset Backed Commercial Paper (ABCP) before 2008, but that market suffered during the financial crisis and did not come back in a meaningful way.

Money market funds allow investors to purchase a pool of securities that generally provided higher returns than interest-bearing bank accounts. There are many kinds of money market funds, including ones that invest primarily in government securities, tax-exempt municipal securities, or corporate debt securities. Money market funds that primarily invest in corporate debt securities are referred to as prime funds. Money market funds are supposed to be extremely safe (investors use it to park cash and do not expect high returns), and there was an uproar when a fund "broke the buck" and traded below par (implying a loss of principal), prompting regulators to design a new set of rules, where all "prime" money market funds (which invest in non-Treasury paper) will have a floating NAV (which can go below par), and can charge liquidity fees and stagger redemptions in case of mass withdrawals. This has caused large outflows from prime funds.

Figure 2.1 shows the amount outstanding of the major fixed income markets over time. The mortgage market grew exponentially in the early 2000s, but has tapered off after the 2008 crisis. In contrast, the issuance in the Treasury markets surged after 2008, prompted by the Federal Reserve's monetary policy. Corporate debt has also grown substantially during the last few years, because of the low interest rates, which prompted corporations to issue debt to buy back shares.

Major Asset Classes and Markets

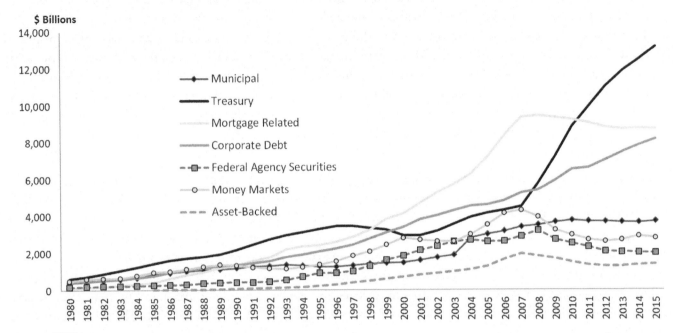

Figure 2.1 Relative Size and Growth of various Fixed Income Markets over time

Source: SIFMA

Equities

Equities include stocks and baskets of stocks, such as indices and ETFs, which trade as a single unit like a stock. We discussed stocks towards the beginning of this chapter when we discussed different instruments, and have detailed chapters later. Derivatives (options) on many of these securities trade actively, as do futures and options contracts on stock indices.

Commodities

Commodities are broadly divided into Agricultural (Wheat, Soy Bean, Corn), Energy (Crude – WTI and Brent, Natural Gas), Industrial Metals (Copper, Zinc, Nickel) and Precious Metals (Gold, Silver, Platinum, Palladium). Futures contracts for many of these commodities (precisely specified – grade, delivery location, etc.) trade actively, on multiple global exchanges (CME, LME, etc.). Some of these futures are physically settled (i.e. at expiration, the party that is long needs to take delivery of the contracted amount of the commodity and pay the price) as opposed to cash settled (i.e. only cash equal to the difference between current market value and contracted market value is exchanged), so for financial investors, it is necessary to "roll" existing exposure close to expiration to a further date or unwind the position completely. . The slope of the futures curve is also critically important in commodities; getting long a long-dated futures with a steep curve can cause large losses, even if the spot rises slightly.

Currencies

This is predominantly an institutional off-exchange over-the-counter (OTC) market, run by the large dealers. Forwards are the most common instrument, where (like a futures) parties enter into a contract to buy/ sell one currency for another on a specific date in the future at a pre-decided exchange rate. , which is different from todays' *spot* exchange rate.

Capital Markets and Investments

As an example, by convention, EURUSD of 1.05 denotes the price of 1 USD in terms of EUR i.e. an investor need to give up 1.05 USD to get back 1 EUR[10]. Annexure III has a section on currency markets, which delves into some more detail.

Emerging Markets

Usually, issuers from non-developed markets constitute Emerging Markets. These are divided into sub regions, such as Asia-ex-Japan, MENA (Middle East and North Africa), Africa, Eastern Europe, Latin America, etc. This is predominantly an equity market, listed and traded in local markets. Equity shares of some corporates are cross-listed in the local market and the US market via ADRs. There is some bond issuance, mainly by sovereigns. Some EM corporates (Petrobras, Gazprom, etc.) are large bond issuers too. Large corporates from well-regarded EM countries issue bonds in "hard" currencies like USD and EUR, and in their local currency.

> Major Asset Classes:
> - ✓ Fixed Income (mainly bonds): Government Bonds, Interest Rate Swaps, Mortgage-Backed Securities, Agencies, Municipalities, Corporate Credit, Securitized Products, Money Markets
> - ✓ Equities (mainly shares/ stock)
> - ✓ Commodities (mainly futures, some stock-like ETFs)
> - ✓ Currencies (mainly forwards and swaps)
> - ✓ Emerging Markets (all security types)
>
> All these asset classes have derivatives trading on some securities.

CONNECTIONS BETWEEN DIFFERENT MARKETS

All these different markets/ asset classes are tethered together by the returns they offer, relative to each other. The investor needs to be compensated for the risk that he takes (and adjusts the initial price he is willing to pay accordingly), and the relative prices/ yields/ expected returns of these instruments/ asset classes need to line up with the investor's perception of risk. The different dimensions of risks are not always comparable, though the quantitative investor might try to impute probabilities of different scenarios and expected cash flows in those scenarios to compute expected returns. While it is possible for prices in some of these markets to move without affecting the others significantly, there are limits to which these markets can fall out of line, relative to one another, unless the prospects of one particular market/ asset class has changed. This is because the investor can always re-allocate assets from the less attractive market/ asset class to the relatively more attractive market.

> - ✓ All these asset classes and markets offer various levels of risk and expected return.
> - ✓ Since capital mostly flows freely (limits to arbitrage notwithstanding), an inadequate risk-return tradeoff in one market will cause capital to get reallocated to other markets, realigning market prices

---

[10] Of course, EUR and USD can be replaced by any other currency pair; the convention remains the same.

3. The Anatomy of the Sell Side

In previous chapters, we've talked about the set-up of the financial system, the various players and their incentives, and the different kinds of securities and asset classes that investors trade in. In this chapter, we will delve a little deeper into one of the key participants, the sell-side. While I will be describing the quintessential large bulge-bracket investment bank, we know (from our discussion in Chapter 1 on specialization and the nebulous firm boundaries) that a sliver of these services can also be easily and profitably provided by a more focused player. These large banks are referred to as *investment* banks to contrast them with *commercial* banks, which accept deposits and disburse loans. During the 2008 crisis, though, several investment banks ended up applying for commercial banking licenses, for regulatory reasons and to gain access to capital.

STRUCTURE OF A BULGE BRACKET SELL-SIDE FIRM

These organizations are very complex, employing tens of thousands of people in various different product lines and geographies. Broadly, these investment banks are split into the Investment Banking Division (confusing, I know), the Capital Markets Division and Prime Brokerage Services (in rare cases, rolled into Capital Markets). Of course, the usual corporate staff departments also exist.[11]

Investment Banking Division

The Investment Banking Division (IBD) *primarily enables primary market transactions*, helping companies conduct an equity *Initial Public Offering* or a *Secondary Offering, arranging* loans or bond deals, or facilitates *mergers and acquisitions* or even *bankruptcy*. The banks get compensated on the successful completion of the deal, as a percentage of the money raised. For complex transactions such as mergers, they often earn fees for advisory services too. There are several other service providers such as accountants and lawyers who also play meaningful roles.

IBD is structured primarily by industry, but there are some specialized groups that run across industries and offer niche advice on topics such as tax efficiency of transactions, etc. The senior-most Managing Directors sit on firm-level committees and talk to the largest clients. Group heads stay in touch with their client counterparts (typically corporate CFOs/ Head of Planning) and pitch ideas. The junior team members typically help with these pitches – research ideas, look up details from client balance sheets, flesh out fund-raising ideas, get a sense of where deals can price, etc. The work is substantive and under tight deadlines, with multiple last-minute changes for client meetings. When a client engages the bank, the team has a live deal and the work content changes to roadshows, working closely with the client, interacting with regulators, etc. At this time, the team is in possession of *material non-public information* from the client. This is why IBD is walled off from the Capital Markets business, which facilitates secondary market transactions. The individuals who thrive best in these IBD roles are well-rounded people who are gregarious, enjoy interacting with people, have strong communication skills, do not mind the long work hours (days start around 8:30 and run late) and the occasional travel, and care about the details regarding accounting and regulation, while not forgetting the big picture that they present in a slide deck. As the junior team members get more senior, they are valued based on how close they are to their clients; when the client has a new request, the bank should hear about it early.

---

[11] Of course, these organizations are rapidly evolving; the general discussion here is merely to give the introductory reader a sense of the lay of the land, and some idea of how business gets done.

Capital Markets and Investments

Capital Markets

This book is about Capital Markets, so we will talk about Capital Markets divisions in more detail. This is the public side of the sell-side business, *walled off from any private information* that IBD may have.

These divisions facilitate secondary market transactions – once securities have been issued and the buy-side already holds them, the capital markets desks, as brokers, facilitate the transfer of financial risk among various buy-side clients. The exact mechanism depends on the specific instrument and how it is traded; we will discuss this in depth later in the chapter. At any time during the trading day, every security/ instrument has two prices (not one!), a lower, *bid price*[12] where the bank/ broker buys from the client (i.e. the client sells) and a higher, *offer/ ask price* where the bank sells and the client buys (Note, the client buys at the higher offer price and sells at the lower bid price). When a client first reaches out to a broker, the client sometimes asks the broker to *"make a market"* before telling the broker what it wants to do. The broker (in this case a *market-maker*) then *quotes* both sides of the market (without knowing whether it will need to buy or sell), and the client then announces which side it wants to transact on. In some markets, quotes are like advertisements and emailed out several times a day for context; market makers don't need to honor them. In general, the broker can facilitate the transaction by either acting as an *agent* (a quote is less relevant here except for pricing context; the client often simply places an order to buy or sell), where it needs to find the participant on the opposite side of the trade before the sale is executed (i.e. *work the order*), or the bank itself can take the other side of the trade (i.e. *commit capital*), fill the trade with its client (i.e. a market maker), and then try to lay off the risk by trading the opposite leg. In both these situations, the bank can look to both its other buy side clients and other sell-side brokers to fulfil the other side of the transaction. When the bank temporarily takes the other side of the trade, it is exposed to price movements in the position (both positive and negative, although the bid-offer spread provides some cushion) until it can trade out of it, whereas as an agent, it simply earns commissions.

The *agency brokerage* model lends itself to setting up of small firms – such firms need relationships, with a few buy-side accounts to get order flow and also other sell-side firms to find the other side of the trade. For a few individuals with little infrastructure (phones, Bloomberg, etc.), the commissions can be lucrative. These agency brokers often cannot *"clear"* trades, and need to *"give up"* the trade to a *clearing broker*, who is a large established firm and has a membership with an exchange/ clearinghouse, which stands in between the counterparties and insures them against default. This is part of the post-trade settlement process; at this point, money gets wired, and securities are put in the buyer's account. The large sell-side integrated firms can clear their own trades, and also clear for other smaller agency brokers. The buyer accounts can be of two main types – either custodian accounts, or prime brokerage (PB) accounts. We discuss this more in the Prime Brokerage section below.

Just like the rest of the business, Capital Markets is divided based on security types/ asset classes; each of these businesses is often referred to as a "desk". For each product line or desk, most front-office people primarily work in *Sales & Trading*. In agency desks, the sales and trading roles are combined; *sales traders* talk to either principal buyers or other brokers trying to show and execute orders. But, in most desks, sales and trading are different functions; the salesperson speaks with the client, whereas the trader makes markets and actually transacts. The trader usually speaks or chats via instant messenger with the desk salesperson, who deals with the external client, but for a detailed question or right before the execution, the trader briefly takes the client call. Sometimes, a buy-side client has a sales coverage relationship, who points the client towards the correct product-focused salesperson. This is useful because, while specialization exists in all parts of the chain, the sell-side is even more specialized than the buy side; a single buy-side trader may need to interact

---

[12] To introduce more jargon, if a trader buys some stocks/ bonds, he has *lifted* the other person's offer (in other words, the trader's bid has been *hit*. So, you *hit* bids and *lift* offers.

The Anatomy of the Sell Side

with multiple desks on the sell-side. It is important for every desk to track their own contribution to firm revenue, so for orders that multiple desks collaborate on, the revenue from that trade is also "shadowed" by the desk that assists in the transaction.

While the buy-side typically does its own analysis, it typically expects the sell side to provide some summary of market data and market commentary. Since the sell-side sees flow from many clients and talks to other brokers, it is well-placed to do this. Also, to provide a more differentiated offering, the sell-side also provides trade ideas for their clients to consider. The skeptical reader might wonder whether the trade idea actually stands on its merit, or is meant to help the bank exit certain positions that it holds (either through market-making or otherwise), but that is a different issue. To help with these tasks, most well-staffed trading desks have *Desk Strategists*. Depending on the exact needs for the role, the strategist could be a programming-heavy data cruncher, or a big-picture commentary writer (or both); in either case, they are a product specialist.

Most product desks in large investment banks are market-making or *"flow" desks*; their job is not to accumulate positions, but to buy and sell securities. They are expected to make money primarily through volume (bid-offer spread / commissions). Their risk limits are usually tight i.e. they cannot warehouse large positions in securities. So, as they keep responding to client requests to quote securities (in liquid markets, this may just be reading off a screen for the most part), they need to keep in mind what securities they hold in inventory, and whether they are better buyers or sellers, and shade their quote accordingly. Of course, there are nuances to this process – in exchange traded products such as equities, the market maker is bound by exchange rules for illiquid securities; for very liquid securities the market maker has very little leeway because the prices are well-known and he can always lay off the risk in the market right away if he chooses to. As we discussed earlier, instead of giving the client a quote and committing capital, the flow desk can also suggest "working the order" by calling other dealers. In this situation, they get price limits from clients and update them if/when the order gets filled. Some desks are pure agency desks, discussed above, where their main role is to also to find the other side of the trade, but they always work orders and do not take temporary positions. In some situations, the sell-side broker reach out to *inter-dealer brokers* who can call others on behalf of this broker, maintaining his anonymity.

The other kind of trading desks at the large banks, which regulations have shrunk, are *proprietary trading desks*. These desks traded the bank's own capital, instead of client capital, and were able to hold positions and "make bets". In the aftermath of the 2008 Financial Crisis, regulators (primarily the *Volker Rule*) determined that, irrespective of walls, it was a conflict for the bank to trade extensively on their own account, while also trading on behalf of clients. Also, the potential for losses from prop desks was higher, because those desks actively take price risk. Along with leverage, these risks get easily amplified.

As regulations make it tough for the sell-side to hold positions, prop desks have largely shut down or spun off. It has become difficult even for flow desks to operate smoothly, since their risk limits for warehousing positions (albeit temporarily) get even tighter. They are working more orders, rather than taking the other side, so execution times have gone up. Even in liquid markets, for large-sized orders, the sell side is unable to step up and take the other side momentarily (or they need large compensation to do so), so prices have become move volatile, intraday. The desks are no longer in a position to provide a liquidity buffer to functioning markets, an unintended consequence of strict regulation. A prop desk and a flow desk with a lenient risk limit may indeed look similar from a regulatory lens; flow desks (incentivized to maximize desk P&L) can disguise an active proprietary position as temporary warehousing of bonds, so this isn't an easy problem to resolve.

Capital Markets desks also have *Research/ Strategy* departments, which have some similarity with the desk strategists. These research departments supposedly have views of the market independent of the trading desks and their objective is purely to analyze and recommend positions, so the reporting lines are independent from the

Capital Markets and Investments

trading desks. In reality, the performance of the research team is closely linked to how much business accrues to the trading desk as a result of clients valuing the research, so while the reporting may be different on paper, their interests are related. The credibility of a research team is also built gradually, based on the quality of research it puts out and the accuracy of its recommendations. These teams publish research pieces, usually on a pre-set calendar (from daily pieces to annual outlook), which are widely distributed to clients. These teams also have to follow strict information sharing codes, so that the research reaches all clients simultaneously. Compliance teams vet everything that goes out from Research, so trading desks like the flexibility of having desk strategists to send out quick notes with a big legal disclaimer.

The Capital Markets business also has product-focused *Structuring* desks. This term, primarily used in European banks, is currently less in vogue, but the business exists, rolled into the product desk or as part of the Index business. These desks come up with customized solutions for client needs by providing them exposure to different (often difficult-to access) markets in composite form often through total return swaps; the bank takes the other side of this trade and hedges itself out. In some shops, the desk strategists double up at the structurers. For example, suppose, hypothetically, it was not possible to access emerging market equities from outside the native country. A global investment bank, which has offices in most emerging markets, might create a structured product which promises investors the arithmetic average of the daily returns of the stock markets of Brazil, China, Russia and India, after neutralizing the currency risk. If a buy-side firm was bullish on these emerging markets, they could potentially find other ways to invest here, but this structured product is probably the simplest way to get this exposure. In fact, the buy-side firm may be willing to even pay a small fee for the convenience. A different buy-side firm may request a variant of this "product" with four different countries, which the desk could create too, just for this firm. Even if the products is simple and easy for the buy-side firm to access directly, it may be more lucrative for the buy-side firm to use a structured swap (which doesn't require a large allocation of capital but provides exposure to the returns) instead of blocking its own capital. The fees paid for the swap may be lower than leverage/ borrowing costs for the buy-side firm, if it doesn't have capital freely available and needs to borrow to put on the trade.

The *Index* business has been a growing franchise in capital markets, with high entry barriers. Traditionally, the index providers publish a rules-based index (e.g. S&P 500) value at set frequency (anytime from continuous to monthly). These indices are meant to be broadly representative of that market; buy-side portfolio managers use it to benchmark portfolios and evaluate performance. The market can be defined in a broad or narrow manner, and the index inclusion rules can be mundane or creative. So, these groups usually collect, archive and process large volumes of security-level data, and publish aggregate summaries. As the market evolved, there were demands for more exotic indices, which these index providers are well-placed to provide. Currently, even the more exotic products created by structuring desks are published as indices, and the Total Return Swap products use these indices as reference. Many buy-side clients have restrictions to invest only in index products; that has fueled this demand too.

The Capital Markets business has become increasingly *quantitative* over the past few decades. Analysts and traders have had to become more quantitatively oriented, especially in the liquid fixed income markets. More data is now available, and not analyzing this quickly will put certain participants at a disadvantage. As the buy-side expects the sell side to provide insightful commentary, this may be one way to distinguish the desk from competition. Many more data-intensive businesses, such as index, structuring have become important. More instruments are being introduced, some of which require technology and model-intensive quantitative techniques. All this has led to a large demand for *Quants*, of varied skill-sets. Some quants are essentially traders with a quantitative mindset. Others are a step removed, analyzing data for traders or structuring trades. There are also quantitative researchers, who primarily put together research based on historical data, or simulate data based on a pricing model to test efficacy. Finally, we have programming-heavy quants, who are responsible

The Anatomy of the Sell Side

for coding financial models and developing pricing engines that the desks use. Risk management roles are also often quantitative in nature. The skill sets and reporting lines for each of these roles vary. For the most technical quantitative roles, it's not uncommon for the best technology brains to step up and assume that responsibility, if they have had some quantitative / modeling exposure.

Risk Management is an important part of Capital Markets, covering several aspects of the overall business. *Market Risk* is responsible for monitoring the amount of risk the firm has to movement in market prices of securities. Each desk of the firm has its own risk limits (e.g. the maximum position it can hold temporarily when it is making markets). Market risk computes suitable risk measures and makes sure that desks don't breach their limits; when that happens, it needs to be escalated, potentially leading to positions getting pruned. Over the years, several units of the Risk Management division has been more closely tied to Compliance (see below), especially in Model Risk and Model Validation units. These roles employ a large number of quants.

Prime Brokerage

Prime Brokerage (PB) Services has become a key growth engine for sell-side firms in the last fifteen years, primarily because of the growth in the assets managed by the hedge fund community. While it has large overlap with capital markets, it has been walled off into its own division/ reporting line, because it works closely with clients that also trade with capital markets desks. Prime brokerage traditionally provided clearing and custody services, but over the last 15 years has developed a platform to leverage (i.e. amplify returns of) a wide variety asset classes, and also the plumbing to borrow and short securities. Over time, the hedge funds have become a lucrative counterparty, as they trade often, and use a wide array of services.

Like in any business, *Origination* is a key component, and involves signing up new clients to the platform. Prime Services typically house *Capital Introductions* groups, which introduce hedge funds to the investor community in hedge funds, and help younger hedge funds get off the ground by hiring people, introduce them to the suitable service providers across accounting, legal, operations, risk and more mundane tasks such as finding office space.

The trading infrastructure involves necessary plumbing such as *Clearing* and settlement functions (analogous to an individual's bank account, and the check clearing process, except here cash is exchanged for securities), through which monies are exchanged and securities change hands. Generally, most trades can be thought of as either bilateral (where the two trading parties face each other and risk the other party not honoring its commitments during settlement, either because of large price moves between the trade execution and settlement times, or the party having larger solvency issues) or centrally cleared, where every party that trades the product is either a member of a *clearing house* (an institution capitalized by members so that if one member goes under, the institution has the solvency to stand behind the trade; every counterparty faces the clearing-house) or represented by a member. In situations where an agency broker is the investor's point of contact, the agency broker *"gives up"* to a clearing house member with whom the investor has a PB account. Any instrument that trades on an exchange (e.g. equities) is centrally cleared; most OTC products are bilateral, but some are centrally cleared. Securities owned by a client can either be stored in the client's PB account, or in a separate *custody* account. The custody account is separately carved out, and distinct from the prime brokerage or the investment bank's credit risk, so the securities should be untouched even if the investment bank goes bankrupt. There are also separate specialized custodian firms that many investors use, in which case the PB transfers securities to that firm, with the client's account details. In some cases, the securities are housed in the client's PB account, especially if the securities serve as collateral for short positions or derivative trades that the client may have on.

The sell-side effectively ends up taking buy-side credit risk in several ways; some trades where the client might owe the broker-dealer money (e.g. swap/ futures) is managed by maintaining *margin accounts*, whereas financial

Capital Markets and Investments

leverage for securities is provided by the *Repo/ Securities Lending* unit. This unit lends capital (i.e. money) to clients, using the security as collateral[13]. A portion of the security's value (70% - 95%) is lent out against the security (the other 5% - 30%) is referred to as the *overcollateralization* or the *haircut*. The haircut is a cushion to protect the lending desk if the security's value goes down; haircuts are low for less volatile assets. The borrower also pays interest on the money that is borrowed. If the security against which money is borrowed loses value (i.e. declines in price) after the purchase, the buyer (i.e. client) gets a *margin call*, which requires him to either put up cash or more collateral to replenish the margin (i.e. collateral) account. Often, this leads to the buyer having to sell the security at the current low price (at a large loss), because the buyer may not have other available resources to fund the account. Alternatively, if the investment was not levered and funded fully with the buyer's own cash, then the client could wait for prices to rebound if he felt that the selloff was temporary.

The desk also interacts with the securities lending programs at the large mutual funds/ buy side institution, and borrows securities from these funds to provide other clients (mainly hedge funds), who might want to *short* it. The mutual fund earns a fee lending a security that it anyway was holding, the other client gets a "borrow/ locate" on a security to short. For this, the client pays a fee (the *borrow cost*), and the broker pockets the difference between the two fees. The cash proceeds from the client's short sale collateralizes the borrowing (i.e. a security in this example) also earns an interest; any fee that the client pays is net of this interest. If the price of the security goes up, the collateral is now insufficient and needs to be topped up. If the short seller does not have additional available resources, this can lead to the short position being unwound at a loss (i.e. the discussion on leverage in the previous paragraph in reverse). The *Counterparty Risk Management* division manages the credit exposure of the sell-side firm to each of its clients.

Support Functions

Most of the roles described above are "front-office" roles. In addition, there are "mid-office" and "back-office" roles too. Front office roles are roles that require direct client interaction or are directly related to generating profits for the firm. The mid-office works very closely with front office members to reconcile post-trade verification records, trades settlements and other operational tasks, run firm-level market risk reports, make sure that the firm is in compliance with all regulatory requirements, etc. In that sense, Counterparty Risk and Clearing roles are closer to the mid office roles. A junior trader would also be working very closely with mid-office, though his reporting lines would be different.

Information Technology is a critical division that supports each of the businesses described above, provides the interfaces by which people in different divisions exchange information. While some IT resources are also dedicated to firm-wide initiatives, whereas most resources are mapped to businesses. In rare cases, some technology personnel report into business heads rather through the technology teams, so their fortunes are more closely tied to the performance of that particular line of business.

Compliance (often combined with Legal) has become much more prominent over the last few years. In some banks, this has been integrated with the CFO's office. This is because the regulatory changes after the 2008 Financial Crisis have required compliance to play a more active role to make sure that the roadmap for adherence to new rules (Dodd-Frank, Volker, Basel 3, as the case may be) is being strictly followed. The large fines imposed on the banks has brought this more in the spotlight, and more resources are being allocated to hire staff. The skill sets required in the unit is also evolving, with more people required to interact with regulators, work closely with certain internal risk departments, and have a more quantitative perspective. In fact, several technology startups have been launched, aiming to supply tools to compliance teams for better surveillance and monitoring.

---

[13] From the buyer's (i.e. client's) perspective, this is a levered (long) investment.

The Anatomy of the Sell Side

In addition, there are several corporate divisions such as Marketing, Legal, Human Resources, Compliance, Accounting & Finance (CFO's office), Strategy/ Planning. Figure 3.1 shows the organization structure of a hypothetical sell-side bank, with the divisions discussed above.

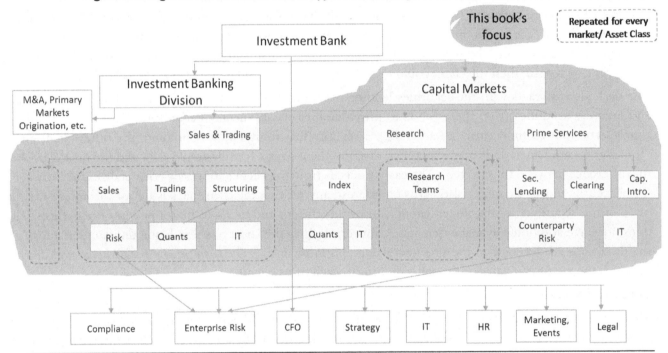

Figure 3.1 Organization Structure of a Hypothetical Bulge Bracket Investment Bank

✓ The sell-side investment bank comprises many departments, as detailed in the chart above. Capital markets broadly comprises Sales & Trading and Research for every product/ asset class. Prime Service is a closely-related department focusing on back-end processes and hedge fund clients.

BASIC MARKET MICROSTRUCTURE

An academic study of *market microstructure* would necessarily get into details about asymmetric information across various market regimes, and how the market maker protects himself by widening the bid-offer spread as he worries about being more uniformed than the counterparty. Here, we take a different approach, and discuss the mechanics of markets governing different instruments.

How do instruments trade?

Now that we have some understanding of how desks work, and the various instruments, we discuss how instruments trade. While we discussed the role of desks in facilitating trades, there are large differences in how different products trade i.e. the market microstructure varies. This is because of the specifics of the product, legacy/ historical reasons, technological evolution, and to some extent regulatory landscape. Broadly, markets can be categorized as Exchange-traded or Over-the-Counter (OTC).

Exchange-Traded Markets

Many popular asset classes trade on exchanges – equities, equity options and futures, Treasury futures, commodity futures and options. These markets have only *one centralized order-book* i.e. market participants put in

Capital Markets and Investments

buy/ sell orders (usually at a specified price); these orders are all consolidated and sorted based on price. The highest price to buy is the best bid, and the lowest price to sell is the best offer. If the best bid is higher than the best offer, trades keep getting executed until this is no longer the case. At the same time, new orders come streaming in and the book continually gets refreshed. When the best bid is lower than the best offer, no more trades are executed until a new order is placed to buy above the best offer or sell below the best bid. Until that time, of course, this bid-offer quote is only relevant for the order size that is available at that price. This bid/ offer quote is firm until cancelled; if an order were to be placed right away at that price, it will definitely get executed (provided the initial order is not cancelled before the new order hits.

Even in this very simple example, there can be various *order types* – a limit order, which specifies the worst price (i.e. floor price for sell and cap price for buy order) at which the order is to be executed, and a market order, which executes the order, at the current/ best possible market price. When an order is placed, the order type needs to be specified. While most ideas in this section can be applied to all the exchange-traded markets (to varying levels), the specifics below relate to the equity markets, which are the most evolved.

Exchanges have undergone a metamorphosis in the last 15 years. Not so long ago, there were only a few main exchanges - NYSE, AMEX & NASDAQ. NYSE and AMEX were hallowed buildings with frenzied activity on the "floor/ pit", and large volumes of trades got done there. Over the years, with the popularity of computers, more trading shifted to the electronic platforms – NASDAQ was the pioneer, set up in 1971 as primarily a quotation system with offline execution, which evolved into automated trading in the late 1980s. The exchanges were modernized. New electronic exchanges were set up; the barrier to entry decreased. There are 12 major exchanges in the US, as of July 2017. Exchanges, being for-profit institutions, figured out that they could sell faster access to data at a higher price, while keeping the infrastructure for the rest of the market at the earlier slow speeds. This led to several perverse incentives, and fueled the growth of high-frequency trading shops. The very low volume on physical exchanges has almost reduced these headquarters to being primarily TV studios[14]!

These listed markets have variants, primarily based on transparency. The market described above (i.e. the transparent centralized order book) is usually a traditional *lit* market because the entire order book is visible.[15] So, it's easy for a trader to see if there is a big block (i.e. large size) order right below the current market. This may not be in the best interest of the party that placed the large order. To get around this issue, some firms (including investment banks) developed *dark pools* or *Alternative Trading Systems (ATS)*[16], with opaque order books. In these *marketplaces*, clients can place orders without others being able to see the order. If the order gets filled, the client is sent a trade confirm. Unlike lit markets, dark pools do not publish quotes (and the order book), and the client's order is not visible to outsiders. The drawback of "hiding", though, is that hidden orders are not on public feeds, so such orders may get "traded through" and not get executed even if the price limit is reached on another venue (i.e. it does not get the benefit of NBBO, or *Rule 611 of Reg. NMS*); had the same order been lit, it would have been executed against the order on the other venue. Also, dark pools, like exchanges, support many order types, allowing clients a lot of flexibility (maybe too much) in how their order is executed, and what information is revealed.

Dark pools initially presented themselves to institutional investors as trading venues where firms could trade without publicly displaying their order, and also trade with similar types of counterparties (i.e. not get picked

---

[14] Even though one sees a few traders on the floor, the actual trading happens off-site in data centers, mainly in New Jersey.

[15] It is possible to trade "dark" on an exchange; certain order types allow it.

[16] An Electronic Communications Network is an ATS that is registered with the Securities and Exchange Commission (SEC) either as a broker or an exchange, and publicly publishes quotes. ECNs only act as agents, matching other participants, and cannot execute their own trades, unlike other ATS.

off by investors with different horizons, objectives and constraints), since the pool operator (unlike exchanges, who need to abide by the *fair access* rule) can control who can trade there. In reality, though, the composition of market participants at these venues is similar to exchanges. Regulators have fined dark pool operators in cases that accused operators of misrepresenting their pool to clients, and even using client orders to inform their own trading. While there is little transparency on order disclosure at these alternative venues, FINRA has recently required them to report volume statistics and report trades to the Consolidated Tape (exchanges have always reported trades to the tape).

Over the last decade, more and more volume has shifted to the dark market from the lit market; most estimates suggest that at least 40% of trading volume is off the traditional exchange. Investors wishing to enter into trades can either reach out to a broker (more expensive), or use electronic *Order Management Systems (OMS)*, which can get significantly cheaper, depending on size and order type. These OMS have made business tougher for equity agency brokers. The ATS and exchanges have also modified their revenue models. Two decades ago, they priced based on volume, and taking a commission on every trade. They have now evolved to *maker-taker models*, where they charge a fee (only) to the client requiring/ taking liquidity and provides a small payment (*rebate*) to the client that provides (i.e. makes) liquidity[17]. This has spurred the growth of high-frequency strategies focused on earning these rebates. With faster (more expensive) access to data/ quote feeds, these firms can algorithmically decide when and what price to provide liquidity, and try to lay it off almost instantly. OMS algorithms have been getting smarter, chopping orders into small pieces and routing it to various exchanges/ dark pools. This trend of more trades shifting off exchanges may be poised for a reversal, as new regulations get implemented, and new exchanges such as IEX establish themselves.

Retail brokers (such as Charles Schwab or TDAmeritrade) do not send their client orders directly to the exchange; instead they send it to a wholesaler (such as Citadel or KCG Securities), who then executes the trade to get "best execution", which is not clearly defined (may be the fastest execution, best price, etc.). Supporters of this argue that this lowers trading costs for small investors; opponents complain about conflict of interest.

Over-the-Counter (OTC) Markets

An OTC market is a bilateral market, where the buyer and seller transact with each other one-on-one, often through an intermediary. The big difference from an exchange-traded market is that there is *no consolidated order book* (lit or dark). This gives the impression of an opaque market, where the principal risk takers are completely at the mercy of the intermediary. The intermediary, on the other hand, might worry about temporarily holding the instrument (he will be on the hook for price changes) if this is a one-off trade in a security, in case there is some recent adverse news that he might have missed. And, if he decides to lay off the risk later, that may not be easy. Despite this apparent opaque nature, OTC markets are very useful when there are a plethora of very similar products available to trade, e.g. bonds issued by General Electric. General Electric issues bonds very frequently to finance operations, and it is unrealistic to expect a deep liquid consolidated order book for every bond issue that GE has launched (in contrast, GE has only one kind of equity share). But, it is likely to be very easy to find the other side of that market, if the broker were to make a market to his client. If the broker is constrained by capital limits, it would be relatively easy to work a bond order in this name. As we move to less popular corporates who are not prolific issuers, this situation gets more acute; a OTC market is probably the only way any risk will get transferred in this situation. The OTC market can also provide *anonymity*

---

[17] Market orders that are executed immediately (or buy orders with limit price at/ higher than best ask price and sell orders with limit price at/ below best bid) and take liquidity from the market. Limit orders that are outside the current bid-offer and get added to the order book (queue) provide (make) liquidity.

Capital Markets and Investments

to the principal risk taker; apart from the intermediary, no one needs to know who the participant is, much like a dark pool. OTC markets also work well when the trade can be customized. Often (but not always), custom products are traded in OTC markets, and the dealer manages his risk by trading in other products with similar risk profiles. This is especially true of interest rate swaps. Of course, customization makes the market less liquid, when someone tries to get out of a swap (which was previously entered into) in the secondary market. Markets have tried to work around this, by standardizing certain aspects of the instruments, such as maturity dates (e.g. *IMM dates*).

Some large and heavily-traded markets (mainly fixed income), such as the bond market (Treasury, mortgages, etc.), the swap market (interest rates and credit default), the currency market (forwards and swaps), etc. are OTC. The primary reasons for this are legacy-related and the diversity / number of bond issues; while the awkwardness of several (hundred) issues by the same issuer is an impediment, it should be possible for modern technology to circumvent part of that problem, especially for bonds (which are not customized for the client). While some market players might argue that the sell-side has a vested interest to keep as much trading in the OTC world as it possibly can, the market has evolved to using systems such as E-Speed and Tradeweb, which offer real-time quotes in the Treasury market from multiple dealers for different sizes and put them in competition with each other. Additionally, the buy side (or other dealers/ potential traders) can issue Request-For-Quotes (RFQs) on these platforms. If the order sizes are not too big, most large sell-side banks have algorithms running to spit out automatic real-time quotes based on current market prices, order flow, recent trades, etc. Treasury and Currency markets, while technically OTC, have seen huge technological and institutional changes; some of these issues are discussed in the chapter on Treasuries, where we discuss market microstructure specific to that product.

In most other OTC markets (municipalities, corporates, CMBS, ABS are examples), the primary mechanism to disseminate quotes is through emails, also referred to as "*dealer runs*". Depending on the market, these quotes may be firm or indicative (i.e. essentially an advertisement). Usually quotes with a size next to them are considered more reliable. While the buy-side relies on these quotes to get a sense of what prices they may be able to trade at, index providers and pricing services use them as a source for prices, based on which they mark index constituents. Firms with risk positions speak with the brokers one-on-one to get a sense of what's bid for/ on offer. Since the order book isn't centralized, multiple sets of people need to stay in touch with one another (instead of checking a central repository) to understand the supply demand dynamics. Depending on the market, post-trade reporting varies – regulators such as FINRA (i.e. *TRACE*) and MSRB have regulatory systems where the dealers need to enter details of the trade soon after it is executed; sizes of large trades are masked. Often, firms with a large inventory of bonds that they need to clear will electronically send out *Bids-Wanted-In-Competition (BWICs)* listing the inventory. Interested parties will be able to bid on one or more positions (like an EBay auction) by a certain deadline; the highest bidder gets the bond, assuming the reserve price is met (seller can choose to not sell the bond after seeing the bids).

Electronic trading is getting more common in many of these OTC markets, with various firms setting up engines to match buyers with sellers. Auto-quoting, discussed in the chapters on Treasuries, is also more common in fixed income and interest rate derivatives, where models spit out real-time executable 2-way markets for small size, based on client inquiry. These quotes are generated by computers, based on movements in various markets and the dealer inventory. Depending on the platform, these systems may be all-to-all (anyone can trade with anyone else), or bilateral (where a participant can control the counterparty). For example, a Greenwich Associates report said that electronic trading venues garnered 20% of U.S. investment-grade corporate bond trading volume in 2015. More generally, though, while these units have grown exponentially, they remain a small part of most markets but are poised to get larger.

The Anatomy of the Sell Side

Even the traditionally exchange traded markets can have some OTC trades. For example, a buy-side firm which needs to do a large trade (e.g. half the daily trading volume or larger) will sometimes call a large sell-side firm and trade the entire block instantly at a guaranteed price – a slight discount to the current screen price, or *Volume-Weighted Average Price*. The broker, who in this case takes temporary price risk, works his way out of the position by trading throughout the day, possibly hedging part of the exposure. If the firm had instead tried to trade it directly on the exchange/ screen, it's likely that size/ volume wouldn't be available; at the very least it would be disruptive and market-moving. Even if the firm used a sophisticated OMS (automated rule-based algorithm), the execution may eventually work out to be cheaper, but an instant fill is not guaranteed, or even likely.

Trade Date and Settlement Date

Strictly speaking, the trade is not completely over when two parties agree to buy/ sell an instrument (the *Trade Date*). Of course, the economics are decided at that point in time, but the actual physical exchange (of security for cash, for example) still needs to happen. This is usually effected by making electronic transfers to various accounts by the back offices of both parties, after the broker has passed on necessary instructions, often through a clearinghouse/ exchange, depending on the market. All this is not instantaneous and takes a few days, depending on the market (Treasury Bills settle same-day). This final exchange is called *settling* the trade, and date on which that happens is called the *Settlement Date*. There are market conventions for how long settlement should take – Treasuries usually settle the day after the trade (T+1 settlement), equity stocks settle T+3, currencies settle T+2, corporate bonds settle T+3, etc. To be clear, any price changes between the trade date and the settlement date does not affect the trade price, but it affects the new buyer's income (unless, of course, he sold out of it soon after buying).

Capital Markets and Investments

Market Microstructure:
- ✓ Exchange-Traded Markets – All orders get aggregated in a centralized limit-order book.
  - Lit Markets: This order book, comprising size, direction and price limit is public
  - Alternate Trading Systems: Comprising dark pools and ECNs, these venues do not publish the quotes or the order book. Clients face a confidentiality-better execution trade-off.
    - At least 40% of trading happens through these platforms.
    - Large client orders are not publicly displayed, providing confidentiality. But the client loses the opportunity to trade against better prices at other venues.
    - Dark pool owners can see client orders, and potentially act inappropriately.
    - Some exchanges are slow to calculate the best bid-offer. High-frequency clients who pay extra can get the raw data very quickly, calculate prices before the exchange, and predict and be positioned for the exchange price when it is published. Some clients put in many orders, intending to give a different impression on the book and cancel them before execution.
  - Increasing number of order-types. Orders that provide (make) liquidity are usually compensated. Retail brokers are paid by venues to direct order flow towards them
  - All trades (lit and dark) are posted to the Consolidated Tape.
- ✓ Over-The-Counter Markets- Bilateral trading between buyer and seller
  - Provides confidentiality, easier to move large blocks.
  - Difficult for customers to get a sense of the exact demand/ supply, especially in less liquid bonds. But, many markets (e.g. corporate and municipality bonds) have to report trades within a few minutes to a centralized reporting engine, enhancing transparency.
  - Dealers send out emails with runs, although some markets trade on electronic platforms
  - To sell a large list of bonds, dealers send out BWICs, and conduct a secondary auction.

FURTHER THOUGHTS

The large sell-side bank is a behemoth, with lots of opportunity for cross-selling products to clients. At the same time, it involves many small teams / desks, who are strongly incentivized (their compensation is closely tied to desk profits) to earn large profits for the firm. Their losses are limited to the desk being shut down if it fares poorly. In a world with many sell-side firms, it is conceivable that this desk would find a home elsewhere; the negative track record affects prospects, but firms willing to grow aggressively will possibly look through it. Because of the very desk-centric culture, it is difficult to foster collaboration across desks, especially if they do not roll up to the same manager. Especially when different sales desks need to work together, it's not straightforward to precisely allocate credit; no wonder the total P&L that each desk reports sometimes aggregates to many multiples of the firm's P&L!

The 2008 financial crisis brought into focus the level of interconnectedness of the large sell-side firm, and its effect on the broader economy. Regulators concluded that the problems were exaggerated because these banks were also owners of large volumes of securities, rather than simply putting buyers and sellers in touch. The

The Anatomy of the Sell Side

banks were taking price risk (in many different ways/ businesses), rather than relying primarily on bid/offer spreads, commissions and fee income for the capital markets profits. The regulators figured that this would be controlled if they forced these banks hold high levels of capital on their balance sheet i.e. make it punitive for the banks to allocate capital to various businesses. While this has reduced the banks' exposure to security price movements (speculative positioning or otherwise) and potentially reduced their profitability, it has also affected their ability to conduct their market-making business effectively, especially in less liquid asset classes/ names[18]. This has reduced liquidity in these markets, and increased potential price volatility, as investors don't have the comfort of the sell-side stepping in to cushion minor speed bumps, when a primary investor may be reducing risk. Some buy-side firms have toyed with market-making in the past; a couple of them (e.g. Citadel) have gained market leadership in specific asset classes. But no grand buy-side only trading platform has emerged so far.

- ✓ The sell-side is a complex behemoth, with small teams tied together with nebulous linkages.
- ✓ These firms were the focus of the 2008 financial crisis; regulatory changes designed to make them safer have also constrained their businesses, causing their clients to worry about how to continue transacting efficiently, especially in stressful markets.

---

[18] Volker Rule allows firms to make markets and set position limits based on reasonably expected near-term demand (RENTD) of clients, which gives banks some leeway while holding positions.

4. Overview of Buy Side Firms

In the previous chapter, we discussed sell-side firms, and the various intermediaries. Sell-side firms play an important role in transferring financial assets from one institution to another, provide infrastructural support and customized solutions. But, most assets are invested by *buy-side* firms, also known as *asset managers*.

WHAT DO BUY-SIDE FIRMS DO?

The buy-side refers to the part of the financial services industry that is focused on investing capital. In a broad sense, these firms are simpler to understand than the sell-side – they raise money from clients (the *asset owners*) and invest it in the financial markets, respecting the guidelines that they agreed to with their clients (and any applicable laws). They earn a fee based on the amount of money they manage, and in some cases a performance fee, based on how well their portfolios perform. If they perform poorly, their clients can take back the investment capital, and allocate to another manager.

There are some standard pools of capital (i.e. retail clients saving for college or retirement, pension funds with beneficiaries, rich individuals and families, university endowment trying to generate returns on its corpus, corporate treasuries, proprietary trading desks, Central Banks, etc.), but capital may be sourced pretty much anywhere. Most buy-side firms are third-party (i.e. external) professional managers who raise capital from one or more capital sources (i.e. asset owners/ clients), and then manage (i.e. invest) the capital on behalf of their clients for a fee. When discussing the buy side, we will refer to this client as the *allocator* or asset owner, and the investor as the manager.

Allocators either choose managers to manage their assets, or invest directly by hiring the relevant investment professionals in-house (or some combination of both). Direct (i.e. *principal*) investment saves them the fee that the manager would charge, but some allocators may not have the expertise to invest directly in specific asset classes. In many cases, institutional allocators (e.g. pension plans) retain *consultants* in an advisory capacity to evaluate and perform due diligence on various managers; these consultants effectively act as gatekeepers between the asset managers and the allocators. In other cases (e.g. proprietary trading desks), investments are completely self-directed without any external asset managers.

Asset managers usually raise capital from these asset owners and hold it in "*funds*" (a legal vehicle that houses investment assets and makes investments) either pooled across clients (commingled funds) or in separate accounts. The holding company or sponsor, i.e. an *Asset Management Company*, invests in the financial market through these funds (which end up holding some combination of securities and cash) and earns a fee from the fund; thus, asset managers are also called fund managers. The fee structure varies widely depending on the terms of the fund, driven in turn by the reputation of the sponsoring team, their track record, asset class, competition in the marketplace for funds, etc. Like the sell-side, the buy-side also uses several vendors for specialized non-core services like accountants, lawyers and IT.

The fund tasks are often separated. The *fund sponsor* "brands" the fund and raises capital with the help of an underwriter, the *investment (sub-) advisor* actually manages the assets (in many cases these two roles are combined), the fund *administrator* verifies whether the financial assets in the fund are being valued correctly and following applicable laws, the *transfer agent* executes shareholder transactions and maintains records, the *custodian* holds fund assets, and the *accountant* certifies fund financial statements periodically.

Since asset managers usually invest on behalf of their clients, they typically abide by certain regulatory and self-imposed guidelines. These asset managers have their specializations and mandates, which reassures allocators about which slivers of the market their capital gets allocated to. The allocators themselves have strict

Overview of Buy Side Firms

guidelines to ensure that they do not deviate from their own investment objectives, given their obligations, investment horizon, risk appetite, etc. Since this system of asset management involves a lot of delegation and gives the manager discretion on where to invest, guidelines are a mechanism to keep managers in check and prevent "style drift".

In the retail investor's world, many of the same issues are present, with private wealth managers (or Robo-advisors)/ brokers acting as intermediaries, evaluating mutual funds, ETFs and single names. Since smaller retail investors rarely allocate money to multiple intermediaries, asset allocation guidelines are less strict; however regulatory requirements are higher. And of course, may retail investors invest directly, without an advisor.

At the institutional allocator's end, the process begins by the board assessing the macro environment and coming up with an asset allocation plan – what percent of their capital they want to allocate to various asset classes – equity, liquid fixed income, rates, credit, alternatives (i.e. private equity, hedge funds, real estate), etc. The (sometimes semantic) distinction between what constitutes an asset class versus an investment style (e.g. are hedge funds an asset class?) and how exactly to divide up the investment universe varies across firms. The next part of the exercise involves selecting managers to manage these sleeves of capital. For some esoteric asset classes, allocators sometimes (increasingly less so) use fund of funds, who are specialized in evaluating a certain kind of manager and can often decide, on behalf of the allocator (instead of merely advise, like a consultant) which manager to pick. Fund of funds involve a separate layer of fees, one of the reasons why that business is receding.

> ✓ The buy-side comprises asset owners/ allocators, investment managers, and intermediary consultants.

INVESTMENT STYLES

Managers can manage assets either passively or actively. *Passive fund managers* usually manage their portfolio to closely mimic a *benchmark* index (e.g. S&P 500 for equities), for very low fees. Such managers are suitable for allocators who want broad exposure to an asset class at low cost, but care less about security selection skills of managers. Passive investment products are available for most asset classes, through a variety of product offerings discussed below. Such managers are evaluated based on how closely their performance mirrors the benchmark; *tracking error* measures how correlated the portfolio's returns are to that of the benchmark. This aside, portfolio implementation (construction/ rebalancing), trading costs and management fees are also important variables affecting the divergence between a portfolio's return and that of the benchmark.

In contrast, *active management* products allow the asset manager more flexibility in picking securities within an asset class, without necessarily anchoring the portfolio to a benchmark. Since this involves the manager analyzing individual positions (instead of semi-mechanically replicating security/ sector weights in the benchmark and periodically rebalancing), active management products usually have higher fees. Active management products also come in various flavors and are available in a variety of products. Over the years, as algorithmic data processing capability has grown stronger and some hedge fund strategies have become widely known and discussed, strategies which were earlier accessible only through active management platforms are now being made available more passively, as "smart-beta" products. The lowest-fee very-similar-to-index product is often referred to as a *Core* product, a benchmarked product which makes some active bets is called *Core Plus*. As discussed above, more dynamic products are called active; the most esoteric investments are often part of the alternatives pool. . A subset of active management is referred to as *absolute return investing*; where the

Capital Markets and Investments

investor is not evaluated relative to a market index but purely based on the absolute level of return the portfolio generates. Most alternative managers fall in this category. These products could either be *long-only* (i.e. 100% long, no shorts allowed), *relaxed constraint* (e.g. 130% long, 30% short), or *market neutral*.

There are multiple flavors of active investing and the idea-generation process; the broad classification is top-down versus bottom-up. The *top-down process* begins by examining the macro landscape, forming a view on how that is likely to evolve, and then identifying investment opportunities that will do well if the view is correct. The contrasting style, *bottom-up*, starts with the individual company or the security, analyzing whether the market is pricing it fairly, and buying positions that the analysts view as undervalued (i.e. the market is pricing it too low) and more likely to go up, and selling / shorting positions which the market is paying too much for. Many firms employ a hybrid process, with investment committees allocating capital across various sector/ asset class specialists, who do the deep dive on single names.

The styles described above, which actually involve understanding and forming an opinion of the securities invested in, are broadly labelled as *fundamental*, and form the bulk of active investment assets. A different (polar opposite) investment style, *quantitative*, generates investment ideas by looking through reams of historical data through the lens of quantitative models and analyzes potentially a large universe of securities efficiently and, depending on the firm, either shortlists them or automatically generates trade lists.

A closely-related (and arguably more precise) taxonomy of investment styles describes them as either *discretionary* (where the individual portfolio manager can decide whether (and how much) to buy or sell a position) or *systematic* (where computer programs analyze data and apply models to pick investments). The exact reasons why one position in a systematic strategy is a buy whereas another is a sell may often appear to be in a black box (except, maybe, to the quant who designed the algorithm). Quant modelers become far more important in the systematic arena; the kinds of models deployed depend on the asset class. Some smart beta strategies discussed above can be implemented systematically.

While fundamental and discretionary are often used interchangeably (as are quantitative and systematic), in reality a systematic strategy can use information on company fundamental performance in its models, whereas a discretionary manager can also use quantitative techniques as a guide or a screening criteria. Recently, *quantamental* has often been mentioned as a separate class of strategies!

- ✓ Investment managers can choose securities passively (replicating a benchmark's holding) or actively (deciding that some specific securities are likely to do better than others and holding more of them).
- ✓ Active management can involve top-down or bottom-up processes, using fundamental and/or quantitative analysis, in systematic or discretionary processes.

INVESTMENT PRODUCT OFFERINGS

Investment managers package and present the above ideas / concepts to investors in the form of different product offerings. Asset owners can either buy specific financial instruments, to the extent they can access them, or buy holdings in Investment products differ in terms of their target audience, which also decides how they are regulated. Of course, these investment products are often specialized by the asset class or sector the managers invest in. Regulation spells out the constraints under which funds operate, and determines whether they are allowed to short (i.e. *long-short*) or not (*long-only*); most regulated funds are long-only, or have limits on how much they can short (e.g. *130-30 funds*). These details are listed in the fund prospectus, fact sheets and annual reports. The prospectus also includes the fee structure of the firms, as well as the other investment

Overview of Buy Side Firms

terms. Institutional fund management agreements are tailored between the client(s) and the manager; regulatory restrictions are fewer but guidelines play a big role. We now discuss the different kinds of investment products offered by asset managers. Most of these products can be offered for any particular asset class, or industry sector, or other specialization.

Mutual Funds

These are funds sponsored by asset managers such as Fidelity, Vanguard, Blackrock, PIMCO etc., primarily targeting retail individuals. Mutual funds can be either actively or passively managed. A board of directors (appointed by the sponsor) oversees the fund manager. The two prominent types of mutual funds are closed-end and open-end funds; open-ended structures are much more common. All mutual-funds publish an end-of-day *Net Asset Value (NAV)*, which is an aggregation of the value of all the securities that they hold. *Open-ended funds* allow investors to buy or redeem fund units with the fund sponsor at the end-of-day NAV every day through retail brokerage account platforms, so the Assets Under Management (AUM) for these funds fluctuate every day. One cannot transact intra-day in open-end funds (they can in ETFs; more on that on the next page).

Closed-end funds raise capital only when they are launched (secondary offerings aside, below), and trade on an exchange like a stock. Their trading prices are market-determined, and usually trade at a discount to NAV. These funds can borrow (within limits) to supplement the equity capital that they initially raise; thus they can amplify returns through leverage. In rare situations (e.g. PIMCO High Income Fund), the fund may trade at a premium to NAV, possibly because investors are willing to pay a premium (beyond the fees) for good management. In such a situation, the fund can do a secondary offering of units to raise more equity capital. Unlike open-end funds, closed–end funds raise permanent capital and do not face redemption risk; investors trade these like a stock in the secondary market.

Mutual funds provide daily liquidity to investors; open-ended funds provide end-of-day liquidity at NAV whereas closed-end funds provide intra-day liquidity through the secondary market (at a premium or discount to NAV, depends on where it is trading). These funds charge a management fee. In a few cases, funds also charge an entry and/or exit load fee. Fees are usually calculated as a percentage of the total assets under management.

In the US, investment funds have to make public all their holdings every quarter, through 13-F filings. Besides, like all investors, they have to file a 13-D form if they own more than 5% of a company. Mutual funds are regulated by the Investment Company Act of 1940 (the "1940 Act"), and are restricted in their leverage (can only borrow from banks, a maximum of 50% of their pre-borrowing assets) and their exposure to derivative investments (cannot be liable for more than fund AUM).

These products are heavily regulated primarily because they are targeted at the small retail investor. So, fund sponsors often market a version of the mutual fund with fewer restrictions to institutional clients, which may allow them to freely use derivatives or take on leverage, etc. Of course, these products will not trade on an exchange or offer daily liquidity; investment terms (including fees) are negotiated for every investor separately. These funds can be commingled or provided through a fund-of-one/ separately managed account structure.

Exchange Traded Funds (ETFs)

Exchange Traded Funds (ETFs), which also earn management fees based on their AUM, have features of both closed-end and open-end funds – Like closed-end funds, they trade intra-day on an exchange like a stock but, like an open-end fund, they can also have AUM changes on a daily basis. This is facilitated by a set of

Capital Markets and Investments

ETF manager-appointed intermediaries called *Authorized Participants* (APs)[19], who, apart from trading the ETF in the secondary market like a stock, can also turn in a basket of constituent securities (the *Creation basket* – decided by the fund manager and changes daily) to the ETF manager to get back a *unit* of the ETF, thereby increasing the fund AUM (by the number of units "created" times the NAV). If there is a lot of demand for the ETF and the AP is receiving many buy orders, the AP can either create new units (by buying the constituent securities in the creation basket and turning them in for units), or search for sellers of the ETF in the secondary market by trading on the exchange. Conversely, if many investors want to sell the ETF, the AP can either resell the ETF to someone else or turn the units in to the ETF manager to receive the *Redemption Basket* of securities (again, ETF manager-determined and changes daily), thus leading to a decrease in the ETF's AUM. The AP has a strong incentive to redeem if the ETF is trading at a discount (below its NAV), and create when the ETF is trading at a premium (above NAV). This mechanism to create or redeem keeps ETFs fairly close to NAV, compared to closed-end mutual funds. The ETF manager publishes the creation and redemption baskets daily, keeping in mind what the ETF needs to hold and sell, to track its benchmark closely.

Professional investment managers sometimes use ETFs to quickly adjust exposures in their portfolio, treating the ETF like a stock. However, if professional managers use many ETFs as their primary means of exposure, the asset allocators may not be thrilled, because they are now paying two layers of fees, for an off-the-shelf product.

While ETFs started out as being predominantly passively managed or quantitative strategy-based products (rule-based portfolio construction), actively managed ETFs are now also available. . *Levered* ETFs and *Inverse* ETFs, which provide a multiple or the inverse of the returns of a benchmark, have also become popular. To maintain the appropriate exposure, these products need to buy when markets rise, and sell when the markets sell off, thus performing poorly when markets are choppy and do not trend. Regulators have been scrutinizing levered ETFs and insisting on better disclosure.

Alternative Investments

Alternative investment funds are less-regulated investment vehicles targeting institutional capital and in some cases, ultra-high net worth individuals; investments are only open to Qualified Institutional Buyers. They are expected to be highly specialized and employ more risky/ sophisticated strategies, often with much less liquidity.

These funds also differ from other funds in terms of the investment fees that the investment managers (often called *General Partners*) charge asset owners (often referred to as *Limited Partners*), and other restrictive terms, related mainly to transparency and liquidity. For example, liquidity constraints may require clients to commit (i.e. *lock-up*) their capital to the fund for various lengths of time (1 year – 10 years, depending on the type of fund), provide advance notice for withdrawals, be subjected to "*gates*" if many clients redeem at the same time, etc.

Alternative investment funds also have distinctive fee structures – aside from a flat management fee as a percentage of AUM, the fee structure also often has *performance fees* built in, if the fund does well. The details of the performance fee (sometimes called *incentive fee* or *carried interest*) calculation matters, in terms of whether performance is absolute (relative to zero) or relative to a benchmark, and whether there is a hurdle return after which incentive fees are calculated, and of course, the percentage of the outperformance that is paid as an

---

[19] Often, there are market-makers who traffic in these ETFs (like any stock), between the ETF end-investor and the AP (very often, the AP also doubles up as a market-maker).

incentive fee. The return net of all these fees (and sometimes some out-of-pocket expenses) accrues to the client.

There are two main kinds of alternative investment funds: Hedge funds and Private Equity/ Venture Capital[20]. At the simplest level, hedge funds primarily invest in securities that a mutual fund would potentially invest in; they buy relatively small holdings in companies that have raised capital in the public markets. So, while their liquidity terms are more stringent than mutual funds, clients can typically get their capital back in a quarter. Private equity firms typically raise multi-year locked-up capital (similar to a closed-end fund, but with a redemption date) to make concentrated bets in a few companies, and take board seats. That said, lines are getting blurry, as hedge funds now trade in less liquid assets and participate in private offerings and bankruptcies, pursue activist strategies to get on company boards and effect change. Private equity Incentive fees (carried interest) are usually earned only based on realized profits, unlike most hedge funds where fees are earned on mark-to-market profits (albeit with a high watermark).

Hedge Funds

Hedge funds differ from each other in terms of "style" – asset class and the investment process/ philosophy. Some common *styles/ strategies* include Macro, Equity Long/short, Fixed Income Arbitrage, Merger Arbitrage/ Event Driven, Credit/ Distressed, CTA/ Managed Futures, Emerging Market. They also vary in management style and structure – *centralized* top-heavy funds which have very few portfolio managers (PM) making investment decisions, with several analysts supporting each of them. While good investment ideas are still tracked individually and rewarded, the employees are much more exposed to overall firm performance, than they are to their own team's. Risk management is more straightforward, as it relates to one large book, rather than multiple separate pods.

Decentralized funds have many semi-independent PMs. They highlight their PM selection, retention and capital/ risk allocation process to clients; in such funds, each PM has significant flexibility in picking investments (less top-down), as long as he remains within his risk limits and expertise. Every team's/ PM's profits are calculated separately, which determines how much PMs are paid (often formulaic) and/or their contract renewed. Hedging and risk managing the overall book requires being vigilant about PM risk levels (as PMs are incentivized to take as much risk as possible, since their employment contract pays them on profits), and also understanding the net effect of the strategies of all the PMs on the firm. The fund manager also takes *netting risk* in terms of performance fees, since the manager needs to pay (the contractual incentive fee) out to PMs who have made money, whereas PMs who lose money can get no lower than a zero incentive fee. If the overall fund hasn't earned positive returns (and so hasn't received a performance fee from its clients), but there are some PMs who have done well, the fund manager is in the difficult position of having to pay incentive fees to some of its employees, while not having received any. .

Liquidity terms (i.e. how often clients can withdraw money from the fund) in *investment management agreements* between hedge funds and their clients vary according to the strategy and asset classes. While quarterly liquidity is common, it may be monthly or even fortnightly (often with a *notice* period) for liquid strategies such as equities. As markets have become increasingly less liquid, some investors have tried to raise locked-up capital to the extent possible, by offering lower fees.

Private Equity (PE) / Venture Capital (VC)

Unlike other funds, venture capital and private equity fund managers raise "locked-up" capital from their investors. These funds differ in liquidity terms; investors can get back their money only after a pre-decided 7-

---

[20] Mutual fund companies now offer liquid versions of (erstwhile) hedge fund strategies through a class of mutual funds referred to as *Liquid Alts*.

Capital Markets and Investments

10 year period, unlike other funds which allow investors to redeem much more frequently after giving a few months of notice. This allows PE and VC funds to purse much less liquid strategies, since they know that they have the capital for several years, and will not be subject to liquidity demands. VC firms typically have concentrated positions in young start-ups, whereas PE firms invest in later-stage companies about to go public, or blocks of equity in public firms, or buyout/ going–private deals. There is no liquid markets to value these positions, so they are periodically valued by third-party experts.

Liquid Alts

Liquid Alts are a type of mutual funds (with daily liquidity, like regular open-ended mutual funds) and cater to retail investors, but hold assets and follow strategies (i.e. investments) similar to that of a hedge fund. In many cases, they represent a push by the ETF and hedge fund community to access more of the retail capital by offering new investment styles, which have not been available to the retail community this far. Some of these funds use liquid underlying assets such as stocks or futures to replicate popular factors such as momentum or value (examples of smart beta), across several asset classes. But, many of the liquid alt funds also comprise funds which hold illiquid instruments, such as bank loans or high yield bonds, while offering daily liquidity to their investor base. Market commentators have been concerned about this mismatch in liquidity (same argument is valid for high yield bond and loan ETFs), suggesting that these funds may be unable to withstand a large one-way flow in assets, especially since the dealers now do not have the balance sheets to step in.

Separately Managed Accounts

So far, all the investment products that we have discussed are *commingled* products; i.e. the investors all invest their capital in the same fund, which the fund manager manages. Different investors may have different terms (i.e. fees, liquidity, etc.), depending on the exact share class that they own.

Some fund managers also allow their larger institutional clients to have separately managed accounts. A separately managed account, funded by a single investor, can have separate investment rules, constraints and fees, based on the investor's requirements. The liquidity terms are also more lenient, because now one investor's redemption doesn't affect the portfolio that other investors end up holding. Since each separately managed account is effectively its own fund (*fund-of-one*), these get operationally tedious for the fund manager to administer and maintain. Allocating securities that have just been purchased across different funds is also an issue, and is most properly dealt with through a pre-investment allocation system, where the proportion of total firm purchases that each fund gets is spelt out before the purchase (and before the end of day closing price is determined).

High-Frequency Algorithmic Trading Products

This paragraph could fit into this chapter in one of several sections – an investment style, a product offering or an investor type. *High-frequency trading*, a subset of quantitative investing, uses very fast computers and extremely high-speed access to exchange data, to put on several thousand trades every second, based on order flow information and price movements. Some industry observers laud them for providing liquidity, whereas others blame them for manipulating markets, trading on information that others don't have, etc. High-frequency trading hasn't yet achieved an institutional pedigree; almost all the firms are small mom-and-pop players raising money from friends-and-family or high-net-worth individuals.

Sell-side Index Swaps

Institutional investors usually pick buy-side managers to manage their investment capital. The sell-side firms have also become serious players competing for these assets, especially the more passive low-fee assets or the assets which can be invested using (low-frequency) quantitative algorithms.

Overview of Buy Side Firms

These sell-side firms usually guarantee the client a return corresponding to a chosen index – equities, high yield, commodities (anything that the sell side can replicate/ hedge). The instrument is structured as a swap, where the client receives the index return, and pays a short-dated floating rate (e.g. LIBOR). For the investor, the economics are similar to investing in an index fund, and the sell-side can execute the initial ramping trade and the rebalancing more efficiently than the asset manager. The fees will likely also be lower than a regular asset manager. For more exotic strategies, the recipe is similar – the sell-side desk will come up with an algorithm based on the strategy, publish an index based on the portfolio that the algorithm chooses, and offer a swap on that index. The important detail is that the sell-side, being a potentially biased counterparty, should have no discretion in deciding what goes into the portfolio comprising the index; the rule-based algorithm ensures that. So, this is a convenient platform for quantitative products. We discuss this further in the chapter on indices.

> ✓ Investment managers offer various investment products such as mutual funds, ETFs, Liquid Alts, Separately Managed Accounts, Alternatives (Hedge Funds, Private Equity and Venture Capital) and Index Swaps.

CAPITAL OWNERS

The section above discussed the various forms that the investment offering is presented to clients. Not all products (or underlying asset classes) are suitable for all investors. Below, we list different kinds of end-investors and their motivations. Some of these asset owners invest in asset managers and securities directly, whereas others use intermediaries to advise them or decide on their behalf; intermediaries are discussed in the next section. While many institutional allocators may appear similar, differences exist in the kind of return profile they need from their capital. For example, most pension plans will have approximately 40% in bonds (Core mandate, safe), 50% in equities (passively managed, and 10% in alternatives – private equity, hedge funds, real estate, infrastructure, farmland, opportunistic, direct lending, etc.).

Retail Investors

Regulatory watchdogs like the SEC consider it part of their responsibility to ensure that these investors do not end up investing in products they do not understand; thus retail investors have a somewhat limited menu of investments to choose from – stocks, bonds, mutual funds, ETFs, options on stocks and ETFs, etc. They comprise individual investors managing their brokerage accounts – either retirement savings or regular taxable accounts, high net-worth individuals who use an individual broker / asset manager on a wealth management/ private banking platform (such as Merrill Lynch, UBS, Morgan Stanley, JPMorgan etc.) to invest in regulated retail products, or ultra-high net worth individuals (similar, but have access to less regulated products as well, and investments with larger minimum ticket size, as well as tax-efficient investing). Since much of the investments are in standard retail products (discussed above), in the last few years, a few "robo-advisors" such as Benchmark, Betterment and Wealthfront have used asset allocation models to roll out automated wealth management services for smaller-ticket investors and also charge lower advisory fees.

Private Wealth Managers/ Registered Investment Advisors (RIAs)

Private wealth managers (sometimes called RIAs) manage money for retail clients. Some retail clients are either *High-Net-Worth (HNW)*, who get more customized service, or *Ultra-High-Net-Worth (UHNW)*, who are have relaxed regulatory protection and allowed to invest in more esoteric products because they are similar to *Qualified Institutional Buyers (QIBs)*. But most retail investors either trade through their own electronic brokerage account, or have a RIA to invest on their behalf. Some retail clients provide investment discretion to their manager, whereas others employ managers purely as agents; clients pay these wealth managers a fee based on

Capital Markets and Investments

the amount of assets they manage. These RIAs also play a very important role in the mutual fund distribution channel, since mutual funds are sold primarily to RIAs who allocate to their clients, whose money they manage. Mutual funds pay these managers very high fees to get their clients invested in the funds. The funds charge management fees to the investor, as discussed above. This process is ripe for abuse, as the investment manager can invest the client capital in high fee funds, incentivized by higher initial commission from the fund. Most advisors are currently held to a *suitability* standard, which prevents them from suggesting unsuitable investments to the client (but the investments need not be the lowest fee); industry advocates have been talking about migrating to a (higher) *fiduciary* standard, where the manager has to invest capital as if it was his own (thus incorporating the cost aspect).

Family Office

A family office manages assets for rich families (richer than the UHNW clients discussed earlier), who either have inherited wealth, or have achieved great entrepreneurial success. It may manage assets of a single family, or pool assets from multiple rich individuals. Most of these offices pick managers, sometimes with the help of consultants, but a few also invest a portion of their assets directly. Their objective is to preserve the wealth of the family, while also in some cases generating tax-efficient supplementary income. Some family offices are large enough to be considered institutional, discussed below.

Institutional allocators

State Pension Plans

These pension plans are usually government entities, which manage the pension assets of government entities. They almost always use consultants, and occasionally manage some capital in-house. The large Canadian pension plans are an exception, as they manage significant assets in-house and have large sophisticated investment teams. Public pension plans are often specialized by state/ profession e.g. Texas Teachers or only by region e.g. New York City, and are tasked with generating enough cash flows to satisfy future pension obligations. Actuarial studies are the starting point to formulate their investment plans.

Corporate Pension Plans

Corporate Pensions are also ERISA-regulated entities, charged with managing the assets of defined benefit/ contribution plans of a particular company. They are similar to state pension plans, but are perceived as more dynamic. They usually have less internal red tape, and have similar capital preservation and liability management objectives as their state-run counterparts. Liability-Driven Investing (LDI), which matches their return profile with their projected outflows (immunization), is an important concept to help them plan their investments.

Endowments/ Foundations

Endowments are university-owned pools of capital, usually collected from their donors and trustees. Over the decades, some endowments (such as Yale) have earned the reputation of having groomed some of the best money managers, who went on to launch large successful hedge funds. The *Yale model* (more an approach or framework) emphasizes the benefits of a carefully selected portfolio of alternative investment managers like private equity and hedge funds, to access return streams that are not easily accessible by liquid market instruments, and picking less correlated assets to form a portfolio. It also highlights getting most risk exposures passively, in-house, and relying on specialist external managers only for sources of risk not accessible internally (core/ satellite framework). Most endowments invest for the long term; they treat their capital as permanent and often do not need to satisfy near-term liabilities. Most endowments heavily use external managers; some have sizeable internal pools of capital.

Overview of Buy Side Firms

Fund of Funds/ hedge fund seeding platforms

Fund of Funds specialize in selecting hedge fund and private equity managers and more complex investment products. They raise capital from allocators, and often have discretion regarding which managers to fund. They also seed new hedge funds, where the manager may have a strong reputation and record elsewhere, but is launching his own fund now. As a seed investor they get significant fee breaks and also a part of the management company proceeds. Fund of funds also often charge performance fees if the returns from their managers are above certain thresholds, so the allocator is left paying two layers of fees, once to the fund manager, and then to the fund-of-funds manager. Fund of funds initially used to advertise their value-add as getting a small institutional investor access to a top-hedge fund; over the years, this has ceased to be a selling point. The best fund-of-funds negotiate directly with prominent funds for a separate share class (or a separately managed account) only for the fund-of-fund's clients, at lower fees than the market.

Insurance Companies

Insurance companies receive large amounts of premium inflows periodically (monthly/ annually). The investment teams are responsible for deploying this capital wisely, using a combination of direct investments as well as external managers for the more esoteric asset classes. Like pension funds, their investment horizons are usually long-term since their liabilities are usually long-dated (again this varies for life insurance versus P&C; actuarial tables play an important role). They are more concerned with book yield. In many cases, their securities are held in held-to-maturity accounts, which does not require them to mark to market. So, unless there is permanent impairment of capital, these portfolios have the appetite to ride out market volatility. Most investments are straightforward low-fee implementations, though some firms adopt a more total-return focused approach. This is because financial markets value insurance firms based on their combined ratio, which causes them to be return-focused.

Corporate Treasury Departments

Companies often generate surplus cash from their operations or raise capital from the financial markets. This is invested in the financial markets, until the capital is needed for investments, acquisitions, operations, etc. The corporate treasury department is responsible for investing surplus funds in suitable investments (from a risk and maturity/ liquidity standpoint). They are usually direct investors and invest mainly in liquid instruments to have ready access to capital; it often is directly connected to working capital management.

Proprietary Trading Desks

These desks used to be part of large investment banks, usually separated from their sell-side operations through "Chinese Walls". These desks used to invest the firm's own capital, directly. With the new regulatory regime after the 2008 financial crisis, Volker Rule, in particular, has made it very difficult for the banks to hold assets on their balance sheet. This has caused almost all proprietary desks to be dismantled.

- ✓ Retail investors own and allocate investment capital either individually, or rely on financial advisors or family offices.
- ✓ Institutional capital allocators comprise pension plans, endowments, foundations, fund-of-funds, insurance companies, corporate treasury departments, etc.

INTERMEDIATION – CONSULTANTS, OCIO, FUND OF FUNDS

Allocators to institutional asset managers vary in levels of financial sophistication. At one end, the large Canadian pension plans behave like asset managers themselves, hiring the best talent and taking significant active

Capital Markets and Investments

risk. At the other end of the spectrum, we see plans sponsored by associations of firemen, etc., with a volunteer-run board without the bandwidth or the knowledge to take an active part in the investment process. Several layers of intermediaries exist to fulfil these various needs.

Process of picking an institutional manager

An institutional allocator, such as a pension plan, often decides on their risk appetite and return requirements internally or through a consultant, after going through a detailed asset/liability analysis. Depending on the allocator, they may or may not update their asset allocation views every year, based on whether they view it as market timing or not. Once the asset allocation is decided, they then need to come up with a shortlist of managers for each of these asset classes / sleeves. Different allocations approach it differently; some use an approved short-list from their consultant as a starting point, others send out RFPs whereas some may also be influenced by inbound calls from asset managers.

The initial step involves a discussion between the marketing staff at the fund manager and the investment specialists for the asset class at the allocator. If there is a fit, the allocators meet the asset manager's investment professionals, then visit the office physically if there is still interest. The final steps include operational due diligence, which involve meetings with the back office and examining the systems. This often reduces the shortlist to two or three firms, who are then invited to a finals presentation, after which mandates are handed out.

Several layers of intermediaries exist to fulfil various needs of the allocators:

Consultants

They serve as gatekeepers between asset managers and allocators. Depending on the exact relationship, they advise their clients (the allocators) on various aspects from asset allocation to manager selection. Consultants also routinely visit managers to be fully up-to-date on what their current investment thinking is. Their manager research division rates various asset managers, whereas the field consultants actually cover the asset owners and advise them which asset managers might be a good fit. Examples of large consulting firms include Towers Watson, Russell, Hewitt, Mercer, Aksia, Cliffwater and Albourne.

OCIO (Outsourced CIOs)

Many allocators (small pension funds, family offices and endowments) are thinly staffed, so they cannot undertake the tasks outlined above. For this reason, they outsource their operations to OCIO (Outsourced Chief Investment Office) firms, which have economies of scale because they do it for several small entities. These firms are similar to fund-of-funds, but focus on core/ core plus mandates too in addition to alternatives. They also maintain accounts for each of their clients and provide a complete turnkey service, including back office, accounting, legal, etc.

> ✓ Intermediaries such as consultants, OCIOs and fund-of-funds often provide services to the asset owners and advise them regarding asset allocation and manager selection.

WORKING AT A BUY-SIDE FIRM

The key business focus areas of most finance firms are attracting and managing clients, and finding lucrative investment opportunities. Depends on what exactly the firm does, and the role of individual within the firm, the emphasis on these activities varies. For most buy-side firms, continually assessing investment opportunities is critical, more than on the sell-side, who serve as specialists/ facilitators. Of course, since buy-side firms have fewer people, they are less specialized and straddle across functions, so members of the investment team often spend a lot of time with clients. Marketing teams on the buy-side are primarily tasked with raising assets and fulfilling existing investor requests (more IR).

Overview of Buy Side Firms

Buy-side firms are fairly heterogeneous when it comes to their internal organization, so there is no one-size-fits-all. Many of the differences stem from their primary mandate and the products they offer, discussed above. Other differences result from them being smaller firms (compared to non-agency sell-side investment banks) in terms of number of employees, so tend to be more "clubby". But, there are some common features, which we will summarize.

Broadly, every buy-side firm is divided into investment and non-investment teams. The role of the investment team is to identify investment ideas, and be responsible for monetizing them. The two broad styles are top-down (i.e. building the portfolio from the asset class, working down to the security level), or bottom-up (i.e. finding the best investment ideas within the boundaries specified by the mandate). In reality, portfolio construction is often a blend of both approaches, with the Investment Committee (headed by the Chief Investment Officer) periodically deciding on asset (or sector) allocation targets, and handing them down to more specialized investment professionals, who find the best ideas within their focus areas based on these specifications. Risk targets are also often pre-specified, using metrics suitable to the asset class. An important distinction across firms is the degree of autonomy the focused investment teams have, relative to the instructions and the boundaries that are handed down to them by the investment committee (i.e. the balance between top-down and bottom-up); for example, professionals at a decentralized hedge fund manager will have more investment flexibility within their specialization.

Within the focused investment teams, the exact nature of tasks depends on the kind of buy-side firm it is – quantitative or fundamentally-oriented, asset class and sector-focus, liquid markets or one-off private deals, etc. Depending on these details, relevant skill sets vary from programming, to understanding business landscape, financial markets and instruments and Excel-based models, staying on top of news and announcements, to even appreciating legal and taxation aspects.

Most of these roles have counterparts on the sell-side (discussed in detail in the previous chapter), who these investors face. For example, the research analysts on the sell-side have similar skill-sets as the corresponding buy-side investment professional on the buy-side. The difference is that the sell-side individual is expected to be more in the weeds and know every detail in a narrow field; the sell-side usually has more people covering the same domain that one buy-side person would. So, an important quality of a mid-level buy-side manager is to know who to reach out on the sell-side for reliable information, without having to reinvent the wheel. He needs to be discreet, so that he doesn't indicate which way he is inclined to invest.

The buy-side also has large teams of non-investment professionals, who are responsible for either helping the investment teams make decisions, or are involved in physically running the non-investment activities in the firm. They include Marketing & Investor Relations, Technology, Quants, Risk, Operations, Compliance & Legal, Finance/ Accounting etc. Again, depending on the exact nature of the firm, some of these groups (e.g. Risk, Quants) can be closely aligned to the investment process. These divisions report up to the Chief Operating Officer/ Chief Executive Officer. The roles are similar to the corresponding roles on the sell-side, but the above comment for investment professionals is valid here too – the buy side departments contain fewer people spread thinner, so the requirement is to synthesize more and connect the dots, rather than know one focused sub-area really well and be siloed.

Marketing / IR roles do not really have an analogous position of the sell side; their main role is to acquire new clients, explain the investment philosophy and current strategy of the firm, understand evolving market needs and come up with ideas for new funds, etc. They also service the existing investor base and handle their day-to-day requests and facilitate meetings with the investment staff.

While an important issue in the entire industry, buy-side (non-mutual fund even more) investment professionals are particularly sensitive to compensation contracts (it is true of the sell-side too; but to a lesser extent,

Capital Markets and Investments

as the economic drivers of business profitability are different). On the buy-side, it's easier to assess an investment team's skills simply by analyzing their returns, whereas on the sell-side one can always argue that it's the seat and the franchise value and not the individual that is responsible for profits. So, investment teams are often compensated based on the portfolio's return performance, whereas non-investment employee compensation is more standardized. This is more so in hedge funds/ private equity, where the manager earns an incentive fee for high returns, part of which may be passed on to the team (sometimes explicit in employment contracts, especially for key hedge fund employees, often discretionary), especially in the decentralized set-ups described above. Marketing teams are recognized based on assets raised.

Other non-investment teams like technology, risk, operations, compliance and finance are also more streamlined and tightly staffed, especially in smaller hedge funds, with the same individual wearing different hats within the group. The roles are less focused and more varied than larger sell-side firms.

Smaller buy-side firms (especially hedge funds) are usually secretive about their ideas and thought process. The large mutual funds are often heavily regulated and need to disclose their portfolio every quarter, so secrecy may appear to be a little less relevant (although hedge funds file 13-D/ 13-F forms too). But, regardless, when a position is being added to or reduced, it's important to be cautious with information to avoid being front-run by other more nimble firms.

5. Indices, Benchmarking, Risk Models and Performance Evaluation

We've gone through a fairly detailed introduction on the various asset classes, markets and the major participants. In this chapter, we discuss a few elements of how investors manage and organize portfolios; we focus less on the individual positions within the portfolio (the rest of the book deals with that), but more on portfolio aggregates, and examine the portfolio from a top-down perspective. We start with an introduction to indices and benchmarks, and why they are useful. We then move to a discussion on portfolio risk measures, and finally end with a summary on how professional investment managers are often evaluated by asset owners. With this background, let's dive right into Indices.

INDICES – WHAT ARE THEY? WHY DO WE NEED THEM?

An Index (e.g. S&P 500) comprises a *basket* of securities (e.g. 500 stocks), all (usually, except some *multiverse* indices) within the same asset class (e.g. equities). These names are included in the basket according to pre-stated rules (e.g. US-listed Stocks with the 500 largest market capitalizations), and then weighted according to a pre-specified algebraic formula (e.g. by market capitalization)[21]. Traditionally, an index was meant to "represent" a market; its movements captured the overall moves in the market, and served as a quick summary. Over the decades, as more money started being managed professionally, indices evolved to serve as benchmarking and performance evaluation tools for the buy-side. Academic literature (and empirical performance) suggests that active management does not significantly outperform a market index; in fact active managers routinely underperform. This has led to renewed interest in index funds, which incidentally are also the least expensive from the investor's perspective.

Anyone with access to data can "*publish*" an index. To do this formally, they need announce a *set of precise rules*, and then following the rules meticulously to refresh the index calculations and statistics (detailed below) at a certain pre-specified frequency (continuous, end-of-day or even less frequently). If the rules and the data required to calculate the index (i.e. the prices and the weights) are transparent, anyone should be able to replicate the index calculations. This is especially important if the index publisher (e.g. Standard & Poor's for the S&P500, a sell-side bank for a customized index) has any vested interest in manipulating the value of the index (e.g. the sell-side bank is the counterparty on a swap referencing that index); in that situation, there should be absolutely no room for ambiguity, on even the smallest detail. In most cases, an index is sufficiently transparent if it follows well-defined rules and the index constituents and their weights are known in advance.

As the index provider needs to process huge volumes of data, credibility in their systems and processes is critical. For example, even during the Lehman Brothers' bankruptcy in 2008, the Lehman Fixed Income Indices (e.g. the Bond "Agg" Indices) continued to be computed and published. Index providers license the use of the index and its constituents, and earn revenues from the license fee. In many cases, the providers also offer products related to the index.

Criteria for a Good Index

An index can serve several purposes –a reference for market performance, benchmarking, performance evaluation, investment theme etc. While the primary purpose of the index should drive its construction, some general principles to keep in mind are:

- Transparency: What rules determine the index composition?

---

[21] Inflation indices are calculated a little differently, and represent the price difference of a basket of goods, suitably weighted, in two periods.

Capital Markets and Investments

- Replicable: Are the index returns replicable?
- Investable: Are the index constituents easily investable? Are the weights known ahead of time?

Index Rebalancing

An index is essentially a portfolio of securities, the constituents and their weights determined by a set of well-defined rules. Since these rules themselves do not change often for benchmark products (unless the market itself has evolved and rules need to keep up), the index, once created, often has the same portfolio (i.e. constituents) for several months. For example, a market value weighted equity index, once created, has the same constituents for months. Constituent weights move only because their prices move; these changes in constituent weight do not require the index provider to buy/ sell securities; these index portfolios are almost *buy-and-hold*. Periodically, the index rules are applied to make sure that every constituent continues to meet the criteria to belong to the index, and to check if there are any new members to be included. This process is called *index rebalancing*. Some other indices (such as fixed income indices) need to be maintained/ rebalanced more frequently, as new bonds constantly get issued and need to be included and old bonds leave the index because their maturity is too short to satisfy index rules. Most bonds pay coupons, so the index generates cash which needs to be reinvested. Most indices try to minimize turnover, so the index rules are crafted to represent the market fairly (for which the index is a benchmark), but to minimize trading and associated costs.

Examples of Popular Indices

S&P500 and Russell 2000 are the most popular US Equity Indices. Eurostoxx50 is the popular European equity index. MSCI publishes a frequently used global equity index – the MSCI World Index, covering equities in 23 developed countries. Within fixed income, many investment grade investors are benchmarked to the Bloomberg Barclays (erstwhile Lehman) Aggregate Index, or sub-components of that. In the high-yield space, the Merrill HY Index is also popular, at par with the Bloomberg Barclays HY Index. In Commodities, the S&P- GSCI (erstwhile Goldman Sachs Commodity Index) and the Bloomberg Commodity Index (erstwhile Dow Jones –UBS Commodity Index) are popular benchmarks. MarkIt Partners publishes the CDX and ITraxx indices (indices on credit default swaps, discussed in Chapter 10) and the IBoxx cash credit bond indices.

> ✓ An index is a basket of securities, constituted using preset rules. Popular indices serve as benchmarks for different parts of the market.
> ✓ A good index should have transparent rules, which allow outsiders to replicate the returns of the index. Its constituents should be easily investible, with the weights known ahead of time.

EFFICIENCY OF INDEX INVESTING

We mentioned that indices can serve as a reference point (i.e. benchmark) to measure performance of other funds/ asset managers. At the same time, there are several funds (referred to as index funds) whose main objective is to mimic the returns of the benchmark index. At the risk of oversimplification, mimicking the index is fairly straightforward, since the index rules are well-known and constituents/ weights are known ahead of time; blindly following the index rules and buying the constituents in the correct proportions will get to a portfolio that will replicate the index performance; a big team of research analysts is not necessary. No trading is required, except at inception and during index rebalance, again according to the index rules. In fact, in liquid markets, this can be done with very little manual intervention. The sell-side is also well positioned, through program trading desks, to facilitate large executions in multiple names at the market closing levels (in equities). So, it should be far cheaper for investors (and it is) to use the services of an index fund manager.

Indices, Benchmarking, Risk Models and Performance Evaluation

In less liquid asset classes, index managers have a somewhat more complicated task because it may not be feasible to buy all the index constituents instantly in exactly the right proportions. In these markets, managers try to mimic the risk characteristics, sector exposures and market structure of the index, and use *stratified sampling* to get to a replicating portfolio. Apart from generating returns close to the index return, they are measured based on the *tracking error volatility (often referred to as TEV or tracking error)* of their portfolio, which is the standard deviation of the return difference between the index fund and the index over time (so, you need historical data to calculate this).

Besides the low cost, there are compelling theoretical reasons to use index funds. Over the last six decades (discussed in Chapter 12), many strands of academic research have concluded that holding the entire market is optimal for *every* investor, regardless of his risk tolerance. According to this theory (often termed *two-fund separation*), risk averse investors should hold only a small part of their wealth in the form of the market index, whereas investors with a higher risk appetite should hold more. But, for both investors, the composition of the "risky" portfolio should mimic the market.

This said, the allure of active investing remains; investors are hopeful that there are managers that can consistently beat the index and are willing to pay up to get access to active management. We discussed this in detail in Chapter 4.

> ✓ Index funds passively and mechanically replicate their stated benchmark index, whose constituents are known in advance, and track them closely.
>
> ✓ Most index funds have low management fees; besides there are theoretical arguments suggesting that index funds are optimal for most investors.
>
> ✓ Tracking error (volatility) is the historical standard deviation of the difference between a portfolio's return and that of its benchmark, and measures how closely a portfolio tracks its benchmark.

BENCHMARK INDICES VS STRATEGY INDICES

Investors with a variety of objectives, constraints, strategies and trading styles use indices for various functions - investing, benchmarking, tracking a market or even trading swaps on the index (in some sense a subset of investing). *Benchmark indices*, which broadly represent a market, are well-suited to fulfilling these needs. However, if an investor needs a fairly nuanced but well-defined (i.e. rules-based) exposure to the market, a broad index may not be very useful.

In this situation, the investor needs a "custom index", which can be built (e.g. by the structuring desk of an investment bank, or a solutions team on the buy-side) to capture the essence of the exposure the investor needs. This is done by creating a rules-based (long, short or long-short, as the case may be) portfolio of securities, which screen favorably based on the criteria the investor cares about. This portfolio could be optimized/ rebalanced periodically to maintain exposures, or could be a static basket. Often, indices are created based on these baskets. These indices do not really represent a broad market, and are referred to as *strategy indices*. The investor can easily obtain exposure to this index by entering into a Total-Return *Index Swap* with the sell-side counterparty, to receive the future returns of this index (receive positive returns and pay negative returns) and pay a financing cost. The sell-side hedges this exposure by transacting in the underlying basket, and charges a fee for this service. In many cases, trading swaps allows institutional investors a convenient mechanism to express a view or trade a product that they may not be set up to trade (as long as they are fine trading swaps – e.g. investors with a fixed income mandate trading equity swaps). The sell side formally publishes a plethora of these strategy indices with tickers on Bloomberg, etc., often to restricted audiences. If a

Capital Markets and Investments

client wants a customization, the providers usually make that available for a large enough investment. If a solutions team on the buy-side provides this custom portfolio, the investor may simply take exposure in funded form (by transferring cash to the provider, like any portfolio). The strategy indices need to be maintained and rebalanced far more frequently and often with more turnover than the benchmark indices.

The most popular strategy indices, especially if they are intended to mimic a popular theme or factor (often called Smart Beta Indices), such as momentum, FX carry, value, hedge fund styles, etc., or replicate the returns of an otherwise inaccessible market, get tweaked to be provided through many buy-side distribution channels such as mutual funds, ETFs, wealth management, etc. So, in summary, there are several ways to invest in Indices – directly using futures, ETFs, Index funds, Total Return Swaps (TRS).

> ✓ Benchmark Indices are designed to track broad markets and reflect overall market moves.
> ✓ Many investors want specific exposure to a focused market but are set up to invest primarily in indexed investment products; tailored strategy indices have been created in response. Strategy indices themselves are not well-publicized, but several products based on these indices are marketed.

INDEX MECHANICS AND TERMINOLOGY

The most relevant statistic of any Index is its value (i.e. the *Index Value*), often a weighted average price. Now, this value is scaled assuming that the value on a specified day in the past (i.e. Base Date, e.g. January 1, 1982) was 100. From that time onwards, to any arbitrary date until the present time, the growth rate in the index value will match the growth rate in the weighted average price (or any other variable that the index is tracking) of the basket of securities.

To be precise, the index value described above is an example of a Price Index Value; its time series tracks reflects the movements in the prices (and potentially, the weights) of the index constituents. For the same index, one can also compute a *Total Return Index Value*, which also captures all other cash flows that the holders of the constituent securities may have received, such as interest or dividends. Until the first additional cash flow that any index constituent receives, the price index value and total return index value series are identical. On the date that any index constituent receives a payment for the first time, the coupon/ dividend is added to the price index value for that date to calculate the total return index value; following this, the two time series diverge, even if there are no additional cash flows. Total Return Index Values are very useful, since their relative change directly gives the total rate of return for the Index. In some cases, investors also care about the price return in isolation; the relative change of the Price Index Value provides that. Interpreting price returns for equity indices is misleading, since prices drop after a dividend payment. For fixed income indices, though, price indices provide useful information on price appreciation, since periodic cash flows are tracked separately through accrued interest and not incorporated in the price.

Other *index statistics*, specific to the asset class, are also published. As a simple example, equity investors may care about the dividend rate; fixed income investors care about the coupon rate. Since this data is available for each constituent, a weighted-average coupon rate for the index can be calculated using the same weighting mechanism as the index value. These index characteristics are published along with the index value, to give investors an idea of what the representative index security would possibly look like, and how the index (i.e. the index value) is expected to behave if the market conditions change. Stated differently, an index characteristic is the (market value-weighted) average of any security attribute across all index holdings.

For the same purpose, investors often study "*market structure reports*" on the index to understand the distribution of any index characteristic (e.g. market capitalization, rating) across the index holdings (i.e. what proportion of the index contains large cap stocks versus small cap, or how much of the index contains high

Indices, Benchmarking, Risk Models and Performance Evaluation

yield names versus investment grade). While the simplest example of this is an exposure (i.e. market value) report, grouped by some security attribute (e.g. size or market capitalization group), there is no standard way to do this. It can be as simple as studying a distribution of coupons in a mortgage index, looking at sector concentrations of an equity index, ratings distribution of a credit index or getting a sense of the exposure of a Treasury index to different points in the yield curve. To be clear, readers should keep in mind that an index is a basket of securities, so all these analytics and reports that are created for indices can also be created for any security portfolios, including portfolios that investors actively manage. Comparing portfolio characteristics to that of the benchmark is a quick way to get a sense of the conditions under which the portfolio is likely to outperform the benchmark.

Index rules also detail other critical implementation aspects such as:

Index inclusion rules - What criteria is used which securities (constituents) are part of the index and which ones are not. As the criteria is applied periodically, some new securities become eligible to be part of the index, whereas some securities eligible earlier are no longer eligible

Constituent weights – How are the index constituents to be weighted to compute a composite index value? Usually indices are weighted either equally or by market capitalization (what proportion of the overall index-eligible universe is this particular constituent), but fundamental weights (e.g. by sales, EBITDA, book value, dividends etc.) and GDP weights (for multi-country indices) are sometimes seen. Some of the older (but popular) indices such as the Dow Jones Indices are price-weighted.

Rebalancing frequency - How often does the provider change the constituents of the index based on reapplying the index rules? Note, weights of the securities in an index, their prices and the index value can potentially change continuously. This many not require a rebalancing, if the index is market-value weighted. But, some index rules specify a security/ issuer concentration cap; if that cap is hit, rebalancing will be required according to the rules of the index. Reapplying the index inclusion rules will usually require a rebalance.

Holidays - How does the provider treat holidays, if some securities are priced and others are not? This is especially relevant for international and multiverse indices (and custom indices), as some markets may be open whereas others may not.

Interim cash flows - When to reinvest interim cash flows (dividends/ coupons)?

Data Sources - What are the data sources to be used for pricing? Which exchanges (for the listed market), or pricing service providers (e.g. MarkIt, IDC, Moody's, for the OTC market) are to be used

Market close conventions - What assumption to use for when the market "closes"? This is usually End-Of-Day for equities, but especially relevant for OTC markets, which are technically open all the time.

- ✓ Index values are the main input into calculating returns of the index.
- ✓ By averaging security attributes, other index statistics are also published. Investors examine the distribution of these attributes across index holdings to identify risks in the index return performance.
- ✓ Index rules have many details, relevant in valuing the index constituents to calculate the index value.

Details

If p_t and q_t are vectors of prices and quantities of the securities in an index (therefore, same dimensions) at time t, the Index Value at inception (i.e. 100, by convention) equals $p_0.q_0$. So, in the simplest

Capital Markets and Investments

case, the Index Value at any time t equals $Index\ Value_t = \frac{p_t q_t}{p_0 q_0} \times 100$. For an Index with intermediate cash flows (i.e interest/ dividend) etc., to calculate the (Total Return) Index Value, we also add all the dividends and coupons (since index inception) and the current accrued interest to the numerator $p_t.q_t$.[22] Essentially, we are trying to get to the current value of the index portfolio if we invested $100 in the portfolio at index inception and followed all the index rules.[23] The total return of any index[24] between time periods t_1 and t_2 is $Total\ Return_{From\ t1\ to\ t2} = \frac{Index\ Value_{t1}}{Index\ Value_{t2}} - 1$.

As discussed above, indices provide the baseline again which most financial assets are managed. We now turn to frameworks that help us understand, ex-ante, the implications of portfolio characteristics, by introducing risk models. Said differently, we analyze how the portfolio is expected to behave if key variables in the market were to move around. We then turn to ex-post portfolio performance, i.e. explain why the portfolio made or lost money in a prior period, based on broader market moves. Since indices are also portfolios, these exercises can be conducted for an index (i.e. what are the key sources of risk for an index's market value to decline), or the portfolio of an investment manager, or the difference between a portfolio's holdings from those of the index (which indicates how much the portfolio is likely to diverge from the index). We also delve into these issues in Chapter 12.

MEASURING RISK – RISK MODELS

Risk definition

Risk is conceptually thought of as the uncertainty of the expected future return. This is often measured as the historical standard deviation of returns (implicitly assuming that the future will be like the past). So, the risk in every security/ asset class/ index can be quantified, as long as historical returns are available.

An alternative characterization of risk decomposes total risk into *systematic* (or *market*) risk and *idiosyncratic* risk. Systematic risks are risks that are essentially broad market-based risks, which this security may have (little or substantial) exposure to. Idiosyncratic risks are company-specific risks that are unrelated to markets, so should be possible to eliminate if the security is held in a well-diversified portfolio, as the idiosyncratic risks should ideally cancel out across securities in the portfolio. For example, the risk that the CEO suddenly quits a company or gets embroiled in a scandal is an idiosyncratic risk. The portfolio will likely remain exposed to market risks (i.e. the portfolio moves just because the overall market moves), since all securities are exposed to the same market risks to varying extents. Investors, therefore, need to be compensated for taking on market risks.

Risk factors – Factor-based Risk Models

This idea of systematic risk is formalized by defining several *risk factors*[25] (sources/ dimensions of market risk) to characterize market risk. Time series of returns can be constructed for a one unit exposure to each risk factor (referred to as *factor returns*). Then, the security's exposure (i.e. return sensitivity) to the risk factor is derived. This is often (but not always) done by running time-series regressions of the security's return history

---

[22] We can also come up with a *Price Return Index Value* in addition to this, by ignoring coupons and dividends.

[23] Of course, the number of securities in the portfolio may change over time (e.g. during the rebalancing), so the number of elements in the vectors at different times will vary (but $p_t.q_t$ will always return a scalar, since both p and q have the same number of elements at any time).

[24] Treat the Index Value like a price (of the portfolio) and use the return formulae in Annexure I. Multiply by 100 to express as a percentage.

[25] A risk factor is often expressed as a long-short *factor-mimicking portfolio* - long securities with high exposure to a particular dimension of market risk, and short securities with low exposure. Hopefully this portfolio neutralizes all other risk exposures except the particular dimension it tries to capture.

on returns of the market risk factors (regression limitations apply; Annexure IV)[26]. The regression coefficients are referred to as *factor exposures*, or *Betas* (which represents how much exposure the security has to that facet of market risk), whereas the intercept is referred to as the *Alpha*, or the return above and beyond compensation for taking on market risk (i.e. the (excess) return that cannot be explained by factor exposures). The standard deviation of the residual is referred to as *idiosyncratic volatility*, and considered a measure of *active risk*. A recent trend in the index has been the creation of *smart-beta* indices, which provides exposure to such risk factors. We will discuss this later, when we talk about equity risk in Chapter 12.

A *risk model* is a model that measures the risk (i.e. the uncertainty of future returns) in a portfolio of securities. This can be done in different ways; the alpha-beta risk characterization described above is a simple characterization of a *factor-based risk model*. As risk has more to do with volatility of returns (than the actual level of returns), the main role of the risk model is not to generate expectations of future returns[27], but more to characterize the volatility of security (and portfolio) returns. In a single factor model, this is equal to the volatility of factor returns times the factor exposure. In a multifactor model, though, the correlations across factors matters; lower correlation may reduce total risk[28]. This is captured by *computing volatilities and covariances of factor returns* (essentially, estimating a covariance matrix of the risk factors), and using the beta coefficients to calculate the volatility of security/portfolio returns (as a combination of factor volatilities and covariances), and adding on the idiosyncratic volatility. The formula is detailed in Chapter 12.

Instead of worrying about extracting risk factors and estimating their volatilities and covariances, we can certainly consider simply working directly with security returns (and their variances/covariances) instead. While this is certainly possible, it is not useful and practical, especially for portfolios with hundreds or thousands of securities[29]. From a technical perspective, it is far easier to estimate and work with sensitivities and covariances (e.g. invert matrices) of a smaller number of less correlated factors than a massive set of highly correlated factors[30]. The whole point of picking risk factors (an art as much a science) is to pick fundamental "forces" which drive returns in the market, and characterize the portfolio in terms of how exposed they are to those factors. In fact, while estimating betas, modelers often force some betas to zero to get more meaningful estimates. When we discuss the CAPM, we will also see that a one-factor model is often very useful.

The above framework (by construction) measures the systematic risk of a portfolio; the idiosyncratic risk can be assessed by examining the volatility of the factor model/regression residuals. To calculate the total portfolio risk, the idiosyncratic risk and the systematic risk are simply added together, since these components are uncorrelated to each other.

While several large financial institutions have developed their in-house risk models, it requires a large undertaking of data and model maintenance. Off-the-shelf models such as Barra, Riskmetrics, Axioma, Northfield,

---

[26] An alternative regression technique to achieve the same final result involves running cross-sectional *Fama-McBeth regressions*. Other statistical techniques such as *Principal Component Analysis (PCA)* are used to extract risk factors, especially in interest rates/mortgage products. Further, in a few cases, the connection between factor and the security is not estimated statistically, but specified apriori, based on a formula (e.g. in a one-factor fixed income framework, *Duration* is a factor exposure, yield change is the factor return)

[27] One can certainly calculate expected returns using this framework, based on the regressions above, though most models normalize and redefine the factors (by subtracting the factor mean) so that the factors have zero expected return.

[28] The calculation uses the portfolio variance formula.

[29] In an extreme example, to mirror the factor framework, we can define every security as a risk factor, and have as many risk factors as securities. For any security, the regression would trivially generate a beta of 1 to the risk factor corresponding to the security and zero elsewhere. This is equivalent to working with security returns directly.

[30] As we will see in Chapter 12, while computing variance for a portfolio of a few securities (or macro asset classes), we sometimes simply work with security returns, their variances and covariances. But the risk factor framework is definitely useful and relevant for risk management of larger portfolios.

Capital Markets and Investments

Aladdin/ Blackrock Solutions (or even Bloomberg) are available, and do a reasonably good job for most liquid asset classes. However, for less liquid portfolios, each tool has its own strength, and often involves a time-consuming initial mapping to the software's framework, and frequent maintenance as new positions are added to the portfolio. These models generate *risk reports*, which detail the portfolio's risk exposures and are reviewed by risk analysts and portfolio managers daily.

Risk Measures

VaR (or *Value-at-Risk*) is a common risk measure. An $x\%$ VaR is a dollar amount, indicating the maximum that the portfolio/ security is expected to lose $x\%$ of the time. So, if the 95% VaR of a portfolio is $10mm, it means that the portfolio is expected to lose less than $10mm 95% of the time; it is likely to lose at least $10mm 5% of the time. A related concept measures *Expected Shortfall*, which computes the expected loss in the worst 5% of the cases (i.e. when losses are more than 10mm). To estimate either of these measures, a time-horizon needs to be pre-specified (daily/ monthly / weekly) over which to compute the expected losses; statistical assumptions regarding the distribution of security returns (often normally distributed with mean zero) and their covariances need to be made. Usually, 95% or 99% VaR limits are set (often as a % of current portfolio value), and portfolio risk needs to be reduced when these limits are breached. These risk measures can be estimated either by using the distribution (volatilities and covariance) of risk factors and the portfolio exposures to the risk factors, or alternatively, by using just the volatilities and covariance of the security returns history (without using risk factors or estimating factor sensitivities). A normal distribution, while statistically simple and providing useful thumb-rules, understates the likelihood of extreme outcomes relative to the actual financial world[31]; risk managers need to be fully aware of this while using risk models and reading risk reports.

VaR is a fair measure for liquid markets, where prices are reliable and it is easy to transact. For less liquid markets, it is difficult to apply statistical models, since the distribution of security prices implied from historical data is very imprecise. Besides, covariances are notoriously unstable and increase in times of stress, so VaR values computed with historical data of calm market periods understate the true risk in times of stress. To get around this, even for liquid markets, analysts use price histories from volatile market regimes to compute distributional parameters.

To supplement this methodology, risk managers sometimes shock specific factors in isolation and compute portfolio returns after that shock. This is particularly relevant in fixed income markets, where the relation between the security price's sensitivity to the risk factor isn't estimated statistically, but specified via pricing formulae (e.g. duration). Spread sensitivities play an important role in credit portfolio risk. In option pricing models, derivatives to various risk factors (i.e. Greeks or sensitivities) are calculated in advance; so the security's hypothetical price change in response to risk factor shocks can be estimated using these Greeks. Alternatively, the security can be repriced (using the pricing formula/ algorithm) using the new values of the risk factor. Shocks of various magnitudes to different risk factors provide the portfolio manager with an idea of the vulnerabilities and exposures in the portfolio. Multiple simultaneous risk factor shocks can be combined into a composite *Scenario*, essentially to capture how much (and which parts of) the market will sell off in certain adverse regimes (e.g. a Lehman-type financial crisis), and sense what would happen to the portfolio if something similar were to unfold.

Role of Risk Models in Portfolio Construction

Understanding the risks in a security and a portfolio is a critical aspect of portfolio construction. These risks can often be characterized relative to a benchmark for benchmarked investors, or on an absolute basis for absolute return investors. If the manager doesn't like the risk profile of the portfolio, the risk needs to either

---

[31] Using jargon, distributions of asset returns have "fat tails".

be hedged or the position size be trimmed. Most portfolio management decisions can be reduced to deciding which risk factors to get exposure to, after assessing whether the market is compensating investors adequately for those risks. While active managers may not always be thinking in these terms (because they focus primarily on the fundamental attributes of the securities they own), some academically-inclined finance professionals often evaluate opportunities by comparing the current *risk premia* (expected return per unit exposure to the risk factor or market) versus their guesstimate of the future level of the risk premia. If a particular risk premium is expected to compress, the investor would like to be heavily exposed to that risk factor, as a reduction in risk premium will lead to an increase in prices of securities exposed to that factor, leading to higher realized returns (and a possible lowering of expected returns going forward from that point in time), all else equal.

- ✓ Risk is conceptually visualized as the uncertainty in (future) expected returns. One way to operationally calculate this is by calculating the standard deviation of historical returns.
- ✓ Total risk can be decomposed into market-dependent systematic risk, and security-specific idiosyncratic risk.
- ✓ The systematic risk is allocated across several risk factors, using statistical techniques. Each risk factor represents a particular dimension of market risk; the factor's inherent risk and a security's exposure to this factor are both calculated. Correlations across factors affect total risk.
- ✓ VaR, Expected Shortfall and Scenario P&L are important risk measures.

PERFORMANCE EVALUATION

Professional money managers make most investments in the global markets on behalf of their clients, who need to assess their performance. In some structures (alternative investment funds), the performance assessment directly drives fee payments to the manager; in most situations, the clients can move their money to another manager if performance is not satisfactory. Since benchmark indices track a broad market, they represent a baseline for judging performance and also provide an investible universe.

Much of this performance, of course, is *marked-to-market* (i.e. based on valuing the portfolio at the current price) and not *realized* (cash in the bank, after the asset has been sold). In private equity mandates, performance fees are usually paid on realized gains and exits, but for hedge funds, fees are based on mark-to-market values (usually books are marked based off third-party index pricing, etc.). In either case, the managers have incentives to take on large amounts of risk, because they get paid much more for outperformance, relative to the penalty for underperformance.

Broadly, the questions investors/ clients would care about, are:

- Did the manager make or lose money? How much?
- How did the market fare during the same time? Did the manager make more or less than the market?
- Adjusting for risk in the portfolio compared to the market, did the investor outperform or underperform? Does the manager's performance relative to the passive benchmark justify his (high) fees?

One would hope that the answer to the first question is easy. But, there are markets (such as private equity) where portfolio positions are one-off and very difficult if not impossible to value. Even in the corporate bond market, most bonds trade once or twice a month at most, in small size, so a price that is used to value a portfolio may not be transactable in large size. However, for most liquid markets, this question is fairly straightforward, as the third-party pricing is reliable, unbiased and comprehensive. Returns based on these prices (and intermediate cash flows) are referred to as *total returns*.

The second question, on market returns, is important for asset owners and managers who are benchmarked to an index (the market in this case). *Excess return* measures the additional return beyond what the benchmark (or, in most cases, the risk free rate) earned. In some cases (especially in fixed income), where the benchmark isn't explicitly stated, excess return refers to the return over Treasuries. A closely-related concept, *alpha*, which calculates the portfolio return above a certain multiple (*beta*) of the benchmark return, is the portfolio's (market) risk-adjusted excess return. We will discuss this further in Chapter 12. Some managers are paid on absolute returns rather than returns relative to an index, so may worry less about the benchmark, but comparisons are always inevitable.

The last question, on risk adjustment and fees, is the most subjective, potentially quantitative and ambiguous. The idea is that a simple excess return calculation is not sufficient if the manager's investment portfolio has a very different level of "risk" compared to the market index. For example, if a manager takes a long position in an index swap that pays twice (2X) the returns of the S&P500 Index, and the index has a +1% return, the manager will earn a +2% return. A simple excess return calculation will suggest that the manager outperformed the index by 1% (or earned double the returns) but hides the fact that the manager ended up taking double the risk compared to the market. Most risk models will indicate that the manager's exposure to the S&P Index was high, and that generated the excess return. The question then reduces to whether that high exposure to S&P Index is something that the manager should be compensated for, or not. This relates to the earlier issue about returns being generated from alpha or beta, which we will return to in Chapter 12.

Performance Evaluation Measures

The ratio of the security's (or portfolio's) average (or expected) excess returns (over risk-free rate i.e. Treasuries) to its total risk (i.e. standard deviation) is its *Sharpe Ratio*, which measures the excess return of the security per unit risk; higher Sharpe ratios indicate more attractive risk-adjusted returns. A similar Sharpe ratio can be computed for the benchmark. To evaluate the previous period's performance, a Sharpe ratio using the previous period's return instead of average returns in the numerator can be computed for both the benchmark and the portfolio[32]. *Information Ratio* is a similar concept, but uses a time series of portfolio excess returns over the benchmark to compute average excess returns and standard deviation. The annualized standard deviation of the portfolio's excess returns over the benchmark is referred to as the *Tracking Error Volatility* (TEV) or, simply, the *Tracking Error*. The concepts of *Alpha* and *Beta* introduced above are also central to performance measurement, especially for absolute return managers. Good security selection and accurate market timing both contribute to excess returns, but it is often difficult to decompose their effects precisely.

Performance Attribution

An essential aspect of portfolio management is understanding the sources of a portfolio's return, almost a post-mortem of performance. For benchmarked investors, this involves examining the industry sector / asset class exposure of the portfolio relative to the benchmark, and the extent of outperformance or underperformance of this sector/ asset class compared to the benchmark. So, an over-allocation to a sector (having a greater proportion of market value in that sector relative to the index) that outperformed the benchmark would have generated excess returns. This incremental return because of differences in sector / asset class exposure between the portfolio and the index is referred to as the *Asset Allocation* effect. Within each sector, securities in the portfolio may be held in different proportions than in the benchmark; this is another source

---

[32] The Sortino Ratio modifies the Sharpe Ratio by using downside deviation (relative to a benchmark or target return) instead of standard deviation, so that the manager is not penalized for deviations to the upside. The Treynor Ratio divides excess returns by beta instead of standard deviation; this may be more suitable if one believes that systematic risk alone (i.e. not idiosyncratic risk) drives returns.

Indices, Benchmarking, Risk Models and Performance Evaluation

of returns and is called *Security Selection* effect. Security selection (within a sector) generates excess returns when a subset of the portfolio that comprises one sector has higher returns than the corresponding sector sub-index i.e. holdings of a particular sector in the portfolio have more/ larger winners than the sector sub-benchmark. Empirically, asset allocation has usually been a bigger driver of excess returns than security selection i.e. picking which asset class or sector to overweight/ underweight has been more important than picking names within a sector.

Formally, this intuition of performance attribution is summarized in the *Brinson-Fachler* model. Suppose there are s sectors. Portfolio returns for the i-th sector are denoted r_{pi}, portfolio weights are w_{pi}, benchmark returns are denoted r_{bi}, benchmark weights are w_{bi}. Portfolio total returns (r_p) are the product of portfolio's returns in the various and their weights in the portfolio, i.e. $r_p = \sum_{i=1}^{s} r_{pi} w_{pi}$. Similarly, total returns for the benchmark (r_b) are given by $r_b = \sum_{i=1}^{s} r_{bi} w_{bi}$.

The difference between portfolio returns (r_p) and benchmark returns (r_b) can be written as Eq. 5.1:

$$r_p - r_b = \sum_{i=1}^{s} \left[\underbrace{(w_{pi} - w_{bi}) r_{bi}}_{\text{Asset Allocation}} + \underbrace{w_{bi}(r_{pi} - r_{bi})}_{\text{Security Selection}} + \underbrace{(w_{pi} - w_{bi})(r_{pi} - r_{bi})}_{\text{Interaction}} \right] \qquad \text{Eq. 5.1}$$

The three terms above in Eq. 5.1 can be interpreted as the Asset Allocation, Security Selection and *Interaction* term respectively, where asset allocation and security selection have the same interpretation as explained in the previous paragraph. The interaction term relates to both these effects. It is positive when the manager is overweight sectors in which the portfolio outperforms the benchmark (and vice versa); it is tougher to interpret and usually has smaller values.[33]

For absolute return portfolios without an explicit benchmark, it also makes sense to examine whether these portfolios have been invested in sectors which did well, and whether the sector sub-portfolios did better than corresponding sector sub-indices. For a buy-side manager, this attribution also forms a basis for compensating analysts for their recommendations.

With most portfolios now being mapped to their risk factor exposures, an alternative approach to performance attribution involves computing how closely the portfolio's realized return during a time period lines up with the sum of the product of the portfolio's (ex-ante) risk factor exposures and the returns realized by the factor mimicking portfolio during that period. Any realized returns in excess of this sum-product can be attributed to *alpha*.

Finally, it may also make sense to check whether the latest (actual) portfolio returns are close to the estimated security/ sector/ portfolio returns, using the latest realized risk factor returns and the estimated factor sensitivities of the portfolio (discussed in the section on risk model). While one wouldn't expect these to line up closely, they provides an out-of-sample test for the quality of the beta and alpha estimates in the risk model and give analysts an idea of model performance.

---

[33] Some systems collapse the interaction term into security selection, by using w_p in the formula instead of w_b.

Capital Markets and Investments

- ✓ A manager is evaluated based on absolute returns or returns relative to a benchmark, depending on the investment guidelines.
- ✓ The primary question is whether the manager made or lost money, on an absolute basis (total returns) and relative to the suitable market index (excess returns).
- ✓ It is important to tease out whether the manager did better than the market because he took on more systematic risk (Beta), or if the manager picked less risky positions that did better than market expectations (Alpha).
- ✓ Sharpe Ratio and Information Ratio are measures of risk-adjusted returns. Portfolios with high Tracking Error are more likely to deviate from the benchmark.
- ✓ Performance attribution frameworks allocate historical excess returns (relative to the benchmark) to Security Selection and Asset Allocation.

PORTFOLIO MANAGEMENT SUMMARY

In this chapter, we've covered a range of common portfolio management issues across various types of asset managers. Different managers have varied objectives and constraints, leading to different implementations of the same ideas across managers. Passive managers want to replicate the benchmark at the lowest possible cost; their main risk is a large tracking error. Active managers are benchmark-aware, but evaluate sectors and securities bottom-up, and make off-index bets. The absolute return investors are often benchmark-agnostic while managing their portfolio, but the capital allocator in his mind likely always wonders whether absolute return investors are doing what they are supposed to and compares them to passive benchmarks casually. Since performance evaluation and attribution is easier for more passive mandates, it's easier to have an opinion on such managers. Morningstar publishes manager ratings for many mutual funds.

REFERENCES

The Barclays Capital Global Risk Model: A Portfolio Manager's Guide. Barclays Capital Research

Lazanas, A, C. Sturhahn and P. Zhong (2010). *The Barclays Capital Hybrid Performance Attribution Model.* Barclays Capital Research

6. Topical Issues in Capital Markets

The capital markets are currently at the intersection of several critical cross-currents. Two broad forces at play are defining this– technology is revamping the way business is done, and there is increased regulatory scrutiny on firms and individuals affiliated with the financial services sector. All these topics are "cutting edge", and there is no dearth of reading materials; here we simply mention these as potential structural issues that are significantly affecting the market.

MARKET MICROSTRUCTURE

We have discussed the evolution of market microstructure while discussing the sell-side (Chapter 3), and will again bring it up when discussing the asset classes in detail (especially Chapters 7 and 11). Without repeating those discussions, we emphasize that electronic order execution, high frequency trading and big-data analytics have all coalesced to have information feed into prices almost instantaneously, asset classes to commove together, markets appearing to be seemingly liquid for small trades, but liquidity becoming very systemic and rapidly withdrawn at the slightest uncertainty, causing markets that have momentarily plunged for little apparent reason. This has prompted several established players to cry foul, causing regulators to take a close look at the mechanics of how the various prominent markets work.

- ✓ The traditional market microstructure of securities either being traded OTC bilaterally between a broker and a customer, or traded on an exchange with a centralized order book is no longer true:
    - Exchanges have been deregulated, leading to greater opportunities and incentives to generate revenues.
    - Electronic venues offering varying levels of anonymity, order types, execution mechanisms and trading speeds, etc. have cropped up, driven by technological advancement
    - Day-trading firms use high speed data feeds and superfast computers to process information instantly submit (and cancel) massive volumes of quotes, and trade with very high frequency.
    - Regulatory changes have shrunk dealer balance sheets, and their ability to warehouse risk.
- ✓ This has led to:
    - Information being incorporated into prices much faster, often without complete analysis.
    - Asset classes and securities co-moving together
    - Market seemingly liquid for tiny volumes, but liquidity becoming rapidly (and more homogeneously withdrawn at the slightest uncertainty. This leads to markets with erratic price movements.

Capital Markets and Investments

RESPONSIBLE INVESTING

Most of this book emphasizes the "rationality" of financial investors, who worry only about the cash flow returns of any financial instrument and the uncertainty associated with those cash flows (and the return correlation across various financial assets), in assessing the relative attractiveness of investment alternatives. Over the past decade, many investors have moved from this unidimensional approach to also incorporating *Environmental, Social and Governance (ESG)* factors in selecting investments; these may not form a part of the traditional financial metrics, but may affect a company's performance significantly in the long term. This has become an important trend; about $8.1 trillion in the US (and $22 trillion globally, i.e. one of every six dollars)[34] is currently allocated to investment mandates that consider ESG factors, with individual investors (especially millennials) and Europe taking the lead. Managers controlling $62 trillion in AUM are signatories to the Principles for Responsible Investment

Socially Responsible Investing (SRI) started out with lists of companies to be excluded from such mandates (negative screening to exclude "sin" stocks)[35]. It was almost morally defined, and such investors implicitly accepted that returns from such portfolios would be lower. As the scope broadened, SRI was renamed *responsible/sustainable investing*. Investors realized that ESG issues, apart from their moral implication, are a form of (long term) risk mitigation[36], and returns of such portfolios need not be lower on a risk-adjusted basis. In fact, some of these issues, mainly elements of governance, were already being covered by financials analysts for years. At the same time, third-party providers have developed ESG indices and are providing ESG scores to companies, which are being incorporated to align investor portfolios with goals and avoid unintended ESG exposures.[37]. This also fits neatly into the trend of thematic investments (Chapter 11), with ideas such as gender diversity, pollution, etc. Currently, managers who are the strongest ESG advocates try to integrate ESG issues into the investment process and discussion. For example, environmental issues are most material in companies belonging to the energy sector, whereas access and affordability may be most important for healthcare companies.

In hindsight, ESG-constrained portfolios have not performed any worse than non-ESG portfolios. Regulatory agencies have confirmed that it is appropriate for managers that are held to a fiduciary standard (historically interpreted as return-maximizing) to also consider ESG portfolios for their clients. This has resulted in more managers offering ESG-aware portfolios, in response to client demand.

Current ESG methodologies suffer from lack of standardization, weak disclosure, low transparency, poor data quality and high subjectivity. They also provide a lagged picture of the companies. In fact, the correlation between ESG scores for the same companies from different data providers is very low. Further, companies that ranked high in ESG models (like Volkswagen) subsequently had large scandals. So, while managers recognize the appeal and importance of ESG ideas, the credibility of these tools is stretched. New start-ups are trying to use big data techniques to come up with ESG scores that address some of these concerns.

---

[34] State Street Global Advisors publication, August 2016

[35] Common exclusions were tobacco, arms and ammunition, alcohol, gambling, human rights, etc. A few corporations are choosing to get certified as B-Corps, which confirms that they meet rigorous standards of social and environmental performance, accountability and transparency.

[36] This is often referred to as the "values versus value" debate. *Impact investing* blends both these approaches, and focuses on financial returns while creating positive measureable social benefits.

[37] It can even be expressed in the form of a constrained optimization problem, with ESG constraints.

> Many investors consider Environmental, Social and Governance issues (apart from standard financial metrics) while selecting investments:
>
> - ✓ ESG-aware managers and strategies have attracted large sums of capital.
> - ✓ ESG portfolios have not performed worse than non-ESG benchmarks, suggesting that this does not hurt returns. Rather, ESG issues are considered part of longer-term risk management.
> - ✓ Current ESG methodologies suffer from lack of standardization, weak disclosure, low transparency, poor data quality and high subjectivity. There is very little relationship between ESG scores provided by different vendors. Some providers are trying to use big-data to improve this.

CENTRAL BANK POLICY

The Federal Reserve cut policy rates (Target Fed Funds Rate) to stimulate the economy during the financial crisis in 2008, and raised rates only at the end of 2015. The idea is that low rates incentivize firms and individuals to borrow and invest/ spend, creating jobs, etc. This has happened, but maybe less than what the policymakers expected, suggesting to many observers that the slowdown is structural (i.e. jobs getting outsourced to cheaper regions, etc.). The Fed traditionally targets only the short end of the yield curve actively to ease or tighten monetary policy but, after 2008, the Fed decided to target even the long end through *Quantitative Easing* (buying long-dated bonds to reduce long-term interest rates), and greatly expanded its balance sheet. This has been a trend globally across central banks, including the European Central Bank, Bank of England, Bank of Japan, etc. In fact, European Central Bank decided to buy corporate bonds, and the Bank of Japan bought bonds and stocks. As a result, some European corporates have been able to issue bonds at negative yields in mid-2016! In late 2015, the U.S. Federal Reserve began raising short term rates slowly. It has indicated that it will begin to "reduce the size of balance sheet" or stop reinvesting the proceeds from existing coupon and principal payments; this may lead to an increase in longer-term rates as the demand for these Treasuries goes down, leading to potentially lower prices if other buyers do not step in.

Some market participants have been critical of the Central Banks and their *Zero Interest Rate Policy (ZIRP)*, saying the keeping interest rates this low for this long (and buying financial assets) does not necessarily stimulate physical demand incrementally, instead this inflates the value of financial assets because of cheap borrowing. Instead, this hurts savers and retirees. . Keeping interest rates low hasn't helped Japan for decades. We discuss this more in Chapter 9.

Capital Markets and Investments

> Central Banks across the world lowered interest rates after the 2008 global financial crisis. While this is a normal monetary policy reaction during a slowdown, this time was different in many ways:
> - ✓ The rates have been kept lower for a much longer time
> - ✓ Central bank actions appear to be more coordinated globally
> - ✓ Central banks have embarked on quantitative easing programs by buying bonds of longer maturities, thus directly moving long dates rates lower
>
> Many analysts have been critical of central bank policies because:
> - ✓ The bond buying program and low rates have encouraged firms to financially reengineer their balance sheets by taking on debt and buying back equity instead of starting new projects. This has inflated financial assets, but corporate profitability has not risen nearly as much.
> - ✓ The prolonged period of low rates has hurt savers, who rely on interest income for living expenses. While the argument for low rates is that companies/ individuals will find it cheaper to borrow and spend, many people have had to save more (not less) because of low rates.
> - ✓ The US economy has not shown signs of high growth or inflation. Some labor market indicators appear tight, whereas others indicate slack. This suggests that there might be structural economic issues related to skill mismatches, demographics, etc.

REGULATION

After the 2008 financial crisis, the deep interlinkages between various banks were exposed; it was clear that one bank's failure could cause the financial system to stutter and cause systemic liquidity crises, leading to spillover effects throughout the economy. This promoted the notion of some banks being Too Big to Fail, implying that such banks would always shielded to protect the economy, giving their management comfort to take excessively risky decisions. This tone, coupled with reports of serious financial transgression pre-crisis (false disclosure during mortgage product sales, LIBOR manipulation, etc., caused regulators to come down hard on sell-side institutions, declaring some to be Systemically Important Financial Institutions (SIFI), and requiring them to hold large amounts of capital. Several lines of business were no longer remunerative because of the high capital requirements; banks started exiting the businesses. Public scrutiny on employee compensation forced banks to trim employee costs and reduce headcount, except in compliance roles. Banks are now required to hold more tier-1 equity capital, through regulations such as Dodd Frank, which imply lower leverage for the business going forward. The Volker Rule has restricted investment banks from trading on their own account and limited bank investment in hedge funds, caused proprietary trading desks to be cut. Many derivatives that were earlier traded bilaterally now need to be centrally cleared. The outlook for the return on capital from the business is therefore lower than it was earlier, prompting managers to complain that banks are being regulated as utilities. Financial institutions now have to face much higher regulatory costs, and present regulators with complex analysis such as Comprehensive Capital Analysis and Review (CCAR) stress tests in the US and European banking Authority (EBA) EU-wide stress tests in Europe and the Prudential Regulatory Authority (PRA) tests in the UK. . Existing laws (e.g. insider trading) are also being enforced more strongly, leading to large fines and reputational risk for financial institutions and some individuals.

There has been a regulatory upheaval in the retail finance space as well. Most Registered Investment Advisors (RIAs) or private wealth managers who manage brokerage accounts of individual clients have been held to a *suitability standard*, where they were required to recommend products that fit the client's need. This was a nebulous standard, because needs aren't clearly defined, and many RIAs ended up recommending "suitable" products that charged the clients high fees, some of which may be paid back to the advisor. This led to a backlash for several years, and the Department of Labor (DOL) has recently come out with recommendations requiring advisors to be held to a *fiduciary standard*, which is a higher standard that requires advisors to act in the client's "best interests", which requires keeping fees in focus. This threatens to change the advisory business model significantly, and also has large implications for the markets as a whole since fewer advisors will have discretion, but just trade model portfolios of the platform they belong to and ETFs.

The regulatory agencies have also been focused on the ability of retail funds (most of them offer daily liquidity) to meet redemption requests. They have now allowed prime money-market funds to vary their NAVs daily. In times of heavy outflows, these funds are now also able to charge liquidity fees and stagger redemptions. Many investors used these funds predominately as a cash substitute to earn a little more than bank accounts with the same assurance of principal; protection; a flood of capital has thus left these funds. SEC has also mandated that mutual funds (and some ETFs) hold no more than 15% of their assets in positions that they cannot liquidate in 7 days, if necessary. They also permit funds to employ swing pricing and charge investors a price different from the true NAV in periods the fund experience large flows, so as to not disadvantage fund investors who do not participate in that large liquidity event.

The President of the US, elected in November 2016, has commented that regulation has shackled industrial activity, and is reviewing laws and proposals with an eye to repealing many of them, so the regulatory landscape remains in flux.

One of the biggest regulatory changes is MiFID II (Markets in Financial Instruments Directive), which will be implemented in Europe in January 2018. At a high level, it aims to increase transparency of markets, shift trading towards more structured marketplaces and promote more orderly trading behavior, reduce the cost of market data, improve execution quality and make trading costs more explicit. At the practical level, the regulation insists that the buy-side pays for research in an unbundled manner, rather than allowing the sell-side to provide research and be compensated through commissions/ order flow. This is leading to upheaval on the sell-side research units, as their work needs to be explicitly priced. Many top researchers are encouraged to form their own research units, serving a small set of exclusive clients. Also, some research-heavy boutique firms used to get paid for their research by the buy side through *Commission Sharing Agreements* (CSA)[38]; that practice is now getting restrained, with firms now needing to use them under a *Research Payment Account* (RPA). Some firms may also consider using quants and big data more actively for research. This will also place restrictions on dark pools; systematic internalizers may get more popular. *Transaction Cost Analysis* (TCA) will get more prominent and mainstream rather than only used by a few large buy-side firms; specialized TCA and order-routing systems will become more popular.

---

[38] In such a practice, the buy side pays a generous commission to their regular execution broker, part of which is shared with the research house.

Capital Markets and Investments

> Regulatory agencies have been partially blamed for the 2008 financial crisis, and accused of being lax with the financial services sector. This has prompted a flurry of regulation. Some key changes:
> - ✓ Dodd Frank requires banks to hold more capital and reduce leverage, thus hampering profitability. Many sell-side businesses such as repo-lending and market making have been affected.
> - ✓ Volker Rule has restricted proprietary trading in investment banks, including investing in hedge funds. Investment banks are not supposed to trade on their own account.
> - ✓ Bank regulators have also increased bank regulatory burden, through stress tests.
> - ✓ The SEC is regulating the amount of illiquid assets that mutual funds can hold, and allowing prime money market funds to have floating NAVs limit redemptions during mass exodus.
> - ✓ The Department of Labor has issued a rule directing retail financial advisors to be held to a fiduciary standard, instead of the existing suitability standard.
> - ✓ In Europe, MiFID II will impose higher disclosure standards, and will have a big effect on sell–side research. Fees/ costs will become more transparent throughout the industry.
> - ✓ Existing laws are being enforced more rigidly, leading to large fines and reputational concerns.

FINTECH

Technology has allowed businesses to be more decentralized and distributed, challenging conventional notions of the need for scale, which had provided big firms an advantage. As a result, startups have begun to gain toeholds in markets that were traditionally the domain of the large behemoth firms. It remains to be seen whether these new-age business models can unseat the dominance of the entrenched players, but the business model innovation and demographic shifts in the consumers of the service are attracting the attention of market participants and regulators. FinTech is a broad term encompassing novel uses of technology in the financial services sector. We present a few examples of fintech applications below:

Big Data in Investment Management

Huge volumes of data of various types (images, text, numbers, etc.) are being created, since the last few years. Innovations in computing are facilitating the rapid processing of this data. In particular, Google's public release of the technology and architecture that it developed to process unstructured data on clusters of distributed commodity hardware (the Google File System or GFS) and the development of several third-party solutions (e.g. Hadoop) on this environment has led to new developments in data processing. This is because:

- Both relational and novel file-based (e.g. GFS) databases are being used, so data can be stored in either structured or unstructured forms. Unstructured data can also be stored and accessed more readily within file-based databases, while rows and columns of traditional data continue to be processed in relational databases.
- Behaviors, opinions and sensory feedback can now be quantified (e.g. "datafication" by Facebook)
- Distributed computing and virtualization technologies have become mainstream, so data analysis can be quickly conducted in groups of fairly standard hardware, instead of relying on elaborate single-server systems.

The essential idea is to conduct a quick and "back-of-the-envelope" analysis using a massive dataset, rather than results based on careful statistical work on sampled "clean" datasets which are then applied to the population. The premise is that patterns and correlations in large varied datasets have incremental value, rather than only drawing conclusions using causation-based statistical inference methods. This has been accelerated by more mainstream acceptance of techniques related to predictive analytics and machine learning.

At the same time, new datasets are being created and being made readily available to third-parties. Stand-alone businesses, many of them start-ups, are focusing on data services and becoming vendors of these alternate data sources. Examples of the new data sources include:

- Data-driven Governments – Governments have progressively been using more data and technology for governance and decision-making, and are making some of this data publicly available, such as the award of government contracts. Much of this data is available through commercial databases such as Haver Analytics, which a new set of solutions providers are continually analyzing for new insights.
- Aggregating Historical Sell-side Research – Research departments within sell-side firms are facilitating the archival of data by converting their digital PDF documents into data-digestible formats such as XML. Some buy-side firms analyze this history of forecasts (against actual results) to identify their "favorite" sell-side analysts, and use algorithmic techniques to place instantaneous orders the moment a new incremental research piece is published.
- Geospatial datasets from Satellite imagery – Satellite imagery has become cheaper to procure, with several private players launching satellites. Methods to store and analyze it have evolved, making it easier to incorporate them into investment decision making. This has special potential in sectors such as retail (scanning parking lot images of malls to gauge traffic), transportation (assessing container traffic at ports, etc.) and commodities (scanning agricultural produce while on plantations to get a sense of harvest, shipments and traffic to high-consuming countries like China), but can definitely play a role to supplement channel checks for sales and inventory in most sectors.
- Social, Event and News Media – Data sources such as Facebook are effective at tracking audience reaction to important retail promotions, advertisements, brand repositioning, product launches, etc., especially for consumer-focused companies. Language processing algorithms can also figure out the gist of a news article at very rapid speeds. Technology has also made it easy to incorporate these variables into the investment decision process, if the manager chooses to do so.
- Consumer Financial Data – Consumers often use software from providers such as Yodlee and Mint to aggregate their financial information and understand their personal spending patterns. These providers make the data available in aggregate terms to investment clients, who can then figure out how trends in restaurant spending versus apparel stores and travel are evolving, within different demographics. Similarly, many banks are also extrapolating spending trends using swipe-level information from credit cards issued by them.
- Location-based data and data from smart gadgets (Internet-of-Things) provide data similar to what is available from social media

Figure 6.1 lists the names of a few emerging firms[39].

---

[39] These are start-up companies, so many of these companies may no longer be around, and new names appear on the list, soon.

Capital Markets and Investments

Figure 6.1 Data Providers in Different Market Segments

Government	Social Media	Event Data	Location and Consumer Behavior	Satellite Imagery	Marketing & Publishers
Haver Analytics	Yelp	iSentium	Google Maps	Google Skybox	DataSift
Socrata	Pinterest	DataMinr	Nokia Here	Orbital Insights	AddThis
	Foursquare	Eagle Alpha	Foursquare Pinpoint		ShareThis
	Facebook	Minetta-Brook	Placed		Bitly
	Linkedin	Raven Pack	Airsage		
	Twitter				

Source: Citi Business Advisory Services, Big Data and Investment Management, 2015

Current Impact on Investment Process

Quantitative trading platforms currently analyze large amounts of data, quickly. Systematic trading so far has focused on market timing by analyzing order flow information and trading at very high frequency. On a more institutional scale, it has also tried, at a lower frequency, to extract relative value across a huge universe of securities (factor modeling, and finding securities with positive alpha), sometimes using technical charts and patterns. This has also prompted the rise of smart-beta algorithms, with several ETFs/ mutual funds trying to take advantage of this opportunity. Even traditionally qualitative investment houses are exploring the cutting edge in technology and data.

The latest wave in the evolution of big data into the investment workspace has placed demands on new tools and expertise. For example, linguistic experts are contributing to algorithms designed based on natural language processing capabilities to convert news releases into actionable trades. Military personnel with expertise in analyzing satellite data have been aligning themselves to finance firms. Professionals with skills in analyzing social media to examine consumer activity, and spot emerging trends and demand shifts now generate reports indicating which individual customer-centric businesses are being discussed more actively (and positively) in social media platforms. Computer science experts with skills in machine learning and neural networks are building models of predictive analytics. Firms are employing "data scientists" to focus on data gathering, archiving and analytics.

At the same time, firms are dealing with challenges that one might normally expect with emerging paradigms. They include mismatch between questions and datasets, long time-windows for data patterns to emerge as the datasets evolve, cultural mismatch with investment management staff (big data pioneers belong to Internet firms, gaming companies, military and other consumer-behavior focused companies).

Big data has big potential for investment firms, even beyond the front office investment idea generation and investment process. Compliance teams use such data to check for trade surveillance and compliant use of social media. Marketing teams are trying to figure out how best to use this data for targeting potential clients to raise capital.

Topical Issues in Capital Markets

Quantitative Investing

Investment processes are getting more quantitative, a theme discussed at several places within this book.[40] Quantitative strategies have increased in popularity, even as investment dollars have been moving from active management to passively managed low-fee products, since quantitative strategies are often more scalable, can be offered for lower fees and do not suffer from behavioral biases. At the same time, the quantitative investment process is also being democratized and made widely available. This allows retail investor to have access to quantitative models, tools and processes, through ETFs, smart beta products, etc. It also allows idea generators to code up ideas and submit them to investment platforms, and share in the economic benefits.

Hedge funds have traditionally been exclusive, as an investment vehicle or even as a place to work. Supposedly, these funds attract the smartest talent and investment capital. Hedge fund managers (i.e. owners) almost enjoy celebrity status, because of their supposed ability to generate high investment returns consistently. Firms such as AQR Capital have created a very successful broad-based business using a quantitative approach to factor-based investing (discussed below) in the last fifteen years, whereas firms such a Renaissance Technologies have generated consistent returns for their investors using proprietary high frequency algorithms. Quantopian is an investment startup that turned the halo effect of a hedge fund manager on its head, by inviting anybody to develop their own return-generating algorithm and backtest it on their platform. Quantopian has a team of people reviewing these publicly sourced algorithms, and picks a few ideas to allocate investor capital to. The idea generator gets a slice of the fees that Quantopian earns through the algorithm. Quantopian doesn't need to maintain a huge army of idea generators, can tap a large talent pool (including people such as professors who may not be inclined to work full time at a fund, but would not mind monetizing their ideas. The business model gained legitimacy when Steve Cohen, a well-known hedge fund manager, provided Quantopian with upto $250million of his own capital through Point72, to be managed by Quantopian. Prominent venture capitalists have backed the effort.

Factor-based investing

Over the last five years, quantitative investing, factor-based thinking, smart-beta ETFs have all taken center-stage. Active investors have increasingly started to define their allocation in terms of owning themes (secular stagnation, ageing demographics, cyber security, biotech, etc.)[41], and owning all the names that have high exposure to that theme, rather than analyzing single names bottom up. Further, a larger proportion of investors now choose to own factor exposures such as momentum, value, growth, dividend yield, etc. and invest in (smart beta) products that provide this. At the same time, more money is moving from active investing to passive strategies, which do not pick specific securities, but invest more mechanically to own broader exposures. Idea generation and trading have both become more algorithmic, with computer models scanning price movements and news much faster than humans, and implement trades based on this analysis instantly, without human intervention. There has been some innovation in security design, with Exchange-Traded Funds (AUM changes daily like mutual funds, but they also trade in the secondary market like a stock), discussed in Chapter 4) becoming very popular. All these forces collectively cause sections of the market to often co-move together, more than in the past. Does this result in a more systematized market, or does this provide further opportunities for a fundamental investor to pick out names that initially move with the cohort, but should not, based on fundamentals? And where does this end, with these fundamental screens getting quantified, maybe with the help of big data, or with the realization that thematic and top-down investing, while increasingly relevant, leave ample room for bottom-up fundamental managers to succeed? Time will tell.

---

[40] Chapters 4 and 11 offer perspectives, chapters 5 and 12 (and the Quantitative Credit section of Chapter 10) discuss some tools.

[41] Sectors may be thought of as a special example of a theme.

Capital Markets and Investments

Crowdfunding

This is an example of disintermediation where people with ideas have tried to reach the (predominantly retail) investor community directly. Platforms such as Kickstarter and GoFundMe have provided idea generators with financial capital, in return for an early version of the product or even equity.

Marketplace Lending

Similar to crowdfunding, investors can now invest in pools of loans to (risky) borrowers with a variety of needs, with the lending platform indicating the creditworthiness of the borrower. Interest rates are high and lucrative from the investor's perspective, but the borrowers, who would otherwise probably have to borrow from the informal lending sector, are happy to pay these rates, which are lower than what they would otherwise pay. These peer-to-peer (P2P) models target consumer segments (such as small businesses) underserved by current banking system. Diversification reduces the risk of one borrower defaulting. China has the largest P2P lending market in the world. Prosper and LendingClub are the leading US players in this space. However, it remains to be seen how this unfolds with potential for fraud, very little know-your-customer checks, and how much of the lending market can be effectively disintermediated at rates that appeal both to the borrower and lender.

Robo-advisors

Robo-advisors are automated financial advisors that help retail investors create and manage suitable portfolios (from a life cycle/ risk tolerance perspective), accept clients with low investment assets and charge a fraction of regular investment advisors at wealth management firms charge. Betterment, Wealthfront and Motif are a few examples of such firms in the US. The business models are evolving, with several live financial advisors using these robo-advisors as tools and working independently, instead of signing up with a large wirehouse such as UBS or Merrill Lynch and parting with a large share of commissions. This becomes even more relevant, as regulatory changes are making it less lucrative for many advisors to stick with the large wirehouses. Most wirehouses are also centralizing portfolio construction, and reducing advisor discretion.

Blockchaining

Blockchaining is a decentralized peer-to-peer network technology that maintains a public (or private) ledger of transactions, using cryptography. Unlike a database, which requires a (trusted) intermediary to maintain it, blockchaining allows any "competitive bookkeeper" (*miner*) to update the ledger by solving a difficult cryptographic problem first, in the process appending a "block" of transactions to the existing blockchain. Other members, can verify this solution fairly easily, and the miner that updated the ledger (to include the last block) gets rewarded. Blockchaining can potentially transform the mid-back offices of financial services firms by revolutionizing the clearing and settlement of securities, or the execution of legal documents. Cryptocurrencies work on a blockchain-based infrastructure.

Payment Mechanisms and Cryptocurrencies

The credit card payment systems (VISA, Mastercard, AMEX, Discover, etc.) and the banks have collectively controlled how financial transactions were conductions. With always-on Internet connectivity and mobile phones as powerful as computers, several companies have tried to break into this. The most straightforward attempt was by PayPal, which links to a user's bank account and is a more secure and cheaper way to pay for/ receive money for Internet-based transactions. Square took this a step further, providing a small piece of hardware that can plug into the phone and swipe a credit card remotely with very little equipment (other players like PayPal followed). Apple Pay and other mobile wallet solutions share a similar idea, except that they can be used for physical point-of-sale purchases and have physical (e.g. fingerprint) verification.

Anything that people are willing to accept in exchange for providing goods and services can serve as a currency. How well (and how long) it works depends on the continued willingness of people, which depends on the checks and balances to prevent misuse and boost confidence. Currencies that are primarily virtual/ electronic need different kinds of safeguards, compared to physical bills (special paper, marking, etc.) issued by central banks. Bitcoin and similar alternative currencies (Ethereum, XRP and NEM are the largest), working on a blockchain-based infrastructure, have been proposed as an alternative to central bank sponsored fiat currencies for some retail transactions.

Bitcoin transactions and balances are maintained in a blockchain (public ledger), which is processed by a network of communicating nodes (not by a central authority). These nodes compete to be the fastest to solve a difficult cryptographic problem, necessary to update and append the new transactions (block) to the existing list (blockchain), and broadcast the information for other nodes to verify and update. The process of collecting newly broadcast transactions and converting them into a new "block" is called *mining*. The miners[42] aim to generate a cryptographic transformation (*hash*) of the new block to link it to the earlier chain, by passing the transaction block (includes reference to previous block, transactions, timestamps, etc.) coupled with a *nonce* (i.e. a random number) through an algorithm to generate the hash. Tough targets/ constraints are set for the hash to satisfy, so this cryptographic transformation (or *hash*) is very computer-intensive to generate[43], but relatively easy to verify. Only a very small set of (unknown) nonces will generate a suitable hash, and finding one iteratively is time-consuming. Once the nonce is known, any node can trivially verify the work. This system makes the ledger very difficult to manipulate, as anyone who wants to change a block has to encrypt that block and all subsequent blocks by coming up with multiple nonces[44]. With the passage of time, since new blocks are always getting appended (usually every ten minutes), this process becomes exponentially harder.[45] For each block that is added, the winning (i.e. fastest) miners[46] are paid for their effort through newly created bitcoins and transaction fees; the sole source of bitcoin supply. This elaborate process resolves issues related to double-spending (i.e. spending the same bitcoin twice), since there is just one central ledger with all records. Anyone connected to the network can easily initiate a transaction using reference information, the receiver's digital public key and the sender's private key. Any node can easily validate the legitimacy of this transaction.

While these currencies have sporadically captured market interest and their "exchange rate" to the dollar has been extremely volatile, none of these technologies have (yet) emerged as a realistic alternative for financial institutions trading in the capital markets. Concerns related to legal issues and money laundering are being discussed actively. But, they are certainly emerging from the "counterculture" domain and trying to be more mainstream.

Compliance Software

Over the past several years, many high profile legal cases have been brought by various regulatory agencies on individuals and companies. They range from insider trading, market manipulation, failure to supervise and the gamut of financial crime, rather than the more commonly prosecuted Ponzi scheme. In many of these situations, company employees, driven by aggressive incentives, asymmetric payouts and an overwhelming

---

[42] Some of the largest miners are AntPool, BitClub, Bixin, BTC.com and BitFury; these are groups where members provide the GPU resources of their computers, and share in the gains if these pools win.

[43] Mining involves finding a number *nonce* which when hashed together with the block fulfils some conditions that are very difficult to satisfy.

[44] The old nonces will no longer work since the transactions have been changed.

[45] The original Bitcoin could only add 1 megabyte of data every 10 minutes, thus limiting the number of transactions that can be processed. On August 1, 2017, the Bitcoin community split into two, and a new version of Bitcoin called Bitcoin Cash, which can have blocks as large as 8MB, was mined for the first time. Both versions continue to be mined and traded.

[46] Miners have evolved from enthusiasts to larger institutions and miner pools, which invest in specialized hardware (e.g. ASIC chip cards for mining)

desire to generate profits and please the top bosses at any cost engaged in unethical behavior, violated company policy and broke the law. These individuals had to pay fines and spend time in prisons. Companies also had to explain to regulators what they did to monitor and stop the conduct and prove that they did not grant tacit permission or turn a blind eye; their reputation was damaged and, in many cases, they paid large fines as penalty or settlement. This, coupled with the greater regulatory oversight discussed above, has led to several start-ups (RedOwl and Palantir are most well-known) designing diagnostic tools (some even use artificial intelligence/ deep learning) to allow the companies to monitor and identify any such behavior early, and deal with it promptly. This space is often referred to as *RegTech*. Some of these firms have also branched out into "portfolio-manager / trader coaching" tools, using diagnostics to identify specific areas of weakness that the professionals can be coached to then work on[47].

> Technology has revolutionized most industries, including financial markets. Some trends include:
> - ✓ Big Data in Investment Management
>   - Evolution in database technologies, data collection methods, and being able to measure qualitative feedback are driving this
>   - New data sources (or existing sources getting organized better) such as data-driven governments, aggregation of historical sell-side research, geospatial satellite data, data from social media, location-based services and news and consumer credit card spending data are providing rich novel datasets.
> - ✓ Quantitative techniques are being applied broadly, comprising data analysis, risk factor design and backtesting, investment idea generation screens, trading desk surveillance, etc.
> - ✓ Investment dollars are progressively moving to a factor-based investment style, and picking investible themes rather than selecting securities bottom-up. Along with microstructure issues, this causes markets to co-move together.
> - ✓ Other trends such as crowdfunding, marketplace lending, robo-advisors, blockchaining, alternative payment mechanisms and cryptocurrencies have potential and have acquired niche positions; it remains to be seen whether they become mainstream.
> - ✓ Firms are raising their vigilance of employees, often using compliance software to detect data patterns that suggest illegal activity.

REFERENCES

Citi GPS (Mar 2016). *Digital Disruption: How Fintech is Forcing Banking to a Tipping Point*. Citigroup Publication

Citi Business Advisory Services (2015), *Big Data and Investment Management*

CFA Institute (2015), *Environmental, Social and Governance Issues in Investing*

Kassam, A.A. (August 2016), *ESG Investing comes of Age as Risk, Return and Impact Align in New Approaches*. State Street Global Advisors White Paper.

Harvey, Campbell (2016). *Cryptofinance*

---

[47] This is almost similar to the role sports analytics has played in the major leagues, inspired by Michael Lewis' *Moneyball*.

Bond Markets

7. Introduction to Bonds – Treasury Pricing and Institutional Details

In the previous section, we discussed financial capital markets broadly, the various agents, markets, and different instruments that are traded. In the remaining sections of the book, we will take deeper dives into some specific markets/ instruments. As we get specific, it will help readers to remember that while these markets are important illustrations, they do not comprehensively describe (not even close!) the universe of securities that market participants transact in. However, at the same time, most securities are variants of the core products that we will discuss, and have many features in common (new securities are continually being designed and launched), so readers will be equipped to find suitable frameworks and reference points to understand any security that they may come across. Specifically, the content in this chapter and the next (except, possibly the microstructure and auction details) are relevant for all fixed income instruments. We introduced bonds in Chapter 2; we take a closer look here.

TREASURIES - THE BASIC IDEA

Any national government needs to fund its expenses, which includes the cost of running the administration, subsidy payments to certain sections of society and industries, developmental project costs, etc. Much of this is usually funded by tax revenues of various forms (or, in the Middle East or Scandinavia, many oil-rich nations fund budgets through oil sales), but if there is a difference between the revenues and the costs (i.e. a *primary deficit/ revenue deficit* in the budget), the government needs to borrow to plug the gap. And, of course, to determine the total outflows, in addition to the costs listed above, interest and principal payments on any prior debt also count as relevant expenses. So *fiscal/ budget deficit*, which includes debt servicing payments, is often the relevant concept when discussing government debt. When government expenses rise/ tax revenues fall, the government has to make the difficult choice of raising taxes or increasing the debt burden by selling more bonds to raise money. Readers who would like a macroeconomics refresher are referred to Annexure III.

These government bonds are typically backed with the full faith of the government. They are considered to be *free of default risk in the domestic market* (i.e. the government's *local currency*), because the government can always print more money to satisfy bond obligations[48] (this would likely hurt the exchange rate; in the domestic economy, inflation would probably rise as a result). Thus, the entire interest payment is to compensate the investor for only the time value of money, including projected inflation. Investors often need different rates of compensation (i.e. interest rates) to part with their money for different lengths of time (usually higher rates for longer, but not always), so the government has to spend more on an annualized basis to raise money for longer periods.

The US government, through the US Treasury and the Federal Reserve, issues bonds for the same reason, which are referred to as US Treasuries. Every country has its own variant of these bonds (e.g. the UK has Gilts and Germany has Bunds). While most countries issue in their domestic currency, some countries, especially emerging market nations, issue in a popular global currency too (i.e. they borrow from abroad instead of local institutions). Foreign investors are usually more interested in these global bonds than local bond issues by the same country, since it reduces the investor exposure to issuer currency fluctuations. In some cases it also prevents the risk of their repayments being frozen if the country institutes capital controls, since global bonds are often subject to jurisdiction in a foreign country with better investor protection laws than the issuing

---

[48] This line of argument gets complicated the Euro area, because Eurozone governments do not have independent control over monetary policy, including money printing, so many Eurozone sovereigns trade at a spread.

Introduction to Bonds – Treasury Pricing and Institutional Detail

nation. These global hard currency bonds usually trade at lower yields than the local currency bonds, after adjusting for exchange rate hedging costs. Despite these apparent comforts of a foreign currency / jurisdiction, foreign currency bonds issued by Argentina and Greece suffered when the regulatory regime underlying these bonds came into question.

> ✓ National government incur recurring expenditures and debt service costs. They cover part of it through taxes; bond issuances make up the gap.
> ✓ Bonds issued by governments and backed by their full faith in the local jurisdiction are deemed risk free, since they can always print money to pay back these bonds.
> ✓ Emerging market sovereigns often issue bonds in developed market currencies too. These global bonds sometimes trade at lower yields, relative to currency-hedged local bonds.

WHAT IS A BOND?

To recap from an earlier chapter, a bond is a contract between a borrower (issuer) and a lender (investor) which details the terms of a debt agreement. Essentially, the issuer borrows money, to repay it back with interest over the next few months/ years (unless, of course, the borrower ends up getting bankrupt before that). The investor's upside is capped to receiving all the cash flows promised by the contract, in return for the current investment. There are various kinds of bond issues – Treasuries, States/ Municipalities, Mortgage Trusts, Corporations, Money Market Issuers (e.g. Commercial paper), ABS (Auto, Credit Card, Equipment Trusts, etc.). We discuss these in Chapter 2. Most of these have varying degrees of risk of the cash flows not being paid because the issuer defaults (i.e. credit risk). In this chapter we focus on Treasuries, which do not have credit risk.

So, the *issuer* of a simple (plain-vanilla) bond, in exchange for an upfront cash inflow (*issue price* of bond, usually close to the par value, but not necessary), promises to pay a set of periodic payments (interest/ *coupon*), and also return the loan *principal* (often called the *face/ par value*) on a *maturity date*. The interest/ coupon payments are calculated as a pre-specified percentage (may even be set to zero or Paid-In-Kind, by periodically increasing the principal value) of the par amount. If the initial upfront payment or the price of the bond (i.e. the borrowed amount) is the same as the par value, the bond is said to be issued at par; if higher (lower), the bond is said to be at a *premium (discount)*. If the investor buys the bond at a premium, then the investor effectively receives a lower return/ current yield than the published coupon rate. This is because the coupon rate is calculated based on the par value, but the investor is paying more than par since the bond is trading at a premium, to receive the same expected coupon payments.

> ✓ Bonds are a contractual agreement between the bond issuer (who needs money) and investors.
> ✓ The issuer agrees to pay the investors a periodic coupon payment and a final principal/ par value at bond maturity, and receives an upfront payment (initial bond price) instead, in the primary market.

OUR FIRST EXAMPLE – A SIMPLE BOND AND ITS YIELD

As an initial example, suppose a bond issued on June 30, 2015 by the US Treasury is initially priced at 99.5943[49], the coupon rate is 1.625% and the maturity date is June 30, 2020. (As a reminder, coupons in the

---

[49] Treasury prices are usually not quoted in dollars and cents, but in "ticks" (32nds of a dollar) as we will see later in the chapter.

Capital Markets and Investments

US are paid semi-annually, whereas coupons in Europe are paid annually). Bond prices are usually stated as a percentage of par, so all the math and numbers assume a par value of 100, though the technical face value for one bond is often 1000.

This bond is colloquially referred to as $T\ 1^5/_8\ of\ 6/30/20$ (Issuer, Coupon "of" Maturity). Like every other security (other bonds, equity etc.), this bond has unique identifiers – a 9-digit *CUSIP* (912828XH8), 12-digit ISIN (US912828XH83 - CUSIP is often a part of the ISIN), a 7-digit *SEDOL* (BYSKX33). Each of these is unique and suffices by itself; they exist simultaneously because of (some) disparate systems. The cash flows, from the investor's perspective, are depicted in Figure 7.1.

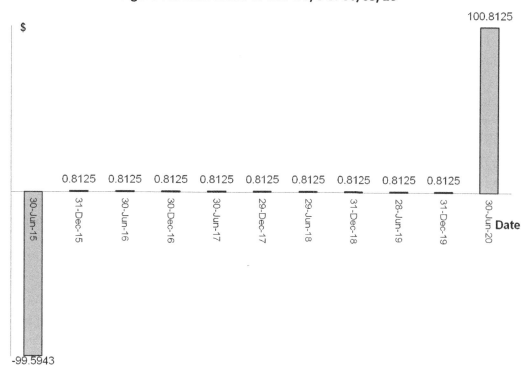

Figure 7.1 Cash Flows of UST 1 5/8 of 06/03/20

How do we analyze this bond? For any such analysis, there are usually two related components – risk and return. $99.5943 will grow to $108.125 in five years, but this simple addition of cash flows is a very imprecise way to think about the investment because money received at different points in time should not be treated equally. More formally, had the bond been issued at par (i.e. 100) and the coupon payments annual instead of semiannual, then the initial outflow would have been 100, and the investor would have earned 1.625% per annum on that investment for the next three years. But in this case, a few additional details matter:

- The investor invests less than 100 (i.e. 99.5943), so the return is (slightly) higher.
- Also, the investor receives money semi-annually rather than annually. Getting money back sooner is usually better (since interest rates are positive), because that money can be re-invested for the remaining period. Very generally, concepts such as *Net Present Value (NPV)* and *Internal Rate of Return (IRR)* capture these ideas (closely related to principles of compound interest and *Time Value of Money*), summarized in Annexure I.

For this example, the NPV is calculated as:

$$NPV = -99.5943 + \sum_{i=1}^{9} \frac{0.8125}{(1+y)^i} + \frac{100.8125}{(1+y)^{10}}$$

Introduction to Bonds – Treasury Pricing and Institutional Detail

where y is the rate of return (an input) that an investor could expect to earn in *a 6-month period* (since that is the periodicity of the cash flows in the equation; there are ten 6-month periods, denoted by i) by taking on a *similar amount of risk*. This is often referred to as *the opportunity cost of capital* and estimated by looking at other available investments. A positive NPV suggests that this project is worthwhile pursuing.

A related concept, IRR, solves for the rate of return that would cause the NPV to be zero. Both NPV and IRR have their pros and cons, related to ranking of projects and multiple solutions to the equations, but are consistent and reliable for straightforward applications as the one above. Here, IRR is the return that solves Eq. 7.1 below[50]:

$$0 = -99.5943 + \sum_{i=1}^{9} \frac{0.8125}{(1+IRR)^i} + \frac{100.8125}{(1+IRR)^{10}} \qquad \text{Eq. 7.1}$$

Computers and calculators solve this equation by trial-and-error recursions. For example, *IRR*, *RATE* and *YIELD* functions in Excel are relevant. In this example, the IRR works out to 0.855%. Calculators such as HP12C and TI BA-II Plus are common financial calculators. If the IRR is greater than the opportunity cost of capital, the investment is a good one. *For the IRR to be equal to the actual return that the investor earns on the bond, intermediate coupon payments need to be reinvested at the same return as the IRR* - a higher reinvestment rate raises the return; a lower one reduces it.

The IRR gives the analyst an idea of the promised return of the investment; this needs to be traded off with the risk of the investment to decide if the risk is worth it. The NPV calculation above requires the analyst first determining what the appropriate rate of return should be for the risk in this project, and then using that return assumption to check if the NPV is positive. While there are models that indicate how much return one should expect for certain risks, this is most directly done by examining other investments with similar risk profiles.

In the US markets, the *yield* (or, more formally, the *Yield To Maturity i.e. YTM*) of this bond is twice the IRR (i.e. *IRR**2, or 1.710% in this example), since yields, like returns, are usually expressed on an annual basis. Note, this is an approximation (but nevertheless the convention and the standard), since it is not completely accurate to double a semi-annual return to get an annual return; according to the Time Value of Money concept discussed above; money received earlier is more valuable than the same amount received later. In fact, the Effective Annual Yield (EAY) corresponding to the YTM is given by:

$$EAY = (1 + \frac{YTM}{2})^2 - 1$$, which is (usually slightly) greater than YTM. EAY is 1.717% in this example.

Although EAY is the actual annual yield, it is almost never used; YTM is universally adopted because of its simplicity. YTM is referred to using several different terms all meaning the same – yield on a semi-annual basis, the annual yield compounded semi-annually, bond-equivalent yield and nominal yield. For non-US bonds which pay an annual coupon, this distinction vanishes; the rate of return from the formula is the YTM (without the need to double it), which is also the precise annual yield. Going forward, any returns (or yields) referred to in the book are annualized returns, unless otherwise stated.

---

[50] The *summation* (Σ) notation is a convenient shorthand for writing expressions without repeating similar terms which are to be added to each other. For example, $\frac{C}{(1+r)} + \frac{C}{(1+r)^2}$ is identical to $\sum_{i=1}^{2} \frac{C}{(1+r)^i}$. In Eq. 7.1 above, we would have to write out nine similar terms, if we did not want to use Σ.

Capital Markets and Investments

The yield of this bond is higher than the coupon; this is mechanically the result of a price lower than the par value. If the bond were issued at a premium (i.e. greater than par), the yield would be lower than the coupon; the IRR equals the coupon rate if the issue price is par. As the bond price increases, a lower IRR (or yield) satisfies the equation above. This is because, as the issue price increases, for the same contractual terms (coupon, maturity, etc.), the investor needs to put up more money upfront to receive the same cash flows; the expected rate of return on this bond goes down. So, *bond prices and yields are inversely related. Given the terms of the bond, every bond price has a unique corresponding yield; using either is sufficient and equivalent*; the lower the yield, the more expensive a given bond. Assuming the opportunity cost of capital doesn't change, at some (high) price it no longer makes sense to invest in this bond; better opportunities lie elsewhere.

The above discussion assumes that the cash flows will definitely be paid when they are due, since the bond has been issued by the government in local currency (the government can print money if necessary). So, the yield compensates the investor only for not being able to earn an alternative return on the investment capital. For bonds where there is a chance that the cash flows do not get paid (e.g. a company with an uncertain future), the yield needs to be higher (i.e. the price needs to be lower) to compensate the investor for the risk of the corporate's default, in addition to the opportunity cost.

These bonds, once issued, also trade in the secondary market (exchange hands among investors). In fact, Treasury markets have traditionally been one of the most liquid markets. As bonds trade post-issuance, their prices fluctuate, depending on what prices investors choose to transact at, which in turn depend on the prices of other assets with similar risk profile. Finally, these perceptions move interest rates, which drives Treasury bond prices. The reasons for this is described in detail over the next few chapters.

- ✓ Bonds are priced using the NPV formula to discount contractual cash flows, using the opportunity cost of capital.
- ✓ Alternatively, the IRR implied by the current market price and the future cash flows is the yield to maturity (YTM) of the bond. This yield can be compared with those of competing investments.
- ✓ Given the contractual cash flows, bond prices and yields have a one-to-one inverse (i.e. negative) relationship. Bond prices and coupons are positively related.
- ✓ If future cash flows are not certain but risky, the bond's yield will be higher (and price lower) than a hypothetical Treasury with the same contractual terms.

U.S. TREASURY AUCTION MECHANICS ***

Armed with a basic idea of bond pricing, we return to the institutional mechanics of issuance, quoting and trading Treasuries. The US Treasury issues securities across the maturity spectrum – "*Bills*" mature in less than a year, "*Notes*" mature in less than ten years, and longer term "*Bonds*" (distinct from generic bonds, which are an asset class) have maturities up to 30 years out. These are issued via auction; the Federal Reserve effectively conducts it on behalf of the Treasury. There are two kinds of bids – *competitive bids* (requiring both yields and quantities), which the institutional players participate in through brokers, and *non-competitive bids* (quantity-only bids that are filled at the market-clearing price, capped at a size of USD5mm, mainly for retail investors). The price is determined through the competitive bid; the non-competitive participants get the same price. When the Treasury announces the auction date, the size and the maturity is known, but not the coupon. Buyers bid the lowest yield that they are willing to accept (lower bid is the higher price), and the quantity they will buy at that yield; the same buyer can put in multiple bids. The buy side places these bids through the sell-side, using one or more of the primary dealers that the Fed has designated. Each dealer presents one aggregate

Introduction to Bonds – Treasury Pricing and Institutional Detail

order book to the Fed. This is an uniform price (Dutch) auction i.e. after the auction, using the aggregated order book from all the primary dealers, the Fed starts from the lowest bid yield (i.e. highest price) and works its way up the yield until the cumulative volume demanded is equal to the auction size less the non-competitive bid size. This yield, at which all the supply is exhausted, is referred to as *the stop-out yield*. The coupon is set, so that the yield on the bond matches this stop-out yield. All winning bids i.e. bids with yields below the stop-out yield will get a full allocation, but pay the price corresponding to the stop-out yield, and not what they bid. Non-competitive bidders also pay the price corresponding to this stop-out yield and get allotted the quantity that they bid for. This auction date usually precedes the bond issue date by about two weeks. The bond begins to accrue interest from the issue date, when monies are exchanged and the bonds are settled.

To describe the extent of success of an auction, market participants often refer to the *bid-cover ratio*. The numerator of this ratio is the total bid amount (across all prices); the denominator is the amount accepted. So, this ratio captures the excess demand or the oversubscription of an issue, ignoring the bid price. When the stop-out yield of an auction is higher than the last *when-issued* yield (see below) prior to the results, it is viewed as a negative; participants refer to the auction as having *tail*ed.

As a side note, some foreign governments issue securities using a discriminatory auction, where they sell bonds to the highest bidders, but each bidder pays what they bid, rather than the market-clearing stop-out yield. This, apparently, maximizes revenue for the government, because it extracts all the revenue it possibly can, by charging every investor the maximum he would be willing to pay. But, the moment the bond starts trading, it will trade at the market-clearing stop-out yield, so, the investors who paid up will have to recognize an immediate loss (essentially, *the buyer's curse*) if they are marked-to-market (some long-only investors are not). This causes investors to shade down their bid, and it may lead to much higher market clearing yields in the first place.

When-issued Market

Well before the auction, on the announcement date (usually around two weeks before), a *when-issued* market develops. This is effectively similar to a forward/ futures market for the not-yet-issued bond, which settles once the bond is issued. No cash is exchanged at trade inception. Between the announcement date and the auction date, the when-issued market trades on yield (since the coupon is not known); once the auction results are posted and the Treasury sets the coupon, the when-issued market trades on price. This is similar to the TBA market for mortgages.

Treasury *Bills*, (i.e. short-dated, with less than one year maturity) are quoted on a *discount basis*. The quote represents an (annualized) discount to face value, and is the yield if this investor holds the bill to maturity, to get back par. These bills do not pay a coupon. The major investors in the Bills market are Money Market Mutual Funds, which are considered cash substitutes and need to be invested primarily in securities with less than a year to maturity.

For example, if the Bill is quoted at (a yield/ discount of) 0.65, the price of USD10,000 par amount is:

$$Bill\ price = 10000 - 65 * \frac{Actual\ Days\ to\ Maturity}{360}$$

Intuitively, if 65bp is the annualized yield, then 65*Fraction of year to maturity should be the approximate discount to par. The ratio *Actual days to Maturity/ 360* is the *day-count convention* in the Treasury bills market. We'll discuss more on that in a later section.

The last-issued (i.e. newest) Treasury in any maturity bucket is referred to as *on-the-run*. This is usually the most liquid Treasury, with tight bid-offer spreads and large volume. About 70% of trading occurs in the on-the-run

Capital Markets and Investments

bonds. Older Treasuries are generically referred to as *off-the-run*, comprising of sub-classifications such *on-the-run*, and *old-old on-the-run*.

> ✓ Treasury securities have various maturities, from short-dated bills to bonds maturing in 30 years.
> ✓ Treasuries are initially priced using an auction, through the primary dealers, where investors bid on the yield and the quantity they would buy at that yield. All winning bids receive the market-clearing yield. The bond's coupon is set based on this yield, to keep the price close to par.
> ✓ A forward market for a yet-to-be-issued Treasury, called the when-issued market, is active from the time the Treasury auction is announced until the bond starts trading, about two weeks later. Investors trade based on yield, and settlement occurs when the bond actually begins to trade.
> ✓ For any maturity, the most recently issued Treasury bond is called on-the-run and is very liquid.

FINANCING TREASURY PURCHASES – THE REPO MARKET ***

A *repo market* is a form of a securities lending/ borrowing market, where investors use securities as collateral while borrowing cash to finance security purchases. Often the security used as collateral is the same security that the investor wants to purchase, so the complete transaction is:

> The investor spends x dollars of his own capital to buy security A, to borrow cash to buy much more (suppose an additional y dollars) of security A. So, $x+y$ dollars is the total amount of security that is bought (and that is the investor's economic exposure). This allows the investor to gain $x+y$ dollars of economic exposure by putting down only x dollars; hence repos are also considered a form of leverage. This is often a seamless transaction; while buying the bonds, the investor would simply let the dealer know that he would want to finance this by repo, instead of paying cash. The entire asset base of $x+y$ is used as collateral for the loan of y dollars; x is the amount of *overcollateralization*. $x/x+y$ is referred to as the *haircut*, and the interest rate to borrow y is referred to as the repo rate. The haircut is set primarily based on how volatile security A is; the higher the volatility, the larger the collateral required. High yield bonds may require a 30% haircut; Treasuries need more like 2%. If the price of the underlying security decreases materially after the agreement, the lender can demand additional collateral at the time of renewal.

The repo market is probably the single largest source of financing for Treasuries. Since they are liquid, default-free and not volatile, the haircuts are small; market participants can put on large trades with very little capital. Since this is a secured loan, the repo rate is often lower than the Fed Funds rate, at which banks borrow and lend overnight to each other in the interbank market.

The mechanics of the repo transaction usually involve the lender of capital buying these securities from the borrower at trade inception, with an agreement to sell them back at an agreed upon (higher) price at the end of the repo term (usually overnight, but can vary). This higher price for the future sale (i.e. the repo rate) primarily reflects the cost of capital, at least for liquid securities such as Treasuries, since it is collateralized by the most secure assets. This rate is referred to as the *GC (General Collateral) rate*. Now, the lender of capital owns these bonds for the duration of the repo term; aside from earning the repo rate as interest, these securities can also be lent out to people who need them (e.g. as a borrow for a short) and earn a lucrative borrow rate. If a security is in high demand, the repo rate for that security may be very low (i.e. the security can trade *special* in the repo market) because the lender of capital would rather lend capital against this security (hence the low *special repo rate*) to earn the large rents from subsequently lending this security out, or to cover an

Introduction to Bonds – Treasury Pricing and Institutional Detail

existing short position. The lender of capital is said to enter into a repo; the borrower of capital enters into a *reverse repo*.

A significant amount of Treasuries are bought using repo financing, where the economic buyer needs to come up with very little cash (sometimes as low as 3-5%), getting the remaining amount financed via repo (mechanics discussed above) from the dealer (typically a large investment bank). After the 2008 financial crisis, regulators require these banks to hold significant amounts of capital against these assets. Since Treasury repo is a low-margin business, and capital is scarce, it often doesn't make sense for the investment banks to allocate much capital to this business. Consequently, banks have been cutting down the amount of repo financing that they are willing to provide. This causes investors who require leverage to use the swap market (discussed later, in chapter 8) instead, thereby causing swap spreads (the difference between swap rates and Treasury rates of similar maturity) to be very tight.

For less liquid asset classes such as corporate bonds, the repo market is more specialized. Instead of rolling overnight agreements security by security (also fairly common), agreements are often struck based on a pool of securities for a longer term, allowing the borrower to substitute similar securities. Haircuts are higher, as are repo rates.

MICROSTRUCTURE OF THE US TREASURY MARKET ***

Treasury quoting convention

Instead of the normal decimal system of dollars and cents, *US Treasuries are quoted in units of "ticks"* instead of cents. In this market, each tick is $1/32$ of a dollar, or 3.125 cents. In the last decade, bonds have been quoted in half-ticks, denoted by a "+" sign after the quote. So, 97-19+ (or sometimes 97.19+) refers to a bond price of 97 dollars and 19.5 ticks, i.e. 97.609375. In some obvious situations (e.g. the ask price, when the bid price is quoted fully), dealers will only quote 19+, i.e. the number of ticks. The implied yield to maturity is usually also part of the quote.

Treasury Trading and Execution

The Treasury market is a multi-dealer OTC market, but is nonetheless one of the largest and most liquid markets. Information is disseminated quickly, and large trades used to be very easy to execute. To facilitate this, there is a hierarchy of Treasury brokers. The highest level comprises the *Primary Dealers*, who participate at Treasury auctions, submitting bids on behalf of their clients, and are authorized to trade with the Fed. There are also a group of *Inter-Dealer Brokers (IDB)*, who facilitate trades across dealers, while keeping their identities anonymous. Historically, these brokers aggregated orders, and dealers could see the best bid and offer on electronic screens, and executed by (voice) calling the IDB. This market structure, along with a thriving Treasury futures market, was enough to keep the market orderly and very liquid. Over the last fifteen years, this format has evolved considerably – the increase in electronic trading, the changing roles of market intermediaries, and new investor profiles, have changed how liquidity is provided and taken in the Treasury (cash) bond market, and the features of this liquidity.

Electronic trading has increased significantly in the cash (i.e. non-derivative) Treasury market. This began with innovations in the interdealer market about fifteen years ago, with the movement in electronic dissemination of prices and quotes from voice-assisted brokers using GovPX, Bloomberg to Electronic Communications Networks (ECN) platforms such as eSpeed (a Cantor Fitzgerald product), BrokerTec (by ICAP), Tradeweb, etc. Such ECN platforms evolved to electronic trading, and eventually enabled automated trading, which provides for electronic order manipulation, processing and clearing of trades. While initially only primary dealers had access to these systems, over the years, the IDBs provided access to more and more participants, including *Principal Trading Firms* (PTFs), which often trade at very high frequency using algorithms, holding trades for milliseconds. PTFs now account for more than half the trading activity on inter-dealer platforms. Some platforms also provide incentives for the PTF to provide liquidity. So, the nature of liquidity providers has changed, as the market-making revenues are distributed across a broader set of players with different incentives and constraints. At the same time, regulatory constraints have made it difficult for traditional dealers to make markets as easily as in the past. While over 90% of the inter-dealer on-the-run volume trades either on BrokerTec or eSpeed, the ECN market share for off-the-run issues is much lower (below 10%); voice-assisted trading is still very relevant.

Some technological changes have also affected the dealer-customer market, where the traditional brokers continue to dominate. While much of this market still operates by voice, large sell-side firms now use "autoquote" algorithms to respond to smaller orders from the buy-side, which quote based on the dealer's inventory and the levels seen in the ECN. From the inter-dealer broker's point of view, the distinction between a broker, dealer and an end-customer has also blurred, as more end-customers transact on the IDB platforms, with many PTFs providing two-way quotes.

Over the past few years, regulatory changes have affected the Treasury market, as discussed above. One would think that this affect liquidity in the markets. *Liquidity* of a market refers to how *quickly* a buyer or seller can transact in large *size* without moving market prices, and if the cost to buy is close to the cost to sell. Liquidity cannot be directly observed, and is usually tracked through proxy metrics like bid-ask spreads, volumes, etc. Examining the data, bid-ask spreads appear tight and healthy at most times (the electronic networks, increased technology intensity and the PTF quotes all feed into this), but much of this liquidity is "phantom" and can be withdrawn in a matter of milliseconds at the slightest indication of adverse news. This causes the end-users (who transact when there is news) to not find enough counterparties when they need them, and the market to gap down, severe bouts of volatility are likely to be more common, despite the apparent calmness of the market. Market players are still figuring out this changing liquidity pattern.

THE SIMPLE EXAMPLE RE-VISITED – SPOT CURVE AND ACCRUED INTEREST

The earlier example on the 5-year Treasury, while helpful, simplified some important details. At issuance, the bond is priced based on a bidding process, as detailed above, where investors use yields of other bonds as reference points while submitting bids. But once the bond begins to trade, what is the fair value of the bond? Also, we conveniently worked with situations when the bond was just issued. What changes need to be made for pricing *at any time* after issuance? Let us take up these issues one by one.

Different discount rates for different payment dates – the spot curve

The yields of bonds with similar time to maturity (and similar risk) serve as a useful starting point in coming up with an estimate of a fair yield. Once the bond is trading post issuance, investors value the bond based on the Present Value/ IRR formula in Equation 6.1. Now they assume a bond yield to solve for the bond's "fair" price. Again, they use yields of bonds with similar characteristics as a starting point, but is there a more formal way to get to a more precise yield? There is also a chicken-and-egg issue here – once you know the yield, you can get to the price, and once you know the price, you can get to the yield, but you need to figure one of these out first.

More importantly, in equation 6.1, we solved for one value of IRR. Conversely, if we use that equation to price bonds, we will use one yield, regardless of the timing of the specific cash flow. Principally, the yields associated with discounting each of the cash flows could be different, because they occur at different points in time; indeed, the primary justification for the Treasury yield is compensation for the time value of money. So, we can write the equation more generally as Eq. 7.2:

Introduction to Bonds – Treasury Pricing and Institutional Detail

$$\text{Bond price}(P) \equiv \sum_{i=1}^{n} \frac{C*0.5}{(1+{r_i}/{2})^i} + \frac{\text{Par Value}}{(1+{r_n}/{2})^n} \qquad \text{Eq. 7.2}$$

where C is the contracted annualized coupon rate, n is the number of *semi-annual* periods to maturity (i.e. $n/2$ years to maturity), and r_i is the *annualized* discount rate (or required yield) associated with time period i.[51] The IRR that we referred to earlier is essentially a (complicated) average of these r_i.

The important point is that the discount rate associated with each cash flow above could be different (i.e. all the r's don't need to be the same). The relation between these yields/ discount rates/ expected returns and maturity is referred to as the *yield curve* or *term structure of interest rates*. While the yield curve is usually upward sloping (i.e. higher yields are associated with longer maturities), flat or downward sloping yield curves have also existed several times in the last few decades; we'll discuss that later. Figure 7.2 shows various shapes of the yield curve.

Figure 7.2 Various shapes of the yield curve

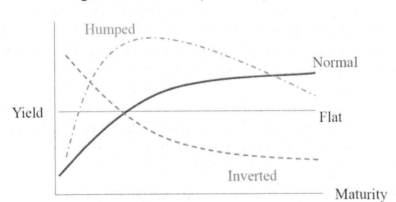

To simplify our discussion, let's momentarily consider a 4-period bond, with a 1% coupon, so our problem reduces to deducing r_1, r_2, r_3 and r_4 in Eq. 7.3 below:

$$\text{Bond price}(P) = \frac{0.8125}{1+{r_1}/{2}} + \frac{0.8125}{(1+{r_2}/{2})^2} + \frac{0.8125}{(1+{r_3}/{2})^3} + \frac{100.8125}{(1+{r_4}/{2})^4} \qquad \text{Eq. 7.3}$$

In many systems, the i-th period discount factor is separately calculated as $\delta_i \equiv \frac{1}{(1+{r_i}/{2})^i}$, so the bond's price can be expressed as Eq. 7.4:

$$P = \sum_{n}^{i=1} (CF_i \times \delta_i) \qquad \text{Eq. 7.4}$$

Where CF_i is the cash flow for period i.

Our aim is to find suitable values of r_i for each time period. The expected return for lending money to the US Treasury for 6 months is most precisely available by looking at the yield of a T-Bill maturing in 6 months.

---

[51] So, r_1 refers to the annualized rate for six months. In the first term, we are compounding for 6 months by dividing r_1 by 2, and raising to the power 1 (i.e. 6 months). The discount rates are always annualized, so they need to be divided by the compounding frequency to get the rate per period.

Capital Markets and Investments

This is the "cleanest" data because there are no other intermediate cash flows, and risk is identical to other US Treasury bonds. So, once we have that yield, we know r_1. Similarly, by looking at a 364-day T-Bill, we can figure out what r_2 is. How about r_3 and r_4?

At this point, we need to look at other types of US Treasury bonds. The STRIPS (Separate Trading of Interest and Principal Securities) market can potentially give us zero-coupon (i.e. only one terminal cash flow) yields longer than one year. Investors can turn in a coupon-paying Treasury bond to the US Treasury, and receive a portfolio of STRIPS, one for each coupon/ principal payment. Each STRIP entitles the holder to only one cash flow of a specified amount at a specific maturity. These can be traded individually, though the market for them is not very liquid. Assuming, we have prices for STRIPS maturing on the payment dates for our bond, we can use the yields of these STRIPS to get the relevant yields, including r_3. Unlike STRIPS, which are generated by breaking apart a regular coupon bond, a zero-coupon bond (ZCB) is actually issued by the US Treasury in that form and also has only one payment, on maturity. ZCBs are quoted/ priced at a discount to par. The pricing for a ZCB is $P_i^{ZCB} = \dfrac{100}{(1+r_i/2)^i}$, so given the ZCB or STRIPS price, we can back out r_i; here we use this principle to calculate r_3 and r_4. Note that, unlike T-Bills, ZCBs and STRIPS are not quoted on a discount basis; they follow a convention similar to regular Treasuries. Once we have r_1, r_2, r_3 and r_4, we can substitute in the above formula to get the bond price. If this were a longer maturity bond, we would have used longer-maturity ZCBs/ STRIPS to get the other r_i. The yield of the ZCB/ STRIP is called the *spot rate*.

Principally, we tried to isolate the price of the exact risk (lending to the US Treasury for i 6-month periods), found how that risk was priced in another security, and used that same discount rate (essentially a price of risk) to discount the cash flows in our bond. Suppose, as owners of the bond, we expect to receive $81.25 at the ends of each of periods 1, 2 and 3 (6, 12 and 18 months) and $10081.25 at the end of period 4 (24 months). The price of our bond should be identical to the prices for $81.25 par in a 6-month T-Bill, $81.25 par in a 364-day T-Bill and, $81.25 par in an 18-month STRIPS/ ZCB and $10050 par in a 24-month STRIPs/ ZCB. This is because both the bond and this portfolio of Bills/ STRIPS/ZCB have identical cash flows, so by the principle of no arbitrage, they should have the same price. So, in many situations, multiple STRIPS could be used to simply calculate the discount factor for all the payment dates, and then these factors are multiplied by the bond payments on those dates to price the bond, as shown in Eq. 7.4 Above. This becomes a scalable process, because the discount factor calculation can be done just once; pricing a bond is then a series of multiplications and additions. The discount factor is essentially the price of a ZCB which pays a dollar at maturity.

It is often not easy to isolate risks exactly (e.g. if the STRIPS is not liquid but our bond is, the STRIPS' yield also includes compensation for liquidity). So these yields serve as a starting point, and may need to be adjusted further.

Bootstrapping – from bond prices/ yields to spot rates

Liquid STRIPS and ZCBs may not be available for every payment date of the bond. But, it is likely that liquid regular coupon bonds may be available, with reliable prices/ yields. This provides yet another alternative to extract spot yields, referred to as *bootstrapping*. For example, suppose the 18 and 24-month STRIPS are illiquid (so we do not have r_3 and r_4 yet), but a coupon-paying Treasury maturing in 18 months trades frequently. If we substitute the values of r_1 and r_2 that we obtained from the T-Bills (always available) and the price of this 18-month Treasury in a 3-period version of Eq. 7.3 (Eq. 7.3 is the 4-period version), we find that r_3 is the only unknown and can solve for it. Or, if the 364-day Bill hasn't been recently issued, we can use a 1-year coupon bond (e.g. a two-year bond issued one year ago), and first calculate r_2 by substituting r_1 and the price

Introduction to Bonds – Treasury Pricing and Institutional Detail

of this 1-year coupon bond into a 2-period version of Eq. 7.3, before proceeding with the step above. Similarly, using the price of the 24-month Treasury and the values of r_1, r_2 and r_3 in Eq. 7.3, we can calculate r_4. With r_1, r_2, r_3 and r_4 now available, we have the spot yields and can price any four-period bond. . The general idea is to start with T-Bills and short dated Treasuries, use a version of Eq. 7.2, with discount rates (r_i) for all periods except one known, solve for that unknown r_i (using the equation, the known r_i's and the price of the bond), and then repeat the process using all these earlier discount rates and the one just computed, and a one-period longer Treasury to calculate a discount rate one more period out. [52]

There are several variants of the spot rates. One common variant is the par rate, which is the coupon rate of a bond issued at par. This value, C, is obtained by solving Eq. 7.5:

$$100 = \sum_{i=1}^{n} \frac{C \times 100/2}{(1 + r_i/2)^i} + \frac{100}{(1 + r_n/2)^n} \qquad \text{Eq. 7.5}$$

For a bond trading at par, C, the coupon rate, is also its yield. This can be done for all maturities (i.e. different values of n), thus generating a par rate curve.

More generally, bootstrapping is the methodology used to derive a yield curve from Treasury prices. Unlike our simple example, this requires several qualitative decisions – which bonds to pick as the liquid precisely-priced bonds (usually the on-the-run bonds), what kind of model (e.g. cubic spline) to use to "connect the dots" between the liquid yields for intermediate maturities, how to use the information in the prices of the other not-so-liquid bonds (set error bounds between model prices and observed prices), etc. Once an avenue for active quantitative research, these models have been largely standardized.

Bond prices on non-coupon payment dates – Accrued Interest

We can use the same framework to price bonds on dates that are not coupon payment dates, since coupons are paid at discrete intervals. We can calculate a NPV to obtain the price just as we did earlier, but if we are two months from the next coupon payment (four months from the previous payment, for a bond that pays semi-annually, unless this is the first coupon payment). The relevant discount rates, using the format in footnote 52 are $r_{0.16}$, $r_{.66}$, $r_{1.16}$ and $r_{1.66}$. We refer to this cash-flow based price below as the *Dirty Price*.

However, market participants do not quote bonds using the dirty price, since the periodic coupon payment is very predictable. Since coupons are paid at discrete time intervals, there are deterministic drops in bond price on the coupon payment dates, as cash flows drop off. For example, the bond's dirty price right before the coupon payment would be higher than the bond's price after the coupon payment a day later by the amount of the coupon payment. The bond price does not spike up right before the coupon payment, but builds up progressively as the time, from one coupon date to another, as the present value of the next coupon payment gets closer to the coupon (i.e. the discount factor goes to 1, as the time to payment goes to zero), and then instantaneously drops as the coupon is paid out, before beginning to rise again. Analyzing the historical return pattern of a bond can get confusing because of this price fluctuation.

---

[52] Most software and reports prefer to represent the time periods (subscripts) in terms of years, so the relevant notation in this framework will be $r_{0.5}$, r_1, $r_{1.5}$, r_2. Only the notation changes; the rates remain annualized and need to be divided by two; the time exponent has the same value. So, if the time period i increases in increments of 0.5 in the above formula and represents half-years, the time exponent will be $i \times 2$. The formula is:

$$\text{Bond price} = \sum_{i=0.5}^{\text{Years to Maturity (in steps of 0.5)}} \frac{\text{Annual Coupon}_i \times 0.5}{(1 + \frac{r_i}{2})^{i \times 2}} + \frac{\text{Par Value}}{(1 + \frac{r_{\text{Years to Maturity}}}{2})^{2 \times \text{Years to Maturity}}}$$

Capital Markets and Investments

The market convention is to adjust the discounted cash flow-based price (the *"Dirty" Price*) for this fluctuation related to the coupon payment and come up with a *"Clean" Price*, which is the price used to quote the security and discuss it among market participants. The adjustment, called the *Accrued Interest*, computes the coupon accrued between the last coupon payment and the current date (in reality it is the settlement date assuming a trade today). The buyer pays the seller the sum of the Clean Price and the Accrued Interest, i.e. the Dirty Price. The Dirty Price is almost never talked about, except on the transaction invoice (so, also called the Invoice Price).

Dirty Price – Accrued Interest = Clean Price

We now discuss the mechanics of calculating the Accrued Interest. Accrued Interest on any day is the coupon rate for the period times the fraction of the period that has elapsed since the last coupon payment. Immediately after the coupon is paid, the Accrued Interest drops to zero, and starts building up again over time. Figure 7.3 shows this for a bond paying a 10% per annum coupon, semiannually on June 30 and Dec 31. The Accrued Interest is computed mechanically by the back office and is added to the Clean Price during settlement, usually one working day after trade date for US Treasuries.

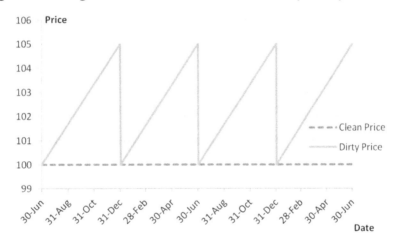

Figure 7.3 Changes in Accrued Interest between Coupon Payment Dates

All bonds (not just Treasuries) with periodic interest payments have an accrued interest component, but the exact calculation mechanics differ slightly, based on the asset class. Eq. 7.6 shows the formula:

Accrued Interest = Coupon Rate × Day Count Convention   Eq. 7.6

The *Day Count Convention* varies depending on the market. For Treasuries, it is calculated as *Actual/ Actual*, i.e. Actual number of days elapsed since the last coupon date/ Actual number of days between two coupon periods.[53]

---

[53] The corporate bond market uses a 30/360 day count convention; i.e. it assumes that the year has 360 days, every elapsed month counts as 30 days, but the days in the current month are counted on an actual basis.

Introduction to Bonds – Treasury Pricing and Institutional Detail

- ✓ Time value of money concepts suggest that investors will often demand larger premium to lend money for longer horizons; discount rates for different time periods are generally different. The bond yield that we calculate using IRR combines these different discount rates.
- ✓ In practice, we need to infer these different period-specific discount rates (called spot rates) from the quoted prices of coupon bonds. This method is called bootstrapping.
- ✓ To price bonds on non-coupon payment dates, we need to consider the time elapsed from the previous coupon date and compensate the bondholder who has held the bond during that time but has not received a coupon. That compensation is called Accrued Interest; and is mechanically added to the price of the bond, based on coupon rate and time from the previous coupon date. Different markets have different conventions to count days.

FORWARD CURVES

The term structure that we derived above is referred to as the spot yield curve, because it is based on the current zero rates. This lists the interest rates at which the US Treasury can borrow today, for different maturities. Implicit in this term structure are *forward curves*, which detail the rates at which one would expect the Treasury to be able to borrow in future (say, one period ahead), *based on today's spot rates*. For example, given r_1, r_2, we can derive f_1^1 i.e. *the one-period rate in one period* as $f_1^1 = \dfrac{(1+r_2)^2}{1+r_1} - 1$. We can similarly derive every point on the 1-period ahead forward curve.

While there is an expectation element to this curve, it is completely determined by today's rates, using no-arbitrage principles. Intuitively, there are two ways to lend for two periods – either directly at r_2, or lend for one year at r_1, and simultaneously lock in f_1^1 today to lend for one period next period. f_1^1 is a transactable rate; there is a FRA (*Forward Rate Agreement*) market where investors can sign a contract today to transact one period ahead on a pre-decided notional. If, at the end of one period, the 1-period rate is higher than today's f_1^1, the lender would have been better off not locking into f_1^1. Unless investors have a view on rates, they would be indifferent taking either side of the FRA at inception. Then, as rates move, one side of the trade becomes profitable, and the other leg is at a disadvantage. If investors want to terminate this before expiration (on period 1 in this example), they may be able to do that; they will either pay or receive the value of the leg upon termination, depending on which way rates moved after the trade was put on. So, expectations for the future get embedded in the back end of today's spot curve, which generate the futures rate/ curve consistent with the expectations.

- ✓ The current (spot) yield curve has embedded expectations about what this spot curve will look like in future, since we can extrapolate what rate an investor is willing to lend for one year one year from now (i.e. the one-year rate one period ahead) by examining the current one year and two year rates, and applying the no-arbitrage principle.
- ✓ Repeating this with the current two-year, three-year rates, etc., we can infer the entire spot curve one year ahead.

Capital Markets and Investments

EXPECTED PATTERNS IN BOND PRICE MOVEMENTS

Bonds are priced by discounting their future contractual cash flows by an appropriate discount rate (risk-free for Treasuries). Treasury discount factors are almost completely determined by market interest rates, so interest rate movements have a big role in pricing Treasuries (and most bonds). We will discuss this aspect in the next chapter. But, even if yields do not move, there are certain predictable patterns in bond prices. We repeat the pricing formula below, to discuss this further:

$$Bond\ price\ (P) \equiv \sum_{i=1}^{n} \frac{C*0.5}{(1+{r_i}/{2})^i} + \frac{Par\ Value}{(1+{r_n}/{2})^n} \qquad Eq.\ 7.7$$

Pull to par

Pull-to-par captures the fact that, while longer maturity Treasuries (and bonds in general) can trade in a wide band, as a bond gets close to maturity, its price is anchored pretty much around par, because the bond will pay off par at maturity. So, over time, discount bonds tend to appreciate and premium bonds tend to decline as they converge to par. The solid lines in Figure 7.4 shows this expected price trajectory (over time) for one premium bond and one discount bond in 2016 (assuming a flat yield curve), maturing in eight years. Discount bonds naturally appreciate in value (and premium bonds lose value) as the maturity date approaches, if market conditions do not change[54].

Thinking through the pricing formula in Eq. 7.7, as the time to maturity shrinks (and gets close to zero), the price gets closer to par (since the discount factor gets closer to one and the discount rate gets less important). For example, with the passage of time, a three-period bond becomes a two-period bond. The price of this two-period bond with be closer to par, compared to the price of the same bond one period ago (when it was a three-period bond), if the yield curve didn't move and is flat/ upward sloping. This is true of both discount bonds (which will increase in value, as the investor needs to bear one less year of a below-market coupon) and premium bonds (which will lose value because the investor will get one year less of an above-market coupon). This holds if the spot rates are the same for all time periods (flat yield curve) or getting lower (positively sloped yield curve). The effect of a positively sloped curve is discussed further in the next paragraph.

---

[54] Although the final payment is the sum of the par value and the final coupon, the bond price pulls to par (and not par + coupon), since we are referring to the clean price here (and the coupon is part of the accrued interest).

Introduction to Bonds – Treasury Pricing and Institutional Detail

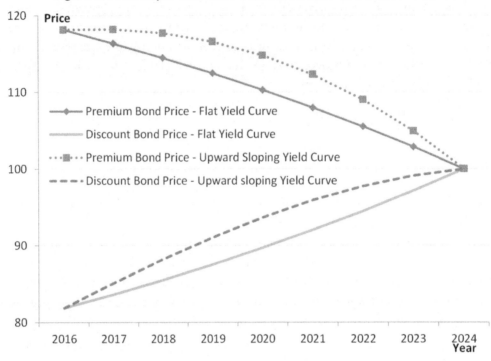

Figure 7.4 Pull to par and Roll Down in Premium and Discount Bonds

Rolling down the yield curve

We discussed, above, the concept of pull-to-par, and illustrated it with a flat yield curve. In the real world, most of the time, the yield curve is often upward sloping and steep, especially at the short end (0-3 years). So, it is likely that a bond with three years to maturity will have a lower yield a year later. It will then be a two-year bond, with a lower yield than the three-year bond because of the positive slope of the curve. In addition to the pull-to-par effect above, this lower yield will also contribute to meaningful price gains.

This issue is related but not identical to the pull-to-par discussion above. A bond will likely pull to par over time (can be a gain or a loss) as it gets close to maturity regardless of the shape of the yield curve; pull to par is more a function of the time to maturity going down. Rolling down the curve is an additional benefit, driven by the steepness of the curve at the very short end. [55] The dotted lines in Figure 7.4 illustrate the combined effect of the pull-to-par and roll-down in an environment with an upward-sloping yield curve.

> Interest rate movements are the most important factor determining Treasury price movements, discussed in the next chapter. This aside, there are a few stylized bond price patterns.
>
> ✓ Pull-to-par: Bonds which are expected to pay back the entire contractual amount pull to the par value at maturity. So, discount bonds tend to appreciate; premium bonds lose value over time.
>
> ✓ Rolldown: A three-year bond today will be a two-year bond a year from now. So, if the yield curve is unchanged a year from now, this bond's future price can be predicted. If the yield curve is upward sloping, this price will go up, faster than the pull-to-par effect.

---

[55] If the yield curve is inverted, the two forces (pull-to-par and roll down) work in opposite directions. In fact, flipping this argument, when a distressed corporate issuer is trading at recovery price, the implied yield curve is negatively sloped.

Capital Markets and Investments

SUMMARY

This chapter explains what Treasury securities are and discusses some institutional details. It also elaborated on the mechanics of pricing and auctioning these bonds. The next chapter will build on this material, explaining the risks embedded in these securities, and some popular trades using these securities.

REFERENCES

Joint Staff Report: *The U.S. Treasury Market on October 15, 2014*. U.S. Department of the Treasury, Board of Governors of the Federal Reserve System, Federal Reserve Bank of New York, U.S. Securities and Exchange Commission, U.S. Commodity Futures Trading Commission

Gibbs, David, J. W. Labuszewski, M. Kamradt. *Understanding Treasury Futures*. The CME Group

Sundaresan, Suresh. *Fixed-Income Markets and Their Derivatives*, Academic Press

Fabozzi, Frank. *Bond Markets, Analysis and Strategies*, Pearson

Fisher, M. *Special Repo Rates: An Introduction*. Federal Reserve Bank of Atlanta Economic Review 87, no. 2 (second quarter 2002): 27-43.

8. Factors affecting Treasury bond prices

The last chapter introduced Treasuries, and discussed how they are auctioned, quoted and priced. Having covered the mechanics of the instrument, we now discuss the risks in holding Treasuries and how to manage these risks. The issues we discuss here are relevant for other fixed income instruments too; however, we ignore credit risk and credit spreads in this chapter because, while usually central to fixed income, they are non-issues for Treasuries.

REVIEWING BOND PRICE-YIELD RELATIONSHIP

The relationship between a bond's price and yield is determined by the formula in Eq. 8.1. The price depends on its coupon, maturity and other contractual features, in addition to the market's assessment of compensation required for the combination of risks embedded in the bond. This shows up in the bond's yield (i.e. the IRR used to discount future cash flows) and depends on how much other investments with similar risk profiles are offering the investor. For Treasury bonds, the yield is essentially a (credit) risk-free rate, driven almost completely by market interest rates for risk-free assets, which is determined by the return that investors require to lend risk free for different time horizons.

$$Bond\ price\ (P) \equiv \sum_{i=1}^{n} \frac{C*0.5}{(1+y/2)^i} + \frac{Par\ Value}{(1+y/2)^n} \qquad Eq.\ 8.1$$

As a reminder, bond prices and yields move in opposite direction, so the higher the yield, the cheaper the bond. If investors perceive an existing bond to be riskier now than it used to be earlier (i.e. investor perception changed), its price will decrease and yield will go up. If the bond's yield is less than its coupon, the bond is trading at a premium (its price is greater than par i.e. 100). Similarly, yields are greater than coupon rates for discount bonds; they are equal for par bonds. This is a mechanical implication of the pricing formula in Eq. 8.1.

Price-yield graph

The price-yield relationship can be depicted in a graph like Figure 8.1, obtained by solving Eq. 8.1 repeatedly using different values for the yield[56]. It shows how price of a bond varies with different yields and its price sensitivity to yield changes. The negative price-yield relationship is apparent; we also observe the graph to be convex to the origin i.e. prices increase "more than proportionately" for yield decreases, and "less than" proportionately for yield increases. Algebraically, this is simply an artifact of polynomial nature of the pricing formula.

---

[56] Other variables in the equation capture contractual features such as coupon and maturity, which do not change with market conditions.

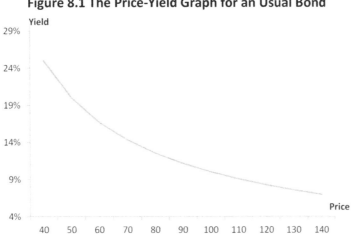

Figure 8.1 The Price-Yield Graph for an Usual Bond

CHOOSING BETWEEN BONDS

Since a bond's price depends on coupon and maturity, from an investor's perspective, comparing the prices of two bonds does not usually provide an apples-for-apples comparison of their relative attractiveness, even if the underlying default risk of receiving those cash flows is the same (i.e. issued by the same party).

Last chapter, we learned that the bond's yield (i.e. *YTM*) is the bond's realized rate of return if:

- The investor holds the bond to maturity
- Investor re-invests the coupons at this yield (not relevant for zero coupon bonds)

So, for bonds with similar default risk and contractual profiles, comparing the yields (i.e. the expected rate of return under certain assumptions) is a good first step to assess their relative value. For bonds with different risk profiles, comparing their yields gives investors a good sense of how much extra the market is willing to pay for different levels of risk.

An alternative return measure, the *Current Yield*, defined as the ratio of the Coupon to the current Price (i.e. $^{C}/_{P}$), tells investors the annual return (as a percentage of investment) if the bond's price does not change. Unlike the YTM, this simply considers coupon income (as a percentage of current price) and does not incorporate pull-to-par effects, so it does not reflect risk/return as accurately. These distinctions also become important for tax planning, as ordinary income (e.g. coupons) is treated differently from capital gains (e.g. price appreciation) by the tax code.

The above measures (YTM and Current Yield) capture elements of the bond's expected return, but are silent about the levels of risk. *While Treasuries have no credit/ default risk, they are exposed to the risk that market interest rates (and hence this bond's yield) changes post-investment, thereby changing the discount rate for discounting cash flows (and thus, the bond's price).* So, an investor should buy Treasury bonds if he expects market interest rates (for the specific time horizon/ maturity related to the bond) to decrease, and sell Treasuries if he expects rates to rise.

Measures such as YTM and Current Yield are more important in regimes where market conditions are expected to persist as is (i.e. interest rates are not likely to move materially), or the investor is planning to hold the bond to maturity (and does not care about interim price fluctuations, as long as he gets paid timely interest and principal). The shape of the yield curve, and any benefits from *roll down* are also relevant. Further, as discussed below, different Treasuries have different exposures to interest rate movement i.e. for the same interest rate move, price changes vary predictably across different bonds. So, in general, *a bond's sensitivity to interest rate movements is also a key risk and an important consideration in choosing between bonds* – investors who want to bet on rate movements will likely prefer more sensitive bonds. Treasuries are fairly easy to lever using the

Factors Affecting Treasury Bond Prices

repo markets are discussed in the last chapter; so buying more of a less sensitive bond is also a viable choice for investors who are allowed to lever.

> *Example:* The ongoing discussion makes bond analysis and selection appear precise and scientific; this example will illustrate the subjective elements involved in choosing bonds. Suppose an investor has an investment horizon of 5 years (i.e. he needs the money for college or retirement 5 years from now, but doesn't need it until then). He is trying to earn the maximum total return over a 5-year period. His alternative choices are the 4 following (default-risk free) bonds in Figure 8.2 of equal credit quality; which should he pick?

Figure 8.2 Example - Alternative Bonds available to the Investor

Bond	Coupon	Maturity	YTM
A	4%	3 years	8.0%
B	5%	20 years	7.6%
C	10%	15 years	8.2%
D	7%	5 years	7.0%

Based on our earlier thumb rule, one would begin with a yield comparison. There is some variation in yield, with Bond C yielding 8.2% and Bond D yielding 7%. But, that is not the whole story.

But, if he picks Bond C, not only does he have to worry about re-investing the 10% annualized coupon each time he receives it, but at the end of 5 years, this bond is still outstanding with a remaining maturity of 10 years. The investor has to sell this bond in the market at that time, to raise money. But, if interest rates are high at the end of 5 years, the bonds cash flows will be heavily discounted and the price will be low, detracting from the investor's returns. The investor is exposed to price risk, especially at the 10-year point 5 years from now.

The arguments involving Bond B are qualitatively similar, with lower reinvestment risk (since the coupon to be reinvested is 5%) but the *price risk* (because of changing interest rates) exposure in 5 years is to the 15-year point on the yield curve; a low 15-year rate in 5-year helps the investor earn a high return.

Bond A has the opposite issue. *Reinvestment risk* of coupon aside, the investor receives the principal too early, at the end of 3 years. The investor then has to invest in a 2-year bond at that time, so is exposed to reinvesting at the 2 year rate in 3 years; the higher that rate, the better it will turn out for the investor.

Bond D has the reinvestment risk associated with the 7% coupon payment, but no price risk since the bond maturity is exactly in 5 years. So, this bond probably has the lowest risk, among the alternatives presented, but the yield is also lowest.

The absolute lowest risk would be in a 5-year zero coupon bond (not among the options above), because it would not have any reinvestment risk and price risk (i.e. interest rate risk).

So, there is no objective correct answer. The most suitable bond depends on what risks (and how much risk) the investor wants to take on (reinvestment risk or price risk), and whether he feels adequately compensated for those risks.

Capital Markets and Investments

QUANTIFYING INTEREST RATE RISK IN TREASURIES

The discussion above indicated that some bonds (Bonds B and C) in the example have price risk from interest rate movements in 5 years, but did not comment on where (i.e. in which bond) the price risk (price volatility from a yield move) was higher. To understand this better, let us examine Figure 8.3, each row of which discusses a separate bond (8 bonds in all). We consider maturities of 6 months, 5 years, 10 years and 30 years; for each of these four maturities, we list two (default-risk free) bonds, one with a zero coupon and the other with a 10% coupon (shaded in grey). Let us assume that the term structure of interest rates is flat at $r_i = 3\%$ for all periods, and ask ourselves how the prices of these four bonds would move if rates rise or fall by various magnitudes, for example 100bp (remember, 100bp equals 1%, just a different unit). We can figure this out by computing the old and new prices for these bonds at various yields by using the pricing formula in Eq. 8.1. Columns 3 to 7 of the top panel of Figure 8.3 show the price of these bonds at various yields; the bottom panel uses this price data to shows price returns for the same bonds if the yield were to change from an initial yield of 3%.

Figure 8.3 Interest Rate Shifts affect Bonds of different Maturities and Coupons Differently

Time to Maturity (yrs)	Coupon	Price at various Yields				
		2.00%	2.95%	3.00%	3.05%	4.00%
0.5	0%	99.01	98.55	98.52	98.50	98.04
	10%	103.96	103.47	103.45	103.42	102.94
5.0	0%	90.53	86.38	86.17	85.95	82.03
	10%	137.89	132.55	132.28	132.00	126.95
10.0	0%	81.95	74.61	74.25	73.88	67.30
	10%	172.18	160.67	160.09	159.51	149.05
30.0	0%	55.04	41.54	40.93	40.33	30.48
	10%	279.82	239.71	237.83	235.97	204.28

Time to Maturity (yrs)	Coupon	% Price Change (deviations around 3.00%)				
		-1.00%	-0.05%	0.00%	0.05%	1.00%
0.5	0%	0.50%	0.02%	0.00%	-0.02%	-0.49%
	10%	0.50%	0.02%	0.00%	-0.02%	-0.49%
5.0	0%	5.06%	0.25%	0.00%	-0.25%	-4.80%
	10%	4.24%	0.21%	0.00%	-0.21%	-4.03%
10.0	0%	10.38%	0.49%	0.00%	-0.49%	-9.36%
	10%	7.55%	0.36%	0.00%	-0.36%	-6.89%
30.0	0%	34.49%	1.49%	0.00%	-1.47%	-25.53%
	10%	17.66%	0.79%	0.00%	-0.78%	-14.11%

(98.04 - 98.52) / 98.52

Focusing on the second panel, we notice that, for the same interest rate movement (i.e. looking down any column), the eight bonds have experienced very different returns. We observe the following:

- *Larger moves in interest rates lead to greater (positive or negative) returns.*
- *For the zero coupon bonds (especially the shorter-dated ones), the percentage returns are close to proportional to maturity* (therefore, equal to maturity for a 1% move, less than proportional for the longer bonds); for the coupon bonds they are a little lower.
- *For an identical move in rates, the longer maturity bonds have lost or gained much more*; this is to be expected from the polynomial pricing function – maturities further out are hit by a higher exponent of the change in rates.

Factors Affecting Treasury Bond Prices

- o For a given coupon rate, the longer the time to maturity of the bond, the greater the price volatility i.e. comparing the four grey rows (10% coupon bonds), the return is larger (in absolute terms) as we move to longer maturity bonds. The same observation holds if we compare the four (unshaded) rows above the grey rows, containing zero coupon bonds.

- *Percentage price changes are larger for low (in this case, zero) coupon bonds, compared to higher coupon bonds with same maturity.* In the table above, across any horizontal maturity band, the % return of the 0% coupon bond (the white row) is higher (in absolute terms) than the return of the 10% coupon bond (the greyed row). Hence low coupon bonds behave as if they have (slightly) longer maturities.

- For positive and negative yield movements of equal magnitude, *the returns are symmetric for small changes in yield*, but asymmetric for large changes in yield.

We can validate these observations by re-examining the price-yield graph shown in Figure 8.1. While this convex pattern holds broadly, as we saw above, different bonds have different sensitivities to yield changes. Figure 8.4 shows the price-yield graph for two bonds (10% of June 30, 2024, and 10% of June 30, 2054) as of June 30, 2016. As we can see, for a similar change in yield, price moves are larger for the longer maturity bond. For the same bond, as the bond's yield changes, the price sensitivity to the yield movement (i.e. the slope of the curve) also changes. For small changes in yield, the slope does not vary much, so small rate moves up or down lead to returns of similar magnitude. For large rate moves, the curvature matters.

Figure 8.4 Interest Rate Shifts affect Bonds of different maturities differently

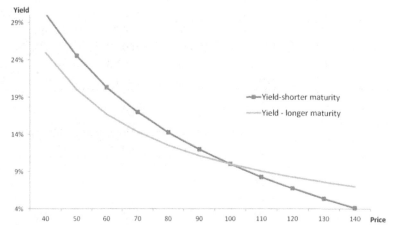

Macaulay Duration – How long is a bond?

Let us now formalize these ideas, and come up with measures to indicate price risk (i.e. price sensitivity to yield changes). *Since longer-term bonds appear to have more price risk, let us try to measure more carefully how long a bond actually is.* For almost all bonds (except zero coupon bonds), there are multiple cash flows (which the investor receives at different times), so focusing solely on the bond's time to maturity as a measure of how long it takes to get back cash is inadequate.

(Macaulay) Duration is an estimate of when (i.e. one number, an average time) an investor will receive the cash flow payments for a bond. This is an average of the time periods when cash flows are received, weighted by the (discounted) cash flows received at the respective times. We need to be mindful of the fact that cash flows at different points in time need to be discounted suitably before they are considered equivalent. Getting more specific, this weighted average can be written as $Macaulay\ Duration = \dfrac{\sum_{i=1}^{n}(w_i \times i)}{\sum_{i=1}^{n} w_i}$, where the weight w_i is the discounted cash flow for period i. Substituting the bond's pricing formula from Eq. 8.1,

$$Macaulay\ Duration = \dfrac{\sum_{i=1}^{n}(\dfrac{CF_i}{(1+y)^i} \times i)}{P} \qquad \text{Eq. 8.2}$$

where y is the yield of the bond per *period* (i.e. $^{YTM}/_2$ for US bonds), and CF_i is the undiscounted cash flow in period i i.e. Coupon + Principal in the last period, Coupon in all periods before the last (For US bonds, we will use $^{Coupon}/_2$ instead of Coupon to calculate cash flows for any period). Note also, the sum of discounted cash flows (i.e. the sum of weights in this example) is the bond price P, by definition. Calculated this way, the units of Macaulay Duration can be interpreted in units of 6-month periods for US bonds (which is then divided by two to express in years), and in years for most bonds in other geographies.

Put differently, *Macaulay Duration represents the weighted-average time to maturity, with the discounted cash flows as the weights*. This is similar to elasticity formulae in economics and engineering courses. Most analytical software, though, will convert the duration to "number of years" in the risk reports.

Price Sensitivity (Risk) of Bonds – Modified Duration

We have anecdotally noted that a bond's price sensitivity appears to be related to how long it is. So, it is no surprise that a bond's price sensitivity to yield changes (i.e. interest rate risk) happens to be closely related to Macaulay Duration. In fact, (the absolute value of) the % change in bond price for a 1 per cent (i.e. 100 basis point) change in yield turns out to be the *Modified Duration* (Dur_{Mod}), defined as $\dfrac{Macaulay\ Duration}{(1+YTM)}$, [57] i.e.

$$\dfrac{\Delta P/P}{\Delta y} = -Modified\ Duration \equiv \dfrac{Macaulay\ Duration}{(1+YTM)} \qquad \text{Eq. 8.3}$$

So, for a given change in bond yield, the return on the bond (i.e. % change in bond price) is:

$$\Delta P/P = -Modified\ Duration \times \Delta y \qquad \text{Eq. 8.4}$$

The duration of a bond is often thought of as a known stable value (given the current market conditions), since it changes very little day over day, so this Eq. 8.4 is a convenient short-hand to compute returns from yield changes (interest rate changes in the case of Treasuries). For bonds with higher duration, the price sensitivity to a given yield change is higher. Duration increases with time to maturity, and decreases as coupons or yields increase (i.e. the convex shape of the curve).

Price Sensitivity (Risk) of Bonds – DV01

The Dollar Value of a Basis Point - DV01 (alternatively, Present Value of a Basis Point – PVBP or PV01) captures exactly the same idea of interest rate sensitivity, but expresses it in different units. It measures, in

---

[57] This can be shown by taking the first partial derivative of the Price (P) in Eq. 8.1 with respect to the yield (y), and rearranging. For bonds which pay coupon multiple times a year, $Modified\ Duration = \dfrac{Macaulay\ Duration}{1+\frac{y}{k}}$, where y is the annualized yield and k is the compounding frequency.

Factors Affecting Treasury Bond Prices

dollar units, the profit or loss for a one basis point move in yields (modified duration measures sensitivity as a percentage of the current price instead of dollars). Eq. 8.5 states this algebraically[58],

$$DV01 \equiv \Delta P / \Delta y = -Modified\ Duration \times P \qquad \text{Eq. 8.5}$$

Graphically, for any yield, DV01 (or, Modified Duration, scaled by price, so that it provides a dollar value change instead of a percentage change) is the slope of the tangent to the price-yield curves in Figure 8.1 and **Figure 8.2**. The negative sign captures the inverse relation between price and yield changes. For small changes in yield (yield changes over short time intervals are usually small), price changes are approximately symmetric and Eq. 8.4 and Eq. 8.5 are excellent approximations. Since duration represents a percentage change in price, the value remains the same regardless of the size of the position. But DV01 represents a dollar profit/ loss, so scales with the position size. The formula above calculates the DV01 for one bond; for a larger position one would substitute the market value of the position instead of the price (which is the market value for one bond).

To quantify how risky an investment in Treasuries is, one needs to understand how much Treasury yields typically move (maybe by looking at the historical volatility of the time series of Treasury yields) and how sensitive the value of a particular position is to a movement in Treasury yields (by checking Duration or DV01).

We have discussed duration through three lenses – a nuanced version of the bond's tenor, relative price sensitivity for a given basis point move in the yield, and dollar value (or P&L) changes for a 1bp shift in yields.

> *Example:* Suppose a bond's price is 99, modified duration is 4 (i.e. Macaulay duration is 4*1.07) and yield is 7% (per annum). Eq. 8.4 implies that this bond's price is expected to decrease by 0.40% (i.e. change to 98.604) if the yield increases to 7.10%, and increase to 99.396 (a 40bp increase in price) if its yield drops to 6.90%. This can be verified by using the pricing formula in Eq. 8.1, or by applying Eq. 8.4 (0.10% change in yield multiplied by a modified duration of 4 gives a 0.40% price move.)
>
> The DV01 of this bond is 0.0396 per $100 of par (calculated directly by taking the difference of two prices before and after moving rates by 0.01%, or by multiplying the modified duration i.e. 4 by the price i.e. 99). So, if we have $1mm face value invested in this bond, the DV01 will be $396 (i.e. 0.0396*1000000/ 100).

> ✓ We have discussed price sensitivity of bonds through three (similar) lenses:
>   - Macaulay Duration: A nuanced version of *when* the investor receives bond cash flows
>   - Modified Duration: A bond's return (in % points) for a 100bp change in yield. Numerically similar to Macaulay Duration in many common situations.
>   - DV01: Dollar profit (or loss) if rates move 1bp.
>
> Conventionally, these numbers are reported as positive for long-risk positions (negative for shorts)
>
> ✓ These approximations work well for small yield shifts, when the yield curve moves in parallel.

---

[58] We need to be extra careful about units and scale here. Eq. 8.5 as shown calculates the change in dollar value for a 1mm par value portfolio. This related to P actually being a percentage of par i.e. a price of 99 is actually 99% (or 0.99) of par, and one basis point is 0.0001. So, when we replace P by 99 and Modified Duration by units of similar order of magnitude as time to maturity, we end up calculating the change in a $1mm par value portfolio for a 1bp shift in rates. The example in this section makes explains in more detail.

Capital Markets and Investments

Interest Rate Risk of Portfolios of Treasury bonds

So far, we have examined the interest rate risk of a single bond. The same idea flows through if we consider portfolios of Treasury bonds, since a portfolio is essentially a linear combination of single bonds. So, we can easily calculate *portfolio duration* and DV01, and interpret/ use them similarly.

For example, if V is the value of a portfolio of n_1 and n_2 units of two bonds with prices P_1 and P_2, i.e.

$$V = n_1 P_1 + n_2 P_2,$$

Taking derivatives with respect to y, and applying the definition of DV01 from Eq. 8.5, it follows that

$$DV01_V = n_1 DV01_1 + n_2 DV01_2 \qquad \text{Eq. 8.6}$$

Note, n_1 and n_2 are number of bonds, i.e. par value in the bond/1000, if DV01 is expressed per bond (i.e. per $1000 par).

Similarly, portfolio duration (both Macaulay and Modified) can be evaluated as:

$$Duration_V = \frac{n_1 P_1}{V} Duration_1 + \frac{n_2 P_2}{V} Duration_2 \qquad \text{Eq. 8.7}$$

Note that, to calculate portfolio analytics, we use bond market value as a proportion of portfolio value to weight individual bond duration, whereas we use par amounts to weight DV01.

Once we have the modified duration or DV01 for the portfolio, we can calculate approximate price sensitivity of the portfolio by imagining the portfolio to be a bond with these characteristics, and using Eq. 8.4 and Eq. 8.5 to calculate portfolio returns/ P&L for different values of yield changes. This is a critical part of assessing the interest rate risk in a portfolio.

> *Example: Calculating interest rate risk measures for portfolios*
>
> Consider a portfolio manager who, on July 7 2017, has a $20mm position in one bond *T 1.75 of 06/30/22* (let us call it *A*) and a $10mm position in another bond *T 2.375 of 05/15/27* (*B*). The modified duration of these bonds is 4.73 and 8.70 respectively, and the bonds are trading at prices 99.41 and 100.48. Multiplying modified duration by price, the DV01 of (1mm par) of these bonds is 470 and 874 respectively. The DV01 of $20mm market value of bond A is 9456 (i.e. $470 * \frac{20}{0.9941}$) and $10mm market value of bond B is 8698 (i.e. $874 * \frac{20}{0.9941}$). So, the total DV01 of the portfolio is 18154 (i.e. 9456 + 8698), also obtained by applying Eq. 8.6[59]. Applying Eq. 8.7, the modified duration of the portfolio is 6.04.
>
> Now, let us suppose that the portfolio manager wants to neutralize the interest rate risk of this portfolio using another bond. Applying what we have learned so far, we can put on a short position in any other Treasury to do this (since we are assuming parallel shifts)[60]; the amount we go short will vary depending on the Treasury we pick to go short. Let us assume that the investor picks T 2 of 06/30/24, trading at 99.14. The modified duration of this bond is 6.46. The DV01 for 1mm par is 640 (i.e. 6.46*99.14). To neutralize the portfolio interest rate risk, we need to short enough of this bond so that the DV01 of the portfolio is 0 (or the modified duration of the portfolio is 0; both should give very similar answers). To neutralize DV01 of 18154 (previous paragraph), we need to be short

---

[59] Here, we need to denote n_1 and n_2 as par values, expressed in millions of dollars, since the DV01 of the bonds have been calculated per million par just before this.

[60] We will see later in the chapter that it is usually prudent to hedge using instruments whose durations are close to the portfolio duration, or use multiple hedge instruments with durations matching the key rate exposures of the portfolio. This minimizes the adverse effect of a non-parallel shift in the yield curve.

18154÷640 or 28.36mm par (or 28.14mm market value i.e. 28.36*0.9914) of this bond. We can verify, by using a three-bond version of Eq. 8.7 and using -28.14 as the market value (note the negative sign) and 6.46 as the duration for the third bond (other two bonds as above), that the modified duration of the three-bond portfolio is close to zero. So, the portfolio is now immune to parallel shifts in interest rates.

HEDGING INTEREST RATE RISK – APPLICATIONS OF DURATION

The standard way to assess Treasury risk, whether for a single bond or a portfolio, is by using the Modified Duration and DV01, discussed above. This risk can be neutralized (i.e. hedged) by adding more positions to the portfolio that would reduce the DV01. This is typically achieved by taking short positions in rate-sensitive instruments. So, mechanically, the manager first decides on a target DV01 for the portfolio, and calculates the gap between the target DV01 of the portfolio and the current DV01. If the current DV01 is higher than the target, then the portfolio needs to be hedged; the manager then chooses the hedge instrument. Once the Modified Duration (or DV01) of the hedge instrument is known, the manager uses multi-security variants of Eq. 8.6 and Eq. 8.7 to decide exactly how much of the hedge instrument to short to get the portfolio DV01 (i.e. price sensitivity to interest rate movement) down to the target level (often zero); the intricate details of how the instrument works becomes secondary. We discuss this through an example below.

Example: Bank lending – ALM Mismatch

A typical bank usually lends money to corporations for longer term projects (e.g. 5 to 10 year loans) by raising overnight or short-term deposits from savers. On the bank's balance sheet, these loans show up as assets, whereas the deposits appear as liabilities. The difference between the assets and liabilities is the shareholders' equity. To simplify, suppose the bank lends out every dollar it raises as deposits as a loan (usually the amount of loans are more than the deposits, because banks typically lend out many multiples of the deposits they hold). The interest rate on the loans, being longer-dated, will be higher than the deposits. Assuming all loans get repaid, the bank makes a profit because of the difference in the two interest rates.

After the loans have been made to the companies, if interest rates rise across the board, the value of the loans on the bank's balance sheet will decrease significantly (usual argument of existing cash flows discounted at a higher rate), whereas the deposits, being much shorter duration, will not get affected nearly as much. Said another way, the bank's loans are now at a below-market interest rate, whereas the deposits will need to be paid a higher interest rate, which will reduce profits. The book value of shareholder equity, representing the difference in the two market values, gets reduced. If interest rates were to go down instead, the book value of shareholder equity would instead go up. If, indeed, the loans were much larger than the deposits, this would amplify the effect. The business model of a commercial bank involves running a duration mismatch between assets and liabilities, which usually generates profits but can hurt if rates go up. Banks may choose to hedge some of this risk; hedging is briefly discussed below.

Immunization

Many investors, such as insurance companies and pension funds, invest their assets with the objective of generating future cash flows that can pay their future liabilities[61]. These may be retirement plan liabilities such as defined contribution pension plans, or insurance related liabilities such as death benefits or general insurance benefits. Future cash outflows associated with these liabilities can be estimated quite precisely, either using employment data or actuarial statistics. These liabilities are discounted to their present value. If the

---

[61] This paradigm of investing has many specific nuances, and is often referred to as Liability-Driven Investing (LDI).

(discounted) present value of the liabilities is less than the assets, the plan is said to be *fully funded*; if the plan's assets only cover 80% of the liabilities, the plan is 80% funded. The right discount rate to discount these liabilities is a critical issue in discussing the funded status of these plans. As a thumb rule, most private pension plans use the AA credit curve to discount liability cash flows, whereas state pension plans often use a (higher) expected return around 7.5% per annum to discount these liabilities. Given the risk appetite in these plans, most market participants would agree that the discount rates (i.e. the expected returns) are too high, relative to the returns that are realistically achievable.

A plan needs to be fully funded to *immunize* its liabilities. In a perfect world, the plan would own assets that would pay off the exact amount of cash that the plan needs each year to pay off liabilities and cover other costs, year after year. If the assets are invested in low-risk bonds (i.e. default next to impossible) and set up to mature on this schedule, then the risk is negligible because the assets essentially become a series of buy-and-hold portfolios, with no interest rate risk, because they do not have to be sold. The bonds are being owned solely for their contractual cash flows, and not the mark-to-market characteristics.

In reality, it is not possible to match every cash outflow with coupon and principal inflows from the assets. Assets need to be either reinvested to put extra cash inflows to work or sold periodically to raise cash to pay liabilities. The more pragmatic solution is often to match the duration of the assets and liabilities carefully, not just at one point of the curve, but at different time horizons. We discuss duration matching further in the next section.[62]

Yield curve movements – parallel versus non-parallel movements

So far, while discussing the interest rate risk of bonds, we've restricted discussion to *yield* changes of bonds. But, as we know, it is more accurate to think of a bond's cash flows as being discounted by different interest rates (or discount rates) for different time periods, as detailed in the previous chapter (since the yield curve is usually not flat); the yield is an "average" of all these different rates. So, in reality a bond's price is affected by several distinct (spot) interest rates (for different time horizons).

Analyzing interest rate risk simply in terms of a bond's yield change (instead of explicitly incorporating the slope of the yield curve) is valid because usually the yield curve moves in a parallel manner (or close to parallel). So, even if we were more precise and considered different spot rates for different time periods, all the rates would shift by the same amount when market rates move, analytically similar to moving the yield. So, as a convenience, we usually work in yield space when measuring interest rate risk.

While parallel shifts are a very good assumption, the yield curve can also shift in a non-parallel manner. In fact, applying *Principal Components Analysis (PCA)* to historical yield movements, Litterman and Scheinkman show that 99% of historical yield curve movements can be attributed to parallel shifts (*level*), changes in *slope* and changes in *curvature*, with parallel shifts contributing to over 65% of the move. But, there can be significant non-parallel yield curve moves too, often policy-induced. We discuss some of the fundamental drivers of shifts in various parts of the yield curve in the next chapter. Market participants actively bet on these slope changes, by putting on steepeners or flatteners, which we discuss in the next chapter.

The duration framework we discussed assumes a parallel shift in yields, as we move the yield of the hedge instrument the same amount as that of the primary portfolio (again not distinguishing between individual bond maturities). In this set-up, non-parallel shifts can be a problem from a hedging standpoint if the yield of

---

[62] Even if all risk/ sensitivities are matched at inception, and the present value of the pension plan assets is greater than the present value of liabilities (i.e. the plan is fully funded and price volatility risk is neutered), this does not imply that the plan will always be fully funded in future, even if there are no "surprises". It is likely that, during the initial years, plan assets may need to be sold to finance payouts (cash flows are not matched period by period; initial liability (out)flow projections may be higher than inflows from plan assets), leading to the plan becoming subsequently underfunded.

Factors Affecting Treasury Bond Prices

the hedge instrument does not move (or moves down), but the yield of the long positions move up (because the Macaulay Duration/ maturity of the long positions may be different from that of the hedge). The workaround is to categorize the constituents of the long portfolio into various maturity/ duration buckets, and hedge the interest rate risk of each of these sub-portfolios with a hedge instrument belonging to the same bucket. Then, the effect of non-parallel shifts are limited to the duration/maturity differences within the bucket, which is a far lower risk (because duration differences are smaller within the bucket)[63].

Formulaically, we can figure out what would happen to a bond's price if *only* one point on the yield curve (for example, the 5-year point) moved, with other points on the curve remaining static. The discount factor related to the 5-year cash flow would change, changing the present value of that cash flow, and the price of the bond. If we move the 5-year point by 1 percent and not move the other points, the resulting bond price change is referred to as the *Partial Duration* (or the *Key-Rate Duration*) to the 5-year rate. We can repeat this exercise for other points on the curve, to get partial durations for other points on the curve. The sum of all the partial durations should equal the total Modified Duration of the bond.

Partial durations are more important for Treasury managers who make nuanced bets on different points on the curve, and bet that some parts of the curve are more susceptible to moves than others. It is also relevant for carefully hedging interest rate risk of portfolios. Portfolios are sometimes analytically decomposed into their exposure to different points (i.e. key rates) of the yield curve, and each of those exposures hedged by the corresponding duration Treasury. For managers that wish to hedge very precisely and carefully, they may want to minimize DV01 key rate by key rate, so that they don't end up making an inadvertent bet on the curve shape. To implement this, the manager would need multiple DV01s for each bond, one for each key rate that they want to hedge. He will then solve multiple equations like Eq. 8.6, one for each key-rate that he wants to hedge. The hedge instruments for different key rate buckets will be different, typically the bond with the duration closest to the key rate is picked.

> *Example:* Operationally, suppose one of the duration / maturity buckets is the 4-7 year bucket. So, we move all the spot rates between 4 and 7 years by 1bp, and compute the price change of all bonds in the long portfolio only because of these moves. This is the DV01 of the long portfolio to the 4-to-7-year rates. To hedge this exposure, we can put on a short position in another instrument in this maturity bucket (say the 5-year Treasury), sizing the short so that the DV01 of this long-short sub-portfolio is zero (the short quantity is negative). Repeating this for other buckets, we will eventually move all the rates that the long portfolio is exposed to, and hedge out the entire DV01 of the portfolio, using hedge instruments from the respective bucket. Of course, we need more hedge instruments if we are hedging this way, using key-rates.

CONVEXITY

Eq. 8.4 is a linear approximation, so ignores the effect of curvature (i.e. convexity) in the price-yield function. For a given bond, the slope of the price-yield relationship (i.e. duration) is different for different levels of yield, since the true pricing function is curved. Convexity is positive for most bonds (i.e. the graphs in Figure 8.1 and Figure 8.4 are positively convex), so the linear approximation in Eq. 8.4 understates the price increase for decreases in yields and overstates price declines for yield increases.

Figure 8.5 shows this graphically. If the initial yield is at y*, the price forecast using Eq. 8.4 is represented by the (negatively sloped) straight line, tangent to the price-yield curve. For small moves in yield such as moving from y* to y_2 or y_3, the price approximation error using the straight line is small, but the error gets significant

---

[63] Yields of Treasury bonds of similar durations usually move by similar amounts (liquidity differences aside), to be consistent with no-arbitrage.

Capital Markets and Investments

for larger moves, to y_1 or y_4. Importantly, for both these moves (increase or decrease) in yield, the linear (i.e. duration-based) approximation is conservative for a long bond position; it overestimates losses and underestimates gains.

Figure 8.5: Convexity

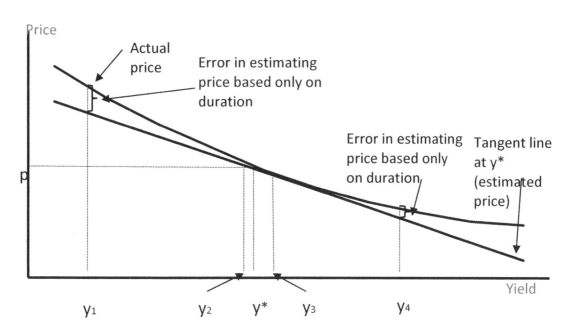

Said another way, the duration gets larger as yields decrease (i.e. the bond's price sensitivity increases) and gets smaller when yields increase. Convexity captures how quickly duration changes (i.e. how much curvature there is in the price-yield curve. The second derivative of the bond pricing equation with respect to yield gives us a formula to calculate convexity precisely. Eq. 8.8 and Eq. 8.9 incorporate convexity and calculate the bond price change more accurately[64]. This effect is negligible for small yield moves, but more important for larger yield changes.

$$\Delta P / P = -Modified\ Duration \times \Delta y + \frac{1}{2} \times Convexity \times (\Delta y)^2 \qquad \text{Eq. 8.8}$$

Where

$$Convexity = \frac{1}{P \times (1+y)^2} \sum_{t=1}^{T} \left[\frac{CF_t}{(1+y)^t} (t^2 + t) \right] \approx \frac{P_+ + P_- - 2 \times P_0}{P_0 \times (\Delta y)^2} \times 100 \qquad \text{Eq. 8.9}$$

While convexity can be used to refine the duration-based price forecasts, there are other, arguably more important applications of the concept. For example, at a portfolio level, *different portfolios with the same duration can have very different convexity profiles*. This allows investors to assess how much convexity costs through various alternative structures. One common example is discussed below in Eq. 8.10. This trade, which aims to take advantage of convexity while being duration neutral, appears to be lucrative at first glance but has hidden risks. It is called a bullet-barbell trade or a butterfly trade, to reflect the fact that the investor has a directionally

---

[64] Many books and software incorporate the "$\frac{1}{2}$" term in Eq. 8.8 within the convexity formula in Eq. 8.9 instead, i.e. in some situations, Eq. 8.9 has an extra "$\frac{1}{2}$" multiplicative term, and the "$\frac{1}{2}$" is left out of Eq. 8.8. This is purely a matter of convention.

Factors Affecting Treasury Bond Prices

similar position in the two extremities (i.e. the wings), and the opposite position (i.e. the hedge) in the middle security (i.e. the belly). Getting long convexity while being duration neutral (through hedges) suggests that one is hedged too conservatively, so when rates go up, the long portfolio doesn't lose as much as the hedge makes. Alternatively, when rates go up, the long portfolio makes more than the hedge loses. This seems like a free lunch, but is actually not. The example below elaborates further.

> *Example:*
>
> Suppose we are long a portfolio of 10mm par 2-year and 12mm par 20-year bonds. We then hedge this portfolio with 10-year bonds. Specifically, we solve for n_3 (negative, because we will be short 10y) such that a version of Eq. 8.6 holds, i.e.
>
> $$0 = 10 \times DV01_{2y} + 12 \times DV01_{20y} + n_3 DV01_{10y} \qquad \text{Eq. 8.10}$$
>
> So, we are immune to a parallel shift in the yield curve.
>
> Now, it can be shown that this long/ short portfolio will be long convexity, since barbelled portfolios are more convex than bullets. Regardless of whether rates rise or fall, one may conclude that the portfolio will make money because of convexity, since duration is hedged. This seems like an arbitrage. What are we missing?
>
> - First, there may be other details like the carry or the initial cost in setting up the position, but these can be ignored for short holding periods, especially since Treasury positions are easy to finance using repos. So, the dilemma remains.
> - The main reason why this isn't an arbitrage is because we are exposed to non-parallel shifts of the yield curve. If the yield curve steepens, pivoting around the 10-year point and causing the 20-year to widen materially, this trade will lose money. Although convexity trades often seem to be an attractive bet, the time horizon and the risk of non-parallel yield curve shifts need to be carefully assessed.

Certain (non-Treasury) fixed income securities can also exhibit *negative convexity* because of embedded options, where the duration decreases (rate of price increase goes down) as rates keep going lower, and duration increases (price decreases become more rapid) as rates keep going higher. US mortgage backed securities and callable bonds, both discussed in Chapter 10, are negatively convex.

FURTHER COMMENTS

Any security whose price is sensitive to interest rate movements has a DV01 associated with it; so far we have only discussed Treasuries. Most other fixed income securities also have rate sensitivity (and hence DV01), but they will not be a suitable hedge for a Treasury portfolio because they will introduce other risks (and/or be difficult to short). But, there are several derivatives of the rates market which are eminently suitable – Treasury Futures, Swaps (and even options on Treasury Futures, Swaptions or ETFs such as IEF, TLT, TBT or several others). We will discuss some of these in the next chapter. That said, even if the details of these instruments get complicated, it is important to remember that, bottom line, these instruments have DV01s (which can be read off a screen), and the investor will decide the size of the hedge trade depending on how much DV01 he needs to neutralize. The security should be viewed primarily as a source of DV01. So, if DV01 were available cheaper using these markets than Treasuries, the investor would be better off sourcing DV01 using these instruments rather than going long Treasuries. But, markets are usually priced efficiently (or there are other liquidity/ regulatory issues), so such "arbitrage" rarely exists.

REFERENCES

Sundaresan, Suresh. *Fixed-Income Markets and Their Derivatives*, Academic Press

Capital Markets and Investments

Fabozzi, Frank. *Bond Markets, Analysis and Strategies*, Pearson

Litterman, Robert, and J. A. Scheinkman. 1991. *Common Factors Affecting Bond Returns*. Journal of Fixed Income

9. Further Topics in Interest Rate Markets

The last two chapters have introduced bonds and the yield curve and mentioned some institutional details, we discussed interest rate sensitivity (risk measurement) and hedging for bonds and portfolios. Treasury bond prices change primarily based on interest rate movements. In this chapter, we discuss fundamental reasons for the movement in interest rates and the shape of the yield curve, and briefly talk about other important interest rate products.

WHY DO YIELDS / INTEREST RATES MOVE?

Treasury yields reflect the investor's compensation for lending money (credit) risk-free for different time periods. Since different financial assets with various risk profiles are competing for the investor's dollar, the investor's preference for investing in risk-free assets depends on how he perceives risk in other assets. Does he think that the risk in the external environment and other assets is high or low, for the compensation that he expects to receive? Is he risk averse and defensive, or does he currently have a high tolerance for uncertainty and is willing to play the odds of the riskier assets moving in his favor? This facet of investor sentiment is based on creating a mosaic of the investment opportunities and risk landscape; we discuss some important considerations for interest rates below. While we discuss these issues separately, they are interconnected, and all part of the same playbook.[65]

Central Bank Policy

The US Federal Reserve and the Central Banks of other countries use interest rates as a cornerstone of monetary policy. The US Federal Reserve, similar to many other Central Banks, is mandated to try to achieve growth targets, while maintaining price stability. Financial stability (macroprudential policy and regulation) is another Central Bank objective.

The Federal Reserve has direct control over the *Fed Funds Rate*, an overnight unsecured inter-bank rate (i.e. a rate at which banks borrow from each other). It announces targets for this rate at FOMC meetings (every six weeks or so), and can intervene in the market by buying and selling securities to keep the rate close to that target. So, historically, the Fed has influenced short rates significantly.

Despite our earlier comment regarding the usual parallel moves of the yield curve, the relation between movements in the Fed Funds rate (unsecured, overnight) and long term Treasury interest rates is not one-for-one. This is because of the difference in the credit risk in Fed Funds rate (bank credit) compared to the risk-free Treasuries (though it should matter much less in an overnight maturity); the (large) difference in maturities is another reason. The current long-term rates also incorporate expectations of future short-term rates and so have other variables affecting them, besides the current short term rates (see the discussion on forward curves towards the end of Chapter 7, and later this chapter). Through this transmission mechanism, historically, long-term rates have usually gone up when short-term rates are raised.

In this manner, the Fed has traditionally had indirect control over the longer end of the Treasury curve. This changed in the aftermath of the 2008 financial crisis, when the Federal Reserve started buying Treasuries across the yield curve to keep interest rates low, as part of the Quantitative Easing program. As the program

---

[65] The previous chapter's discussion on level, slope and curvature factors explaining the bulk of yield curve movements is a "reduced-form" approach, where we rely on historical data to explain data patterns.

Capital Markets and Investments

evolved, there were variants of this policy, such as Operation Twist, with a focus on specific maturities. These purchases have had a direct effect on keeping interest rates low, even at the long end of the curve. [66]

When rates are low, the Fed expects the economy to expand fast, stimulating growth and pushing up prices. Very simply, low interest rates lead to lower discount rates; some projects that were earlier negative NPV may now become positive NPV projects and be worthwhile investments. This is the rationale for the Fed lowering (Fed Funds Target) rates when it foresees a recession (technically defined as consecutive quarters of negative GDP growth). Since monetary policy is not instantaneously effective and works with a lag, the Fed needs to be proactive and act before it sees conclusive proof. When growth is outpacing capacity and prices are rising, the economy is at risk of overheating, and the Fed usually raises rates to slow it down.

Emerging markets have been the engine of global growth over the last few decades; they have predominantly been export-led. As a result, their current account balances (Exports – Imports) have increased significantly, leading to an inflow of USD, Euro and other hard (i.e. developed country) currencies into these economies. At the same time, foreign investment (both portfolio investments i.e. in financial assets and direct investments i.e. in physical projects) has increased, further adding to international capital inflow. The foreign central banks in these markets have invested the USD reserves predominantly in the US markets and have become very large buyers of Treasuries, helping rates stay low. Their long-term orientation has also kept the long end of the yield curve especially low.

Business Cycle

The economy is generally assumed to be exposed to expansions, booms and recessions. During expansionary phases, companies are doing better, macro data is strong and investors are less risk averse and more optimistic, allocating financial resources away from Treasuries into riskier assets. These growth prospects cause the longer term rates to rise and the term structure to steepen. At some point, though, the Central Bank may decide to raise (short-term) rates too, to keep price levels stable. Conversely, as the economy begins to slow, investors seek safety, and/ or they expect the Fed to reduce rates (from the currently high levels associated with high growth), and hold more Treasuries than they normally do, as a decrease in interest rates will lead to increase in Treasury prices. In fact, the Central Bank policy moves discussed above are essentially their response to where they believe the economy is, in the business cycle.

Economic Variables and News Releases

Economic Variables and Releases help investors and policymakers form expectations regarding where the economy stand in the business cycle. The most popular ones are Non-Farm Payrolls (employment), GDP growth, PMI Indices, Retail Sales, Consumer Confidence, FOMC Fed Fund Futures Target Rate, etc. These are all collected with different lags, are noisy and are revised periodically (sometimes substantially), so provide an incomplete estimate of the economic condition. Besides, data may (or may not) be seasonally adjusted and not all indicators point in the same direction, so interpreting this data requires a lot of subjectivity and attention to detail. Economic data aside, news releases often lead to big market moves, such as the US Treasury announcement regarding discontinuation of the 30-year note, the Taper Tantrum following a Bernanke speech in the summer of 2013, etc.

While investors continue to rely mainly on published macro data sources, the ease of data collection and the big data movement has led to a burgeoning primary data service industry. Here, smaller firms collect focused data (e.g. the demand for taxis in Manhattan, or the number of cars parked in the parking lot of a major

---

[66] Some market participants have been critical of the Central Banks and their Zero Interest Rate Policy (ZIRP), saying the keeping interest rates very low for very long does not necessarily stimulate physical demand incrementally, instead this inflates the value of financial assets because of cheap borrowing, and hurts savers and retirees. Firms making capital investment decisions probably do not care whether the Fed Funds Rate is at 0bp or 25bp. . Besides, this approach hasn't helped Japan for decades.

Further Topics in Interest Rate Markets

shopping mall) and sell this to financial service firms, who use it to anticipate and predict macro data announcements. Some of these predictive services (e.g. ADP, predicting payrolls) have become widely available and macro data announcements in their own right. Also, with trading being increasingly linked to electronic algorithms, and computers also playing a central role in scraping news off news services, markets react to economic announcements instantaneously, often even before the data is flashed on industry-standard platforms such as Bloomberg and Reuters.

Inflation Expectations

The interest rates we have discussed thus far are called *nominal interest rates*, and reflect compensation for two distinct aspects – the fact that the same item will probably cost more in the next period than it does today, and the fact that most people would rather have money in hand today than get the same purchasing power a period later (a pure time preference, also related to the opportunity cost of capital or growth prospects). The former is an *inflation expectation*; the latter is *the real interest rate*. So, *Nominal Interest Rate = Real Interest Rate + Inflation Expectation*. This is referred to as the *Fisher Equation*.

More formally,

$$1 + r_{Nominal} = (1 + r_{Real}) \times (1 + \pi_{Expected}), \text{ or}$$

$$r_{Nominal} \approx r_{Real} + \pi_{Expected} \text{ for usual values of } r \text{ and } \pi$$

Eq. 9.1

Investors form inflation expectations based on the growth prospects and demand in the economy, relative to the productive capacity available. Current price levels/ increases also play a role in estimating future inflation. Treasury-issued financial instruments called TIPS protect investors against realized inflation-related risks; we will discuss them briefly in a later section. Several economic data series track realized inflation or price increases - the Fed follows the Personal Consumption Expenditure series to formulate policy; the TIPS uses the Non-Seasonally Adjusted CPI series.

To summarize, interest rates move because of either changes in growth prospects, term premium or inflation expectations. While these forces are not completely independent, two of these can be observed directly, through the difference between nominal rates and TIPS yields (inflation expectations) and the slope of the yield curve (term premium), so the implied effect of growth prospects can be backed out.

TERM STRUCTURE OF INTEREST RATES – THEORIES OF THE SHAPES OF YIELD CURVE

As we discussed in an earlier chapter (and will detail below), the forward curve is tightly linked to the term structure of the current spot rates, via no-arbitrage. There are a few alternate hypotheses that try to explain the relation between these curves and their shapes.

The *Expectations Hypothesis* says that the current futures rates should be equal to the expected future spot rates. This is grounded in a Rational Expectations framework, which postulates that, on average, people's expectations are realized, else they will learn and adjust the expectations. So, according to this idea, if the marginal investor expects rates not to move, the term structure should be flat, and the futures should coincide with the spot curve. Empirically, the evidence for this theory is mixed. The *Liquidity Premium Hypothesis* goes a step further and suggests that current futures rates equal the expected future spot rates, plus a liquidity premium. The liquidity premium exists because lenders usually prefer to lend short-term, borrowers prefer to borrow long-term (i.e. people like to have the cash with them sooner rather than later), so longer term rates need to be higher to induce people to commit for the longer term, pushing up the forward curve. This is also why the current spot term structure is usually upwards sloping. The *Preferred Habitat Hypothesis* states that different maturity sectors are distinct market segments with their own investor classes and demand-supply dynamics. Investor preferences dictate which part of the curve they will participate in by default (e.g. pension funds and insurance companies prefer long-term bonds); this clientele effect suggests that investors need a premium to gravitate to other parts of the curve. One can view the Liquidity Premium argument as a specific case of the Preferred Habitat idea, where the short-end (and to some extent, the extreme long end) is the preferred habitat.

This explains why the yield curve is usually upward sloping, for the most part. At the very long end (around 30 years), rates are somewhat lower compared to the intermediate part of the curve. This is explained by the higher convexity of these long term bonds, as well as the fact that there are many institutional investors such as pension funds, insurance companies and foreign central banks with structural reasons to strongly prefer the long end of the curve, to match the key rate durations of their liabilities better. Of course, the shape of the yield curve varies materially through the course of the business cycle.

During the expansionary phase of a business cycle, the strong economic data and corporate performance causes investors to be less risk averse, pushing up the long end of the curve as they reallocate to riskier asset classes, and the yield curve gets steeper. As investors worry about the Fed raising rates, the front end starts rising, and the curve begins to flatten. As the Fed raises rates, the front end keeps rising; if this raises concerns of the economy slowing down too fast, investors may start shunning riskier assets to move back into Treasuries, taking the long term yields lower. In fact, *an inverted yield curve has often been considered a leading indicator of recessions*. And as the economy actually slows and gets close to a recession, the Fed may reduce short term rates, leading to a low flat yield curve. This persists until investors feel better about the economy, when the curve begins to steepen. Some typical yield curve shapes have been shown earlier in Figure 7.2.

INTEREST RATE VOLATILITY AND INTEREST RATE MODELS***

Interest Rate Volatility

We have discussed a few reasons why interest rates move around. Movements in interest rates can be summarized in the data by tabulating historical changes in interest rate over time (of a specific term) and computing a standard deviation of these interest rate movements[67]. This represents the historical interest rate volatility for that point on the term structure, and provides an idea of how much rates are likely to move in future (if the future is likely to be like the past).

Interest rate volatility can be expressed as a relative rate movement (i.e. as a percentage of the initial interest rate level); this is referred to as *Black vol*, since it is used in the Black Scholes options model. Alternatively, interest rate volatility can be expressed in basis points; this is referred to as the *basis point or normalized vol*.[68] Using the Black vol to generate interest rate projections assumes that interest rates are expected to follow a lognormal distribution (rates are just as likely to rise by 1% of their initial level as decrease by 1% of the initial rate); whereas using basis point vols assumes a normal distribution for interest rate movements (rates are as likely to go up by 5bp as they are to go down by 5bp). Empirically, the normal distribution for rates is more popular, so the normalized or bp vol is used more often.

Importantly, all interest rates are not uniformly volatile; interest rate volatility is not just one number. We can compute historical interest rate volatility for any interest rate – short-term or long-term. Empirically, basis point volatility for intermediate term is highest; longer term and shorter term rates are less volatile[69].

---

[67] Annexure IV discusses the mechanics of calculating a standard deviation from data, and its economic interpretation.

[68] To estimate basis point vol using historical data, one would work with historical interest rate differences, whereas for Black vol, one would divide the interest rate difference by the initial interest rate before calculating the standard deviation. Basis point vol = Black vol × current interest rate.

[69] If a parallel shift occurred 100% of the time, the bp vol for all rate maturities would be identical.

Further Topics in Interest Rate Markets

Interest Rate Models

Interest rate volatility assumptions are important inputs in designing interest rate models. These models usually treat interest rates as a random variable, and estimate how much rates are likely to move from their current levels within a certain timeframe, using volatility assumptions. These interest rate models also form the basis for pricing/ estimating the value of interest rate options, instruments that pay off only if interest rates reach certain levels.[70]

To elaborate, apart from the level of interest rates, the current value of interest rate options (which will expire in future) depends greatly on interest rate volatility and how interest rates are assumed to evolve over time. The purpose of interest rate models is to come up with future alternative paths for interest rates and their relative likelihood, and use this for pricing options (i.e. estimate how often the option is valuable, and by how much). For this, the models need to make assumptions regarding the distribution of interest rate movements. The forward curve sets the point estimates of expected future values, and model parameters are calibrated to historical data (such as volatility). Running simulations based on these models provide insight into how much rates are estimated to vary around the forward curve.

Apart from the interest rate volatility assumption, the structure of the model itself is also important. For example, some models impose that interest rates are *mean reverting*, while other models do not. Interest rate models are often also classified in terms of the number of "factors" they use – *one-factor* and *two-factor* models are common. In a one-factor model, all rates are 100% correlated, by construction. A multifactor model does not impose this perfect correlation in theory, but the parameters estimated empirically end up implying a much higher correlation between short-term and long-term rates than is observed in the data. Some of this high correlation is often blamed on the "affine" structure of these models, which modelers often impose for tractable estimation. Again, looking beyond these details, the purpose of interest rate models is to generate with possible future interest rate trajectories and their probabilities; once these paths are generated and accepted as given, the specifics of the models are of secondary importance.

Alternatively, instead of using historical interest rate volatility to price options, one can use market prices of interest rate options as given. Along with a chosen interest rate model, analysts can then back out what level of interest rate volatility is *implied* in the current market prices of options (of course, specific to the model chosen). This helps investors decide whether the options are expensive or not, by comparing these implied volatilities with historically realized volatility. Of course, by using option prices, many values of implied interest rate volatility can be obtained (even for the same point on the yield curve), since the price of every option (different maturities and strikes) can potentially lead to a different implied interest rate volatility (respecting no-arbitrage conditions).

INVESTING IN TREASURY MARKETS - EXPRESSING VIEWS USING TREASURIES ***

Most investors in Treasury Markets are drawn to the fact that Treasuries are some of the safest investments. So, much of the investment is by insurance companies, pension funds, mutual funds promising safe returns, etc. As the economic outlook gets uncertain and financial markets get risky and volatile, more investors get attracted to the safe-haven status of Treasuries and start buying them, leading to an increase in their prices (lower yields). This is referred to as a "*flight to quality*".

The most fundamental view that investors express by buying or selling Treasuries is their view on interest rates; *if they expect rates to decline, they buy Treasuries and vice versa*. For benchmarked investors, this translates into

---

[70] We discuss options in detail in Chapters 13 and 14. These interest rate models also make distributional assumptions on interest rate dynamics (normal vs lognormal, etc.)

Capital Markets and Investments

being overweight or underweight Treasuries relative to their benchmark. Of course, as we discussed in Chapter 8, not all Treasuries are equal in terms of rate sensitivity – a five-year Treasury will have approximately half the duration of a ten-year Treasury. So, comparing proportion of portfolio market value is not the correct way to determine exposure to Treasuries; DV01 is more relevant.

Leverage

Treasuries are some of the lowest risk instruments, with no default risk and relatively low price volatility. This implies a low expected return. For investors who are very confident about their view on which direction Treasuries are likely to move, they can amplify their returns through leverage. Less volatile assets such as Treasuries are especially easy to borrow against; the standard mechanism is to use the repo market as described in the previous chapter. Fixed income arbitrage hedge funds use significant leverage to juice up trades in the Treasury market. The difference between the (usually overnight) borrowing rates (i.e. cost of *leverage*) and the asset returns (on a very large notional) shows up directly in the bottom-line; this is a winning trade as long as the asset return does not fall below the leverage cost. The leverage cost needs to be paid no matter what, so if asset returns fall even slightly below the borrowing cost, this can eat into profits very quickly (because of the large notional exposure) and drive firms insolvent. Regulatory / Balance sheet constraints on the sell-side are drying up the repo market, making these trades less common than they used to be.

Carry Trades

For a portfolio manager, a position such as the one above, in which the investor is long an asset with a higher yield/ interest rate and short an asset with lower yield is called a positive-carry trade. Every day that market conditions remain unchanged, the investor makes some money and is being paid to wait. If duration-mismatches are generating the positive carry, then a rise in rates will usually hurt profits (because of upward sloping term structure); a decrease in rates will be accretive.

All bond investors, including Treasury investors, care about the coupon as a source of return. C/P is referred to as *Current Yield*, and measures *carry* (i.e. how much does it pay / cost to hold the position for a year if nothing changes from today, except the passage of time). The rest of the return comes from price changes of the bond, which depends on whether rates moved in the direction that the investor had anticipated. Also, it matters where the investor had been positioned on the curve, as longer duration bonds have more yield sensitivity. Besides, different points on the yield curve may move by different amounts.

All bond investors care about carry, especially in the credit universe, where coupons can be much higher. But, carry trades are also common among currency investors, who borrow in the currency with a lower interest rate (i.e. the lower yielding currency) to lend in the currency with a higher interest rate. If the currency with a higher interest rate appreciates (or depreciates less than the interest rate differential between the two currencies), the investment is profitable.

Steepeners and Flatteners

Investors often have a view on how different points on the yield curve will move relative to each other (i.e. not parallel), but do not have a view on the level of rates. For example, they may believe that the yield curve is likely to steepen (i.e. long term rates rise more / fall less than the short term rates), but are unsure whether rates in general are headed higher or lower. To express this view, they will go long a short-term note and short a long-term note/ bond, likely setting this up on a low (likely close to zero) DV01 basis using Eq. 8.6 (the short quantity is negative). Since the duration of the short-term note is lower than the long term note/ bond, the investor needs to be long more Treasuries (in dollar amount) than they are short, to neutralize the effect of parallel shifts in the curve. Note, this is likely to be a positive carry trade, despite being short a higher interest rate bond, because the investor is long much more of the shorter-duration bond to be DV01-neutral. Such a trade is called a *steepener*; *flatteners* bet on the curve flattening by putting on the opposite position.

Further Topics in Interest Rate Markets

Flatteners are often negative-carry if set up DV01-neutral. If the trade sets up to be negative-carry, some investors may choose to be carry-neutral, and take on some interest rate risk instead, because they do not want to bleed carry each day that they wait for the trade to work.

Relative Value Trades

While most investors use the Treasury bond market to either meet their long term investment objectives or to express tactical views on the interest rate levels, certain relative value investors (usually hedge funds/ CTAs, etc.) trade one bond against the other. They may buy cheap and short rich (as indicated by their models) bonds at various points of the yield curve, or put on steepeners/ flatteners as described above. Another common trade involves trading the spread between on-the-run and off-the-run Treasuries, a proxy for how liquidity is priced in the Treasury markets. Investors also trade some of the instruments described below against Treasuries (or each other), to express views on the cash-futures basis, swap spreads or interest rate volatility.

To summarize, investors use Treasuries usually to express views on interest rate movements, to hedge interest rate risk, and to bet on how they expect the shape of the yield curve to change. Convexity trades are also common.

OTHER INSTRUMENTS BASED ON THE RISK-FREE RATE***

Forward Rate Agreements

Last chapter, we introduced the concept of forward rates, and Forward Rate Agreements (FRAs). Lenders and borrowers today can negotiate a rate to lend/ borrow a set amount on a specified date in the future. These rates (the *forward rates*) are tied to the spot rate by no arbitrage. For example, an investor can either lend today for one year, or lend for six months today and also decide today to lend in six months for a further six months at the current relevant forward rate. Both these lending plans should lead to the same interest income; the forward rate is thus set by no-arbitrage. More formally, if $_nf_m$ refers to the forward rate in n periods to lend for m periods,

$$(1+r_{m+n})^{(m+n)} = (1+r_n)^n \times (1+{_nf_m})^m$$

$$or, \quad {_nf_m} = [\frac{(1+r_{m+n})^{(m+n)}}{(1+r_n)^n}]^{1/m} - 1 \qquad \text{Eq. 9.2}$$

Note, this Forward Rate Agreement is not an option; it is a firm commitment to lend or borrow (depending on which side the investor has chosen to be) at this rate for a definite notional amount (also decided today). At inception, from a purely financial perspective, the investor should be indifferent between borrowing and lending at this rate, since it is a zero NPV transaction, and no money changes hands today. After the transaction is decided, this becomes either a lucrative trade or a losing one, depending on which way the rates move. Choosing to lend at the forward rate (in future) is similar to being long a bond, at least from the interest rate sensitivity perspective (adding DV01 to the portfolio), since the forward rate will reflect the current expectations of a m-period rate n periods from today (embedded in today's values of r_n and r_{m+n}). So, if rates go up, this forward rate is likely to go up too. By the same argument, choosing to borrow the appropriate notional at the forward rate is akin to being short, or putting on a rate hedge. To unwind this hedge, the investor may have to enter into another FRA with the opposite economics; alternatively, he may be able to cancel the FRA by paying or receiving the losses or gains (because of rate movements) since putting on the initial position.

Treasury Futures

The FRA as described above is an OTC product, where the parties can decide today when in future to borrow and lend, for how long. Because of the bilateral nature of this transaction, it may not be easy to get in and out of the trade at short notice, which is essential for speculators or hedgers. Besides, while losses/ gains may occur instantaneously in a bond portfolio following interest rate movements, cash flows are settled in a traditional FRA only on expiration, thereby rendering hedges using FRAs less useful. A similar product, the US Treasury futures, trades on exchanges (CBOT being the primary exchange) and is very liquid. It is marked to market daily, and cash flows are replenished in the investor's account with the broker daily, depending on rate moves. While maintaining the essence of an unfunded interest rate position, the product has been standardized on several dimensions to promote liquidity, as discussed below.

Treasury Futures are a contract to buy or sell US Treasuries (within a specified maturity band) on a fixed contract expiry date in the future, with the price decided today (no cash changes hands today). These contracts expire on set dates in March, June, September and December, with liquidity mainly in the two nearest expiration dates. Expiration dates aside, these contracts differ from one another based on which US Treasuries (i.e. which maturity band) can be delivered on expiration. For example, to settle a 10-year T-Note Futures contract, any Treasury with a remaining maturity between 6.5 to 10 years can be delivered. These are *physically-settled* contracts, since securities actually exchange hands upon settlement. In some other markets (e.g. equity indices), futures are *cash-settled*.

The value of any Treasury Futures contract (the *derivative* in this case) is based on the price of the US Treasuries that can be delivered against the contract (i.e. the *underlying*). Anytime during the delivery month, the investor who had earlier sold the futures needs to deliver an eligible Treasury; he can choose exactly which Treasury and which day (i.e. the *Delivery Option*). Now, all the Treasuries in the eligible pool do not cost the same, so the futures contract specification makes some adjustments (*Conversion Factor*, discussed below) depending on the Treasury chosen to try to make all Treasuries in the eligible pool look similarly attractive from a delivery perspective. However, since these adjustments are rule-based, even after applying these adjustments, some Treasury bond usually appears marginally cheaper. This is the *Cheapest-to-Deliver* or *CTD* Treasury that the seller will usually choose to deliver, all else equal; the futures price typically tracks the value of this CTD Treasury. A rise in rates will reduce the value of both the CTD and also the future. Because of the high demand for the CTD, it often trades "special" in the repo market; i.e. it's much cheaper for market participants to borrow using the CTD as collateral, compared to other Treasury collateral.

The supply/ demand of contracts in the derivative (i.e. futures) market depends almost completely on the number of investors willing to put on interest rate bets / hedges using these contracts (unlike Treasuries, which also depends on Treasury issuance, aside from investors). The number of futures contracts outstanding is not related to, or bound by the supply of underlying Treasuries available in the market. So, during expiration, it may be impossible to source the underlying, either because it is buried in some long-only asset manager's index portfolio or because there simply aren't enough securities that have been issued. This may cause a "*short squeeze*" in the underlying Treasuries, and lead to delivery "*fails*", for which there are penalties. In reality, most investors in futures do not wait for contract expiration to deliver/ take delivery of underlying instruments; they "close out" their futures position by trading out of it (remember, this is exchange-traded so very easy to trade) close to expiration, often "rolling" to the next expiration to maintain the economic exposure. The exchange publishes the *Open Interest* for every contract daily, which indicates the total number of futures contracts that have not been closed out, an indicator of liquidity.

While leading to pricing intricacies (because of adjustments, etc.), the contract design allows flexibility in delivery – both in terms of delivery date (with a month of the expiration date and underlying security (any security within the maturity band, price adjusted by the Conversion Factor) – to prevent short squeezes, fails, or a general breakdown of the contract. With a wide choice of securities, the seller can likely find a close substitute to the CTD. With a month to deliver, that the market can likely sort these issues out before the final delivery date, increasing confidence. The futures market doesn't need to be constrained by the amount

Further Topics in Interest Rate Markets

outstanding of on Treasury issue. Consequently, despite the complicated details, the Treasury Futures market is very liquid.

Futures contracts for 3-year, 5-year, 10-year (6.5-10 year maturity), Classic (15-25 year maturity) and Ultra (>25-year) are freely available, for the next expiration date. They are quoted in ticks, like Treasuries. Investors use the Treasury futures market to either bet on interest rates or to hedge existing interest rate exposure; the DV01 of a futures contract depends primarily on the underlying Treasury (i.e. the CTD), but is also affected by the adjustments.

Details related to Treasury Futures

Each Treasury Futures (i.e. distinct underlying/ maturity band and expiration) contract has a distinct price, which changes continuously based on market conditions. Both the long and short side agree to transact at this price at contract expiration (if they both end up holding the contract to expiration). For every futures contract, the short investor agrees to deliver Treasury securities of his choice (within the maturity band specified by the contract) with a face value of $100,000. The long position holder agrees to pay the futures price multiplied by the conversion factor, for these bonds.

The *Conversion Factor* for any bond is its price (assuming $1 par) which implies a yield of 6%. Thus, all bonds eligible for delivery are adjusted to be approximately of equal attractiveness. The futures price is multiplied by this conversion factor to determine how much the long position holder needs to pay to receive the bond.

How does an investor decide when to invest in Treasury Futures? Very simply, a Treasury investor has the choice either to buy a Treasury bond or go long the (near term) Treasury Future, which will potentially deliver a similar Treasury in the delivery month. If t indexes the current date, P_t is the bond invoice price (includes accrued interest), CF its conversion factor and F_t be the futures price, these two alternative ways of getting long exposure cost P_t and $CF*F_t$ respectively. The *Gross Basis* B_t is defined as:

Gross Basis = Bond price P_t - Futures Price * Conversion Factor

If the current date (t) lies in the delivery month, for any bond that can be delivered, B(t) cannot be negative, because investors will then go short the futures, buy the bond and immediately deliver it into the futures, and lock in riskless profits. A positive basis does not imply riskless gains for the opposite trade (i.e. long futures and short bond), because after going long the futures, the investor has no control over which bond will be delivered and on which day (and thus may not be able to cover his short bond position costlessly). Even after the last trading date of the futures, the short futures holder has seven days to deliver the bond of his choice. The smaller the basis of a bond, the cheaper it is for the short investor to deliver that bond; this bond is *Cheapest-To-Deliver (CTD)*.

Let us develop this argument further and carefully extend it to months prior to the delivery month. Since the shorting, purchase and delivery cannot be simultaneously executed now, we need to adjust the formula above to recognize that the long bond will earn accrued interest from the time it was bought until it is delivered. Also, the bond purchase needs to be financed in the repo market. The difference between the bond's coupon and the repo rate (usually overnight) is the carry (positive when the yield curve is upward sloping) earned from buying the bond and financing it until it is delivered (say at T, often at the end of the delivery period). This needs to be added to the Gross Basis to calculate the *Net Basis*. So,

Net Basis = Gross Basis - Income from Accrued Interest + Bond Financing Cost

Net Basis = [Bond Invoice price P(t) - Futures Price * Conversion Factor] – (Coupon Rate*(T-t)/365 + Repo Rate *(T-t)/360, assuming Treasury day count is Actual/365 and repo day count is Actual/ 360.

The Cheapest-to-Deliver Bond has the lowest Net Basis. If the Net Basis is negative at any time, it suggests an arbitrage opportunity (similar argument as with Gross Basis). However, this trade is not a definite arbitrage

Capital Markets and Investments

because repo financing is usually short-term and can suddenly rise, especially if the CTD switches. Equivalently, investors use a related concept, Implied Repo Rate, which is the repo rate that sets the Net Basis to zero. If the Actual Repo Rate is lower than the Implied Repo Rate, then an arbitrage possibly exists.

Earlier, we pointed out that the formulaic conversion of all bonds to yield 6% using the conversion factor introduces minor biases, leading to the CTD bond. Usually, when market yields are lower than 6%, the shortest maturity bond in the eligible maturity bucket is often the CTD (ignoring the effect of repo rate differences across bonds). When Treasury yields are higher than 6%, the longest maturity bond is often the CTD.

TIPS (Treasury Inflation Protected Securities)

All the interest rate products that we have discussed so far are valued based on the headline interest rates, i.e. *nominal* interest rates. As explained in the section on inflation expectations, (risk-free) interest rates in general reflect both inflation expectations as well as the pure time preference for parting with capital for one period. While nominal Treasuries are liquid and free from default risk, they are exposed to the risk of inflation.

The US Treasury started selling Treasury Inflation Protected Securities (TIPS) since 1997, and issues them in five, ten and thirty year maturities. The principal value of TIPS is indexed to the Non-Seasonally Adjusted (NSA) Consumer Price Index (CPI) for all Urban Consumers. Other countries such as Australia, Canada, Israel, Sweden and United Kingdom also issue inflation-indexed government bonds. Conceptually, these instruments protect investors from the risk that a dollar in future will probably be able to buy fewer goods and services compared to a dollar today (so the face value is adjusted to reflect realized inflation); investors thus only need to be compensated for their time-preference and the fact that they are deferring consumption to the future. So, yields on TIPS are lower than nominal Treasuries with similar maturities. *The yield on the TIPS is close to the real rate of return.*

Issuing Inflation-indexed securities reduces the incentive for governments to issue nominal debt and pursue inflationary policies. Pricing/ yields on these securities also provides a reference to estimate investor expectation of future inflation trends. These bonds may also reduce the cost of issuing public debt, because inflation-averse investors may pay a premium to be protected against inflation. In particular, relative value investors in government bonds often express their view by trading the *inflation breakeven yield*, by taking opposite positions in the nominal bond and similar maturity TIPS. The breakeven yield includes both the inflation expectations, as well as the inflation risk premium that investors require to hold instruments that do not compensate them for inflation. Investors often assume that inflation risk premium is not likely to change in the short-term, making the breakeven sensitive mainly to changes in inflation expectations, which are often driven by inflation realizations and macroeconomic data.

Details

The principal amount on TIPS issued by the US Treasury is indexed to the Non-Seasonally Adjusted CPI-U, which is published monthly by the Bureau of Labor Statistics. The indexing at month *t* is based on the index value in month *t-2*. Since the periodic adjustment to principal is treated as current income for tax purposes, investors have to pay taxes on this "phantom income", which they will not realize until they sell the bonds[71]. TIPS are issued with 5, 10 and 30 year maturities, and can be stripped.

On any coupon payment date (say *s*), the interest due is calculated by multiplying the stated at-issue coupon rate by the inflation-adjusted principal on that date. Effectively, the instrument pays coupon payments of:

$$Coupon\ Payment = 100 \times \frac{CPI_s}{CPI_{Issue\ Date}} \times Coupon\ Rate\ at\ Issue$$

---

[71] This issue exists for Zero Coupon Bonds too.

Further Topics in Interest Rate Markets

The US TIPS provide investors with a put option at maturity (T). Investors can put (i.e. sell) the bond back to the Treasury at par, even if there has been deflation (i.e. $CPI_T < CPI_{Issue\ Date}$). The maturity balloon payment is

$$Maturity\ Payment = Max[\ 100, 100 \times \frac{CPI_T}{CPI_{Issue\ Date}}]$$

The duration of TIPS is measured with respect to the real interest rate. Since, nominal interest rates are usually higher than real interest rate, TIPS duration is likely to be significantly higher than that of a comparable nominal Treasury bond with respect to its nominal yield. Further, in an inflationary period, TIPS duration, even with respect to nominal yields, are likely to be higher because the inflation-sensitive cash flows are back-loaded at maturity.

LIBOR-BASED INSTRUMENTS

What is LIBOR?

So far, all the interest rates we have discussed were riskless Treasury rates (except the Fed Funds Rate, an interbank rate). We now introduce another interbank rate, LIBOR, London Inter-bank Offer Rate. This is a rate collected and calculated daily by ICE (Inter Continental Exchange) by polling representatives of 18 different banks on what rates they are willing to lend to and borrow from other banks for various (usually short – overnight to 12 months) time periods and currencies. The outlier responses are excluded, and the rate is published around 11:45am UK time daily.

In the past few years, market manipulation scandals have rocked the integrity of LIBOR rates, but they have continued to remain a relevant benchmark for financial products.[72] Corporate bonds sometimes have coupons linked to LIBOR (floating rate bonds) instead of a fixed coupon rate. As more investment products get synthetically created by the sell-side, the opportunity cost of capital is often indexed to LIBOR, more accurately reflecting the bank's cost of funds. LIBOR is higher than Treasury yields for similar maturities because it reflects bank credit risk, but in almost all cases, there is a close correspondence between changes in LIBOR and Treasury rates. This breaks down during financial crisis, when Treasury yields decline because of a flight to quality, whereas LIBOR goes up because investors are more concerned about the solvency of banks. The TED (Treasury –Euro Dollar) spread captures this dynamic over time. If the TED spread remains close to constant, LIBOR-based instruments will behave similarly to Treasury instruments.

EuroDollar Futures

The simplest product linked to LIBOR is the EuroDollar Futures (EDFs). They are exchange-traded and reflect market expectation of 3-month LIBOR rates (i.e. the underlying is 3-month LIBOR) upon contract expiry, every quarter. Unlike Treasury futures, which has very little liquidity beyond the first two expirations, Eurodollar futures are liquid (albeit somewhat less) up to 10 years out, i.e. 40 quarterly expirations. On the electronic screens, the quotes are color-coded – the first four years are colored white, red, green, and blue respectively, and are referred to as such.

This market represents the forward market for 3m LIBOR, for every quarter for the next 10 years. Applying our earlier discussion on the interest rate term structure and forwards, we can back out a spot LIBOR curve, and LIBOR curves at various future points in time. The difference between the Treasury curve and the LIBOR curve has traditionally represented (refreshed) AA financial sector risk, adjusted for the cost of funding and

---

[72] At the time of writing, there is serious talk of phasing out/ replacing LIBOR as a benchmark over the next few years. This will affect hundreds of trillions of dollars of assets.

Capital Markets and Investments

carrying Treasuries on the firm's balance sheet. However, recent regulatory changes affecting the repo market for Treasuries have spilt into the LIBOR market. Further, some OTC derivatives such as interest rate swaps (discussed next) are now collateralized and centrally cleared, making this interpretation less relevant, and causing these rates to be abnormally low.

Details

> The price of this contract (in sharp contrast to a bond) is simply (100 − yield), so if the market's estimate of the 3-month LIBOR on the contract expiry date is 1.5%, this will be quoted at 98.5. So, when the expected rate goes up, the contract price goes down, linearly (no convexity, unlike bonds). As an example, if I am long 4 contracts, and the price on the screen moves from 99.25 to 99.15, it means that the expected 3m Libor at contract expiration changed from 0.75% to 0.85%. Since the notional amount underlying each contract is $1mm, and this is a 3-month rate (i.e. the duration of the contract is 0.25 year), the profit is 4*(99.15-99.25)*0.25/100*1000000 = -1000 (i.e. a loss of $1000). Every basis point move in 3m LIBOR expectations leads to a $25 gain or loss per contract, i.e. the DV01 per contract is $25 (i.e. 0.25*0.0001*1000000).

Interest Rate Swaps

Interest Rate Swaps are another popular LIBOR-linked product. In this product, for a time period decided upfront, an investor agrees to periodically receive (opposite trade is to pay) a fixed interest rate (the *fixed leg* of the swap) in exchange for paying (opposite trade is to receive) LIBOR (the *floating leg* of the swap). A notional amount is also agreed upon, to multiply these rates to determine the net payment. The fixed rate (called the *swap rate*) is set so that the investor is financially indifferent between receiving the fixed leg and the floating leg i.e. the present values of the fixed and floating legs are equal at inception, so the swap is a zero-NPV transaction and no cash flows are exchanged when the trade is set up. In a sense, the swap rate is close to an average of the floating rates expected over the period of the swap. The fixed rate is quoted as a spread (i.e. *swap spread*) over the Treasury rate for that maturity, but once the swap is entered into, the fixed rate stays constant for the length of the swap.

After the swap is entered into, a subsequent rise in interest rates (i.e. LIBOR) is good for the fixed-rate payer (he is now paying too little, since it is based off earlier calculations and is to receive higher rates) and bad for the fixed receiver (he is receiving a low off-market rate). So, in response to the rise in rates, the NPV of the swap now becomes negative for the fixed receiver, similar to that of a long bond holder i.e. the receiver of the fixed leg is long duration, similar to that of a bond owner. Thinking of the duration of the fixed and floating legs separately, the duration of the fixed leg is similar to the duration of a bond with the same fixed coupon and maturity. Since the cash flows of the floating leg readjust in response to rising rates, the PV of that leg does not change i.e. the floating leg duration is close to zero. So, the net duration of the swap is close to that of a fixed rate bond with the same maturity and coupon; this is added to the fixed receiver and subtracted from the fixed payer's portfolio. The notional of the swap is analogous to the par value of the position in a DV01 calculation; it denotes the size of the position and the magnitude of the gain or loss.

Like the Euro Dollar Futures discussed above, interest-rate swaps are also based off LIBOR, since an investment bank is typically the counterparty. But, the *n*-year swap rate is different from the *n*-year rate implied by the Euro Dollar Futures market, because the swap rate is calculated using a PV formula which properly adjusts for the convexity of the swaps, whereas the Euro Dollar Futures rates do not capture convexity (since they are linear products) and will be slightly higher.

Swap rates have traditionally not been risk-free, since they have counterparty risk; they are usually priced as if they were as risky as large financial firms. So, one would usually expect swap spreads over Treasuries (i.e. difference of the two rates) to be positive. But, over the years, the margin requirements of swaps have gone

Further Topics in Interest Rate Markets

down, and swaps are fully collateralized now in most cases. Recently, regulators have taken initiatives to have swaps centrally cleared, which implies that that there will be a clearinghouse guaranteeing the obligations of both the buyer and the seller, until the trade is cleared. All this has meaningfully reduced the risk of swaps, and narrowed swap spreads. In fact, as many foreign central banks are expecting the US Federal Reserve to raise interest rates, they have been selling Treasuries out of their foreign reserve holdings to keep their currencies weak versus the US Dollar. At the same time, new regulations have made it increasingly onerous for financial institutions to have a large balance sheet (including owning Treasuries or providing financing for them, so repo rates are high). This has caused Treasuries to be relatively cheap, and market participants have preferred to add duration by receiving fixed in swaps instead of buying Treasuries. All this has caused swap spreads at some maturities to be negative since 2014.

Investors use swap markets for a variety of reasons. Swap markets give them indirect access to the fixed or floating capital markets, although their debt may originally have been issued in a different manner. Swaps are also useful as a tool for hedging and speculation; investors can manage their asset-liability structure and mismatches using swaps.

Also, these interest rate swaps are distinct from the Index Swaps we discussed in the chapters on the Buy-side and Indices. They are all swaps, and the floating leg pays LIBOR, reflecting the cost of capital of the sell-side firm, but the fixed leg of all these swaps is very different; the fixed leg provides exposure to different risk markets in each of these products. To complicate this further, one can even imagine an index swap indexed to a Treasury index, which will behave similarly to an interest rate swap, i.e. the fixed leg of that index swap will provide exposure to the Treasury market!

Details

> Let us consider a 5-year interest rate swap, between two parties X and Y. Suppose X pays the fixed annualized swap rate (say 6%) to Y (i.e. 3% every 6 months) on a pre-decided notional, for the next 5 years. Y, the floating rate payer, pays X half the prevailing 6m LIBOR rate (on the same notional) at that time. Depending on which rate is higher, one party pays the other the net cash flow. Usually, contracts are based on the 3M LIBOR, in which case Y pays a quarter of the 3M Libor rate times the notional to X every 3 months. Two of those periods also involve Y receiving the semi-annual cash flow associated with the (fixed at inception) swap rate from X, so cash flows in those periods are netted. Figure 9.1 shows this.

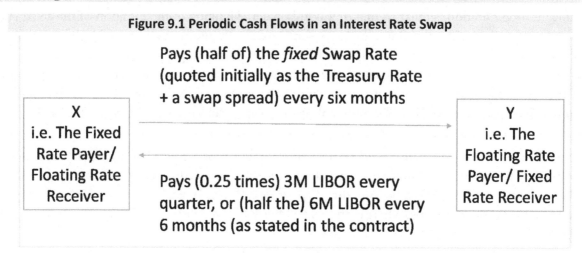

> In the above situation, Y (the fixed payer) is long duration and X is short duration; the duration of the fixed leg is similar to the duration of a fixed rate bond with coupon equal to the swap rate and maturity

equal to the swap term, whereas the duration of the floating leg is close to zero (since its PV will always be close to the notional). If the duration of the swap is known, the instrument can be simplistically used to hedge interest rate risk by neutralizing portfolio duration. The swap rate is set such that, at inception, the present value of the fixed legs and the floating legs are equal. Note that the swap rate is based off the LIBOR term structure (since the floating legs are LIBOR-based), so any swaps position which is hedging a Treasury portfolio is exposed to the basis between LIBOR and Treasury rates; if the two rates diverge from one another, then the hedge will not work nearly as well.

If s denotes the swap rate, and f the forward LIBOR rate for a N year swap indexed to the 6-month LIBOR, then the swap rate is given by the equation below (i.e. PV of both legs are equal):

$$NPV_{fixed} = \sum_{n=0.5}^{N} \frac{s/2}{(1+r_n/2)^{2n}} = \sum_{n=0.5}^{N} \frac{{}_{n-0.5}f_{0.5}/2}{(1+r_n/2)^{2n}} = NPV_{floating}$$

This can be rearranged as:

$$0 = \sum_{n=0.5}^{N} \frac{1}{(1+r_n/2)^{2n}} \left(\frac{s}{2} - \frac{{}_{n-0.5}f_{0.5}}{2} \right) \qquad \text{Eq. 9.3}$$

This shows that, for the correct swap rate, the swap indeed has zero NPV. If we ignore the distinction between Treasuries and LIBOR and replace the forward LIBOR curve with the forward Treasury curve (usually not a big difference, but it ignores the TED spread and excludes an important detail), the swap rate can be written as a function of the zero coupon Treasury bond prices, i.e.

$$s = 2 \frac{(1-Z_N)}{\sum_{n=0.5}^{N} Z_n}$$

The Euro Dollar strip captures the current market expectation for 3-month LIBOR at various future points in time. If we write a version of Eq. 9.3 using 3-month intervals for the floating leg, then the forward LIBOR from the Eurodollar strip can be substituted for f in the formula (the floating leg bit) for different time periods, leaving s (the swap rate) as the only unknown, which can be solved for. Note that we need to use the forward 3M LIBOR corresponding to September for a payment in December (i.e. 3 months lag, these months are just an example), since the floating payment is set a quarter in advance (i.e. not decided on the day of payment, but decided the moment the previous floating payment has been made). Many interest rate swaps pay every six months of the fixed leg, but every quarter on the floating leg, so that needs to be accounted for, too.

ETFs related to Treasury Markets

We discussed Exchange Traded Funds earlier, in the chapter on asset classes. These ETFs contain a basket of securities, and aim to provide access to various specific markets and asset classes. They trade on exchanges like stocks. Some ETFs provide exposure to the interest rates market – a few are listed below (ETF managers in parenthesis).

TLT – 20+ Year Treasury Bonds (iShares)

IEF –7-10 Year Treasury Bonds (iShares)

EDV – Extended Duration Treasury i.e. 20-30 Year (Vanguard)

TLO – Long Term Treasury (SPDR)

SHY – 1-3 Year Treasury Bonds (iShares)

Further Topics in Interest Rate Markets

TIP – TIPS (iShares)

IEI – 3-7 Year Treasury Bonds (iShares)

Investors sometimes trade these products instead of the underlying bonds because it is a simple one stop shop solution. Many of these investors may be equity investors, unfamiliar with the details of fixed income securities and lack dedicated fixed income sales coverage, yet want to express a view on rates or hedge interest rate risk. In this case, it also allows a basket of OTC underlyings to be seamlessly converted into exchange traded instruments. For this convenience, the ETF manager charges a management fee. .

Options on the above securities

We leave a detailed discussion on options and their valuation for our equity markets section. Options on rate-sensitive securities also work in a similar manner. As a quick overview, options, like futures, are financial derivatives whose value is referenced to an underlying instrument. Unlike futures, the option owners have the right, but not the obligation (i.e. they have a choice) to enter into the pre-specified buy/ sell transaction at a pre-decided price (strike price/ exercise price) on the option expiration date. For this choice, the option owner pays the option seller the option premium while buying the option, unlike futures when no cash changes hands at inception. There are two broad types of options – *call options* which grant the right to buy the underlying, and *put options*, which give the right to sell the underlying at the strike price. So, call options end up being valuable at expiration if the underlying has risen above the strike price; put options have value at expiration if the underlying has fallen above the strike price.

Most instruments that we discussed above also have an active options market; options on Treasury Futures and Eurodollar futures are traded on exchanges such the CBOE/ CME, whereas options on ETFs are traded on the equity exchanges. Options explicitly on the interest rate (swap rate/ LIBOR) trade OTC and include:

- *Caps /Floors* on the swap rate: Effectively a sequence of options on LIBOR on every reset date, since the caps/ floors protect for a length of time.
- *Swaptions*. Options to enter into a (receiver or payer) swap in on the option expiration date
- *Mid-curve option*: Options on a forward-starting swap
- *CMS Option*: Option on the swap rate (rather than an option to enter into the swap)

These options all bet on LIBOR/ swap rate and are very similar. People often put on relative value trades across the various instruments.

TOPICAL ISSUES IN THE TREASURY MARKET

The Treasury market is an old established market, so has been time-tested. While most investors believe that exchange-traded market in general work most efficiently (since the order book is centralized), the Treasury market, despite being OTC, has remained a thriving market. Many experts, however, insist that dealer competition alone cannot keep markets honest; they clamor for more transparency in Treasury/ fixed income pricing, for all trades to be posted to a consolidated tape, and for the order book to be centralized, or at least orders being routed to the venue/ dealer with the best price.[73]

Most of asset pricing is based on the investor's perception of risk and return across asset classes, but the supply of securities (like any product) also matters, most of the time. Now, the supply of US Treasuries is driven mainly by macroeconomic considerations. Specifically, the government's budget deficit i.e. how much

---

[73] This is all standard in equities, though the equity markets have their own set of market microstructure issues, which we will discuss in Chapter 11.

Capital Markets and Investments

the government is expecting to spend beyond its tax receipts) determines Treasury issuance (since it is government borrowing). For example, on October 31, 2001, the US Treasury announced that it would *discontinue issuing 30-year bonds*, saying that this maturity was not necessary to meet the government's financing needs and discontinuing issuance at this maturity would save taxpayers money. This supply shock led to a 34bp decrease in the 30-year rate in one day! During this period, from March 2000 to December 2001, the Treasury also conducted 45 reverse auctions to *buy back Treasuries*, motivated by budget surpluses. This buyback program caused the long end of the yield curve to invert steeply.

US citizens and American entities (funds, etc.) hold about two-thirds of the US Treasury bonds, with about a third being held by foreign countries. *Foreign countries, mainly China and Japan, have grown their holdings of US Treasuries over the past fifteen years*, as the US economy went from budget surplus to deficits and increased Treasury issuance. While foreign holders were 26% of the Treasury market in 1996, they are over 40% of the market today (and the market itself has grown from USD 4 trillion to 15 trillion during that time). If foreign governments find Treasuries less attractive going forward (for whatever reason), Treasury yields are likely to rise, especially if the government is facing a budget deficit and needs to continue issuing Treasuries. Figure 9.2 shows the holders of US Treasuries and their relative share over time. Note the increase in Foreign Holders and Monetary Authorities (i.e. Federal Reserve) over time.

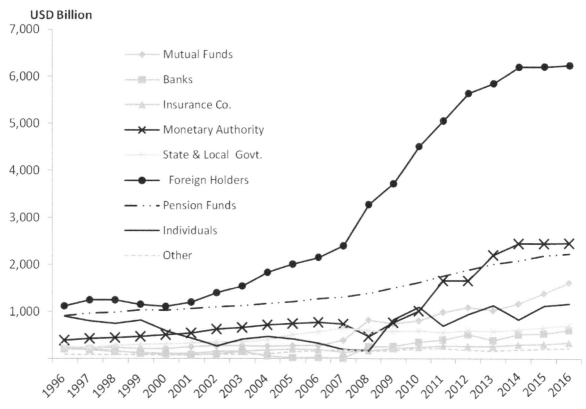

Figure 9.2 Holders of US Treasuries

Source: SIFMA

During the 2008 financial crisis, the US Federal Reserve decided to engage in *Quantitative Easing* (many other Central Banks such as the European Central Bank and Bank of Japan followed), where they bought US Treasuries in high volumes, thereby increasing demand and reducing longer-term rates. Government debt issuance increased rapidly, and the size of the Fed's balance sheet increased from below USD 1 trillion in 2007 to over USD 4 trillion today. While these lower rates have probably spurred some additional economic activity (as people and firms borrowed to spend), they have likely also caused firms to borrow excessively (at cheap rates) to pay shareholder dividends, and financial investors to get cheap leverage to inflate the value of all financial assets. Further, the lower yields hurt the ability of retirees and others to generate income from savings.

The US Treasury market is one of the most liquid fixed income markets in the world. However, even in this market, despite widespread adoption of electronic quoting and trading platforms, the liquidity is sporadic and disappears for large trades or off-the-run issues whenever market conditions are not perfectly normal. This is related to the larger issue of constraints on dealer balance sheets and restrictions on them warehousing bonds. But, the issue is amplified here because most Treasury securities were earlier financed in the repo market, which has dried up because of regulatory reasons (see Chapter 7), reducing the buyer base and causing fewer natural buyers to step up during tight liquidity conditions.

CONCLUSION

The yield on Treasuries is a surrogate for risk free rates, and other risk assets are often priced with that as a reference. The principal risk in investing in Treasuries (or any of the other interest rate sensitive products that we discussed) is that interest rates move against the position; duration captures the rate sensitivity. For fixed income instruments that have other embedded risks (e.g. credit risk) captured through a spread over Treasuries, duration works too. Finally, duration helps calculate price changes from given yield shifts; why the yield has changed is irrelevant for this mechanical exercise. The difference is that, unlike rates, spreads don't often move in a parallel manner, so the idea needs to be tweaked to apply to spread sensitive portfolios.

REFERENCES

Gibbs, David, J. W. Labuszewski, M. Kamradt. *Understanding Treasury Futures*. The CME Group

Sundaresan, Suresh. *Fixed-Income Markets and Their Derivatives*, Academic Press

Fabozzi, Frank. *Bond Markets, Analysis and Strategies*, Pearson

10. Other Fixed Income Markets

We discussed Treasury markets in the last three chapters, and provided a framework to assess interest rate risk of bonds. With this understanding, we now extend these ideas to other common fixed income instruments and introduce their basic ideas in this chapter. We will talk about several products below; they broadly belong to either mortgages, credit or securitized products. While we will breeze through the topics, it is important to recognize that these are all significant asset classes within the fixed-income universe – mortgages are comparable to Treasuries in size, municipals used to be more than half the size of Treasuries before the Federal Reserve expanded its balance sheet post 2008, and credit market size is comparable to that of mortgages. Figure 2.1 provides an idea of the relative sizes of different markets over time.

Each of the products below has different bells and whistles. The important detail is that all these products, with the exception of hybrids and loans, are bonds (hence they form part of fixed income), so the essential framework, introduced in Chapter 7 of contracted cash flows being discounted to arrive at a current price is valid. What is different is that these cash flows are now uncertain (remember, Treasuries are risk free, ignoring potential liquidity issues), so we need to attribute a risk premium in the form of additional required return; the discount rates are not obvious, although they should be higher than Treasuries (for the same cash flow profile). But, if we observe a price for one of these risky securities, we can back out the yield at which it is trading; the yield difference with a similar-maturity liquid Treasury is the risk premium that the market is currently charging. This yield difference is often referred to as the *spread* of the bond[74]. Yield remains a measure of the expected return of the bond under certain assumptions; duration is still a valid measure of interest rate risk. So, simply summarizing instruments in different asset classes by their duration, yield, etc. helps a lot and provides context in understanding how they will behave in different market environments; remembering the details of every product is of secondary importance. Almost all fixed income markets predominantly trade OTC, with mortgages nearly as liquid as Treasuries (TBAs more than pools), and higher spread credit and structured credit less so.

Bloomberg publishes some of the most commonly used fixed income indices[75]. Figure 10.1 shows the market value of these benchmark indices, a proxy for the size of the markets. Note, these numbers will be meaningfully smaller than the actual aggregate size of some of the markets that we have discussed (e.g. in Figure 2.1), since index inclusion rules exclude the less liquid shorter maturity smaller issues, which are a significant part of some markets.

---

[74] So, loosely, Treasury yield + spread = risky bond yield.

[75] These indices were initially published by Lehman Brothers. After the Lehman bankruptcy in 2008, Barclays took over the production of these indices. Bloomberg recently bought the index business from Barclays in 2016.

Other Fixed Income Markets

Figure 10.1 Bloomberg Barclays Fixed Income Indices (Dec 2016)

US Fixed Income Indices	Market Value (USD mm)
U.S. IG Market (ex-144A, TIPS & Munis)	18,822,372
U.S. Treasury	6,768,117
Government-Related	1,466,302
Agencies	736,520
Local Authorities	219,098
Sovereign	201,252
Supranational	309,432
Corporate IG	4,865,746
Securitized	5,722,206
CMBS	321,184
ABS	88,384
U.S. MBS	5,298,027
Covered Bonds	14,611
US TIPS	1,060,217
US Municipals IG	1,382,036
US 144A IG	1,432,208
US Corporate HY	1,339,992
US Loans	716,943
Convertibles	213,003
US Municipal HY	82,728
Taxable Municipals	298,873
Build America Bonds	167,411
Taxable Municipals-ex BABs	131,462
Total US Fixed Income	**24,288,155**

Europe / UK Fixed Income Indices	Market Value (EUR mm)
Pan-Euro IG Market	13,075,990
Treasury	7,960,632
Government-Related	1,862,563
Agencies	845,552
Local Authorities	325,283
Sovereign	126,648
Supranational	565,079
Corporate	2,132,900
Financial Institutions	890,910
Industrial	1,031,970
Utility	210,020
Securitized	1,119,896
ABS ex CMBS	25,931
CMBS	10,228
Covered	1,083,737
Pan-European High Yield	333,007
Pan-Euro EMG Ex PE Agg	50,668
Euro Treasury High Yield	140,469
Pan Euro Total Fixed Income	**13,600,135**

Source: Bloomberg/ Barclays Live

US MORTGAGES

Mortgages are one of the largest fixed income asset classes; prior to the financial crisis, mortgages were a larger asset class than US Treasuries. They are owned by all types of institutional investors.

Most *residential* mortgages in the US are guaranteed by a Government Agency[76] (e.g. Fannie Mae / Freddie Mac/ Ginnie Mae), although they are *originated* by a mortgage bank[77]. Apart from regular *fixed rate mortgages* with 15 or 30 year terms, originators also issue *Adjustable Rate Mortgages (ARMs)*, which have an initial low *teaser* fixed rate; the coupon then resets to a fixed spread over LIBOR after a specified number of years. This may cause interest costs of some homeowners to suddenly increase after that specified time period, especially if their credit has weakened over the years and they cannot easily refinance (more details on refinancing below).

A *Special Purpose Vehicle (SPV)* buys these mortgages from the originator; the originator receives cash which allows the originator to make more loans, and repeat the process. Homeowner mortgages are *pooled* together in the SPV based on geography, loan balance, loan-to-value (LTV) bands, credit (i.e. FICO) scores, which bank originated the mortgage and the coupon of the mortgage loan. Each pool has its own *pool number*. The

---

[76] These agencies were set up by an Act of Congress to support the mortgage markets, but morphed into privately owned companies which borrowed heavily with an implicit government guarantee to actively invest in the rates/ mortgage markets. The 2008 financial crisis caused Fannie and Freddie to fall in government conservatorship.

[77] Prior to the 2008 financial crisis, Agencies used to limit their guarantees to loans that *conformed* to certain criteria such as maximum loan size, credit score, etc. There was a large non-Agency mortgage market, comprising of mortgages that did not meet the agency criteria because they were either too large (*Jumbo* mortgages) or too risky (*Alt-A* and *sub-prime*). Post-crisis, the Agencies have stepped into these market too, and take on more borrower risk, at a higher fee than they used to charge earlier. Pools based on lower-credit collateral is now referred to as *low-FICO*.

Capital Markets and Investments

SPV issues bonds with this pool as a collateral. The cash raised from these bond issuances is used originator for the mortgage loans. The cash flows from the monthly mortgage repayments from th the pool are used to pay interest and principal on these bonds.

Investors buying such bonds[78] (also called *Mortgage Backed Securities* or *MBS*) are not concerned about the default risk of the homeowner (except for prepayment speed considerations, discussed below), since a government agency is guaranteeing the payments. If homeowners default, the Agency makes up the difference; so this effectively replaces homeowner credit with agency credit, and eventually lowers cost of borrowing for the homeowner. The coupon on the MBS is lower than the weighted average coupon on the mortgage loans by about 0.70% per annum because of servicing costs and agency guarantee commission. The guarantee fee is based on the average LTV and FICO scores in the pool, and is read off a Loan Level Pricing Adjustment (LLPA) matrix. Unlike most other fixed income securities (which pay coupons semi-annually in the US and annually in Europe), *most MBS pay a monthly coupon*. Like the underlying mortgages, these MBS also *amortize* i.e. part of the principal is paid back every month, but keeping the monthly annuity payment fixed. In the initial months, the monthly payment comprises mainly of interest and a little principal; as the principal is paid down, the interest component goes down and a larger proportion of principal is paid back each month (but the monthly payment remains same. There are two main kinds of Agency MBS: *Pass-throughs* and *Collateralized Mortgage Obligations (CMOs)*. In this section, we mainly discuss pass-throughs[79], and hold back our discussion of CMOs until we discuss securitization more fully later in this chapter. In some situations (e.g. home equity loans), residential real estate loans may not fit the criteria to be put into any pool; these remain as whole loans on the originator's books and end up being more expensive for the borrower.

Prepayments

In the US, homeowners can prepay the mortgage anytime without penalty. While there are several variables affecting *prepayments*, the most important variable is the current interest rate i.e. can the homeowner refinance to a lower mortgage interest rate? Since mortgage rates follow Treasury yields closely, a lowering of interest rates will lead to easier refinancing at lower rates, causing more mortgages to be prepaid. From the perspective of the bondholder, this is treated as an early repayment of principal[80]. Normally, a decline in interest rates would lead to an increase in bond value (we discussed this at length in the chapters on Treasuries), this upside is lower in MBS because the bondholder is involuntarily saddled with cash (because of faster prepayments, bond cash flows are expected sooner), exactly when rates are low (so reinvestment returns are weak). When rates are high, prepayments are slower than the norm, and the bond maturity *extends* (i.e. gets longer than expected), exactly when the investor would like more capital to invest at the higher rates. So, Agency MBS have *negative convexity* i.e. MBS durations get longer at higher rates and vice versa (exactly the opposite of the desirable convexity features). Commercial mortgage pools also exist; those mortgages have pre-payment penalties, thus making prepayments less likely (and less of a risk).

For the mortgage analyst, it is very important to understand the prepayment dynamics. Besides the interest rate-related factors described above (*Refinancing*), prepayments (in full or partial i.e. curtailments) occur for several other non-rate-related (i.e. non-financial) reasons such as *Turnover* (borrowers moving to new homes either for personal reasons or cashing out home equity), and *Involuntary* reasons such as foreclosure/ servicer

---

[78] These bonds are also called Real Estate Mortgage Investment Conduits (REMICs)

[79] The term MBS, used with further qualification, usually only refers to Agency Parr-through mortgages, in market parlance.

[80] Borrower defaults are also treated like prepayments.

Other Fixed Income Markets

buyout upon borrower defaults (in which case the Agency steps in and prepays), or a loan modification. Macro factors such as seasonality (school year-related) and geographic location also play a role.

Analysts carefully watch current *prepayment speeds*, and also use sophisticated (albeit usually imprecise) models[81] to predict future prepayment speeds, essentially by running simulated paths on interest rates (and occasionally other factors described above, like home prices), and predicting prepayment speeds based on the simulated values of those factors, and the history of (simulated) prepayments. These models are necessarily *path-dependent*; the current value of the factors (interest rates, home prices, etc.) is not enough to predict prepayments; the paths that these variables took to get here matters. Two measures to track prepayment speeds are *SMM (Single Monthly Mortality)* and *CPR (Conditional Prepayment Rate)*. SMM captures the fraction of a pool that makes principal prepayments over a month; CPR is an annualized version of SMM. Eq. 10.1 shows this relationship.

$$(1-SMM)^{12} = 1 - CPR \qquad \text{Eq. 10.1}$$

The Public Securities Association (*PSA*) convention for prepayment speed states that 0.2% of the outstanding principal balance is prepaid in the first month of the life of the mortgage. This rate ramps up by 0.2% each month, until it reaches 6% in month 30, and stays at that level for the rest of the mortgage life. This is not really how one expects the mortgage to pay, but is used as a benchmark for communicating prepayment speeds. A pool paying at *100 PSA* pays exactly at this rate, whereas a pool paying down at 160 PSA is expected to pay at 1.6 times the PSA convention.

The TBA Market

To Be Announced (*TBA*) is a futures market for MBS pass-throughs yet to be issued, similar to the when-issued Treasury Market. Unlike the when-issued Treasury market, where all details of the Treasury (except the coupon) are known, the TBA trades only specify the Agency, program and coupon to describe the security; face value and price decide the economics of the trade. SIFMA decides standard settlement dates every month. The record date to receive the month's cash flows (interest payments, scheduled and unscheduled principal) is the end of the previous month. Only certain *conforming* pools, based on maximum loan size, credit score, etc., are eligible for delivery into a TBA. Like Treasury futures, the seller has the option to deliver any pool within these parameters; analysts assume the worst, most negatively convex pools will be delivered and adjust pricing to reflect this. The exact pools (Pool Number/ CUSIP) are notified two days before delivery. The *worst-to-deliver* pools tend to be the pools prepaying the fastest for TBAs with coupons above the current market rate, and the pools prepaying the slowest for TBAs with coupons below the current market rate. So, specified pools with good characteristics often trade at a pay-up (i.e. premium) to TBA. Some specified pools are non-deliverable into TBAs because of undesirable characteristics.

The TBA market provides liquidity to a heterogeneous market by reducing the variables that can be agreed upon; otherwise, if we think of the granularity in every pool, it can easily get fragmented like the corporate bond market. TBAs also allow originators to hedge their originations by taking positions in the TBA market instead of waiting to collect a critical mass of loans, protecting them from interest rate risk.

Dollar Rolls (Financing TBA positions)

On the settlement date, the investor long the TBA has to pay cash for the pool and take delivery. To continue maintaining an unfunded position, the investor can "roll" the position. "Buying the roll" involves buying front month TBA and selling back month TBA (and temporary paying out cash in the process); "selling the roll" is the opposite. The difference in price between the two TBAs is referred to as the *drop*. The drop is related to

---

[81] Prepayment models from various well-known institutions, all making plausible assumptions, generate prepayment spends that are very different from one another.

Capital Markets and Investments

the repo cost, since they are both financing tools for rate sensitive instruments, but there is no tight linkage, unlike the relation between the Treasury futures market and repo, through the net basis.

The cash flows for the month accrues to the investor if he is long the roll, since he owns the front month TBA on the record date. He will pay out these bonds on the next settlement (unless he rolls again), so he is exposed to the prepayment dynamics for that month. During the next settlement, the identical pool need not be returned; any eligible pool can be delivered.

TBA Coupon Swaps

Instead of investing in a TBA outright, mortgage investors also trade *coupon swaps*, where they buy a TBA with a higher coupon and sell one with a lower coupon (or vice versa). Dealers quote the price spread for swaps with coupons 50bp apart e.g. the Fannie 3.5/3 swap. The prices of different coupon TBAs do not move one-for-one as rates move, since the prepayment speeds (and therefore the durations) are different for different coupons. All else equal, the higher coupon pool will have faster prepayment speeds (and lower duration) than the lower coupon pool, since the prepayment option is more valuable if the coupon on the existing mortgage is higher. The durations will also change at different paces as rates change, making this a convexity play too.[82]

Mortgage Servicing Rights (MSRs)

Mortgage Servicing Rights (MSRs) are the rights to service the mortgage (collect and process the periodic mortgage payments) and get paid a fee (often around 0.25%-0.50% of the mortgage amount) for doing so. This fee is paid out as long as the mortgage is current, so it has much of the same prepayment risk as regular MBS securities. If a borrower defaults on a mortgage, the servicer needs to step in to try to collect, or initiate foreclosure proceedings and liquidate the delinquent accounts[83]. Mortgage servicers (and some commercial banks) hold large portfolios of these MSRs which buy from originators and need to hedge against interest rate movements.

Valuing MBS

When we studied Treasuries, the interest rate sensitivity (duration) of Treasuries was highlighted as an important characteristic/ metric. Duration remains a very important concept in mortgages to capture how mortgage value changes with interest rates; its calculation gets more complicated (and varies across models) because of the relation between prepayment speeds (which affects duration) and interest rates. Also, *Weighted Average Life* is often used in mortgage-land to give a sense of when the bond is expected to mature, and its rate-sensitivity. Prepayment risks are also very important when evaluating MBS. *Effective Duration*, which reflects the change in MBS price for a unit change in its option-adjusted spread (OAS, discussed below) properly accounts for the prepayment option.[84]

Like other fixed income securities, yields and spreads are the most important concept when valuing mortgages. Mortgages are expected to trade at a higher yield/ positive spread to Treasuries (even if we believe that the Agencies do not have default risk) to compensate the investor for the negative convexity profile. Said differently, the investor has provided refinancing options to the homeowner pool, which reduces the cost of the mortgage bond. Three spread concepts are commonly used, of which the first two are *static* (They assume that the term structure of interest rates may have any slope, but is not changing dynamically*)*:

> The *nominal spread* or *yield spread* is the simplest spread concept. We compute the yield of the cash flows of the MBS assuming a fixed prepayment rate, and compare that to the yield of a Treasury with the

---

[82] Further, most pricing models suggest that TBAs with coupons closest to the current mortgage rate are priced tight; bonds with coupons further from the current rate are priced cheap. OAS is materially positive for coupons that are not close to the current rate.

[83] In many markets, a *special servicer* takes over when a mortgage is past due.

[84] The usual modified duration formula takes periodic cash flows to be fixed, and does not capture the prepayment risk adequately.

same average life. We ignore the distribution of cash flows over time, and the prepayment optionality of MBS.

The *zero-volatility spread (z-spread)* adds a fixed spread to the Treasury spot curve to discount cash flows so that the calculated price matches with the market price, so each cash flow can have a different discount rate (unlike the nominal spread). Also, a different prepayment speed can be used to derive the cash flow at each period, consistent with the interest rate at different points on the forward curve. Importantly, prepayment rates drive the average life, which determines the Treasury we compare with to calculate spreads.

The static spread metrics we discussed above are unable to adequately capture the sensitivity of (nominal) spreads and average life when interest rates change. To recognize the embedded prepayment optionality in mortgage securities, we use the idea below.

The *Option-Adjusted Spread (OAS)* assumes that interest rates are not static, but that the forward curve and the terms structure of rates move around over time. It values the embedded option explicitly, and incorporates the interest rate sensitivity of cash flows, at any point in time.

OAS calculation involves first generating (several thousand) possible interest rate paths, by simulating interest rates using the interest rate volatility and other variables that capture interest rate dynamics. Interest rate paths serve as inputs to generate mortgage rate paths. The prepayment model then uses these mortgage rates as input to generate prepayment forecasts, which generate the cash flows along every *point* across every possible path. These cash flows are all path-dependent, so a 3% interest rate in period 5 will imply different prepayments, depending on how we get to this 3% rate. Each of these cash flows is discounted by sum of the relevant interest rate and a constant OAS and added to get the theoretical MBS price associated with that path. This is repeated for all paths, and a probability weighted average of all these prices is calculated to get to the theoretical MBS price. The OAS is the fixed constant value that is added to each interest rate across each path to discount cash flows so that the (average) theoretical price matches the MBS price observed in the market. Importantly, OAS is a model-dependent value, dependent critically on the prepayment model. The different between the z-spread and the OAS is often referred to as *option cost*.[85]

Mortgage investors typically look at OAS of a particular MBS relative to other similar pools and over time, to decide whether the pricing is attractive. This totally depends on how the prepayment speed is being modelled, so investors often also overlay their fundamental ideas about whether the pool is a discount or a premium pool (i.e. coupon above or below market, trading above or below par), seasoned or not, the average life of the loan, the agency backing it, the banks who originated, LTV, average loan balance etc. These fundamental features become even more important while analyzing non-agency residential mortgages.

Mortgage Market Liquidity

Mortgages are traded OTC; the mechanics are similar to how Treasuries trade. The TBAs (and other pass-throughs) are extremely liquid, pools less so, but still very liquid relative to the other fixed income assets. TBAs trade like Treasuries, in ticks, on platforms such as BrokerTec and Tradeweb, with a layer of inter-dealer brokers connecting the various sell-side desks, who interact with the buy side. Pools and CMOs, which

---

[85] To calculate Effective Duration, the OAS is changed by 1bp at each point in each path, cash flows regenerated and the bond repriced. This price change, by definition, is the duration.

Capital Markets and Investments

we will discuss in the section on securitization, trade by phone/ chat, and are quoted in ticks. The non-agency market is primarily a voice market like the corporate bond market.

MUNICIPAL BONDS

The Municipal Bond (*muni*) market has a special status within fixed income, because it is the only market where interest income is exempt from federal taxes, and in some cases from state and local taxes too[86]; this market is also referred to as the *tax-exempt market*. Because of this big benefit, municipal bonds are more expensive (i.e. yields are lower) than similar taxable bonds. To compare yields on a tax-equivalent basis to similar taxable issuers, the yield of a municipal bond needs to be divided by (1- tax rate), as shown in Eq. 10.2:

$$Yield_{taxable} = \frac{Yield_{muni}}{1 - tax\ rate} \qquad \text{Eq. 10.2}$$

The main investor base for this market is high net-worth individuals with high tax rates (hold directly as well as through mutual funds), as well as some corporations that pay taxes at high rates. The large investor base of pension funds is not attracted to this segment because they do not pay taxes anyway.

This market is extremely fragmented, with many issuers with small issue sizes and an active regional market. Many issuers have tapped the market over the decades, as federal funding has declined and demand for public services has increased. California, New York and Texas (the states, and counties within these states) are the biggest issuers.

Municipal Bond Classifications

Municipal bonds come in several types:

General Obligation (GO) – These are backed by the full faith and tax revenue of the issuer (including income tax, sales tax and excise tax for states, and property tax for counties). Investors will assess the growth rates of population, reassessment of property values, per capital debt and other issuer obligations.

Revenue Bonds – These bonds fund special projects, and a portion of the project's revenues are allocated to service the debt; *suitable debt service reserve accounts* (similar to escrow) may be set up to accomplish this. Rate covenants in the bond stipulate that service charges for the project users will be kept high enough to cover debt obligations. These bonds are categorized into sectors such as housing, education, utility, health, etc.

Double-Barreled Bonds – These bonds contain features of both GO and revenue bonds, being backed by the full faith of the issuer and the cash flows of the project being financed by the bond.

Insured Bonds - This section of the municipal market comprises lower rated municipal debt, "*wrapped*" with the guarantee of a monoline insurer; thus the municipal debt takes on the credit quality of the insurer. Post the 2008 financial crisis, the financial stability and ratings of these insurers have taken a hit, thereby affecting the growth of this market.

Pre-refunded Bonds – Some muni bonds (of the above categories) are callable by the issuer. For the bonds that are non-callable, they can be *refunded*, which is lucrative if their yield goes down. To execute this refunding, the issuer uses new debt at the current lower yields (i.e. raises more money), uses this cash to create a collateral pool of Treasuries or other high-quality securities that pays out according to a similar schedule as the original tax-exempt security (i.e. *defeasance*). The issuer now needs to pay a

---

[86] Build America Bonds (BABs) issued in 2009-2010 are an exception; they are taxable. President Obama signed a law permitting states to issue taxable bonds for two years, and to receive a subsidy from the center equal to 35% of the interest payment.

lower coupon (for the new debt) and reduces funding costs; the old debt is serviced by the collateral and trades very tight. This is possible because the muni-coupons, being tax-free, are often lower than Treasury coupons. Regulations prevent munis from profiting from this via arbitrage.

Figure 10.2 shows the size of these various components of the Municipal IG market, as of December 2016. Ratings-wise, 14% of this market is AAA, 54% is AA, 27% A and 6% BBB. There is also a separate high yield muni market (ratings are discussed in the next session on credit).

Figure 10.2: Bloomberg Barclays Municipal (IG) Index (Dec 2016)

	Number of Issues	Market Value (MM)
GO Bond Index	15,274	373,774
Revenue Bond Index	30,603	892,131
Insured Bond Index	156	2,848
Prerefunded Index	4,112	113,284
Total Municipal Bond Index	**50,145**	**1,382,036**

Unlike many other fixed income issuances, where one issue typically has only one bond, most muni issues contain several bonds (vary in coupon, maturity, etc.). In *term issues*, all bonds in the issue mature at the same time, and the issuer makes a bullet payment at the end, like a regular bond. These are quoted in price units and called *dollar bonds;* the secondary market is more liquid. A *serial issue* has several bonds, but each has a different maturity date; maturities are laddered to make it easier to meet repayments and match with tax inflows. In *series issues*, the issuer raises only a portion of the total project cost initially, and then continues to issue bonds on a pre-set schedule until the entire capital is raised. This is an efficient way to fund construction projects, since expenses are staggered. Serial and series issues are quoted based on yield.

High-Yield Munis

During economic slowdowns, tax collections go down, reducing cash flows available to service debt. Usually this is not a huge issue because the larger municipalities typically have large debt capacity; smaller issuers have reinsurance protection. There are specialized parts of the market, though, where market risk remains key. For example, some municipalities have issued bonds backed by the settlement payments by cigarette companies to state and local governments that depend on the smoking rates of the population; these bonds pay down faster if more cigarettes are consumed. Airport bonds backed by airlines traded at distressed levels post 9-11 and the subsequent airline bankruptcies. Counties such as Vallejo and Orange County in California, and cities such as Detroit have also filed for bankruptcy under Chapter 9. Puerto Rico also has a large capital structure that is getting restructured. Jefferson County missed principal payments on sewer bonds and GO bonds, as it could not roll over its debt since the reinsurers got downgraded, during the financial crisis. So, there is a niche area of tax-exempt high yield municipal bonds, which carry significant risk and offer lucrative returns.

Primary and Secondary Muni Markets

In the primary market, the larger generic GO issues are launched using a competitive bid among *underwriters* (usually sell-side investment banks, who commit their balance sheet to buy the bonds from the issuer and then re-offer it to other investors, ensuring that the deal gets done). But, most issuances are negotiated between the underwriting syndicate and the issuer, instead of being competitively bid. In both cases, an *official statement* describing the issue and the issuer is put together, similar to the prospectus or offering memorandum.

Muni bonds, like other fixed income securities, trade OTC. The larger issues are supported by the larger sell-side banks. The smaller issues are traded by regional and local dealers. Standard & Poor's publishes the Blue

Capital Markets and Investments

List daily, which contains the inter-dealer listings for municipal bonds and reflects the supply of bonds available in the municipal dealer community. All trades are also reported to Municipal Securities Rule-making Board (MSRB), which are made available publicly, ensuring transparency in pricing.

CORPORATE CREDIT

Companies issue a variety of instruments (broadly classified into debt and equity) to meet interim cash needs and finance their growth plans. Unlike Treasury instruments, corporate debt instruments also contain the credit risk that the issuer will be unable or unwilling to pay coupon or principal payments when these payments come due (and so trade cheaper than a Treasury bond with the same terms). Depending on market conditions, a company chooses among various instruments to balance its desire to issue securities at low cost but maintain operating and financial flexibility, considering current investor appetite for returns (yield/ spread) versus safety of capital.

Capital Structure

The *Capital Structure* refers to the mix of different debt and equity securities that a company uses for financing itself. These different securities, which are *liabilities* of the issuing firm but *assets* of the investor that holds them, vary in cost (i.e. what investors will pay), and the flexibility they provide to the issuer, so CFOs spend a lot of effort trying to optimize the mix[87]. Understanding the issuer's capital structure is critical to analyzing securities, especially credit. We discuss capital structure here in this chapter, in Chapter 11 when we discuss equities, in the Annexures when we discuss financial statements and, briefly, earlier in the book.

Different instruments vary in terms of their *seniority* (who gets paid, in what order, if the issuer goes bankrupt i.e. the *Absolute Priority Rule*), *maturity* (for example, equity represents permanent capital and legally doesn't need to be repaid, whereas short-term debt needs to be paid in less than a year), compulsion to pay on time (debt needs to be paid on time, dividends on equity and preferred stock can be skipped without legal constraints), other contractual features, covenants and regulatory treatment. Most capital structures are simple (these are the ones we will discuss); capital structures of financial firms sometimes get complicated.

Debt instruments (the bonds/ loans/ hybrids discussed earlier in the book) have a periodic coupon payment for a certain number of years, and a principal payment at maturity. Most corporations "roll over" this debt, i.e. issue fresh debt (not necessarily the same instrument or even same part of capital structure) as maturity date approaches to pay back the earlier principal, so debt servicing costs can jump up if interest rates or spreads are high during this time. Interest payment on debt represents a tax-deductible cost for firms (investors pay tax on interest income, though, except on Treasuries and Munis), dividends on equity and preferred stock[88] are not tax-deductible.

Different firms have different credit quality (we discuss this below), depending on the amount of debt they have outstanding relative to their projected cash flows and risk, so not everything we discuss here is applicable to every firm. But usually, the capital structure follows a *waterfall* structure reflecting the seniority and the sequential payment priority of the liabilities – working capital / revolvers get paid down fully first, first-lien loans (secured) get paid next, followed by second-lien loans, secured bonds, senior unsecured bonds, subordinated bonds, preferred stock and finally equity. Most common capital structures will only have a few of these instruments – working capital debt, senior (unsecured) bonds and equity, whereas some companies can have even more stratifications. As a general rule, non-financial companies with greater credit risk usually have

---

[87] Analysts and academics disagree on how much this mix actually matters, because the cost of different securities of an issuer are linked. Chapter 11 has a more detailed discussion on this topic, in the section on capital structure theories.

[88] Dividends on Trust Preferred are tax deductible, but only a handful of firms (mainly financials) can issue them.

Other Fixed Income Markets

more complex capital structures. Figure 10.3 shows a hypothetical capital structure. When a company issues new securities, they are often issued either *pari passu* (at an equal footing) to some existing bond, or senior/junior to it. Analysts focused on a particular security worry both about whether their security (and other securities above it or at the same seniority[89]) is comfortably covered by assets, earnings or cash flow, as well as the complete debt stack.

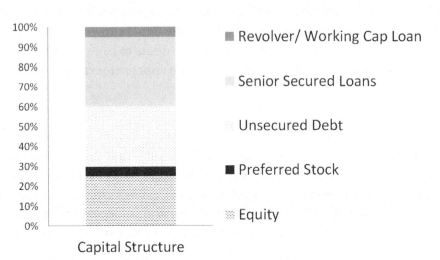

Figure 10.3 Capital Structure of a Hypothetical Company

Bankruptcy

Practically, this pre-specified absolute priority of payment is rarely followed if a company files for bankruptcy. This is because it is hard for creditors to initiate bankruptcy proceedings unless there is an actual event of default that has not been cured, so the equity holders are also given some enticement (some post-bankruptcy equity, release from litigation, etc.) so that the business can file before all the value has leaked out. Usually, most bankruptcies in the US are *prearranged/ prepackaged* according to *Chapter 11* of the bankruptcy code (*reorganization*), where the bankruptcy court supervises the restructuring of the liabilities to continue operating the business, rather than *Chapter 7* (*liquidation*), where the firm's assets are sold to service the liabilities to the extent possible, under the bankruptcy court. For a Chapter 11 liability restructuring proposal to be confirmed by the courts, either every creditor class votes in favor of the plan (absolute priority not necessarily respected), or one impaired consenting (liability) class has to vote in favor of the restructured deal and absolute priority has to be respected[90]. Essentially, any creditor class that has absolute priority violated against it has to vote for the plan. Usually, restructuring involves new money being invested, some existing securities getting cancelled and new securities issued to replace them (usually less than the earlier par amount). Investors take losses, or *haircuts*. Debt obligations get amended or exchanged for new debt and/or equity securities, and some debt holders may have little or no recovery on their investment.

---

[89] All these securities also need to get paid in full, for the security that the analyst is assessing to get paid in full.

[90] A *"yes" vote* under bankruptcy law requires two-thirds of the dollar value of the creditor class and one-half of the number of creditors to vote yes.

Capital Markets and Investments

Quantifying Default Risk

Credit products trade at a (positive) spread over Treasuries to compensate investors for default risk[91]. The default risk can be converted to equivalent spread compensation, if analysts can form an estimate of the *Expected Loss* (for every dollar invested in the security), for which they need estimates of *Default Probability*, and the *Loss Given Default* (which equals *1- Recovery Rate*). Eq. 10.3 captures this relationship:

$$Expected\ Loss = Default\ Probability \times Loss\ Given\ Default \qquad \text{Eq. 10.3}$$

For a one-period security, *the expected spread (i.e. spread times the probability it gets paid) is equal to this expected loss*, applying the no-arbitrage idea. For a longer term bond, we can apply the same principle, but the math gets messy, because we need to recognize that the default probability changes over time[92], the value of the coupon payments that are paid out before the default occurs, etc. Investors choose to invest in a particular bond by comparing its spread to other comparable issuers/bonds, and also taking a view on whether the spread is too wide, compared to the default risk and recovery assessed by the analyst. While the default likelihood is arguably the same for all debt issued by a firm (most debt has *cross-default* provisions)[93]; the *recovery rate* can vary significantly across issues, depending on their relative seniority and claim to company assets.

Credit Rating Agencies

Three major credit rating agencies (Standard & Poor's or S&P, Moody's and Fitch) operate in the USA. Corporate issuers appoint one of more rating agencies to research the issuer's financial health and prospects, and publish reports on them. These rating agency reports (and analysis), unlike sell-side reports, are created using non-public information (of course, the report themselves, once published, become widely available), with the company's cooperation. Each agency also publishes a *rating* (i.e. a letter grade/ score), indicating how risky it thinks the company and its debt is; both issuers (corporate families) and issues (facilities) are rated, separately. Agencies are also required to keep following the company and updating ratings.

Many investors are skeptical of credit ratings because of conflicts of interest (companies pay rating agencies to rate them) and because rating agencies appear to act after the fact, when spreads have already widened to reflect increased risk. But, credit ratings are nevertheless useful because many investment guidelines are driven by credit rating, many financial contracts get voided if credit ratings change significantly, regulators assess capital requirements of banks, etc. Because ratings agencies can access non-public information, their reports sometimes provides a glimpse into company information not otherwise available. But, rating changes lag; the latest information is often reflected earlier in spreads.

Credit ratings take the form of letter grades (much like an academic course grade). For example, S&P publishes ratings from AAA (highest quality, minimal credit risk), AA, A, BBB, BB, B, CCC to D (defaulted). Ratings between AA and CCC have *notches* (+/-), to provide further granularity. Agencies also publish ratings outlooks (positive, negative, neutral) for each issue, and watch-lists. Companies are said to have a split rating if two rating agencies assign different ratings. Ratings below BBB- (i.e. BB+ and below) are considered *high yield (HY)*, ratings above that are referred to as *investment grade (IG)*. Investment guidelines often restrict certain managers to not invest in high yield; market dynamics of high yield securities are also very different from IG.

---

[91] Over the past few years, *Liquidity Risk* has become a very important part of the spread too; we discuss this later in the chapter. So, spreads are typically decomposed in credit and liquidity risks.

[92] A bond issuer is more likely to default in five years than in one, especially if there are large scheduled bond repayments during this time.

[93] A debt security with cross default provisions is assumed to be in default if another security by the same issuer has defaulted; usually the clause clearly lists out which debt is included (or not).

Other Fixed Income Markets

Important Elements of Credit Analysis

An analysis of a corporate's creditworthiness and whether certain securities will be paid (back) in full depends on an evaluation of the company and its prospects (similar for equities or any instrument that the company issues) and depends on industry factors, the company's position in the industry and its projected growth and profitability. Details such as accounting quality, cash flow adequacy, liquidity, maturity of the security, the security's position in the capital structure and its asset coverage matter. The prospects of peer firms and the prices at which their comparable securities trade is also important.

Many of the details we discuss below, while still somewhat relevant, are less used frequently for investment grade bonds, which comprise the vast majority of corporate debt issuance. Most investment-grade investors follow a top-down approach looking at sectors, rating, spread and maturity, instead of digging deep into issuer-level details. This is possible because investment grade debt is usually adequately cushioned by assets; the company needs to satisfy these debt obligations before paying down other liabilities. Even in a difficult market environment, these issuers usually have enough resources to comfortably cover debt payments. The common risk to investment grade credit is spread sensitivity to overall market sentiment and outlook for the sector/issuer, rather than any serious chance of actual default.

Analysts often try to summarize the *financial risk* of a corporate borrower and compare it to others by calculating ratios of some numbers available in financial filings. We introduce this topic in Annexure II, where we discuss financial statements. Common *ratios to assess creditworthiness* include Debt/ EBITDA[94], Debt/ Capitalization, Free Cash Flow from Operations/ Debt, EBITDA/ Interest Coverage. These ratios cover the gamut of liquidity, operational efficiency and the extent of leverage. As mentioned above, it is important to calculate these ratios both using the total debt stack of the company (to get a sense of company solvency, especially as most indentures now contain cross-default clauses) as well as using only debt that is senior to or at the same level as the security being analyzed (to get a sense of how well the security is covered). The yield and these ratios for this security, when compared to other similar firms, provide a good idea of relative value. The other dimension of relative value is time. Like Treasury bonds, different credit securities by the same issuer can have different maturities. So, they can trade at significantly different spreads over the respective benchmark Treasuries; default risk typically increases over time. So, *credit spread curves* exist, similar to Treasury yield curves; offering a tradeoff between return and default risk at different points in time.

The bond indenture/ loan agreement contains *covenants*, which detail the relationship between the lender and the company, and lay out what the company is required to do (*affirmative covenants*) and cannot do (*negative covenants*). Documents also contain *financial covenants*, which can be one of two types. Loan covenants often stipulate *maintenance* covenants, where the companies needs to maintain certain financial metrics at all times (e.g. Debt/ EBIDTA). High-yield bonds typically contain *Incurrence* covenants, which are breached only when the company's explicit acts causes the financial limit to be infringed[95,96]. Investment-grade bonds are issued with very few covenants, mainly a negative pledge (i.e. a commitment to not secure assets against other debt, beyond a certain level). While covenants cannot prevent a fundamentally bad investment or the "view" being

---

[94] EBITDA is Earnings Before Interest Tax Depreciation & Amortization, discussed further in Annexure 2.

[95] For example, an incurrence covenant stipulating a minimum EBIDTA/ Interest Coverage ratio of 4 will not trigger if EBIDTA decline causes the ratio to fall below 4, but a maintenance covenant with the same terms will be. If the company issues more debt that increases interest expense, then both maintenance and incurrence covenants will be breached.

[96] High yield bonds and loans have many covenants to address all kinds of potential issues that compromise their interest – early redemption/ callability, registration rights, reporting requirements, events of default and cure periods, limits on indebtedness, liens, restricted payments, asset sales, mergers, relationship with subsidiaries/affiliates, etc. But, many "standard" covenants in an indenture sometimes have carve-outs that weaken the covenant significantly, while giving the superficial impression of being protected.

Capital Markets and Investments

wrong, it protects debtholders from adverse actions by the company, or holders of other parts of the capital structure. It recognizes the priority of claims, and allows debtholders to demand restructuring if certain covenants are violated and not *cured* in time. Covenants typically get weaker in markets when the demand for new issue high yield instruments is high.

As discussed above in the section on capital structure, the instrument's seniority/ subordination in deciding the priority of payment. Another detail is to be careful about which subsidiary or "box" has issued the debt. The cash flows and the debt may all map to different legal entities; figuring out how much of the business cash flows and assets are available to service the relevant debt is important. The most standard version of this is the operating company – holding company (*opco – holdco*) structure, where debt is issued at both the operating and holding company. All things equal, it is better to own operating company debt (closer to the assets) than holding company debt; the senior-most security at the holdco gets paid from the equity cash flows at the opco. Similarly, it is also essential to watch out for guarantees or other contingent liabilities. Secured debt also sometimes has liens on specific firm assets supporting the claim.

Credit Instruments

Bonds

Much of the corporate issuance is via bonds, which have contractually defined cash flows (like Treasuries) – coupon rate, maturity date, issue size, etc.; additionally, these bonds also have credit risk. So, the agreement formalizing the transaction, the *indenture* (or the *prospectus*[97], during price talk), is an important document which investors (and their lawyers) read in detail. This contains *covenants*, which detail what happens if the borrower does not pay lender dues, and if the bond is secured by certain assets (or not). Many of the terms are boilerplate, but a term sheet laying out the important commercial terms is usually circulated to prospective investors. The bond issue is initially floated with a range of yields/ spreads (*price talk*), and the issue size and the yield are finalized after assessing investor demand.

Analytically, corporate bonds are similar to Treasuries, where the promised cash flows are spelt out, and then a yield (i.e. discount rate) is backed out, at which the discounted cash flows line up with the current price. To compensate investors for bearing the credit risk of the issuer, this yield is higher (i.e. price is lower) than what it would have been if the bond with the same terms had been issued by the Treasury. Like other bond instruments, investors will earn the yield (ignoring reinvestment risk) if they hold the bond to maturity, but they are exposed to bond price fluctuations before maturity if the bond yield changes because of market conditions. Like other (non-Treasury) fixed income securities, the yield of any corporate bond can be decomposed into the similar duration Treasury yield and a spread. The decision to buy a particular corporate bond is based on whether this spread is adequate compensation for the risk of the issuer/ bond, and if this spread is likely to tighten on not. Of course, interest rate movements also change the yield of the bond[98] and have a significant effect on bond total returns, so corporate bond investors either hedge the interest rate risk actively (by being short Treasuries) or end up taking an (long) interest rate view implicitly by being long the bond.

Corporate bonds come in many variants – while most coupons are fixed, bonds with *floating rate* coupons (typically indicated as LIBOR + fixed Spread) are also seen. The floating-rate bonds have very little interest rate risk, since the coupon resets to reflect the current LIBOR periodically. However, like fixed-rate bonds, they continue to have exposure to spread volatility, since the spread is fixed at the original spread at issuance,

---

[97] For loans, the corresponding document is called an *Information Memorandum (IM)* or *bank book*. Loan documents may contain material non-public information, so a version of the IM is also created only containing public information for investors who do not want to be constrained in trading the issuer's bonds or stock, by receiving private information.

[98] Credit bonds (which have a fixed coupon rate), like most other fixed income instruments, have interest rate duration and are exposed to rate movements; higher spread bonds have less rate sensitivity.

Other Fixed Income Markets

even when the LIBOR component resets. Companies whose revenues are related to market interest rates (e.g. banks) may be interested in issuing floating rate bonds. Subsequently, if the corporate is worried that rates will rise suddenly and cause its interest outflows to go up, it can hedge itself by paying fixed (i.e. the swap rate) in the interest rate swap market, and receiving LIBOR. Corporates sometimes take advantage of favorable issuance conditions in one market versus another, and entire into offsetting transactions in the interest rate swap market.

A corporate issuer, based on the terms at initial issuance, may be able to buy back/redeem its bonds (i.e. call back these *callable bonds*) at a price pre-decided at issuance (the *call price*). The issuer is likely to do so in low-yield (low interest rates and/or low spread) regimes, since they can now issue bonds at lower yields / coupons and save interest costs. Such a bond would have been cheaper to begin with, at issuance, since the bond's price is implicitly capped close to the call price and will not rise as much as a non-callable bond when market yields decrease.

Corporates also issue hybrid securities such as *convertible bonds* (i.e. *converts*) and *preferred stock* (i.e. *preferreds*). We have discussed these earlier in Chapter 2; we repeat that here for completeness. A convertible bond is a bond with the additional provision that it can be converted into shares (at the investor's option; but, the issuer can force conversion under certain situations) at a fixed share price (i.e. one bond equals a fixed number of shares), usually well above the share price of the company's stock when the bond was issued. This bond also pays a coupon like a regular bond, but the coupon (more specifically, yield) on the bond is lower than a bond without the conversion feature. While regular bonds have no upside beyond the timely payment of interest and principal, the investor in the convert can benefit if the company does really well and the stock shoots up. If the stock goes down instead, this functions like a regular bond (albeit at a lower yield), so the downside is likely lower than the stock (i.e. the bond floor kicks in). High yield corporates usually issue converts when they want to take advantage of a run-up in their stock price or their stock price volatility and pay a below-market coupon. Investors closely monitor the *premium* i.e. the difference between *parity* (number of stocks one can get times the current stock price) and the market price of the convert. The premium should usually expand when the stock price goes down, and shrink when the stock price increases.

Preferred stock is similar to a bond, with a stated coupon (usually higher than a regular bond), principal and maturity (sometimes perpetual, with a call feature). The coupons payments are optional for the company; non-payment does not constitute a default and preferred stock holders cannot initiate bankruptcy proceedings; this is why the coupons are higher. However, the coupons are cumulative, so if the company does not pay the preferred holders one period, it has to make good on multiple payments the next time it pays. Also, the company cannot declare a dividend to ordinary stockholders before paying off the preferred dividends. Analysts and regulators do not treat preferred stock as debt, since payments are optional, so the company appears less indebted on paper.

Companies, especially in the financial services industry, issue several other less common securities, such as Co-Cos (Contingent Convertible), AT1s and warrants, but we skip these in this book. Start-ups often issue convertible preferred shares, which allows the venture capitalist the seniority above the equity if the company is liquidated, but also the opportunity to convert the investment into stock if the company performs well.

Capital Markets and Investments

Loans[99]

Loans are secured, floating-rate paper issued by high-yield borrowers at a spread over LIBOR[100]. They are often callable near par, and have restrictive covenants about the use of proceeds, as discussed above. Issuers usually *reprice* (i.e. call back, and replace) loans when the company's spread tightens. Loans are also often paid down if the company has excess cash flow, conducts asset sales or issues equity/ debt, according to the terms of the agreement. While loans are at the top of the capital structure; they are often issued by the riskiest companies, so are often not of high credit quality. Aside from the spread over LIBOR, loans (and bonds) may be issued at an *Original Issue Discount* (OID), below par. Some loans also have other fees (that the issuer bears, and the lender earns), such as up-front fee, commitment/ ticking fee, facility fee, etc. Many of these fees exist because the borrower is not required to borrow all the money right away (and pay interest), yet the lender has to keep the money ready, since the borrower can ask for it anytime. These fees are more common with revolvers and working capital loans, which even firms with good credit quality routinely use.

Loans used to be primarily financed by banks in the 1980s; the market expanded dramatically in the late-1990s after loan documents got standardized and syndicated. The securitization market also picked up in the late 1990s; the popularity of CLOs (discussed below) led to a huge demand for loans. Loans had traditionally been a fully private market (i.e. the loan buyer/ lender had *material non-public information* about the issuer, similar to a bank or a rating agency, since the loan covenants required this level of disclosure), but as the loan market attracted more institutions, the concern about some investors (current holders) having private information whereas others (prospective buyers) did not. Further, since some investors transact in both bonds and loans, they cannot be privy to non-public information if they want to keep trading bonds. Some investors sign *big-boy* letters agreeing to transact in loans, although there may be information they are not privy to. Loan issuers who have bonds or stock outstanding also try to make information widely available soon after they have announced anything material to loan holders, through a press release or 8K.

As discussed above, loans, like high yield bonds, have covenants to protect investor interests. Unlike bonds, loans have maintenance covenants (which are more stringent), collateral and mandatory prepayments clauses (to pay down loans with excess cash flow). Loan agreement terms are often changed with a lender vote; different amendments require different levels of approval. In "hot" markets when investors are bidding up new issue loans, *covenant-lite loans*, which have covenants comparable to high yield bonds or even weaker, become more common.

While the loan market has become more standardized and institutional, it remains an illiquid clumsy secondary market, with scarce liquidity, and settlement periods anywhere from a week to months[101]. Over the last two decades, CLOs (discussed in the section on securitization) have emerged as the biggest buyer of loans.

Credit Default Swaps (CDS)

A CDS is an OTC derivative contract between two parties, where one party (the *protection buyer*, who is short risk) pays the other (the *protection seller*, who is long risk) a periodic *premium* (similar to a coupon payment) for a certain *term* (1 year, 3 years, 5 years, etc.). During this term, if the *reference entity* (similar to the underlying in other derivatives) defaults (we'll get into more specifics later), the CDS *triggers* and the protection buyer can deliver one of the eligible bonds (reference obligation or any other bond parri passu to the *reference obligation*) issued by the reference entity and will get paid par from the protection seller; if there is no default during the term, the protection seller gets to keep the premia and needs to pay back nothing. The reference entity and

---

[99] Legally, loans are not securities, but we will ignore that technical detail.

[100] Loan coupons usually have a *LIBOR floor* of 1%, so if LIBOR trades below 1%, the coupon rate is calculated as if LIBOR is at 1%.

[101] Recently, there has been some talk of Blockchaining technology being used to smoothen this process.

Other Fixed Income Markets

reference obligation are clearly stated in the original contract. CDS, like an insurance contract, provides protection from the default of the reference entity in exchange for the periodic premium; further, the protection seller's payoff resembles that of a long bondholder, who receives a periodic coupon, but loses much of his principal (except for recovery). Since the spread is fair compensation for the default risk, this contract, like other swaps, has zero NPV at inception. The CDS premium serves as compensation to the protection seller for bearing the default risk of the instrument. This default risk (at least the perception) changes continuously, so the premium should change very frequently to keep this a fair "zero NPV" contract.

Now, if the premium were to change continually and every contract traded with a different premium (since it was entered into at a different time), it would be inconvenient and hinder liquidity[102], so market participants have made minor changes to the above construct. Over the last several years, CDS contracts, while still OTC, have become more standardized. Contracts now have a standard fixed annual coupon (i.e. premium), either 100bp (for IG names) or 500bp (for HY credits), and standard coupon payment/ expiration dates. The difference between the fair spread for default risk compensation (as discussed in the paragraph above) and the stated contract premium (100 or 500, as the case may be) for the specified term is converted to its equivalent NPV and paid or received upfront. So, under these conventions, cash is exchanged at inception. As an example, if the fair spread is 900bp (flat credit spread term structure), and the CDS coupon is 500bp per annum for a 5-year contract[103], this translates to a bond-equivalent price of 86[104]; the protection buyer has to pay the protection seller 14 *points upfront*. If the spread widens the next day to 1000bp and protection buyer wants to unwind the contract, he executes another contract as the protection seller and will receive 16.36 points upfront; this effectively unwinds the trade (since the coupon payments from the two contracts will now offset exactly, both in amount and timing).

Pricing aside, there are other important details regarding CDS, such as the circumstances under which they trigger (i.e. a *credit event* occurs). The two most common US corporate CDS triggers include the issuer filing for bankruptcy and failure to pay (interest or principal) and moratorium. Some CDS (usually European names) have restructuring (mod-R), obligation acceleration, sovereign CDS have repudiation, etc. Some European reference entities have senior CDS and sub-CDS, where the sub CDS can trigger without the senior triggering. The exact reference entity of the CDS is also important, especially in issuers with multiple subsidiaries. Large financial firms cannot trade their own CDS, because it is believed that they can take actions that cause technical defaults leading to CDS triggering (and CDS holders making/ losing money), without other material consequences.

The ISDA Determinations Committee (DC) votes to decide whether a credit event has occurred. Upon triggering, CDS settlement can be either physical or cash. The textbook physical settlement involves the protection seller delivering one of the eligible bonds and getting the par value in cash, so the effective value of the CDS after default is the difference between par value and the projected recovery. In reality, in many reference entities, the amount of CDS open interest (similar to outstanding) is larger than the debt issued by the company, so the settlement process itself can lead to an artificial scarcity of the bonds. To avoid this, CDS

---

[102] The interest rate swaps market has continuously changing swap rates and investors figure out the NPV difference arising from rate movements from contract inception date to current date, and pay/ receive the difference to unwind or novate the contract. While this can also work in the CDS world (and it did, before the 2009 *Big Bang/ Standard North American Contract* or *SNAC*), it just gets messier because there are so many reference entities (companies) rather than only the one swap rate term structure.

[103] Think of this as a bond with a yield of 9% paying a coupon of 5%.

[104] The bond-equivalent value 86 or (14 points upfront =100-86) is not visually obvious; it's based on a NPV calculation. Bloomberg customers use CDSW to convert running spreads to points upfront.

Capital Markets and Investments

can also settle in cash, following a two-step auction process to determine the recovery rate that the market expects. So, just like the probability of default, the recovery rate plays an important role in CDS pricing.

CDS contracts are unfunded derivatives, so it allows investors to take on (or protect themselves from) credit risk without putting down cash (although it takes up risk capital). Interest rate risk (or even the concept of yield) is not relevant for CDS, because it isolates only the credit risk of the issuer (reference entity). While CDS (running) spreads should be close to spreads (over LIBOR) of bonds issued by the same issuer, there are a few reasons why they are not be exactly the same (the arbitrage trade is often not precise and easy to implement); the difference between CDS and the bond spread[105] is referred to as the *CDS- cash basis*[106]. This is because liquidity differences exist between CDS and bonds, the CDS cash flows (upon default) may be different from bond cash flows since the bond may not be trading near par, bonds have covenants so a cheapest-to-deliver type issue can occur, bonds are difficult to short - financing and borrow costs also affect the basis, credit products have high transaction costs.

Indices of CDS (i.e. a preset portfolio of single-name CDS constituents) are more common and liquid; we introduce them in the section on securitization, when we discuss CDX.

Market Dynamics and Liquidity

Every credit market has its own specific details, and works very differently; it is very difficult to scratch the surface and keep the discussion short and pointed while doing justice to the topic. That said, we mention a few broad ideas and emerging trends below.

The credit markets are *far less liquid* (i.e. less easy/ costly to transact in) than many other markets, such as equity, Treasuries or mortgages. The differences between equity and fixed income, from a liquidity standpoint, relate to the *market fragmentation* (as well as the exchange versus OTC issue). In equity, every issuer usually has just one instrument outstanding; for prolific fixed income issuers such as GE, that number could be several hundred! So, the market volume and attention gets divided across many more issues, and often manual intervention by a broker is necessary to align the buyer and seller on a particular position. This is also the issue with Treasury bonds and mortgages, but investors are more inclined to accept most of the Treasury issues as close substitutes (true to a large extent with GE, but there may be different "boxes"); the *recently issued* "on-the-run" instruments account for a large proportion of the trading volume; the *liquidity is concentrated* there. This liquidity (or the lack of it) shows up in *bid-offer spreads* and *trading volume*. In credit markets, though, bid-offer spreads are not binding, and the real levels are evident only when an investor actually tries to trade. Before the 2008 crisis, broker-dealers would find it financially compelling to buy bonds from one investor, hold them temporarily and sell to another (i.e. use their balance sheet), thereby making it easier for investors to trade in and out of positions. Post crisis, regulatory burdens for the dealers has made this much more difficult; most orders are "worked" or traded on an agency basis to find the other side. This has coincided with apparently tighter bid-ask spreads (suggesting better liquidity) on the dealer runs, questioning the efficacy of the entire quoting mechanism in credit. Analysts now believe that, aside from default risk, a significant component of spreads now also need to compensate investors for liquidity risks.

Liquidity in credit markets is *not uniform*; there is a gradation. Bonds are more liquid than loans, higher quality and larger issuers are more liquid than lower quality and smaller issuers, and for a given issuer, benchmark

---

[105] To be precise, CDS-cash basis usually refers to the difference between the CDS premium and the Asset Swap Spread of the cash bond. The Asset Swap is a transaction when the buyer of a bond pays the bond's coupons for the term of the bond in exchange for LIBOR + the Asset Swap Spread.

[106] *Basis* is a generic term describing the price difference between an unfunded (*synthetic*) and funded (*cash*) instrument; we used it to discuss the difference between Treasury cash bonds and futures.

Other Fixed Income Markets

(similar to on-the-run) and global issues are more liquid that non-benchmarks. Corporate credit bonds settle T+2.

Within the credit bond markets, IG bonds are relatively liquid. They are quoted at a spread over Treasuries, which reflects the compensation for the incremental risk that investors are taking on, beyond the interest rate risk and time value of money that Treasuries compensate for. The highest quality IG bonds trade almost like Treasuries, with credit e-trading platforms making quotes available. Like Treasuries, a particular bond is colloquially referred to by its issuer, coupon and maturity.

HY bonds are quoted on a dollar price basis, which makes sense since the primary risk in these bonds is issuer specific. These bonds trade largely over phones/ chat. The least liquid high-yield bonds trade by appointment.

Loans are an especially illiquid market. Since they are floating rate, and do not remain outstanding for very long in a benign market environment (because they get called/ repriced), they are often priced close to par. But, during periods of illiquidity in 2008 and later, despite being at the top of the capital structure, loans have traded down significantly, albeit with little or no associated volume. While there is a secondary market, the loans settle in weeks, if not months[107]. LSTA, the main association for loan traders, is setting up a scheme to compensate the buyer for settlement delays. Loans trade on phones and BWICs.

Since credit is a bilateral OTC market, it can potentially be opaque, with a seller/ buyer not knowing what the fair price for a specific instrument is. Since the early 2000s, this (big) problem has been resolved through the TRACE system, managed by FINRA, where every trade needs to be reported within 15 minutes of execution, indicating price, size and whether it was another dealer or a buy-side customer on the other side. TRACE does not publicly publish order sizes for large orders, capping the display at 5+mm for IG and 1+mm for HY. MSRB plays a similar role for the municipal bond market.[108]

CDS is traded in spread/ point upfront terms for both IG and HY names. When CDS was introduced, it was envisaged to be a liquid mechanism to trade single name credit. For several years, that appeared to be the case. The liquidity in the single-name market disappeared post 2008. Market participants tried standardizing the contracts (*Big Bang/ SNAC*), but the liquidity did not return. Much of this has got to do with dealer balance sheets shrinking because of regulation, but it also reflects some concern that CDS exposures are bilateral, with significant counterparty risk. Regulators have required CDX Indices to be cleared centrally through a swap execution facility (similar to interest rate swaps), so that the risk is mutualized and borne by the clearinghouse, but single name CDS has still not completed the transition.

Default risk aside, Liquidity Risk has become more important in fixed income, especially corporate credit bonds, because of the reasons discussed about. Over the past few years, several analytics providers have started providing scores to measure bond level liquidity; ingredients include trading volume, age, amount outstanding, bid-offer spreads, number of dealers quoting, etc. Liquidity Cost Scores (LCS), introduced by Barclays, is arguably the most popular. Quantitative measures of liquidity have allowed analysts to decompose the total spread into default and liquidity components.

While electronic trading is still at its infancy in the corporate bond market, about 20% of the investment grade bond market and 6% of the high yield bond market trades electronically.[109] The obstacles to widespread adoption of electronic platforms include the fragmentation in the market with the large number of issuers and bonds, but only a few of them trade actively (yet many can be considered close substitutes). At the same time,

---

[107] The LSTA states that 27% of loans close to par settle in more than 20 days.

[108] Surprisingly, Treasury trades are not posted anywhere!

[109] In contrast, foreign exchange is an OTC market where over 75% of the trading is done electronically.

since the regulatory constraints of the dealers have reduced their ability to warehouse bonds and provide two-way liquidity, some of these platforms may help investors find a market participant willing to take the other side more easily. Dealers have been transitioning some of their equity electronic trading staff to build fixed income platforms. MarketAxess, Electronifie, TruMid (and more recently Tradeweb) are some of the prominent third-party platform providers.

Credit Analytics

Like all fixed income instruments, credit instruments are also compared based on yields and spreads. *Spreads* can be defined several ways – yield spread, z-spread and OAS. We discussed these different spread measures in the section on *Valuing MBS* in *Mortgages*, earlier in this chapter. While the option-adjustment in the case of MBS relates to the prepayment option, in case of credit bonds, it relates to other embedded options such as callability, convertibility into stock, etc.

We discussed the concept of duration extensively when we covered the interest rate risk of Treasuries. Extending the idea to corporate bonds, we can compute a duration exactly similar to the duration calculation for Treasuries, but the (modified) duration here reflects the percentage price change for a one basis point change in this particular bond's yield (or yield curve)[110]. But, if we assume that a one basis point change in market interest rates leads to a 1bp change in this bond's yield (i.e. spread remains constant), then we can use analytical durations calculated the same way to measure interest rate sensitivity for corporate bonds.

Conceptually, we can discuss a credit bond's sensitivity to spread widening. This may be even more relevant, because most credit investors are more concerned about spread movements. Analytically, for a fixed rate bond with no embedded options, this is the same calculation as the interest rate duration (numerical values may be slightly different), because a one-basis point change in a bond's yield will have the same effect on a bond's price regardless of whether the change originates through spreads or interest rates (since yield is the arithmetic sum of both spreads and rates). This is the *spread duration* (or *CS01*, similar to DV01 for interest rate movements) of a bond; by interpreting this as the bond's price sensitivity to spreads, we are assuming that spread shocks translate one-for-one into yield shocks.

Importantly, for floating rate bonds, the concept changes. The interest rate component that is part of the coupon payment and the discount rate frequently updates, implying that there is very little interest rate sensitivity. But the credit spread that is part of the coupon payment is fixed at issuance for the life of the bond, whereas the spread that is part of the discount rate (which reflects current risk) continuously updates. So, for floating rate bonds trading close to par, the spread duration or CS01 remains significant, similar to a fixed rate bond, whereas the interest rate risk disappears.

The above spread duration (or CS01) metrics provide price sensitivities if the spreads move parallelly i.e. high spreads move by the same absolute amount as low spreads. This is not empirically true, as high spread bonds move more than low spread bonds when there is a spread shock; in fact the spread move happens to be close to proportional (i.e. if s denotes spreads, $\Delta s/s$ is a constant). Formalizing this by referring to Eq. 8.4, and adapting it for spreads (spreads move yields one-for-one if rates do not move).

$$\Delta P/P = -Spread\ Duration \times \Delta s \qquad \qquad \text{Eq. 10.4}$$

By multiplying and dividing by s, we can rewrite Eq. 10.4 as:

---

[110] In case of Treasuries, a one basis point shift in market interest rates translates to a 1bp shift in the particular bonds yields; in the case of the corporate bonds, (potentially negative) correlation between spreads and interest rates makes the effect on yields more ambiguous.

Other Fixed Income Markets

$$\Delta P / P = \underbrace{-Spread\ Duration \times s}_{DTS} \times \frac{\Delta s}{s} \qquad \text{Eq. 10.5}$$

Now, since $\Delta s/s$ is constant across positions, the relevant metric to track while measuring or neutralizing risk exposures is the product of spread duration and spread (also called *Duration Times Spread* or *DTS*). In the interest rate world, since rates usually move parallelly, Eq. 8.4 (a version of Eq. 10.4 using yield instead of spread) is more useful because Δy is constant across positions, so matching durations makes sense to hedge rates. Duration calculations for callable bonds gets more complicated; this is usually computed numerically similar to mortgage bonds, by first coming up with interest rate paths, then computing a OAS to match the bond price, then bumping the OAS up/down and repricing the bond.

Quantitative Credit

Credit investing is almost always fundamentals driven. IG investors often follow a top-down stratified sampling approach to get a sense of their portfolio characteristics (including risk measures), and compare it to a benchmark index. Many investors line up spreads next to fundamental credit metrics, within a sector, and use a simple relative valuation framework to pick a diversified portfolio of credits. More quantitative investors use techniques like the *Altman Z-score* (essentially a weighted average of financial accounting ratios, mapped to historical empirical default data) and the *KMV Distance-to-Default* (discussed below) ideas to pick names.[111]

The *Structural Model* simulates a distribution of firm values. In these frameworks, default occurs when firm value falls below the debt levels. KMV (subsequently bought by Moody's) pioneered this idea, where they computed how far any company was from defaulting, and formalized it in the Distance-to-Default concept (distance between firm value and debt value). They then used their historical default database to map Distance to Default to actual default probabilities (by checking how often firms with a certain specific "distance" defaulted in the next year, to ascertain if certain companies are trading rich or cheap (based on the default probabilities implied by their market spreads).

With the popularity of the CDS market, quantitative investing in credit was taking off pre-2007 (the crisis curtailed this significantly), with investors even betting on correlations of defaults in baskets of credit securities, introduced below in the section on structured credit below. The framework for these was a variant of the Structural Model above, referred to as *Reduced Form Hazard Rate Models*. In these models, default is simulated directly, with the arrival rates for default following a Poisson distribution (see Appendix 3 for details on probability distributions). Using an expected value-NPV type framework, these model parameters (usually assuming a recovery of 40% for IG and 30% for HY) are calibrated to market spreads to back out default probabilities (or survival rates) at different points in time. Default probabilities for different single names are calculated this way. Defaults in equally weighted portfolios (baskets) of single names are simulated using Gaussian (i.e. normally distributed) copulas (joint distributions), using t-distributed marginal distributions for each single name (with the default probabilities as calibrated above). This can generate loss distributions for portfolios, based on a correlation assumption; conversely market prices of various parts of these portfolios can be used to back out an implied correlation.

---

[111] Recently, investors have also begun mentioning factor models for credit, this mainly involves rules-based investing in a portfolio of bonds, depending on what risks these bonds are exposed to.

Capital Markets and Investments

Investing in Credit

The types of trades that Treasury investors usually participate in – yield-based, carry trades, steepener/ flattener, etc. are all applicable to credit investors. There are a few further considerations/ variants that we discuss below.

High Grade Investors

For all the details that we discussed above, most of credit investing is straightforward. Most credit issuance is by highly rated *investment grade* (IG) companies, and investors often follow a *top-down* approach by allocating positions using stratified sampling (or high-level metrics) to buckets of sector, rating, maturity and spread-bands, instead of dealing with issuer-level minutiae. Investors often carve out the investment grade universe into financials and non-financial issuers, since financial issuers are analyzed very differently from other industries. Many investors are benchmarked to an index, so they compare the characteristics of each of these buckets to those of analogous buckets of the benchmark. This approach works because these bonds are high up in the capital structure, with a large liability cushion below them, so they are insulated from most issuer-level shocks. It is not common for equities to move a lot, but bonds to remain unchanged because they are just as likely to get repaid.

Investment grade bonds trade at a *spread over Treasuries*, and is arguably the most important metric investors look at to decide whether the bond is worth buying. Without new information about this issuer or changes in investor's risk perception, this spread (low to begin with) doesn't move much day over day, on an absolute level. But, Treasuries move by the minute (hedging flows, macro news, etc.), thereby changing the yield of the bond. Since bonds are ultimately priced off yields, an unhedged high-quality IG bond is almost like a Treasury bet. For investors that want exposure to only the credit, they *hedge their interest rate risk*, often by going short the Treasury to which this bond is benchmarked. For an IG portfolio, interest rate risk is monitored separately, and often neutered by hedging based on key-rate durations (discussed in Chapter 8). For benchmarked investors, interest rate risk relative to the benchmark (which often also has interest rate risk) is the relevant exposure. Of course, this is a non-issue for floating-rate bonds.

New issue Flips

All credit investors (IG, HY, bond, loan, convert, etc.) routinely mechanically invest in the primary market in new issues, even if they do not want to hold the position long term. The perception is that "hot" new issues with a lot of investor demand will trade up on issue, and they can flip (i.e. sell out of) the position in a day at a profit. Buy-side trading desks maintain good relationship with the sell-side, which helps get good allocations. Of course, this does not work all this time (some new issues trade down), but it works often enough for it not to be ignored.

High Yield Investors

Unlike IG investors, HY investors need to understand their credits well and take active views on the name, because these names are more likely to default. These analysts are more bottom-up, and examines the entire gamut of capital structure, covenants, business risk, relative value, collateral and asset coverage, etc. In practice, most fundamentally-focused professionals will build cash flow models for the next 3-4 years, and apply multiples to the projected accounting/ cash flow variables to arrive at an enterprise value (which comprises of the value of debt and equity, which can be subtracted out)[112]. Interest rate hedges are not nearly as important, because these bonds have more issuer-specific risk and trade on price; further, rate movements and spread movements are negatively correlated in the medium term, because rates usually rise when the economy is doing well (stagflation aside), which drives down the spreads of these risky issuers. In fact, the *empirical*

---

[112] The market value of equity also gives analysts an idea of how much firm value exists beyond the unsecured debt.

Other Fixed Income Markets

interest rate duration is usually much lower than the ones published by the systems, because spread movements offset the rate move partially. These bonds are quoted on price and are often callable, unlike IG bonds which trade on spread. The OAS (Option Adjusted Spread) is a useful metric of value.

Convertible Bond Arbitrage

Convertible Bond Arbitrage (convert arb) used to be very popular pre-crisis (less so in the last few years), where an investor buys the convertible bond and goes short the stock, sizing the short using the *delta* (bond price sensitivity to underlying) to the underlying stock (discussed in the chapters on options) provided by the convert model (based on an option pricing model). Logically, if company does well, the convert will increase in value (and the short position in the stock will hurt i.e. the premium shrinks), but the delta on the convert will increase (the bond now behaves more like a stock as it is closer to conversion price), the position will be under-hedged and make money overall. Conversely, if the issuer performs poorly, the stock (in which the investor a short position), since it is lower in the capital structure, will likely go down more than the convert, which is protected by the bond floor (i.e. the premium increases). The convert delta will also shrink, causing the position to be over—hedged; the stock hedge should make more than the convert loses. So, by putting on this trade, the investor is essentially long convexity. But, if there is an exodus of investors from the credit/ convert market, the spreads can widen massively, more than the stock sells off, and the position will hurt. Alternatively, if the stock is already trading at a high price (so the bond is above par/ expensive to begin with), and the company gets taken over, this may cause the stock to rip and the bond to get taken out at par (based on covenants), making it very painful.

Basis Package

The difference between the spreads of the CDS contract and the cash bond is referred to as the basis. This basis is usually slightly negative because of the issues discussed in the section on CDS. But if the basis moves too much one direction, investors often take positions to bet on mean reversion of the basis. Alternatively, if the negative basis is too wide, ideally the investor can buy a 5-year par bond (with financing rate at LIBOR)[113] and buy protection (using CDS) on the entity[114], thus locking in a positive cash flow every period. If the entity defaults, the investor can deliver the bond and get back par, and use this to pay back the financing. This is trickier in reality because of bonds trading away from par (so principals will be mismatched), maturity mismatched between bond and CDS, transaction costs, and LIBOR changing after trade is initiated (since financing is shorter term than 5-years and needs to be rolled).

Passive Investing / Hedging

Credit investing has more frictions than many other liquid fixed income asset classes. Investors who are not fully dedicated to credit have historically found it more difficult to participate in this market. Understanding the market plumbing is complicated, as well as the number of coverage relationships that need to be maintained. Over the years, instruments have developed to overcome this.

The most common and straightforward passive representation, targeted towards retail investors, are the credit-focused *mutual funds* (mutual funds exist for almost all asset classes that can be invested without derivatives; we discuss them in Chapter 4). These funds are usually benchmarked to a common credit index, and the fund manager usually uses stratified sampling techniques to keep tracking error within acceptable limits.

Over the years, institutional investors have gained access to passive credit instruments. The most common passive credit instruments are the credit *ETFs* (we discuss ETFs in Chapter 4, and several other places in the

---

[113] In practice, a fixed rate bond will be converted to a LIBOR-based floating rate using the *asset swap* market.

[114] Negative basis implies that the coupon on a 5-year par bond is greater than the CDS premium.

book) used just as much by retail investors. Many prominent fund managers have sponsored several credit ETFs, with the universe segmented by quality, maturity, floating rate versus fixed, etc. These ETFs, like credit mutual funds, invest in the underlying bonds and can trade at a discount or premium to NAV, but offer intra-day liquidity. Some common credit ETFs include LQD (Investment Grade by iShares i.e. Blackrock), HYG (High Yield by iShares), JNK (High Yield by SPDR i.e. State Street) and VCIT (Investment Grade by Vanguard).

The two instruments above are funded, require an upfront cash investment and provide exposure to underlying credit bonds. A common mechanism to get *unfunded passive credit exposure* is to invest in the *CDX* IG or *CDX HY* Index, which are baskets/ indices of US Corporate CDS published by MarkIt[115]. The sell-side makes two-way markets on these indices, and investors can get long or short credit in synthetic form by taking positions in these indices (similar to cash settled futures, but trade OTC). Importantly, these indices have many fewer names – 125 for IG and 100 for HY - so the exposure is very different from the credit bond universe. In the recent series, MarkIt has tried to use names so that the sector weights are closer to the popular cash bond indices, so that bond investors can tactically hedge using CDX. New "series" of these baskets (with some changes to constituents) get published every March and September; many investors choose to "roll" their exposure from the older index to the current on-the-run series.

A recent instrument to get unfunded exposure is total return (index) swaps on the IBoxx IG (or HY or Loan) Total Return Index, with some sell-side firms beginning to make markets in them. While these swaps provide unfunded exposure, they reference an underlying cash bond index, thereby allowing investors to express an unfunded view without having to take exposure to CDS-cash basis.

Options are available on ETFs and CDX, with a couple of dealers quoting options on TRS.

Distressed investors

When bonds trade far below par, and the issuer has a serious chance of going bankrupt, distressed firms get active. Their work is a combination of fundamental research, capital structure analysis, legal and covenant review and what deals to strike with which creditor classes, when and how to approach the company, etc. This is very process-driven and illiquid and often takes years, but is idiosyncratic with large potential upside, if the assets were bought cheap. Some private equity players also have teams looking at this market.

SECURITIZATION

Securitization Overview and Motivations

Securitization forms the foundation of structured (credit and mortgage) products. It involves pooling together several stand-alone loans (or other securities that generate cash flows), and creating a composite asset pool from these stand-alone assets. In the simplest securitized products, bonds are issued (backed by this pool) and serviced using the cash flow streams of this composite asset.

Securitization enables the loan *originator* (the finance company that lends to the end-borrower) to get existing loans off its balance sheet (by selling these loans to the securitization entity), and get more cash to make additional loans. Normally, it would be tough for the originator to convince an investor to buy a loan because the investors would worry about *idiosyncratic risk* (what if something goes wrong with the end-borrower) and *moral hazard* (why will the originator lend responsibly, if the originator can turn around and sell the loan off, instead of owning the loan until it is paid off?). Aggregating these loans with several other loans in a pool reduces the idiosyncratic risk to the investor, since this loan is a small part of a large portfolio. Especially in

---

[115] MarkIt European IG and HY CDS Indices are called ITraxx Main and X-Over, respectively. Their US bond indices carry the IBoxx label.

Other Fixed Income Markets

consumer-related portfolios – residential mortgage, auto, credit cards, etc., there are hundreds/ thousands of loans.

The aggregation/ bond issuance is done through a bankruptcy remote Special Purpose Vehicle (SPV), often sponsored by an investment bank, which buys the stand-alone loans (assets) from the originator (often from multiple originators), and issues securities (liabilities)[116] backed by these assets' (also called collateral) periodic cash flows. The revenues from selling the liabilities to investors are used to buy the stand-alone loans. In the simplest case, the periodic cash flows from the assets are simply *passed through* to the security (i.e. liabilities) owners[117], but in many cases there are different kinds of securities that are issued, similar to a company's capital structure. If the bond holders may worry about the quality of the portfolio, the SPV may decide to divide up the liabilities, and issue a class of *junior* securities (let's call it "equity") carved out of the same assets cash flows, which takes the first hit (i.e. the *first loss*) in case of defaults, so the other securities do not get impaired. For this feature, the equity expects to earn a higher return than the bonds. However, the equity securities can take only a certain amount of loss before they are wiped out. Of course, the SPV could have a larger equity piece, but there will now be even lesser cash flow to go around for the bond holders (in case of no/ little default) since equity holders need to be paid, so fewer bonds can be issued (since the bond holders need a certain return/ cash flows). So, it is a balancing game; the SPV needs to issue enough equity to make the bondholders comfortable in buying bonds, but also needs to minimize the amount of equity it issues (equity is issued cheap, because it is riskier and demands a higher return) to maximize its profits. This sliver of equity makes bondholders comfortable that their returns will not be hurt, unless losses are very large (and the equity gets paid back nothing). Equity holders invest knowing fully well that they might eventually lose a majority of their par value because of losses, but the security is cheap enough that they are willing to enjoy the high initial equity cash flows (when all the assets are doing well) and hope that the high cash flows continue for an extra year or two beyond the base case.

In a sense, the SPV is like a company, which receives cash flow from its assets (instead of operations) and sells securities to fund (i.e. buy) these assets, and pays the security holders a return. In some cases, the SPV sponsor may retain a slice of the equity, mitigating the moral hazard issue raised earlier. After paying off the bondholders, the SPV splits any residual cash flows (if any) between the equity and the SPV/ sponsor itself, based on prior arrangement. There are several bells and whistles to this basic structure (e.g. reserve accounts need to be funded before the equity gets paid, so the bondholders have a buffer of cash), which we will gloss over.

One detail here, which doesn't change the basic idea but takes it further, is that the SPV can potentially issue many more types of securities, essentially all bonds with different coupons, but having different priority of receiving payments. This matters if losses in the assets are high enough to completely wipe out the equity (not uncommon since the equity is usually not a large amount), and then the *junior*-most bond effectively becomes the first loss piece. This class of bonds now get impaired until it is completely eroded, after which the next higher class of bonds begins to take the hit on losses. These different slices are referred to as *tranches*, and the process is called *tranching*. The liability structure in which junior securities need to get wiped out by losses before the next higher class of bonds are affected is referred to as *sequential pay*; tranches that are supposed to take losses last are the most senior. Each of these tranches often has a different rating by the rating agencies, and is referred to by its rating or by labels such as super-senior, senior, mezzanine, equity, etc. Tranches above

---

[116] The portfolio that generate cash flows for the SPV is called its *assets*; the securities that the SPV issues and has to pay out cash to are called its *liabilities*.

[117] In some situations, like in mortgages, the asset cash flows are enhanced by third-party guarantees.

Capital Markets and Investments

the most junior (equity) piece are said to be *overcollateralized*; because some collateral can take losses before the tranche is impaired. According to investor terms in some structures, the senior-most liabilities need to be paid down at par when the junior bonds take losses beyond a certain level, thus protecting them even further.

Another detail, less relevant today, but very important pre-2008, is that the assets in the securitization pool need not be funded assets like bonds and loans. In fact, CDOs, which we will discuss later, were primarily created using single name CDS as the assets, and the premiums for those single name CDS served as asset cash flows.

Why does Securitization Work?

The reason securitization works is because investor markets are segmented (Chapter 4 discussed this), so there are certain classes of constrained investors, who are investing in a particular securitized market as a "tourist", to get some extra yield. They do not want to understand the ins-and-outs of the underlying assets in the SPV, and are satisfied with a moderate return. There may be other investors who specialize in understanding the collateral, and are happy to take on the equity risk. The reality is that most capital is of the former kind (non-specialists), which is why the bonds (which are protected from first loss) are priced high (and returns, while satisfactory to the investors, are not very high compared to the asset cash flows), and the equity is priced low (offering a high return relative to cash flows). In effect, this is an *arbitrage* trade for the SPV (i.e. its sponsor), because it gets cash inflows from assets, pays its liabilities (and servicing costs, if any), and has cash left over.

> *Example:* Figure 10.4 shows a simple securitization structure visually, using hypothetical numbers. The structure initially owns 500mm of assets, paying L+350 per annum. Aside from the equity, it has 462.5mm of liability tranches at different spreads, with a weighted average of L+195[118]. So, the cash inflows from assets are 17.5mm (i.e. 500*0.0350), and outflows to liabilities are 9mm[119]. Assuming no other costs (reserve accounts, fees, etc.), the equity gets 8.5mm every year. Now, the equity has paid 37.5mm upfront (which, like the liability proceeds, is used to buy assets), so equity holders expect to break even in 3.5-4.5 years (if the entire pool survives that long)[120]. If the pool survives beyond that, the equity holders get a large return (22.67%), since equity investors keep earning 8.5mm for each year that the portfolio does not take losses[121]. The AAA investors are getting paid L+150bp and the BB tranche is getting L+500bp, which is likely comparable to/ better than what they could get elsewhere for similar risk.
>
> The equity tranche is the first loss piece and begins to start incurring capital loss from the first loss (0%) until 37.5/500 (or 7.5%), at which point it is completely wiped out. So, in this example, 0% and 7.5% would be the *attachment point* and *detachment point*, respectively, for the equity tranche. The equity tranche would also be referred to as the *0 -7.5% piece*. Similarly, the BB tranche comprises 7.5 – 11.5%, the BBB comprises 11.5 – 17.8%, A is 17.8 – 23.8%, AA is 23.8 – 29% and AAA is 29 – 100%.
>
> Eventually, portfolio losses begin to creep up. Figure 10.5 shows the structure after 10% of the assets have defaulted, and the total remaining assets at $450mm. In a standard sequential-pay structure, losses reduce the equity tranche first, and the higher-in the-capital-structure liability tranches preserve their value until the equity is wiped out. With a $50mm loss, the equity (which had contributed 37.5mm) is actually wiped out, and the BB tranche has lost $12.5mm (62.5%) of its principal and is

---

[118] This example could just as easily have been created with fixed rate asset and liabilities.

[119] L is assumed to be 0 in this math. Any value of L affects the assets and the liabilities equally, since it is passed through.

[120] $37.5 \div 8.5 = 4.4$. This ignores discounting

[121] This is because of the benefits of leverage, which we discuss more fully in the next chapter on equities.

Other Fixed Income Markets

now thinner. It is said to be trading with a *factor* of 37.5[122]. Of course, the attachment and detachment points now change for every tranche.

Figure 10.4 Securitization Initial Cash Flows

Capital Structure	Initial Size
AAA at L+150	355
AA at L+200	26.25
A at L+300	30
BBB at L+400	31.25
BB at L+500	20
Equity (Unrated)	37.5
Total	500

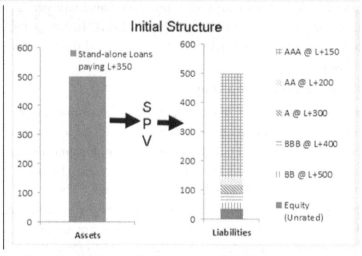

Figure 10.5 Securitization Cash Flows After 10% Losses

Capital Structure	Size post 10% Default
AAA at L+150	355
AA at L+200	26.25
A at L+300	30
BBB at L+400	31.25
BB at L+500	7.5
Equity (Unrated)	0
Total	450

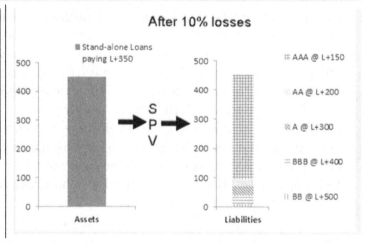

Different Types of Securitization Structures***

There are various different kinds of securitized products, across different asset classes. They use the general framework described above, but add bells and whistles to cater to the needs of their specific asset classes and investors. We mention some of them below, in a few sentences.

MBS

We've discussed the broad structure of mortgage securities earlier; essentially "similar" mortgages are pooled together, and bonds are issued against the cash flows from the pool. Tranched liabilities can be issued against pools of these mortgages (instead of simple pass-through securities); these are referred to CMOs.

---

[122] 37.5=100-62.5. In many securitization structures, there is no explicit equity tranche with a residual claim on cash flows. The first loss tranche also has a specified coupon, and excess spread of the assets over the liabilities is used to build reserves and serves as a cash flow buffer in case of losses.

Capital Markets and Investments

Collateralized Mortgage Obligations (CMOs)

Sometimes, mortgage-backed bonds are put into a trust (as assets in the above securitization example, (often called REMICs in this situation), and the trust issues tranched bonds like the example above. In the above example, tranching addressed credit risk, but credit risk is not an issue in the agency MBS market. The purpose of the tranches in the agency MBS market is to allocate prepayment risk across different bonds/ investors, who are in the best position to manage it (and will therefore require the least compensation to bear the risk). So, one way to understand risk in a CMO tranche is to track the variability of average life across various prepayment scenarios.

The simplest CMO structure is a *Sequential* pay structure, where the collateral's principal is divided into different tranches, paid out sequentially over time. Any given tranche receives principal only after the previous tranche has been completely paid down; all tranches but the one being currently paid are "locked out". Once we assume a prepayment speed, the thickness of any tranche is set to meet a certain average life[123] target for that tranche (except the last tranche, the *last cashflow sequential*, whose thickness and average life depends on the thickness of the other tranches).

The average life of the various tranches changes with prepayment speed assumptions. The shorter sequentials have tight prepayment windows, so their average lives vary less. The average life of the intermediary tranches vary the most; the extension on the last cash flow is limited by the underlying loan's maturity. Different investor types (money market funds, bank, insurance companies, etc.) prefer tranches with different average lives; sequential tranching weakens the connection between the average life of the bonds from the underlying's coupon or refinancing terms. The principal lock-out makes a sequential behave more like a bullet that regular mortgage collateral. This makes CMOs especially interesting in a steep yield curve environment relative to mortgages, since TBAs will not roll down as well as locked-out CMO tranches.

Planned Amortization Classes (PACs) are tranches designed to provide even more stable cash flows (i.e. protect against prepayment speed variability than sequentials. The complementary *Support/ Companion* tranche is therefore more exposed to prepayment risk. The PAC has a target principal payment at each point in time, based on a prepayment speed assumption. If prepayments are more than the target amount (i.e. speeds are faster), then the support tranche receives the excess cash flow beyond the target. If speeds are too slow, then the support does not receive any principal until the PAC is caught up and back on schedule.

PACs are specified in terms of PSA prepayment speed bands (e.g. 100-250 PSA). For any future time period, the PAC schedule is set by considering the maximum that can be paid out at that time if the prepayment speeds are anywhere between the upper and lower limits of the band. So, within those bands, the PAC is expected to pay on schedule[124]. If prepayment speeds are faster than the upper limit of the bound, the PAC will initially pay on schedule, but the support bond will also receive principal payments and get depleted very quickly. Once the support is gone, this becomes a busted PAC, and trades like a regular bond. PACs can also be sequentially tranched (they have a common support).

CMO structurers usually allocate coupons in a different proportion to these tranches that the principal payments; this is referred to as *coupon stripping* (up or down). This is another lever to control the price of the bonds at issuance, since most investors often prefer buying bonds close to/ below par (often for tax reasons). In the extreme, *interest–only* (IO) and a *principal-only* (PO) tranche can be created. The IO pays a coupon as long as the mortgage keeps paying interest (is current), and the PO receives only the principal and gets a large lump-

---

[123] Average life is a similar concept to Macaulay Duration. In this market, investors look at average life more often than duration.

[124] If prepayment speeds are within the band but not constant, there is no guarantee that the PAC can pay on schedule.

Other Fixed Income Markets

sum payment upon prepayment. If interest rates decline, this suggests faster prepayment speeds; so the value of the IO goes down (since interest stream is expected to get cut short) and the PO value goes up. So, an IO tranche has negative duration and negative convexity[125]; the PO has positive duration and positive convexity (similar to a zero-coupon bond). Coupon stripping can also be applied to create (LIBOR linked) *floaters* and *inverse floaters*. The inverse floater has a coupon cap (i.e. *Cap – LIBOR*), since its coupon cannot be negative and the total coupon payment needs to equal the underlying coupon payment[126]. So, high coupon bonds are prime candidates for coupon stripping.

Commercial Mortgage Backed Securities (CMBS/ CMBX)

Commercial mortgaged-backed securities (CMBS) are bonds whose payments derive from a loan or a pool of loans on *commercial* real estate[127]. The CMBS market exists for the same reason that the residential MBS (RMBS) market does – to free up the originating lender's capacity to lend more, and because there are willing investors to invest in that asset class. The big differences between the RMBS and the CMBS market is that the CMBS pools are usually much more concentrated than residential pools, prepayment is a much smaller issue in CMBS because of stiff prepayment penalties and lockouts, and most of the risk borne by investors is credit risk, since very little of this market is guaranteed. Liabilities are serviced solely using the cash flows generated by the assets. In fact, lending agreements between the assets and the originators often incorporate additional safeguards (such as minimum cash balances, etc.) so that the loans are eligible to be put into a CMBS securitization. Because of the reduced role of the government agencies, the servicing of the loans is also an important investor concern. The master servicer, like with residential mortgages, collects principal and interest payments and deposits into the REMIC, but the role of the special servicer, who works out distressed loans to maximize recovery, is much more critical[128]. Figure 10.6 shows the main categories within the CMBS universe.

Figure 10.6 CMBS Sub-Categories

Category	% of market
Retail	25
Office	23
Multi family	15
Hotel	13
Mixed Use	10
Housing	3
Manufactured	3
Self Storage	3
Industrial	3
Other	2
Total Share	100

Source: CRE Finance Council

---

[125] IOs are negatively convex because prepayment speeds usually increase faster when rates go down, and decrease slowly when rates rise.

[126] Coupon rates may not add up directly, because the sizes of the floater and the inverse floater may be different; in some cases the inverse coupon can have a levered LIBOR effect (a scale factor) to allow for the creation of a larger floater.

[127] "Commercial real estate" includes both business properties and multi-family real estate such as apartment buildings.

[128] This is also true for private-label residential mortgages.

Capital Markets and Investments

The liabilities issued against the pool are usually sequentially tranched; each of these tranches is rated by the rating agencies. The AAA tranches are often labelled A-1, A-2, A-J, etc. Classes B, C, etc. represent the mezzanine and junior tranches, which are also referred to by their ratings. The most subordinated (often unrated) class is called the B-piece. In most cases, the special services owns a part of the B-piece, to align servicer incentives with the investor.

In other types of securitizations, the excess spread between the assets and the liabilities is either used as additional credit enhancement (e.g. build reserve accounts) or paid out to equity holders. In CMBS, this excess spread is sold as an interest-only class; there is no explicit residual claimant equity investor.

There are potential conflicts between CMBS participants (such as B-piece buyers, mezzanine buyers, and AAA investors). As an example, a AAA investor may want a delinquent loan liquidated so that the senior bond can get paid down while the B-piece investor (in the first loss position) may want the loan extended in the hope that the loan will improve. Conflicts can also exist involving the special servicer. Fees can be generated from a loan being placed with the special servicer even for a short time. Larger fees are generated by a modification that leads to an extension, lower interest rate, or principal pay down. Conflicts of interest involving the special servicer, B-piece buyer, and borrower may harm the interests of the senior bond holders.

The commercial mortgage market is predominantly a non-agency market, but there is a rapidly growing Agency component, comprising mainly Agency multifamily securitizations and securitizations based on small business collateral (part of CMBS because often secured by real estate). Like other forms of CMBS, prepayment is much less of an issue here. Even in these Agency-sponsored structures, credit risk is of primary importance because the agencies usually guarantee only the top of the capital structure.

The MarkIt iBoxx Trepp CMBS cash index comprises all non-IO CMBS securities (and its sub-divisions, such as the IG universe) is the standard benchmark index. CMBX is a synthetic index (published by MarkIt) referencing a basket the largest 25 CMBS deals. Tranches based off CMBX are also traded[129].

Asset-Backed Securities (ABS)

While all; securitized products are essentially securities backed by assets, the Asset Backed Securities (ABS) market formally primarily comprises securitizations of collateral/ assets such as credit card receivables, auto loans, equipment leases and student loans. More esoteric ABS (e.g. aircrafts) also exist; niche investors focus on these areas. Like other securitizations, the quality of the assets is far more important than the originator since the structure is secured by the assets and not the originator's balance sheet. The originator often gets financing cheaper through ABS, because the rating of these securitized tranches are often better than that of the originator. About three-quarters of the ABS issuance has average life of less than three years. Depending on the underlying asset, the pools may be heavily diversified with hundreds or thousands of loans, with very low concentrations, or less diversified concentrated pools with investment grade obligors, where it is less of a statistical distribution analysis and more bottom-up. Investors typically worry about delinquency rates, loss severity, prepayment characteristics, portfolio yield and spread, etc. Since the issuer is often the servicer of these pools, origination policies, underwriting guidelines, servicing infrastructure and collection procedures as well as the originator's reputation are also important.

Auto ABS, which comprises prime loans and leases and subprime loans, is currently the largest consumer new-issue ABS sector. Most issuers are captive financing arms of the auto makers. This is a typical sequential pay structure, with additional credit enhancements through cash reserve accounts, over collateralization and excess spreads. Prepayments are important, while a robust used-car market leads to high recovery of defaulted loans.

---

[129] There are some similarities with CDX, discussed later.

Other Fixed Income Markets

Credit card ABS, comprising bank cards and retail store cards, have shrunk since the 2008 financial crisis as credit card usage has shrunk, but remain a prominent part of the market. The important distinction with credit cards is that the loan balances are revolving, which is handled by a master trust. Multiple series of bonds are issued from the trust, which are supported by the cash flow from all the loans. The issuing bank maintains a pro-rata interest in the trust to align interest with the ABS investors. Since the underlying loans are revolving, the principal payments are separately stored in a reserve account, which are paid to the ABS investors on the maturity date of their bonds (similar to principal payments of any bond). Alternatively, these principal payment can also be used to purchase additional receivables for the trust.

Collateralized Loan Obligations (CLOs)

The basic structure of a CLO is similar to the other securitized products – the assets (collateral) are leveraged loans issued by high-yield companies. On the liability side, the SPV issues a series of notes to investors rated from AAA to B, representing sequentially tiered claims on the cash flows from these assets. Both assets and liabilities are usually floating rate (LIBOR-linked). There is also an equity tranche subordinated to the notes, which receives residual cash flows. CLO liabilities, like the assets, are also callable (equity holders decide to call), but have a non-call period. The CLO manager can continue to trade the initial collateral after the initial investments are made during the reinvestment period. After the reinvestment period, maturities and prepayments in the collateral pool are used to amortize the notes sequentially. Loans have to satisfy certain eligibility criteria to be included in the portfolio; the portfolio must also satisfy or maintain/improve certain concentration and quality tests. The manager receives a periodic fee and incentive payments based on the performance of the CLO.

Like other securitized products, the CLO is an attractive vehicle for the issuer because the investor clientele is segmented. AAA investors take on very little risk and are willing to participate in the senior part of the capital structure because it yields a little more than their alternative investment choices. If a large enough AAA tranche can be placed at a low spread (as discussed in **Figure 10.4**), this creates enough excess spread (between the assets and the AAA liabilities) that the lower-rated riskier tranches can get compensated adequately and have excess cash flows left over for the equity holders.

A CLO is a finite-life vehicles, which winds down after a pre-specified time (or sooner if it gets called, or amortizes if it fails an interest coverage test). It typically has a ramp-up period, re-investment period and amortizing period. CLO managers usually buy collateral and hold it in a "warehouse" several months before the CLO is launched. In situations when the CLO is not fully ramped-up (i.e. invested) at closing, CLOs often get an additional three to six months to fully invest (ramp up) the portfolio. During the re-investment period, the manager can reinvest loan principal payments/ sales proceeds into new collateral, subject to satisfying certain portfolio quality and cash flow tests (average life, overcollateralization, average rating, etc.). Aggregate portfolio statistics need to be kept within certain limits (or need to be improved if the limit has already been breached) before reinvestment is allowed. After the reinvestment period ends, during its amortizing period, the CLO has to use principal repayments and sales proceeds to sequentially redeem the liabilities, beginning with the most senior AAA liabilities. In most cases, CLOs are called by the equity holders soon after the reinvestment period ends (since paying down the AAA notes reduces the excess spread and hurts the CLO equity returns, as described above), but if the CLO lives through its reinvestment and amortization period, it needs to be redeemed by its final maturity date.

After the non-call period, a majority of CLO equity holders can direct the manager to redeem the liabilities; this happens when the economics of the equity tranche have deteriorated because the excess spread has gone down (either because the assets have repriced, or AAA notes have been paid down or liability coupon payments have gone up without a corresponding increase in asset coupons). This redemption is funded either by selling the assets or refinancing the entire capital structure by repricing it (at a tighter spread).

During the regular life of the CLO, the SPV receives payments from the collateral and pays the notes. Several Quality tests (Diversity, Weighted Average Life, %CCC, Max Rating Factor, etc.) and Coverage tests (Interest Coverage Ratio (IC) and Overcollateralization (OC)) need to be satisfied for the notes to be paid as per the original schedule. These structural safeguards were important in ensuring that the CLO noteholders did not face defaults during the 2008 financial crisis.

Typically, if a CLO is failing a Quality test, the manager may not trade except to improve the failing test, but no cash flows are diverted from the lower tranches to the senior parts. In contrast, Coverage tests protect the senior note holders. The OC tests measures the amount of notional of the assets (with haircuts for excess CCC and defaulted assets) and IC tests measures the amount of excess spread. Assets are usually valued at par, unless they are distressed, in which case they need to be marked to market. If these coverage tests are not satisfied, the interest payment to lower tranches are diverted to partially repay the senior-most notes, so that the tests are satisfied again.[130]

Collateralized Debt Obligations (CDOs), synthetic CDOs

This market is almost non-existent after the 2008 crisis, but we include it for the sake of completeness. In the case of CDOs, the collateral typically comprised bonds. The interest payment from the bonds were used to pay the interest on the liabilities. In many cases, the collateral was synthetic (i.e. single-name CDS), and the premium on the CDS was used to pay the interest on the liabilities. If a name in the collateral pool defaulted, the assets would reduce by the loss (i.e. par – recovery) incurred times the exposure to that name.

It was easy to create these synthetic CDOs for the sell-side pre-2008 crisis because they did not have to source physical bonds and build warehouses; this quicker process caused the market to grow massively.

CDX, Tranches - Bespokes

Every six months in March and September, MarkIt publishes CDX and ITraxx Indices comprising single-name CDS constituents. There are various types – CDX.IG comprising 125 equally weighted US Investment grade issuers, CDX.HY contains 100 US HY issuers, ITraxx Main contains European IG issuers and ITraxx X-Over contains European HY issuers. Indices with 5-year underlyings are most popular. These indices do not rebalance, but a new series of these indices (with some new constituents) is issued every 6 months. The constituents remain unchanged for a given series, unless there is a default (when a new *version* of the existing series, excluding the defaulted name, starts trading). Options are also traded on these CDX/ ITraxx indices.

The assets underlying a synthetic CDO are single name CDS contracts; any portfolio of single-name CDS can potentially fulfil this role. Liabilities can then be issued against this pool, with the CDS premia being the cash inflows from the assets. Applying the same principle, liabilities are issued against these CDX indices; equity, mezzanine and senior tranches are common and fairly liquid. The attachment and detachment points for these tranches depend on the specific underlying index (IG equity tranche has a 3% detachment point, whereas HY equity tranche has 15%). Like the original synthetic CDO market, tranches can also be issued against *bespoke* (custom) CDS portfolios too, instead of the CDX indices.

---

[130] The exceptions are the Interest Diversion/Par Preservation/Reinvestment Tests (similar to OC tests); if the portfolio fails these tests, interest cash flows are diverted to buy more assets rather than to redeem the senior notes.

Other Fixed Income Markets

Current Role of Regulation

Securitization was at the center of the 2008 financial crisis, and has consequently earned a bad reputation and significant regulatory scrutiny. One of the issues highlighted was that the sponsors had no incentive to prudently buy/ originate loans since they could offload all the risk to other investors. As a result, after years of discussion, regulators now insist that the sponsor (or an affiliate owns) 5% of any new deals, as a form of *risk retention*. This could either be a vertical slice (5% of every tranche) or the bottom 5% of the capital structure. This affects a range of securitization vehicles, from CLOs to CMBS.

CONCLUDING COMMENTS ON FIXED INCOME

Over the past four chapters, we have discussed the basics of bonds, the details of the Treasury market, how participants use fixed income instruments to express views and take / hedge risk, and an overview of the other prominent fixed income markets. This should equip readers to be fluent in fixed income, and enable them to read more advanced discussions on these topics. As a final note, Chapter 12, which discusses portfolio analysis, is just as relevant for fixed income assets, although it uses equity examples since the theory was developed with equities in mind. Readers interested in portfolio construction would do well to read that, almost as an extension of Chapter 5

REFERENCES

De Groot, Peter, A. Chan and J. Vallecillo. *Barclays Municipal Markets Primer*. Barclays Research

Sundaresan, Suresh. *Fixed-Income Markets and Their Derivatives*, Academic Press

Fabozzi, Frank. *Bond Markets, Analysis and Strategies*, Pearson

Maxwell, William & M. Shenkman. *Leveraged Financial Markets*

Antczak, Stephen J., D. Lucas & F. Fabozzi. *Leveraged Finance*. John Wiley & Sons

Kessler, Mike (2013). *Barclays CLO Market Mini Primer*

Preston, David. *Wells Fargo CLO Primer*

CRE Finance Council CMBS Primer

Gauthier, Laurent, A. Bisla & V. Prasad. *An Introduction to CMOs*. Morgan Stanley Research

Equity Markets

11. Equities - Valuation

Equities are certainly the most "popular" asset class, in terms of the attention it receives on the financial media. The equity market is generally considered a barometer of the economy's health. Below, we discuss what equities represent, and frameworks for valuing them. While this section assumes some familiarity with the first section (Chapters 1-5) and the annexures, it does not assume any knowledge from the chapters on fixed income, discussed earlier. Before moving on, students should make sure that they are fully familiar with the NPV, IRR and cash flow discounting concepts in Annexure 1.

WHAT IS EQUITY?

Early on in the book, in Chapter 1, we discussed the example of a young firm with ideas but no capital. It needs to raise capital from external investors to try to put these ideas to fruition. In return for the investors' capital, it promises the investors a part of the future cash flows of the project. When investors evaluate whether to participate in the investment, they assess the size and uncertainty of the future cash flows of the project, the portion of that cash flow that investors would be entitled to, the initial investment amount, and how much they could potentially earn elsewhere. Together, this information provides investors a perspective of risk and return, relative to other opportunities.

The specifics of the investment agreement (i.e. how, exactly, investor compensation is determined) defines the asset class. For example, if a fixed periodic cash flow is promised to the investor, regardless of how well the company performs, it is a debt contract. Alternatively, if the investors receive an ownership share of the firm in return for their investment, they are entitled to a proportion of residual firm earnings, after the firm pays out whatever it owes non-owners. This is an *equity* investment, as described in Chapter 2. The company does not have any legal cash flow obligations towards equity holders but may sometimes choose to pay shareholders a *dividend*. To complete the picture, *hybrid* securities like preferred stock and convertible bonds, which have flavors of both stocks and bonds, may also exist in the capital structure. These hybrids are conceptually closer to bonds, but may have additional features that make the securities convert to stock, or get special regulatory treatment by making coupon payments non-mandatory. We have discussed them in Chapters 2 and 10.

> The specifics of the terms in the investment agreement between the company and the investor determines whether the security is a debt instrument (bond/ loan), equity or a hybrid (preferred stock and convertible bonds) security.

EQUITIES AND THE CAPITAL STRUCTURE – ROLE OF LEVERAGE FOR A CORPORATION

Equities represent an ownership share of the company, but what does this practically mean? Let's suppose the firm has an *Enterprise Value* of F (determined by one of several approximate methods, discussed later), which is collectively held by all investors. This value F is spread across the capital structure (i.e. the gamut of sources of external funds). Let us assume, for simplicity, that the capital structure comprises only (one kind) of debt and equity. Debtholder claims (suppose, D) can be easily valued, based either on face value or market yields, since the cash flows to debt are well-defined. The debt investors are more senior in the capital structure (i.e. they have priority in receiving cash flow repayments), so their investment is less risky than equity and therefore trades at lower yields. The residual firm value (F-D), after all other parts of the capital structure are paid out, belongs to equity holders. Equities are the *junior-most instrument type in the capital structure*, paid out only

Capital Markets and Investments

after all other financial obligations are met. If the firm has S number of shares outstanding (this is an arbitrary number decided by the company when it decides to raise capital/ formalize ownership documents), then the value per share is (F-D)/S, which can be compared to the firm's share price to decide if the stock is trading cheap or rich relative to this calculated price.

Almost all of the growth in a firm's value after the debt has been issued goes to the equity holders, since the cash flows to debt are fixed (a decrease in bond yields will increase debt value a little, but the bulk of the benefit trickles down to equity). Similarly, if a company's growth prospects fade, equities take a big hit right away, whereas bond values can remain relatively stable as long as investors believe that the company can generate enough cash to service debt. So, as long as a company can invest in projects that earn a return greater than the debt servicing costs, it is profitable for the company to keep issuing debt to invest in these projects. The benefit of these excess returns over and above debt service costs show up directly in the equity bottom line, which is why debt is referred to as "*leverage*". The same identical operating firm, when financed with a mix of debt and equity, will generate higher returns for the equity holders than if it were financed completely with equity. Similarly, if the company's debt-financed projects end up earning less than the cost of debt (maybe because market conditions changed), the equity holder value gets eaten into, because the debt needs to be serviced regardless of the project performance, unless the company files bankruptcy if it cannot fulfil debt payment obligations. In that situation, the equity value gets wiped out to zero, the bond holders get the keys to the firm and they can either restructure or liquidate the firm to salvage whatever value is left.

An equity investment is always riskier than bonds (i.e. expected cash flows are far more uncertain) in the same company, so investors will usually demand a higher return on equity than bonds.

- ✓ Different securities have different rights to cash flows. For example:
  - Debt securities are paid fixed cash flows, decided when the initial contract is signed. If these cash flows are not paid, debt holders can take control of the company
  - Equity securities get whatever value is left over after paying out all liabilities, including debt. It is a residual claim on company assets; the company does not have any legal cash flow obligations towards equity holders but may sometimes choose to pay shareholders a dividend.
  - Equity holders also have limited liability; their maximum loss is the amount they have invested in the company as an equity investor, even if the company does something egregious towards other stakeholders. The minimum possible value of the equity is zero, not negative.
  - Hybrid securities assume debt-like or equity-like characteristics depending on the situation.
- ✓ The same project cost (or company) can be financed using various alternative mixes of debt and equity (often called leverage).
  - If the project has more debt (and less equity) and performs really well, the equity holders will make much more money than in a situation when the project has less debt and more equity. But, a project performing poorly is better off with less debt. This is because the debt payment is fixed regardless of project performance, and equity receives what is left over.
- ✓ For the same project, equity is riskier than debt (cash flows more uncertain), so the required return for equity is higher than interest cost of debt.

Equities - Valuation

CAPITAL STRUCTURE THEORIES - TAX BENEFIT OF DEBT

A firm can choose to finance its projects with various combinations of debt and equity. The *Modigliani-Miller hypothesis*, based on no-arbitrage arguments, is that this choice of capital structure has no effect on a firm's total value. If the proportion of debt is higher, then the company may think its saving on capital costs because debt is cheaper, but the cost of equity gets more expensive because the cash flows to equity gets more volatile. According to this idea, capital structure choices do not influence the weighted average cost of capital. Further, if investors prefer/ dislike leverage, they can borrow/ lend at a personal level to effectively undo any capital structure choices that the company has made.

This also draws attention to all the "frictionless markets" assumptions in the theory. For example, any interest payments that a company makes is part of its cost, and is therefore paid out of pre-tax revenues. Dividend payments to equity holders are made from after-tax profits. So, when a company is choosing between debt and equity, the difference between their costs get amplified because of tax reasons. So, this creates a bias in favor of more debt, to reduce total cost of capital.

Theories of asymmetric information between lenders, firms and external equity investors have tried to address the issues related to optimality of capital structure. The final answer depends on the tradeoffs between the tax-savings and the incentives for equity holders/ managers to hide or reveal information (i.e. signaling models), assignment of control rights in various outcomes and the wasteful cost to verify firm returns or enforce bankruptcy.

Most practitioners will agree that capital structure matters in creating or destroying firm value. Large amounts of debt can cause operationally viable firms to file for bankruptcy, or amplify returns to equity shareholders during strong operating conditions.

Does the financing mix (i.e. Debt/ Equity) affect the enterprise value of the firm (i.e. total value of firm debt + equity)?

- ✓ Initial answer is no – the cost of equity goes up as the equity in the project reduces relative to the debt. The weighted average cost remains the same because of no-arbitrage.
- ✓ The next level suggests that more debt creates a more valuable firm, because tax laws allow interest cost to be deducted, but not equity cost of capital. This tax deduction increases firm value.
- ✓ The final answer is ambiguous and depends on agency cost issues.
- ✓ Practitioners feel that a suitable capital structure can create firm value.

CORPORATE GOVERNANCE

Most corporate decisions are either taken by management or a board of directors appointed by shareholders. Some directors are nominee directors appointed by original owners, some appointed by financiers such as lenders, shareholders, etc. The exact details vary by firm, and are set out in the Bylaws at the time of incorporation (or subsequent amendments). Many important items (such as director appointments, merger tender offers) actually require a shareholder vote, with shareholders voting in proportion to their holding. Institutional shareholders, with their large block holdings, usually control these decisions. In the last few years, several institutions have bought shares in the open market to accumulate a sizeable holding, and then pursued an *activist* strategy to reform the company's operations and strategy, and pushed management to take actions they otherwise wouldn't. Theoretically, by having a voice in appointing directors (who are supposed to act on behalf of all shareholders) and by having a vote in important decisions, equity holders control the firm. Over

Capital Markets and Investments

the years, there has been significant issuance of several *share classes*, with some shares not having voting rights. Google (now Alphabet) is a classic example of a company being widely-held but tightly controlled; Facebook recently adopted a similar structure. Each year, the board of directors also decide how much of the firm's cash balance can be used to pay shareholders right away (i.e. *dividends*), instead of ploughing cash back into the business. Many companies do not pay dividends to their shareholders; those shareholders hold the stock because they expect the stock price to rise significantly. Companies can also choose to *buy back* some of their outstanding stock from existing shareholders with their cash balance; companies typically engage in buybacks when they feel that their stock is undervalued, thus representing a good investment of company cash. At the heights of booms, companies may even borrow money to pay their shareholders a big dividend, or to buy back stock.

Companies communicate publicly during earnings releases (every quarter in the US) and when there is material news, discussed in Annexure II. The earnings (press) release and the subsequent investor call provides investors with context about the company's financial/ operating performance, its plans and strategy going forward, and its outlook for the business in general. Companies also have board meetings in which the senior managers of the company are answerable to the board about executive decisions and performance, and an Annual General Meeting, which all shareholders and the press attend. To facilitate information flow to institutional investors, the company's Investor Relations department also organizes investor days and speaks at industry conferences. Larger companies have sell-side analysts covering them; this greatly increases transparency and scrutiny, which also facilitates a larger institutional investor base. Investors who believe that a company has significant value, but are unhappy with its performance, management or governance (which are leading to value destruction), sometimes take an *activist* position, trying to buy a significant shareholding in the public market, and then try to get themselves elected to the board to effect change, by influencing or changing management.

> Since Equity holders have no firm commitments but only a residual claim on the firm, they are very interested in ensuring that the firm is run in the best possible manner, because they receive the entire benefits of efficiency and bear the full pain from poor operations. This is done through:
> - ✓ Appointing a Board of Directors that meets at least quarterly; the management technically reports to the Board. Some equity investors try to play an activist role.
> - ✓ Analyzing all the information that the company puts out in its financial statements, press releases, etc. Investor Relations holds investor days.
> - ✓ Sell-side analysts, who cover the larger firms, and publish reports for their investor clients

VALUING EQUITIES

Setting the Stage

Since the value of equities is the residual value of the firm after other parts of the capital structure are paid their full dues, equities cannot be valued in isolation, without valuing the entire firm and valuing what these other more senior securities are worth. In most cases, though (except for distressed firms), the cash flows due to these non-equity securities are relatively easy to predict and value (the range of disagreement within these values is fairly small), so much of the equity valuation analysis centers on the value of the firm itself.

To provide a simple but specific illustration, Debt (Fixed Income) and Equity are two (extreme) forms of financing. Cash flows for debt-holders are "guaranteed" by the company, whereas, for equity holders, there are no promises. Both these types of securities can be valued using Discounted Cash Flow (DCF) methods,

Equities - Valuation

by performing a Net Present Value calculation exercise. The difference is that the cash flows are contractually specified in the debt contract, whereas it is difficult to come up with the cash flows to equity. So, analysts have to spend a lot of time coming up with pro-forma financial statements after making assumptions on future revenues, costs (to estimate interest cost, one needs to assume debt levels) and one-time spending / inflows. After tallying these numbers, it is possible to come up with estimates of cash flows to equity holders, for the next year and further ahead. This is referred to as a *financial model*.[131] Of course, for existing stable companies, the historical financial statements can serve as a starting point for this exercise. For companies without suitable history, this model has to be built from scratch.

Coming up with cash flows is only one part of the exercise. Deciding on the suitable rate to discount these cash flows is another critical aspect, since these cash flows are not risk-free. So, while Treasury rates can serve as a reference, the likelihood of receiving cash flows, and the recourse in case cash flows are not received (i.e. bankruptcy) need to be assessed. The discount rate reflects the investors' *required rate of return*, given the risk profile of the company (alternatively, the investors' *expected return* on the stock assuming they invest at a "fair" price), and depends on their *opportunity cost of capital* (i.e. their expected return from other investments). While there is no precise method to come up with a discount rate, it can be implied from the prices and cash flows of other similar securities (essentially, an IRR calculation). Some asset pricing models (e.g. CAPM/ factor models, discussed in the next chapter) help provide required return estimates consistent with varying levels of risk. Whatever the exact valuation methodology, it should be apparent that, for the same company, the required return (i.e. the discount rate) for equities should be higher than the required return (i.e. yield) for bonds, since the bonds are much safer investments than the equities; there can be no situation when the bonds do not get paid fully but the equity does. For most of our discussion on valuation in the next section on models, we will assume that the expected returns are given to us. Once we have estimates of future cash flows to equity, and a suitable discount rate, it is straightforward to value the equity stock by discounting cash flows in a NPV framework. Alternatively, to get around the need for estimating discount rates, people often use "multiples-based valuation", discussed below. To do this, having near—term projections of future cash flows, and a sense of the valuation of similar companies, is adequate.

One method to conceptually approach this is to try to value the firm as an entity. Suppose C_t denotes the net cash flow projections for the firm in period t (to pay both debt holders and equity holders), and the firm lives on forever. Using a variant of the NPV formula, the firm value (V) is calculated by $V = \sum_{t=1}^{\infty} \frac{E[C_t]}{(1+WACC)^t}$, where WACC (Weighted Average Cost of Capital, average of expected returns on the firm's debt and equity) represents the suitable discount rate for these cash flows, and incorporates the firm's leverage. We can deduct the market value of debt from V to calculate the value of equity. We leave a detailed analysis of calculation WACC to later; for the moment, we assume that the firm in question has only equity in its capital structure.

Equity Valuation Models [132]

As we begin discussing equity valuation models, we emphasize that these models take the cash flows and discount rates above as given, so any errors or misleading assumptions in estimating these values get amplified in the model. Also, these models are almost meant as frameworks to think about valuation, rather than taken

---

[131] Investment bankers, corporate finance professionals and fundamental investors often refer to organized cash flow forecasting as modeling, whereas quantitative finance folks use the same term to refer to the quantitative techniques used to value financial instruments.

[132] Much of the Valuation theory we discuss here is rooted in the seminal work by Benjamin Graham and David Dodd, in the 1930s, and Myron Gordon in the 1940s.

Capital Markets and Investments

too literally. Often, we do not have good information on all the variables necessary to form the complete picture, and use formulae based on simplifying assumptions. We discuss some of these below.

Dividend Discount Model

We begin with the highly stylized Dividend Discount Model. The idea is that, if an investor invests in the shares of a publicly listed company, the only cash flow that he will get from the company are the periodic dividends (maybe buybacks, etc.). So, the current fair value of the stock has to be equal to the present value of the expected future dividends (from the next dividend to the end of time). Of course, the current investor probably expects to sell the stock at a price in a few years, but the person who buys the stock from our investor is paying our investor a price, based on discounting further future dividend payments (argument can be repeated for every future investor). As discussed above, we also need a discount rate to discount future cash flows (in this case dividends); for the purpose of these models, we will assume that the discount rate is given to us.

We consider an all-equity firm. Conceptually, its share price is given by:

$$P_0 = \sum_{t=1}^{\infty} \frac{E[D_t]}{(1+r^*)^t} \qquad \text{Eq. 11.1}$$

where D_t represents the cash flows (usually dividends) to the shareholder in period t and r^* is the constant expected return on equity. Estimating D_t (or any financial variable) very far out is almost impossible, but right now, we are simply formulating the framework. We will apply assumptions to how D_t evolves over time to get by.

A special case of this is when no cash flow growth is expected (i.e. constant dividend), then $P_0 = \frac{D}{r^*}$.

> *Example:* Suppose an all-equity firm has 1 million shares outstanding, currently priced to yield 10%. The firm earns $4mm net profit after tax, and distributes the whole amount as a dividend.
>
> This is a no growth situation, so the value of the firm is simply 4mm ÷ 10%, or $40mm. The firm has 1 million shares outstanding, so this translates to $40 a share.
>
> Now, suppose that a new project with a very similar profile to the firm's existing operations becomes available for $4mm. The project is expected to earn $1.2mm each year in net cash flows. The firm wants to buy this project, and finance it with a new share issuance program. How many shares should be sold, and at what price?
>
> Let us first value the new project i.e. 1.2mm ÷ 10% (since similar risk profile) = $12mm[133]. The value of the firm will increase by 12mm after taking on this project, so the new value of all the shares has to equal $52mm. Also, the latest share price (say x) times the number of newly issued shares (say y) has to equal the cost to buy the project. This reduces to a system of two equations and two unknowns i.e. $(1+y)x = 52$ and $yx = 4$ (all numbers in millions). So, substituting the second equation in the first, $x = 48$. $y = 4/48 = 83,333$ shares.

Alternatively, we can also make an assumption on future stock price and write Eq. 11.1 as

$$P_0 = \sum_{t=1}^{k} \frac{E[D_t]}{(1+r^*)^t} + \frac{P_k}{(1+r^*)^k} \qquad \text{Eq. 11.2}$$

---

[133] It is important to wonder why a project worth $12mm is being sold for $4mm (maybe seller has some constraints, and there are few buyers), but let us ignore this question for the moment.

Equities - Valuation

Essentially, we project dividends for the next k periods, and then make an assumption on the share price k periods ahead. This essentially is the point of view of an investor who is thinking of selling the shares k periods from now. The valuation critically depends on P_k or the *terminal value*, and makes these dividend discount models difficult to use, except for stable companies with little uncertainty.

Extensions to the Dividend Discount Model

We now extend the above model to assume that cash flows (i.e. D_t) grow at a constant rate g. If the expected return on equity (i.e. opportunity cost of holding equity) is fixed at r^*, then [134].

$$P_0 = \frac{D_1}{r^*-g} = \frac{D_0(1+g)}{r^*-g} \qquad \text{Eq. 11.3}$$

Eq. 11.3 is called the *Gordon growth formula*. The idea can also be applied to a situation with multiple growth regimes. For example, if the analyst has a sense of the dividends during the next two periods, and then expects the dividends to grow at a stable rate g, the formula gets rewritten as:

P_0 = PV of cash flows in years 1 and 2 + PV of cash flows thereafter, i.e.

$$P_0 = \frac{D_1}{(1+r^*)} + \frac{D_2}{(1+r^*)^2} + \frac{1}{(1+r^*)^2} \frac{D_2(1+g)}{r^*-g} \qquad \text{Eq. 11.4}$$

> *Example:* A venture capitalist takes an equity stake of 20% in a start-up by investing $2m. The start-up has negative cash flow in the first year of $2m, and earns a positive cash flow of $0.5m in year 2. From years 2-5, the firm is able to maintain a constant monopoly growth rate g. After year 5, the firm is expected to grow at the industry average of 10% per annum. What is the required monopoly growth rate for years 2-5 to give the venture capitalist a required return of 20%?
>
> Let us write down the projected cash flows, below:

Time Period	0	1	2	3	4	5	6
Cash Flow	-10	-2	0.5	.5(1+g)	.5(1+g)²	.5(1+g)³	.5(1+g)³(1.10)

We then discount these cash flows (using a version of the Gordon growth formula), set the NPV (including the initial investment) to zero, and solve for g.

$$0 = -10 - \frac{2}{(1+0.2)} + \frac{0.5}{(1+0.2)^2} + \frac{0.5(1+g)}{(1+0.2)^3} + \frac{0.5(1+g)^2}{(1+0.2)^4} + \frac{0.5(1+g)^3}{(1+0.2)^5} + \frac{1}{(1+0.2)^5} \frac{0.5(1+g)^3(1.1)}{0.2-0.1}$$

The only unknown in the equation above is g. While it may be possible to solve it analytically, using the Goalseek function in Excel is convenient in such cases.

Equity Valuation using multiples –Relative Valuation, P/E and other Ratios

The above DCF techniques need precise estimates of cash flows far out into the future and discount rates, both of which are difficult to obtain. Near-term cash flow projections are arguably easier, starting with prior financial statements as a baseline, and overlaying company guidance to come up with estimates for the next 2-3 years. We now present valuation ideas that use these near-term cash flow forecasts as the primary input, and try to come up with an estimate of firm value, by looking at what levels other "comparable" companies (or "comps") are valued, and using cash flow-based "multiples". These models essentially help answer if the

---

[134] Let us accept this result at face value. For interested students, the proof follows from the properties of geometric series.

Capital Markets and Investments

company being analyzed is being valued cheap or expensive relative to other similar companies. So, principally, these techniques are more about equity valuation relative to comparables, which is then mapped to an absolute value. This also related to the Ratio Analysis section that we discuss in the Annexure on financial statement analysis.

For example, analysts often compare EV/EBITDA across companies within a sector to get a sense of which companies are valued cheaper than others. There may either be a good reason for one company to have a lower ratio (e.g. weaker management team, older assets), or it may be mispriced. .For a forward-looking version of this measures, analysts typically use the next period's EBITDA from financial projections (instead of the current value).

Of course, we can come up with several alternative measures or ratios. Some of these are industry-specific, relating to physical assets and replacement cost of capacity. Many ratios are also more relevant for some asset classes – e.g. Net Debt/ EBIDTA and Interest Coverage ratios matter more to credit investors; Price/ Earnings Per Share (i.e. P/EPS) ratios are primarily used by equity investors. For example, analysts may remark that unsecured bonds of a company has a Net Debt$_0$/ EBIDTA$_1$ (multiple) of 3.5 and is trading at a yield of 7%, whereas its peer companies have Net Debt$_0$/ EBIDTA$_1$ of 4 and trade at 6% yield. An equity analyst can similarly contrast P$_0$/ EPS$_1$ of companies in a certain sector, or over time.

Creative uses of ratios can help determine where the company's value/ risk is coming from –operations (revenue side or cost side), capital structure decisions, etc. The *Du Pont Analysis* framework is a convenient starting point to decompose top-level ratios to its various constituent drivers.

Many of these relative multiple-based ratios can be mapped to special cases of the discounted cash flow models we discussed in the previous section. To provide some conceptual foundation for P/E-based valuations, let us continue with a version of the dividend discount model discussed earlier. Suppose the dividend payment is a constant fraction, a (the *payout ratio*) of the firm's earnings X_t, which grows at the rate g every year, then Eq. 11.3 changes to:

$$P_0 = \frac{D_1}{r^*-g} = \frac{aX_0(1+g)}{r^*-g}$$

$$\text{or,} \quad \frac{P_0}{X_0} = \frac{a(1+g)}{r^*-g}, \quad \text{and} \quad \frac{P_0}{X_1} = \frac{a}{r^*-g} \quad [\because X_1 = X_0(1+g)] \qquad \text{Eq. 11.5}$$

We can also express the value of a stock as the sum of the value of a no-growth stock and the *Present Value of Growth Opportunities* (PVGO), i.e.

$$P_0 = \frac{X_1}{r^*} + PVGO = \frac{aX_0(1+g)}{r^*-g}$$

$$\text{or,} \quad PVGO = \frac{X_1[g-(1-a)r^*]}{r^*(r^*-g)} \qquad \text{Eq. 11.6}$$

$$\text{So,} \quad \frac{P_0}{X_1} = \frac{1}{r} + \frac{g-(1-a)r^*}{r^*(r^*-g)}$$

From either Eq. 11.5 or Eq. 11.6, a high P$_0$/X$_1$ implies either a low required return on this stock r^*(i.e. perception of low risk), or high expected growth rate g (which raises the PVGO term). Stock prices can rise because of higher earnings estimates, or higher P/E multiples (or both). How P/E (market assessment of growth potential/ risk aversion) is expected to change with earnings estimates is an important determinant of the future outlook for stocks.

Equities - Valuation

> Equities are valued using:
>
> ✓ Discounted Cash Flow (DCF) models, which use cash flow projections (by extrapolating key variables related to future cash inflow and outflow) and discount them.
>
> - Assumptions on the evolution of cash flows (constant in perpetuity, constant growth, etc.) are necessary to make these models tractable.
>
> ✓ Multiples-based relative valuation helps compare equity values across a peer group of companies, by expressing current equity values as a multiple of common ratios. If multiples for a company are low, then this company is undervalued (maybe for good reason) relative to the peer group.
>
> - Under certain assumptions, multiples-based valuations can be reconciled with DCF-based tools.

EQUITY VALUATION IN REAL LIFE

The sections above discussed the relevant tools, models and concepts that equity investors consider while evaluating investment opportunities. In practice, most fundamentally-focused professionals will build cash flow models for the next 3-4 years, and apply multiples to the projected accounting/ cash flow variables to arrive at an enterprise/ equity value. This section mentions some real-world issues and themes that come up.

Role of Macro Analysis in Equity Valuation

Equity valuation depends critically on identifying relevant information that helps project future cash flows/ earnings, as well as investor sentiment (which affects market-wide discount rates/ multiples). Fundamental analysts aim to accomplish this at the company level, and by tracking macro trends, since company-level, sector/industry-wide and economy-wide issues affect a company's prospects and performance. Some academics believe that the effect of company-level issues on stock performance cancel out once several companies are aggregated in a large portfolio (discussed in detail in the next chapter); the empirical evidence is less obvious. Regardless, the macro (i.e. economy and sector) environment is very important to assess; in fact most investors will agree that except for smallest and riskiest companies, the macro outlook usually dominates the company outlook and is a key determinant of equity performance. Revisions to estimates of companies' future earnings move closely with macro PMI data.

The starting point for this analysis is getting a sense of where in the business cycle the economy is currently in. Policy rates (i.e. Federal Reserve statements), inflation trends, employment reports, purchasing manager surveys, and other economic indicators (e.g. the Conference Board Leading, Coincident and Lagging indicators) provide a sense of the current and future state of the economy. This helps investors sense which way the economy is likely headed, which has important implications for the sectors and companies they cover. Investment committees are especially watchful of these trends, to decide between risk-on/ risk-off allocations, as well as picking sectors within the cycle. For example, investors typically expect cyclical sectors such as consumer discretionary, financials, Housing, energy, industrials and materials to do well when the economy is expanding. When the economy slows, defensive sectors such as utilities, consumer staples and healthcare are likely to do well. Investment styles such as Growth (including small cap equities) do well when economic prospects are improving; Value does better during slowdowns. Over the years, though, as sectors have become more diverse, there are cyclical and defensive opportunities within each sector too. . Finally, all of these concepts will come together in the estimate for cash flows, growth rates, discount rates or multiples that are required to populate the models discussed above.

Economic cycles have historically lasted for varying periods of time, so simply being in a certain stage of the business cycle does not tell us what will happen next. Changes in policy rates (lower), inflation trends (decreases) and strength in some key sectors such as housing usually help support a growth cycle. As conditions tighten (usually because of the Fed raising rates or inflation rising e.g. oil prices going higher), the economy slows down. Since the financial markets themselves are a leading indicator of the economy (i.e. investors' view of the future outlook are incorporated in today's security prices), if investors are trying to predict future stock (or bond) prices, they need to go beyond developing a sense of the future economic outlook. Rather, the issue is often about deciphering what future conditions are priced into the market today, and whether the analyst's opinion of the future macro outlook is different from that. Analysts track global central bank behavior, interest rates, relative performance between early-stage cyclical stocks (e.g. housing, consumer discretionary) and late-stage cyclicals (e.g. energy, materials) to sense where the leading economic indicators are headed[135]. They track leading economic indicators (survey data such as PMI is a common one, as is housing starts/ permits/ prices), which are usually co-incident with the stock market, to look for divergence between the future economic activity indicated by this data and what is being indicated by current security prices. At the same time, they are mindful of secular or structural trends (i.e. retail moving online, ageing demographics, etc.) and whether these forces have gathered enough momentum to overwhelm shorter term cyclical effects, or if cyclical effects will dominate. Over the last few years, as institutional liquidity has reduced in less popular names, investors have become more focused on the *flows* in each market; who is buying, for what reason and how much. There is research suggesting that (mutual fund) flows chase performance, but some investors anecdotally feel that exogenous flows may move prices, in relatively less liquid markets, especially as much of the buying (ETFs/ algorithms) is often mechanical. The boom-bust cycles in the market have typically become shorter, over the years.

Taking a step back as we emphasize the importance of the macro environment, the entire relative value argument can be extended beyond stocks, starting with asset classes (i.e. are equities more attractive investments than bonds?) to sectors (i.e. is healthcare more interesting than energy?) to industries and individual securities. At every stage, there is a choice regarding how an investor should be positioned. In many asset management firms, each of these questions is answered by different sets of people, with the investment committees deciding on asset and sector allocation, individual portfolio teams picking securities. Of course, the last step of picking securities is the most resource intensive, since it involves studying companies individually. In fact, depending on the investment firm's philosophy, some firms skip the last step and hold baskets of securities in a sector or theme, instead of picking names. This style of investing has become more popular, as people search for investible themes.

Fundamental versus Quantitative Investing

Investing in equities, as discussed so far, involves studying the economy, industry and company's history, and assessing future prospects. This is a predominant qualitative exercise, supported by several data points, which finally comes together in the cash-flow based model. This approach is commonly referred to as *fundamental*, because it involves forming an opinion on the business, operations and outlook of the company. For a firm that adopts this approach, it is labor intensive, since an analyst can only be responsible for a few dozen companies at most. So, position sizes are often relatively large, and portfolios more concentrated. This being said, the role of data in fundamental investment processes is becoming more important; Chapter 6 discusses some of these advancements.

---

[135] Choosing the appropriate lags while trying to decide which variables lead markets (and by how long) is important, albeit imprecise.

Equities - Valuation

In contrast, quantitative investment approaches are more interested in getting their investment right "on average", and often have no specific insight about a particular company, even when they have investments in them. These methods reduce a company to a few easily observable company specific metrics, then map this combination of metrics to share price or expected return using a model, and then run the model on several (hundreds) of securities to find a subset that screens attractively, based on this model. They then invest in this large list, exiting positions when certain other data-driven criteria are met.

A closely-related taxonomy of investment styles describes them as either *discretionary* (where the individual portfolio manager can decide whether (and how much) to buy or sell a position) or *systematic* (where computer programs analyze data and apply models to pick investments). While fundamental and discretionary are often used interchangeably, as are quantitative and systematic[136], in reality a systematic strategy can use information on company fundamental performance in its models, whereas a discretionary manager can also use quantitative techniques as a guide or screening criteria. Recently, hybrid approaches such as "quantitative, with discretionary overlay" are being mentioned by some managers; in fact, *quantamental* has often been mentioned as a separate class of strategies!

Discretionary investors tend to do more in-depth analysis for a smaller set of companies, whereas systematic investors try to get the broad strokes right over a large universe of names. Consequently, discretionary portfolios are usually more concentrated and built bottom-up (and managers are often more specialized), and bet on "home-runs". In contrast, systematic investors have smaller positions in many names, and may have very diversified portfolios across sectors, geographies, company size, etc. Systematic strategies are more easily applied to the liquid markets, allowing strategies to trade/ rebalance their books more frequently. More liquid underlying securities also allow the systematic portfolios to be financed more easily, and run higher levels of leverage. Discretionary investment processes are more likely to be exposed to behavioral biases; systematic processes are rule-based and avoid this drawback. Backtesting is easier done for systematic ideas, and impossible to do for a discretionary process. But, systematic strategies are exposed to high model/ statistical risk, and the risk of "garbage in-garbage out" (from data quality or over-fitted model perspective) and the risk that the future might evolve to be materially different from the patterns discerned from past data.

Value Investing

Value Investing is a style of long-term fundamental investing, which involves buying out-of-favor (but solid) companies at low prices (with high margin of safety), focusing on why you are on the right side of the trade, and why the other person who is selling to you might be wrong. This approach highlights being on the other side of behavioral or institutional biases. It is not about forecasting earnings a few quarters out and applying discount rates of multiples; rather the philosophy emphasizes developing a specific focus area with deep knowledge, working patiently to be able to buy large positions at sizeable discounts to their intrinsic values. Smaller less glamorous companies not covered by hundreds of analysts are more likely to be suitable candidates.

Non-traditional data sources

Security prices depend on the outlook for the economy, as well as for specific sectors and companies (and, of course, all these outlooks are related). Investors have been traditionally getting data from organizations (either economy-wide/ government run or trade associations, etc.), broadly disseminated at a scheduled time, or relying on company announcements/ earnings releases, to create their investment mosaic. With the explosion of data collection tools and proprietary data, there are several new sources of data that have become relevant.

---

[136] This is because discretionary managers almost always rely on predominantly fundamental information, whereas systematic strategies depend almost exclusively on quantitative model output.

Capital Markets and Investments

Satellite imaging (how many cars are parked at key Walmart parking lots), credit card swipes (what are people buying, in what quantities), shipping and trucking data (what items are moving across the country and landing in ports), taxi and Uber usage, hotel bookings, scanning text files and news releases etc., are all available for a price. Big-data technologies have made it easier to analyze this information. What data is truly useful (how, exactly, to use it) and leads market movements is the big question. These types of data are changing the role of data as purely an input for quant teams to a more relevant investment decision-making ingredient across investment styles. We discuss this more in Chapter 6.

Role of Algorithms

Quantitative techniques have permeated every part of the investment process, from idea generation to order execution. We've discussed the various effects in different parts of the book; the overarching result is that markets react very quickly to all kinds of information – be it order flows, price action, stock-specific news flows as well as macro headlines. Idea generation and trading have both become more algorithmic, with computer models scanning price movements and news much faster than humans, and implement trades based on this analysis instantly, without human intervention. The proliferation of ETFs and text/ news parsing machines has led to even the more tangential relationships showing up immediately in co-movement across instruments and asset classes, and markets increasingly becoming either risk-on, risk-off or flat, with low dispersion. Regulation is also exacerbating this trend, as decision-making gets more centralized.

Model Robustness

Model Robustness is an important part of the investment process. In the fundamental investing world, this essentially translates to recognizing how sensitive the cash flow-based model outputs (e.g. project cash flows, stock price) are to the inputs/ assumptions (e.g. revenue growth rate). In terms of model organization, all assumptions should be explicitly listed in a separate section, and every cell in the model should link to either the assumptions and/ or other formulae. Hardcoding within the model should be minimized; all hardcoded numbers should reside in the assumptions section. This makes the model transparent, and allows for easier model auditing. Sensitivity analysis to model inputs is also easier, when the model is laid out this way.

In quantitative investing, model robustness relates to the specification of the quantitative model, the estimation of the model parameters, and the suitable testing of the model with out-of-sample data. These analytics drive several modeling decisions; a balance needs to be maintained between economic intuition and statistical performance, while actively recognizing the drawbacks of the methodology.

Thematic Investing

Over the last five years, as quantitative investing, factor-based thinking, smart-beta ETFS have all taken center-stage, active investors have increasingly started to define their allocation in terms of owning themes (secular stagnation, ageing demographics, cyber security, biotech, etc.)[137], and owning all the names that have high exposure to that theme, rather than analyzing single names bottom up. Further, a larger proportion of investors now choose to own factor exposures such as momentum, value, growth, dividend yield, etc. and invest in (smart beta) products that provide this. At the same time, more money is moving from active investing to passive strategies, which do not pick specific securities, but invest more mechanically to own broader exposures. The influence of algorithms have become more pervasive. All these forces collectively cause sections of the market to often co-move together, more than in the past. Does this result in a more systematized market, or does this provide further opportunities for a fundamental investor to pick out names that initially move with the cohort, but should not, based on fundamentals? And where does this end, with these fundamental screens getting quantified, maybe with the help of big data, or with the realization that thematic and

---

[137] Sectors may be thought of as a special example of a theme.

Equities - Valuation

top-down investing, while increasingly relevant, leave ample room for bottom-up fundamental managers to succeed? Time will tell.

Shorting Equities

Investors (unless barred by regulations or guidelines, such as mutual funds) can take a short position in stocks to express a bearish view. As a reminder, a short position involves selling a security that you do not own at the current (presumably high) market price, with the hope of buying it back (i.e. covering it) later at a lower price to close out the position. Mechanically, this involves getting a "locate" for the stock from a prime broker so that the investor can borrow it (only a certain amount may be available for borrowing in securities lending programs), sell it at the current market value, and using the cash proceeds (and additional collateral) to collateralize the borrow; sometimes other securities can also be used as collateral instead of cash. The short seller pays the prime broker the borrow cost (compensation for borrowing the security, works similar to interest) for being short the stock; this fee varies significantly depending on how much supply of the stock is available for borrowing. Most borrows are overnight, and typically get renewed, but borrow costs can change. The short seller is also responsible for any dividend payments while he is short the stock. If interest rates are high, the seller can earn some interest on the short proceeds. So, being short has significant costs that tick every day; the price has to go down by more than this amount for the trade to work. This is why investors often look for (or try to create) short-term catalysts when short a name. A rip up in the stock (a short squeeze) can be painful, since it will now cost more to buy back (i.e. cover) the short. This also leads to potential margin calls.

Real-life equity valuation has several facets; we touch on a few in this section:
- ✓ Macroeconomic analysis is often the first step in projecting future stock returns.
- ✓ Fundamental investors qualitatively project future cash flows and earnings, whereas Quantitative investors analyze data quantitatively, and put on diversified positions across many names.
- ✓ Algorithms have proliferated both quantitative idea generation and trading mechanics.
- ✓ Robustness and stability of models (i.e. large changes in output for tiny changes in inputs) is key.
- ✓ A plethora of new data sources have emerged, with the advent of big data.
- ✓ Investors are more macro-driven than earlier, leading them to pick themes instead of specific stocks, causing broad sections of the market to co-move together. Quantitative models, which scan news feeds and immediately put on trades, incorporate news into prices of related securities instantly, causing broad-based co-movement.
- ✓ Value investment is a philosophy which tries to understand which positions the investor is likely to have a comparative advantage.
- ✓ Short-selling is important in keeping prices close to their fair value. The regulations and the mechanisms surrounding short sales create frictions.

EQUITY INSTRUMENTS

Investors can trade equities using various vehicles. They broadly include single name stocks (equity shares) and portfolios/ baskets of single names. These baskets, which often have themes often have themes (sector-based, broad index replication, smart beta, etc.) come in various flavors – ETFs, closed end funds (both of which trade intra-day) and open-ended mutual funds (which trade at market close at their NAV) these is discussed in detail in the section on buy-side products in Chapter 4 of the book.[138]

Derivatives are also common instruments to get equity exposure; these include equity index futures, equity (single name and index/ ETF) options and (less common) equity swaps (i.e. total return swaps on equity ETFs or indices, similar to the ones discussed in Chapter 5). We will discuss equity options in Chapters 13 and 14. This section discusses forwards and futures.

Forwards

Equity index futures, introduced in Chapter 2, are derivative instruments that cash settle to the index value on the settlement date. The S&P500 E-mini Futures is the most popular futures contract, which settles every quarter to the S&P500 Index. To derive the fair value of a futures contract, we motivate it by considering the (more straightforward but economically very similar) forward contract.

Forwards are instruments using which one party agrees to buy (and the other party agrees to sell) a specified underlying (in this situation, an equity index) on a specified date in the future, at a price decided today. While no money or underlyings are exchanged today, the parties are bound to follow through with their side of the contract on the pre-specified future date. The value of the forward contract reflects the price at which market participants expect the cash index to trade at expiration and the cost of financing. While the forward value may appear to be (and is!) related to market expectations of the future value of the index, its value is usually given by a no-arbitrage argument. If the cash index is trading today at S, an investor could short it, receive S, invest it in the bank account and earn r per cent from now until expiration (*not annualized return* but only for this period), at which time he would have S(1+r) in cash. For there to be no arbitrage trade, the cost for him to close out him the initial short cash trade should be exactly S(1+r).

If the forward price F is lower than S(1+r), the investor would short the cash index at S, receive $S and go long the forward at F (no cash requirement at trade inception). At expiration, he would use a part of the short proceeds (with interest) to go long the underlying at F (this is where the long forward contract comes into effect; the market price on that day does not matter), and use that underlying to close out the initial short position and have S(1+r) − F left over, risk free. Similarly, if F were greater that S(1+r), the investor would sell the index forward at F, borrow S at interest rate r, use this borrowing to buy the index with cash. On the forward maturity date, the investor would use these index securities to fulfil the obligations under the forward contract by providing these securities for sale at price F. A part of these sales proceeds, [S(1+r)], would be used to pay off the borrowing, and the investor would pocket a risk-free F − [S(1+r)]. Eq. 11.7 summarizes this no-arbitrage relationship:

$$F = S(1+r)$$
Eq. 11.7

So, the forward price, to be transacted on at a future date, is completely based on variables known today – the current underlying value (S) and the interest/ financing rate (r). This is not inconsistent with the idea that forward prices should reflect market expectations of the future, but emphasize the fact that market expectations of the future value of the index (at any time horizon) are captured in the current index value; if most market participants expect the index value to be high in future, this will raise the current index value. We used a similar argument while discussing the relationship between forward and spot interest rate term structures.

This relation between forward and spot values of an underlying asset holds not just for equities but most other assets as well. Some refinements include incorporating dividends paid between now and expiration date of

---

[138] Of course, fixed income investors also use these baskets to access the markets, so there is nothing specific to equities that relates to these products.

Equities - Valuation

the forward (the underlying price will go down once the dividend is paid; own the underlying directly today entitles the owner to the dividend, but not the forward. The other common consideration is storage costs (for physical underlying), which increases the cost of carrying the underlying, like financing. Some underlying products also have a convenience yield associated with them, relating to the value of having the asset in hand, rather than a financial contract that promises the asset in future. If d is the dividend rate and c is the storage cost per cent between the current time and expiration (i.e. not annualized), Eq. 11.7 would be rewritten as:

$$F = S(1+r-d+c) \qquad \text{Eq. 11.8}$$

In a no-arbitrage world, the difference between S(1+r-d+c) and F is often attributed to the convenience yield. In general, the return difference between a cash instrument and the associated derivative is often referred to as the *basis*. Traders who plan to trade one of these and neutralize the risk by taking the opposite position in the other are exposed to the basis risk.

If the forward-spot arbitrage is not easy to implement (for whatever reason), then the points on the forward curve can move around independently of the spot price. This is often seen in certain difficult-to-store commodities or even the VIX futures (discussed in Chapter 14), where the underlying (VIX) is not a tradable spot market instrument.

Futures

The above discussion on forwards is fully relevant, as we discuss futures. Futures are very similar to forwards, with some differences in institutional mechanics. Futures trade on exchanges and are arguably more liquid, but they cannot be customized like a forward contract (which is a bilateral agreement between two parties). Like forwards, no money changes hands when an investor enters into a futures contract (the investor may choose to take a long or short position), but the investor agrees to execute at a price (the futures price) on a future date (the expiration/ maturity date). Futures contracts mature only a few times a year (the exchange on which the contract is listed announces standard expiration dates well in advance), so unlike forwards (where both parties agree to a date), futures traders can only choose expiration dates from the menu that the exchange provides. In reality, not all the expirations are liquid at all times; it is common to see the vast majority of the trades in the nearest maturities, with longer-term investors "rolling" maturities further (selling out of the nearest future which he is long, to simultaneously buy a future further out to maintain exposure to the underlying) out as the expiration of the nearby futures contract gets closer. The price of the futures contract will be close to the formula in Eq. 11.8, to be consistent with no-arbitrage (the specifics of the exchange rules of futures contracts can cause minor deviations). Assuming r, d and c do not change often, the futures (like the forward) will move one-for-one with the spot market, and are referred to as a *delta-one derivative*[139].

Apart from the expiration dates, the futures contract also standardizes other details. For example, for the S&P500 E-Mini Futures contract which trades on CBOE, each contract is denominated as $50 times the value of the S&P500 Index, so a one point move in the index leads to a $50 gain or loss in the contract.[140]

Since the futures contracts are traded on the exchange, it is easy to find out how much the investor's initial futures trade is worth, post trade inception (but before expiration). The current market price of the futures, relative to the futures price at trade inception, times the number of contracts traded, directly provides the gains or losses, like any other listed security. For a forward, it is not as easy as reading the number off a screen.

---

[139] In some markets, the futures–spot market arbitrage is not perfect because of details such as the underlying being slightly different or there being uncertainty in dividend payouts or storage costs; this futures-spot difference is called basis and can move around.

[140] We saw examples of this standardization when we discussed Treasury futures, where there were rules associated with the underlying (which Treasury, and the delivery option for the seller) and Eurodollar futures, where the contract size was $1mm.

Capital Markets and Investments

This *mark-to-market feature* for futures also leads to the investor either receiving or paying the day's gains and losses into his brokerage amount, thereby removing the risk that the futures investor will be unable to pay a large loss if the trade moves against him. At any point during the trade that the investor does not have cash in his margin account to pay that day's loss, the trade is automatically closed out, thereby limiting the extent of *counterparty risk*. To unwind a futures contract, an investor can sell it on the exchange just like any share; unwinding a forward is more complicated.

> Equity instruments include common stock, ETFs and mutual funds. Derivatives include stock options, index swaps, forwards and index futures. We discuss equity futures above:
>
> ✓ A forward/ futures contract does not require any upfront cash transactions at trade inception. But, on the settlement date, both the buyer and the seller have to fulfill their original trades at the previously agreed price (unlike an option).
>
> ✓ Forwards/ futures are priced by no-arbitrage, by replicating the equivalent trade using the underlying instrument and borrowing. Instead of going long the forward today, an individual can borrow cash equal to the underlying spot price and be long the underlying through settlement date. The total cost of this replicating trade should equal the cost of the forward today.
>
> ✓ While forwards are bilateral OTC trades, futures are exchange traded standardized in terms of settlement date, contractual features, etc. This usually makes futures more liquid.

EQUITIES AS AN ASSET CLASS - MICROSTRUCTURE OF EQUITIES

Equities have traditionally been one of the most liquid transparent markets, easy for retail investors (and institutional investors) to access, with SEC regulation guiding corporate disclosure. These markets have also formed the basis for large success stories and spectacular failures, throughout the last century. Venture capital, private equity, large successful IPOs, market crashes have all become part of famous movies, novels and folklore. Equity markets have traditionally been a forward-looking (albeit volatile) barometer of a company's / economy's health, reflecting future prospects in current prices. Investors have found these markets indispensable in growing and preserving their capital, while it has been the prominent form of external financing for corporates. Investors usually could swap their equity holdings for cash at the prevailing market price through their brokers (who sold it to others on the floor of an exchange). We have a discussion on exchange traded markets and their microstructure in Chapter 3; it may be useful to review those ideas at this point. Traditionally, the asset manager would call a broker on the floor of the exchange, who would write out a ticket to a floor broker, who would run to a post and shout or show hand signals to execute a trade, either with another broker who had an order for the opposite trade, or with a specialist market maker. This would take minutes. Over the years, the information dissemination and then the process got progressively automated, with the introduction of computers and the Internet. The competitive structure among exchanges has also evolved, leading to a different set of incentives.

The last fifteen years have completely transformed the way equities trade, and have had material consequences on the markets. Other asset classes, such as foreign exchange, futures, options, even Treasuries have faced this to varying extents; technological advancement (and, in the case of equities, changes in the organization and philosophy of exchanges) has been a transformative force. The influence of technology was felt as early as 1971, when the National Association of Securities Dealers (NASDAQ) began trading as the world's first electronic stock market. At that time, the major stock exchanges were New York Stock Exchange (NYSE), American Stock Exchange (AMEX) and Philadelphia Stock Exchange (PSE). Aside from this exchanges,

Equities - Valuation

Chicago has been home to other exchanges (CBOE and CME) which have large market share in options and futures (equities, indices and commodities). In 2000, NASDAQ members voted to restructure the exchange into a for-profit company. NYSE merged with rival Archipelago and became a for-profit private company. In 2007, NYSE merged with the fully electronic Euronext and became a transatlantic exchange. Around the same time NASDAQ bought PSE. NYSE Euronext bought AMEX in 2008. In 2013, Intercontinental Exchange (ICE) bought NYSE-Euronext. As electronic processing, communication and execution became mainstream, the floor (or the pit) became less important, with the vast majority of orders being routed electronically; executions got much faster. All this consolidation and commercial-orientation of the exchanges prompted them to be more profit-minded.

As trading became computer-dependent, there have been two clear dimensions to it - algorithmic execution and algorithmic investment decision making. Most of the discussion in this section relates to algorithmic execution, which uses computers to optimally submit orders and transact on platforms, once the buy/ sell decision is made. High-Frequency firms, discussed below, also (in addition to execution) make buy/sell decisions using algorithms, as do other quantitative investment firms, which may trade at a much lower frequency and have longer holding periods (many ETFs / smart beta funds are classic examples).[141]

Exchanges are required to make sure that each execution is done at the *National Best Bid/Offer (NBBO)* at that time, which requires looking at prices on other exchanges and routing orders to a different exchange when there are more favorable prices elsewhere. Now, this rule (Rule 611) only requires exchanges to look at the "top of the market" for the best quote rather than the full size of the order (i.e. depth of book), so a part of a large order could get executed at a sub-optimal level if the best quote is for a small size (and so the order gets routed there), but the order is only partially filled at the best level and the quotes below the best price are worse than those on other venues.

While the exchanges were reorganizing themselves, other big changes were taking place in electronic markets as well, facilitated by technology. The big change here was the advent of *dark pools*; unlike exchanges where everyone can see the entire order book and what orders (how much at what price) are in the queue, dark pools function like quasi-exchanges where the common order book is not visible. Participants see only their orders and get posted once their orders are filled. This was advertised as a great benefit to the buy-side; the market would not know of their large orders, which could "hide" until they get filled[142]. The drawback of "hiding", though, is that hidden orders are not on public feeds, so such orders may get "traded through" and not get executed even if the price limit is reached on another venue; had the same order been lit, it would have been executed against the order on the other venue.

There are now more than 60 trading venues, 12 of which (as of July 2017) are exchanges and the others are alternate venues. *Reg NMS* (NBBO) rules also apply here (to the extent the orders are lit); but these alternate venues can also fill orders at the same level as the best price on the exchanges (since they do not publish quotes), essentially free-riding on the public prices at the exchange. These dark pools (and now the exchanges too) also offer a plethora of order types and execution algorithms, either designed to take advantage of less price-sensitive order flow, pace their execution with market liquidity, or break up large orders and not make it obvious that a large order is on the blotter. Other types of Alternative Trading Systems (ATS)[143] were also

---

[141] We discussed quantitative investing earlier in this chapter and in Chapters 4 and 6.

[142] Also, dark pools can restrict who trades on their platform (as long as they remain below a threshold volume in that security), so theoretically clients can be led to believe that they are not trading against a certain type of investor. In reality, though, the composition of market participants at these venues is probably similar to exchanges. Regulators have fined dark pool operators in cases that accused operators of misrepresenting their pool to clients, and even using client orders to inform their own trading.

[143] In Europe, the corresponding term is Multilateral Trading Facility (MTF).

Capital Markets and Investments

set up. ECNs are electronic venues that match buyers and sellers, essentially by-passing exchanges. Most venues offer access fee to orders that provide liquidity (the liquidity *maker*) and charges the order that uses the existing liquidity in the venue (the *taker*). This causes informational biases between the different types of clients on the platform, often exaggerated through the various order types, as well as conflicts of interest between clients and the proprietary desks of the sponsoring firm, since the dark pool owner can trade internal flows against client orders. While there is little order/ quote transparency on all these alternate venues, FINRA has recently required them to report volume statistics and report trades to the Consolidated Tape (exchanges have always reported trades to the tape); most estimates suggest that at least 40% of trading volume is off the traditional exchange. The regulations that apply to these alternate venues depends on whether they register with the SEC as an exchange or a broker (most are brokers).

Retail brokers (such as Charles Schwab or TDAmeritrade) do not send their client orders directly to the exchange; instead they send it to a wholesaler (such as Citadel or KCG Securities), who then executes the trade to get "best execution", which is not clearly defined (may be the fastest execution, best price, etc.). Supporters of this argue that this lowers trading costs for small investors; opponents complain about conflict of interest.

Another development in the equities market has been the rise of high-frequency trading shops. This has been a direct result of the exchanges getting commercial. That prompted them to offer different tiers of service, including providing very fast access to order data, a multitude or order types and "rebates" for providing liquidity. As a result, several high-frequency shops have mushroomed, who operate by putting in, executing and cancelling trades at very high speeds (several thousand trades a second) using sophisticated computers and infrastructure. While high frequency trading has attracted a lot of attention, it has not attracted large amounts of institutional capital. That said, many large market-making/ buy-side firms (e.g. Citadel, Renaissance Technologies, Tower Research) have placed special focus on high-frequency trading.[144]

While most of the discussion above has been on algorithmic execution and order routing (which high frequency firms are very skilled at), high frequency firms also make investment decisions algorithmically. Many of these firms focus on other traders' (retail, institutional buy-side, sell side, other high-frequency traders) motives and optimizes against that. The attributes of the security they trade are almost irrelevant; all relevant information is in the price action and order flow. Speed is of essence; in addition to sophisticated decision making (and execution) algorithms, the aim is to get the information first from trading venues through very fast connectivity and co-locating servers next to the matching engines of the exchange and be first in line with their orders. By getting this information quickly directly from exchanges (through paid direct feeds), processing it quickly and computing a synthetic NBBO, high frequency firms can forecast the public NBBO before it is published through the *Security Information Processor (SIP)*[145]. Because of their very advanced end-to-end technology, they can transact in microseconds.

High frequency trading may involve actual trades (usually tiny), held for very short periods of time before unwinding, or orders that are submitted and cancelled before they are executed. The latter creates noise and deludes the market into believing that abundant liquidity exists, which vanishes when a counterparty tries to execute. The actual trades are very small, so create a semblance of liquidity and very tight bid-offer spreads and volume, but only at the top of the market in miniscule size. Large orders will not benefit from this, which is why some algos (also referred to as *Order Management Systems* or *OMS*) chop these orders into small bits.

---

[144] But, it is not all large players, small firms (few people, with very fast computers, co-located servers at data centers and special data feeds) have created very lucrative businesses.

[145] There are actually two SIPs, one for stocks which have primary listing on NYSE and the other for stocks with primary listing on NASDAQ. NASDAQ is working on reducing the latency in its SIP.

Equities - Valuation

Also, the rebates that exchanges provide participants for "making" liquidity provide strong incentives for high frequency firms to enter into one side of the trade and then immediately unwind, earning the rebate on both legs. High frequency firms are rumored to have very high Sharpe ratios (even double digits; Sharpe Ratio of 1 is usually considered very good for traditional strategies), but are not considered scalable for institutional size. HFTs often invest through their prime brokers, adding another level of anonymity. This also requires very advanced risk systems at the prime broker's end to continuously monitor these firms.

Current Status

Currently the regulators are embroiled in a discussion with market participants on which aspects of high frequency trading help the market, and which aspects don't. The high-frequency supporters highlight that such trades allow efficient flow of information and minimize arbitrage opportunities, provide more liquidity to retail investors, do nothing illegally and are small mom-and-pop operations. The naysayers emphasize that they mislead markets by stuffing quotes, putting in orders with no intent to execute, "front-run" markets because they have access to order flow and quotes before other players and are generally disruptive because they do not "invest" but continually flip positions with no view on how the position is likely to perform longer term. Some of the angst is also directed towards the exchanges and the trading venues. As exchanges got profit-focused, they created differentiated offerings in terms of speed and order–types, which nourished HFT. As dark pools emerged, their opaque process created opportunities and risks; in fact several dark pool operators settled with regulators for not treating their customers equally. Because of the non-transparency, many of these cases were tried with the help of whistleblowers. The ideal world would try to keep all the positive aspects of the HFTs, while minimizing the negative impacts – new platforms such as *IEX*[146] (which recently got SEC approval to become an exchange), or rules such as minimum order fill rates or quote life, control over access fees are all steps in that direction. Even prominent high-frequency quantitative hedge funds like Renaissance Technologies have filed patents for solutions to prevent themselves from being exploited by predatory HFT strategies[147]. While the effect of HFT on the market may be generally benign so far (except for sudden short-lived *flash crashes*), regulation is trying to ensure it stays that way. At the same time, it is trying to ensure that all customers are treated fairly, and one customer's information is not improperly used to benefit another. The SEC is also trying to conduct pilot projects to get a precise sense of what the maker-taker fees actually do to market liquidity.

---

[146] IEX slows down the processing of client orders by about 350 milliseconds by adding 38 miles of redundant cable, which gives the IEX severs enough time to update prices on its exchange, to avoid getting picked off by HFT strategies.

[147] The trading strategies of Renaissance Technologies has high turnover (i.e. securities are bought and sold very often), making this issue especially relevant for them. According to the patent document, like other funds/ brokers, their orders are broken up on a central sever into small bits, which are then routed to different venues, based on price and liquidity; this idea is commonplace. The difference is that these orders are mainly sent to *colocated* servers belonging to the exchange (which offer the lowest latency fastest execution) with specific instructions on exactly when these trades should be executed. The co-located servers are instructed to synchronize the trades, using atomic, optical or GPS clocks, so that HFT firms do not have enough time to identify an order on one exchange and then trade against it on another exchange.

Capital Markets and Investments

Market Microstructure:
- ✓ Exchange-Traded Markets – All orders get aggregated in a centralized limit-order book.
  - Lit Markets: This order book, comprising size, direction and price limit is public
  - Alternate Trading Systems: Comprising dark pools and ECNs, these venues do not publish the quotes or the order book. Clients face a confidentiality-better execution trade-off.
  - Clients run the risk of dark pool owners seeing their orders and acting against them
  - Some exchanges are slow to calculate the best bid-offer. High-frequency clients who pay extra can get the raw data very quickly, calculate prices before the exchange, and predict and be positioned for the exchange price when it is published.
  - Some high-frequency clients put in many orders, intending to give a different impression on the book and cancel them before execution.
  - There are many order-types (a huge change from the old days of market and limit orders).
  - Clients are paid to direct liquidity to the venue. So some trading strategies are solely designed to capture this "rebate", and unwind the trade right away.

REFERENCES

O'Hara, M. *High Frequency Market Microstructure*

Bodie, Zvi, A. Kane, & A. Marcus. *Investments*. Mc-Graw Hill Higher Education

Concept Release on Equity Market Structure. Securities & Exchange Commission

Equity Market Structure Literature Review Part II: High Frequency Trading. Division of Trading and Markets. U.S. Securities & Exchange Commission

Trahan, Francois, M. Kantrowitz, E. Needell. *A Summer Intern's Guide to Understanding Macro's Role in the Investment Process*. Cornerstone Macro Strategy

12. Portfolio Theory, Asset Allocation and Factor Models

The previous chapter introduced equities and their institutional details, and discussed some frameworks for modeling and pricing equity stocks, focusing mainly on cash flows and relative multiples. We also mentioned the different valuation perspectives that institutional investors follow while investing in equities.

In this chapter, we delve deeper into how financial assets can be combined into a portfolio to get the "best" risk-return profiles. We start with specifying risks in an investment, and introduce a stylized characterization of an investor's preference for risk and return (important only for estimating certain empirical numbers later). We then look at combining multiple risky securities to give investors suitable risk-return tradeoffs. This prompts a discussion on what risks are important in pricing equities, and appropriate models to think about expected returns on equities. This leads to a brief overview of CAPM and multi-factor models such as the Fama-French models and other factors such as momentum and a few comments on market efficiency. This chapter presumes knowledge of basic statistics, so students who need a refresher should refer to Appendix II before proceeding.

While the ideas here are presented in the context of equities, the core concepts are just as relevant for other asset classes; investors use these techniques just as often to construct multi-asset portfolios. In that sense, these concepts are also relevant for fixed income securities and portfolios, which we discussed over the past four chapters. At the same time, the risk (sensitivity to interest rate shifts i.e. duration) and cash flows in Treasury portfolios can be clearly specified, so the portfolio construction and risk management is also more direct. Much of the content in this chapter may appear abstract and theoretical, but the ideas are used much more in practice than one might initially guess. In fact, many of the portfolio construction ideas that we talk about here often show up in discussions on *asset allocation*, where the question is to decide how much capital to allocate across different asset classes.

EXPECTED RETURN AND RISK

The starting point of any investment thesis involves coming up with an estimate of the expected return (over a certain specified timeframe) of the financial asset. Investors can get a sense of this by examining historical data (e.g. averaging historical returns, if the future is expected to be similar to the past), or setting expected price targets, based on fundamental analysis. Models (discussed later in the chapter) can also calculate expected returns for a stock if it is "fairly" priced.

The risk of the asset is defined as the uncertainty (or imprecision) of the expected return, since it is simply an estimate. This can be measured in different ways, such as the standard deviation of historical returns (again, assuming that the future is likely to look like the past, on average) or by examining the upside/ downside scenarios in the fundamental analysis.

For our discussion below, we will use historical return averages and historical return standard deviation (or variance) as measures of expected return and risk; other estimates can also be used.

INVESTORS' RISK-RETURN TRADEOFFS – UTILITY FUNCTION AND INDIFFERENCE CURVES

Given our premise of a risk-averse investor, we would expect the investor to take on more risk only if he expects a higher return. So, if we plot the risk and expected return combinations that an individual would equally prefer on an x-y axis, we will expect a positive slope.

Capital Markets and Investments

To build on this, let us assume that investors have a formula for scoring risk-return tradeoffs i.e. they substitute risk and return estimates in a formula and get back a score; the higher the score the more they like the combination. For example, that formula may look something like Eq. 12.1:

$$U = E(R_p) - 0.5 \times A \times \sigma_p^2 \qquad \text{Eq. 12.1}$$

Where U is the preference score (often called *Utility* value), $E(R_p)$ is the *expected return* of the portfolio, σ_p^2 is the *variance* of the portfolio (risk measure) and A, the degree of investor's risk aversion, represents the investor's preference for tradeoff between risk and return. As expected, U increases when $E(R_p)$ increases, σ_p^2 decreases or A increases. Figure 12.1 shows this - the left panel contains a few values of risk and return for which the investor is indifferent, since U = 0.1 for all these pairs (assuming A=1.4).

Figure 12.1 Representing Investor Preferences Graphically

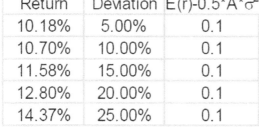
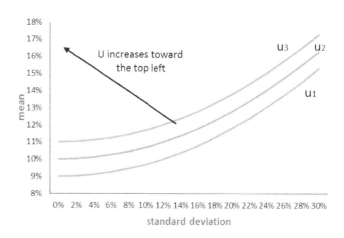

A (Captures Risk Aversion) = 1.4 in this example

The right panel of Figure 12.1 depicts this graphically. Each point represents a different risk-return combination, i.e. an asset, or a portfolio of assets. The values from the left panel are one of the lines in this figure; other lines represent different values of U. Along any one curved line, the investor is indifferent about which point he is on (i.e. which asset/portfolio he owns on that line), but the investor's aim is to move to higher values of U. While stylized, this function and graph captures the essence of investor behavior - for a given return level (i.e. an imaginary horizontal line) the investor prefers the lowest possible level of risk (i.e. leftmost part of the graph), whereas for a given risk level (i.e. imaginary vertical line), the investor prefers the highest return possible (i.e. the highest point on the graph). Both these areas maximize the value of U. Without other constraints, *the investor would prefer points on the top-left corner of the graph.*

> ✓ We assume that investors characterize securities in terms of their expected return and their risk (i.e. how much is the actual realized return likely to deviate from the expected return).
> ✓ Risk is often represented using the standard deviation of the return distribution.
> ✓ Under mean-variance utility investors seek to obtain the highest expected return for a given variance. Investor risk-return tradeoffs can be theoretically represented using utility functions of the form discussed in this section.

DIVERSIFICATION – THE CORE IDEAS

With these building blocks, let us introduce the basic principle of diversification. Compared to holding just one financial asset (and getting exposure to the risk and return associated with that asset), an investor can

Portfolio Theory, Asset Allocation and Factor Models

obtain a higher expected return *for the same risk*, if he holds other financial assets (which are not perfectly positively correlated with the first asset) along with (a lesser amount of) the first asset. Said another way, diversification allows investors to reduce their risk exposure to achieve their target total return, by holding a combination of securities in a suitable proportion, rather than concentrating their bets in only one security. For example, an investor can improve the risk-return profile of his portfolio by adding an international equity index to his existing holding in a US index. This argument also holds for adding additional equity stocks to a single-stock portfolio.

Consider two stocks A and B, with expected returns r_A and r_B, and risk σ_A and σ_B. Diversification implies that a portfolio (denoted by p subscript) which includes both A and B can achieve a better risk-return tradeoff than a portfolio that comprises either only of A or only of B. This is because random components of the returns of A and B can potentially cancel each other, so a portfolio of A and B can be potentially less volatile than either of them held in isolation. Of course, this will not happen if A and B are perfectly positively correlated, in which case there is no benefit to diversification.

Said more formally, the expected return is

$$E(r_p) = w_A E(r_A) + w_B E(r_B) \qquad \text{Eq. 12.2}$$

The portfolio variance is

$$\sigma^2(r_p) = w_A^2 \sigma_A^2 + w_B^2 \sigma_B^2 + 2 w_A w_B \sigma_A \sigma_B \rho(A,B) \qquad \text{Eq. 12.3}$$

with $w_A + w_B = 1$ where $\rho(A, B)$ is the correlation between A and B.

For any return target r^*, and the weights w_A (i.e. Dollar value of asset A in the portfolio/ total dollar value of the portfolio) and w_B that generate this return, the corresponding portfolio variance is lower than the variance in another hypothetical (long or short, potentially levered) portfolio generating the same return containing only one asset (A or B).

> *Example:* Figure 12.2 shows the effect of diversification in a two-asset portfolio, assuming different correlation levels. Each of the lines in the right panel (one for each correlation assumption) traces out the risk-return combinations achievable by varying the proportions of asset A and B in the portfolio (US and JP in the graph, respectively).
>
>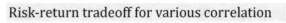
>
> **Figure 12.2 Diversification in a 2-asset portfolio**
>
>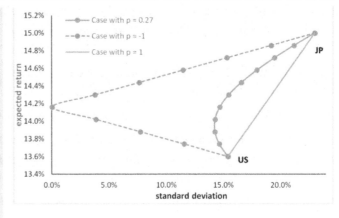
>
> If the correlation is +1, investing in any portfolio of US and JP is the same as a scaled position in either one (hence the straight line). With a correlation of -1, it is possible to reduce risk sharply. For any

Capital Markets and Investments

correlation in between, different portfolios of US and JP offer some reduction in risk. For example (assuming the correlation is 0.27), compared to a 100% weight in US, increasing the proportion of JP modestly (20%) in the portfolio reduces the risk as well as increases the expected return.

From Eq. 12.3, we can calculate the minimum variance of returns for any portfolio of two assets by minimizing σ with respect to w (by writing w_b as $1-w$). The minimum variance is:

$$\min \sigma_p^2 = \frac{(1-\rho^2)\sigma_1^2\sigma_2^2}{\sigma_1^2 - 2\rho\sigma_1\sigma_2 + \sigma_2^2}$$

To identify this portfolio, the weight of asset A in the portfolio with the above minimum variance is:

$$w^* = \frac{\sigma_2^2 - \rho\sigma_1\sigma_2}{\sigma_1^2 - 2\rho\sigma_1\sigma_2 + \sigma_2^2}$$

As a special case, we can consider two assets with equal standard deviation. The portfolio with the minimum variance is the equally weighted portfolio (i.e. $w^* = 0.5$), and the minimum variance is lower than the variance of either security individually.

As we keep adding securities to a portfolio, there are *decreasing returns to diversification*. The rate of risk reduction slows down and eventually tapers off, as shown in Figure 12.3. This is because, as we add securities to a portfolio, the variance of the securities matter less and less, and the *covariance* (similar to correlation, but an unscaled measure whose value depends on the magnitude of returns, not bound by -1 and 1) between the securities matters more and more. The correlation (or the covariance) in a global portfolio is likely to be lower than an all-US portfolio, so the benefit from diversification is higher in the global portfolio.

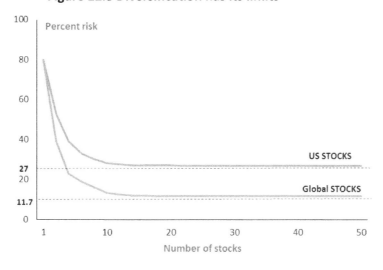

Figure 12.3 Diversification has its limits

To see this clearly, let us write down the formula for variance of returns of an equally weighted portfolio of N assets. The generalized version of Eq. 12.3 with equal weights can be written as:

$$\sigma_p^2 = \frac{1}{N^2}\sum_{i=1}^{N}\sigma_i^2 + \frac{1}{N^2}\sum_{i=1}^{N}\sum_{j\neq i}^{N}\text{cov}(r_i; r_j)$$

$$= \frac{1}{N}\left[\frac{1}{N}\sum_{i=1}^{N}\sigma_i^2\right] + \left[1 - \frac{1}{N}\right]\left[\frac{1}{N(N-1)}\sum_{i=1}^{N}\sum_{j\neq i}^{N}\text{cov}(r_i; r_j)\right]$$

$$= \frac{1}{N}[Average\ Variance] + \left[1 - \frac{1}{N}\right][Average\ Cov]$$

Portfolio Theory, Asset Allocation and Factor Models

As N gets large, the average variance matters less, and the average covariance matters more. If the individual security variances are high relative to the covariance between them, diversification will matter more than in a situation where the variances are small relative to the covariances.

The portfolio variance does not go to zero but reduces at a decreasing rate. Beyond a certain point, portfolio risk cannot be diversified away. But, the risk contribution a stock makes to a portfolio is (usually) less than the risk of the stock if held in isolation. A part of the stock risk gets diversified away (because of imperfect correlation with the rest of the portfolio); some of the risk remains. We will come back to the discussion on when to add a security to the portfolio later in the chapter, after we introduce the concept of Sharpe Ratio.

Portfolio *theory* (i.e. not set in stone, but a theory) emphasizes that investors are expected to hold stocks not in isolation but in well-diversified portfolios. So, the risk compensation that they receive (in the form of higher expected returns) should only be for that part of the stock risk that cannot be diversified away in a portfolio. If we express the expected return of a stock (i.e. compensation for bearing risk) as a sum of the risk free rate and a *risk premium*, the risk premium is a function of (only) the undiversifiable risk.

> The main ideas on diversification that we discussed in this section are:
>
> ✓ Imperfect correlation (i.e. less than +1) across securities reduces risk if the securities are held in a portfolio, than if they were held individually.
>
> ✓ There are decreasing returns from diversification as more names get added to the portfolio
>
> ✓ Expected returns from the stock (probably) depends on non-diversifiable risk. According to this theory, the expected return of a stock is equal to the risk-free rate plus a risk premium. The risk premium is a function of undiversifiable risk.

BUILDING ON DIVERSIFICATION – PORTFOLIO THEORY AND EFFICIENT FRONTIERS

In this section, we try to develop a full-fledged theory of allocating securities to create an "optimal" portfolio, using the principles we just highlighted. The discussion at times will get abstract and theoretical, but it will hopefully provide some insight about the tradeoffs driving the investing world. We start by investigating how a risk-free asset[148] influences portfolio choice, by considering a world with one risky asset (US equity index) and the risk-free bond. We then extend this to a situation with two risky assets (US and Japan) and the risk free asset. This theory (which includes the previous section) is often referred to as *Mean-Variance Optimization*, pioneered by Harry Markowitz in the early 1950s.

Case 1: Optimal Portfolio with One Risky Asset and the Risk Free Asset

If w is the weight in the risky asset, σ the volatility (standard deviation) of the risky asset, and r_f and r are the risk-free and expected risky returns respectively, applying Eq. 12.2, the portfolio return is:

$$r_p = w\,r + (1-w)\,r_f = r_f + w\,(r - r_f) \qquad \text{Eq. 12.4}$$

In the above equation, r is a *random variable* (see Annexure 3); all other values are known. So, using Eq. 12.4, expected portfolio return, variance and volatility are:

---

[148] Of course, as we discussed in the section on Treasuries, the risk-free bond itself is a nebulous concept. To make it completely risk-free, the asset's maturity needs to line up with our investment horizon. T-Bill are also often thought of as a suitable proxy, since T-Bills have low interest rate risk and presumably no default risk.

Capital Markets and Investments

$E[r_p] = r_f + w\,E[r - r_f]$ Eq. 12.5

$\sigma_p^2 = E[(r_p - E[r_p])^2] = w^2 \sigma^2$ Eq. 12.6

$\sigma_p = |w|\,\sigma$ Eq. 12.7

Combining Eq. 12.5 and Eq. 12.6,

$$E[r_p] = r_f + \frac{E[r] - r_f}{\sigma}\sigma_p$$ Eq. 12.8

Eq. 12.8 is the *Capital Allocation Line (CAL)*. Plotted on the $E[r_p]$ and σ_p coordinate axes, it represents the risk-return tradeoffs that are available (feasible) to an investor. The slope of the line **$[E(r) - r_f]/\sigma$** is the *Sharpe Ratio*, and represents the excess return the investor gets per unit of risk he takes. The intercept is the risk-free rate. To emphasize, the line only provides the set of feasible portfolios in this two-asset world; it says nothing about which particular portfolio the investor chooses. To find that portfolio, we need to use the investor's preference for risk versus return.

Figure 12.4 Optimal Portfolio from Capital Allocation Line

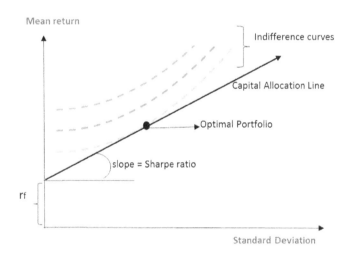

Figure 12.4 shows this graphically, using investor preferences from the curves in Figure 12.1 (which also used similar risk-return axes). The Capital Allocation Line shows the investment possibilities available to the investor. The curves represent investor preferences; the investor is indifferent between any point on a particular curve and is happier on higher curves (i.e. up and to the left). The investor picks the tangency portfolio (the point where the CAL is tangent to a curve) to reach the highest possible curve[149], while constrained to hold portfolios on the CAL.

This is essential a mathematical optimization problem – choose w to maximize the value of U in Eq. 12.1 subject to satisfying the CAL equation Eq. 12.8. i.e.

Essentially we substitute for $E[r_p]$ and σ_p^2 from Eq. 12.5 and Eq. 12.6 into the above function to express U in terms of w, then take first derivatives with respect to w and set that equal to zero, to solve for the optimal w. The solution is:

---

[149] If an indifference curve goes through the CAL, there is a higher curve that just touches the line (i.e. line is tangent), since the curves are a continuum, obtained by changing values of U.

Portfolio Theory, Asset Allocation and Factor Models

$$w^* = \frac{E[r] - r_f}{A\sigma^2} \qquad \text{Eq. 12.9}$$

As A (coefficient of risk aversion) gets smaller (A is usually assumed to be between 1 and 5), the investor gets less risk averse and the holdings of the risky asset relative to the risk free asset gets larger. Also, the relation with the other variables – risk-free rate, expected return and volatility of the risky asset - are all as expected. In particular, the value of w* can exceed 1, if the expected return is high, risk low, and risk aversion low. In this situation, the investor borrows (at the risk-free rate) to hold more than 100% of the allocation in the risky asset.

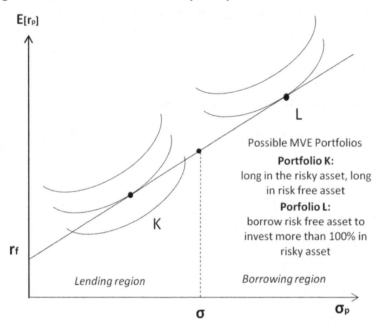

Figure 12.5 Levered Portfolios may be Optimal for Some Investors

Figure 12.5 shows optimal portfolios for two alternative sets of preferences (i.e. two different individuals) represented by two sets of curves. Their optimal holdings are at the (respective) tangency points with the Capital Allocation Line. One individual is risk averse, and invests part of his cash in the risky asset (with risk σ, denoted by the point where the vertical line meets the capital allocation line), and the rest in bonds (i.e. lending at the risk free rate), represented by portfolio K. The other investor wants higher expected return than 100% equity allocation will allow, and is happy to take on the incremental risk, so borrows at the risk free rate to invest the borrowing in the risky asset, represented by portfolio L. The proportion of the risky asset in the investor's total portfolio depends on his risk preference.

- ✓ The Capital Allocation Line describes the menu of possible risk/return trade-offs between a risk-free and risky asset. Its slope is the Sharpe ratio for any portfolio created using these two assets.
- ✓ The optimal portfolio with a risky and risk-free asset for any investor is the tangency point of that investor's indifference curves with the Capital Allocation Line.
- ✓ The tangency portfolio of a particularly risk-loving investor may involve borrowing at the risk free rate to have an allocation greater than 100% to the risky asset.

Capital Markets and Investments

Case 2: Optimal Portfolio with Multiple Risky Assets and One Risk-Free Asset

Let us consider a world with multiple (two in this example, but the idea works for more) risky assets and one risk free asset. To get to the optimal portfolio, we split the problem into two parts. First, limiting ourselves only to the universe of risky securities, we build on the core diversification-related concepts that we developed early on to get a sense of what the optimal risky portfolio should look like. Once we have that, we treat this risky portfolio as a single risky asset and apply the ideas from the prior section, to arrive at the final portfolio.

Figure 12.6 is similar to **Figure 12.2**, extended to short positions (i.e. w<0 and w >1). The sections of the risk-return curve with short (Japan / US) positions are marked.[150] We also point out the minimum variance portfolio, discussed earlier. Importantly, for every point in the part of the curve below (i.e. with returns less than that of) the minimum variance portfolio, the investor can pick a different portfolio (above) to get higher returns with the same level of risk. The part of the curve above the minimum variance portfolio is called the *Efficient Frontier*; the investor's optimal portfolio will always lie in that part. [151]

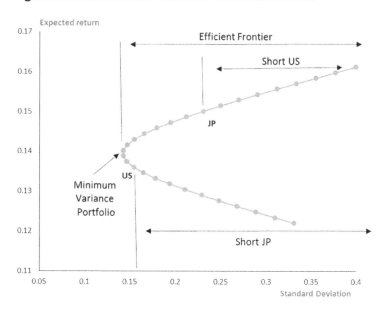

Figure 12.6 Risk-Return Tradeoff - Efficient Frontier

With multiple risky assets (and a risk-free asset), more than one Capital Allocation Line is available. Essentially, a different CAL can be constructed using a different point on the Efficient Frontier (all CALs start from the risk-free rate); investors can potentially access risk-return combinations on any of these CALs. Since the investor finally wants to end up at the highest possible indifference curve, the CAL that matters is the steepest CAL of all these possible CALs i.e. the CAL with the highest Sharpe Ratio. That is the CAL which forms a tangent with the Efficient Frontier. The tangency (risky) portfolio offers the same Sharpe Ratio as the steepest CAL i.e. it has the maximum Sharpe Ratio across all risk portfolios. This tangency portfolio is called the *Mean-Variance-Efficient* (MVE) portfolio. Importantly, this optimal risky portfolio is the same for all investors, regardless of their preferences. It is the portfolio with the maximum Sharpe Ratio, which does not depend on investor preferences.

---

[150] This entire curve is also called the Minimum Variance Frontier, since it maps the lowest achievable standard deviation for each level of expected return. For two-asset portfolios, it comprises all possible asset combinations.

[151] With more than two risky assets, each pair of assets can produce such a curve; the Efficient Frontier is then constructed by taking the outer boundary (envelope) of all these curves.

Portfolio Theory, Asset Allocation and Factor Models

Once we have this portfolio, we can pretend to be back in the single risky asset world, with the MVE portfolio as the risky asset. Then, using the ideas in the previous section, we can find out the proportion of the portfolio in the risky and risk-free asset. This allocation (between risk-free and risky asset) depends on investor preferences, but the composition of the risky portfolio is the same for all investors; it is the MVE. This result (of every investor holding the identical risky portfolio, regardless of risk appetite) is called *Two Fund Separation*. It is as if the investment universe is split into a risky bucket and a risk free bucket- every investor holds both buckets, but the relative weights depends on the investor's risk appetite. If everyone holds the MVE (albeit in different proportions), the MVE has to be the aggregate of all securities issued in the market (i.e. the *market portfolio*), since all assets need to be held, at the market clearing price. This serves as a theoretical foundation to justify the relevance of index funds; they are the optimal MVE portfolio. Figure 12.7 shows this graphically. The CAL through the MVE (i.e. the market portfolio) is called the *Capital Market Line*. To set up the mathematical optimization problem to obtain the MVE portfolio, we can maximize the Sharpe Ratio (slope of CAL) subject to Eq. 12.2 and Eq. 12.3.

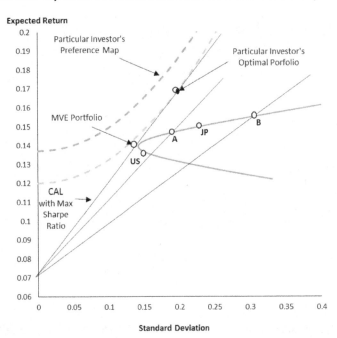

Figure 12.7 Optimal Portfolio with Risk-free and Two Risky Assets

To summarize, the CAL provided the risk-return tradeoffs available to an investor with an investment universe of a risk-free asset and one risky asset. The slope of this line is the Sharpe Ratio. The tangency point of the CAL with the indifference curve decided the optimal portfolio for an investor. With multiple risky assets, the investor can choose between CALs, for every point on the Efficient Frontier. The steepest CAL maximizes Sharpe Ratio, and is tangent to the Efficient Frontier. The tangency point is the MVE portfolio. This implies that the risky portfolio is same for all investors, regardless of risk preferences; the risk free asset and the MVE portfolio are the only two portfolios that matter; this is referred to as Two-Fund Separation. The MVE portfolio has to be the market portfolio in equilibrium, since all assets need to be held. The tangency between the CAL through the MVE portfolio and the indifference curve map provides the optimal portfolio for the investor, and decides the investor's allocation between the market portfolio and the risk-free asset. Every

Capital Markets and Investments

investor, regardless of risk attitudes, holds the same risky portfolio (i.e. risky assets are held in the same proportion by everyone); the proportion of the risk free asset to the risky portfolio changes according to risk preferences.

Quantitatively, this problem can be solved using a sequence of optimization exercises (assuming means, variances and covariances of returns are available). First, we derive the mean-variance efficient frontier by finding the portfolio that minimizes variance for every expected return level. Then we find the portfolio with the highest Sharpe Ratio that lies on the efficient frontier; this is the mean-variance efficient (i.e. tangency) portfolio[152]. Mathematically, these two steps can be completed in the same step. We then find a particular investor's optimal portfolio by maximizing his specific utility function, subject to the constraint that his chosen portfolio lies on the line passing through the risk free portfolio and the tangency portfolio (i.e. the portfolio has the same Sharpe ratio as the tangency portfolio).

When does adding a new security improve a portfolio's risk characteristics?

We discussed the limits of diversification earlier in the chapter. Conceptually, adding a new asset to the portfolio can help only if this new asset increases the portfolio's Sharpe Ratio (SR). If ρ is the correlation between the new asset (subscripted NEW below) and the present portfolio (subscript p), it can be shown that, for small w,

$$\frac{\partial SR}{\partial w} > 0 \text{ if } SR_{NEW} \geq SR_p \rho$$

So, it makes sense to keep adding the new asset until the Sharpe ratio of the portfolio rises such that partial derivative drops to zero, i.e. $SR_{NEW} = SR_p \rho$. That is the equilibrium condition for the optimal portfolio. Rewriting,

$$\frac{E[r_{NEW} - r_f]}{\sigma_{NEW}} = \frac{E[r_p - r_f]}{\sigma_p} \rho,$$

$$\text{or} \quad E[r_{NEW} - r_f] = \frac{\text{cov}[r_{NEW}, r_p]}{\sigma_p^2} E[r_p - r_f]$$

This equation should hold for any security (say security i) and any portfolio (say, the MVE portfolio). We discussed earlier that the MVE is the market portfolio in equilibrium. So, changing the subscripts to reflect this,

$$E[r_i - r_f] = \frac{\text{cov}[r_i, r_{Mkt}]}{\sigma_{Mkt}^2} E[r_{Mkt} - r_f] \qquad \text{Eq. 12.10}$$

Eq. 12.10 is known as the *Capital Asset Pricing Model (CAPM)*, a framework for pricing securities (i.e. estimating expected returns) that has been the starting point of much of financial theory. We discuss this below in more detail.

---

[152] The theory we just discussed postulates that every investor will hold a combination of this portfolio and the risk free asset in different proportions, depending on their risk aversion.

Portfolio Theory, Asset Allocation and Factor Models

- ✓ For a (possibly large set) of securities, one can compute a set of efficient portfolios. These portfolios provide the highest expected return for any level of standard deviation. They comprise the upper part of the mean standard deviation frontier (the efficient frontier).
- ✓ If there is a risk-free asset, the mean-variance efficient portfolio (MVE) is the risky portfolio with the highest Sharpe ratio. This is obtained by drawing the line through the risk free rate that is tangent to the mean-standard deviation frontier. This is the relevant capital allocation line.
- ✓ This tangency CAL is often called the Capital Market Line (CML), since the MVE portfolio is the market portfolio in equilibrium, as every investor holds the same risky (MVE) portfolio.
- ✓ To find the optimal portfolio (combination of the risk-free asset and the MVE), find the tangency point of this CML with the highest possible indifference curve. This portfolio is different for every investor
- ✓ It makes sense to include a new asset in a portfolio as long as the Sharpe Ratio of the new asset is greater than the product of the Sharpe of the portfolio and the asset-portfolio correlation.

Market Frictions - Effect on the Optimal Portfolio

So far, in our current set-up, there are no constraints on what the investor can buy, sell or short. We discussed situations and optimal portfolios when the investor is able to lend or borrow (unlikely) at the risk-free rate, and is able to go long or short the mean-variance efficient portfolio of securities. Let us consider situations when some of these outcomes are not possible.

First, *the risk free asset may not exist* (i.e. all assets may have some payoff volatility over the investment horizon). In this situation, we can consider all assets to be risky, and construct the efficient frontier as before. In this situation, the optimal portfolio will lie of the frontier itself[153], and will be the point of tangency between the frontier and the indifference map (i.e. which point on the frontier allows the investor to reach the highest possible indifference curve).

Next, even if there is a risk free rate/ asset, *it may not be realistic to assume that any financial investor can borrow at the risk free rate*[154] ; typically a regular investor will face a higher borrowing cost than the government. In such a situation, the Capital Allocation Line is not a straight line; it has a kink at the MVE portfolio (the CAL gets flatter as it extends beyond the MVE portfolio; it looks like an inverted V). Like before, the optimal portfolio is the tangency point between the (now kinked) CAL and the indifference map.

There may also be constraints on the maximum amount of leverage/ shorting that the investor can take on, etc. In this situation, the feasible set of outcomes get restricted. For example, if an investor cannot borrow, the solution is restricted to the points on the CAL between a 100% allocation to the risk free asset and a 100% allocation to the MVE portfolio, i.e. only allocations of type K in Figure 12.5 are possible (the CAL gets vertical (downwards) at the MVE, reflecting the impossibly high cost to obtain leverage).

Implementing these constraints in the form of a mathematical optimization problem is also straightforward, since they can be reflected by either rewriting the constraints or adding more constraints. Of course, this

---

[153] There is no concept of a Capital Allocation Line, because there is no lending/ borrowing rate and a risk-free asset (i.e. the intercept on the y-axis of the CAL is not defined.

[154] All investors can *lend* at the risk-free rate by buying Treasuries (government-issued securities).

Capital Markets and Investments

makes it numerically challenging to get robust globally optimal solutions, prompting analysts to consider other methods that we will mention later.

CAPITAL ASSET PRICING MODEL (CAPM)

Assumptions of the CAPM

The Capital Asset Pricing Model is an equilibrium model[155] that follows directly from the diversification/mean-variance optimizing assumptions discussed in this chapter. While Markowitz pioneered the thought process, William Sharpe, John Lintner and Jay Mossin had critical contributions to formalize this into a tangible model (over a decade after Markowitz's original idea). It assumes a single period investment horizon, with perfectly competitive markets (i.e. individual investors are price takers, no taxes, frictionless markets i.e. no transaction costs and freely available information) with investments limited to traded financial assets and mean-variance optimizing rational investors. Investor preferences do not need to be identical (in the last section, we confirmed that preferences did not play a role in determining the MVE portfolio), but arbitrary preferences could lead to violation of mean variance optimization as the optimal investor strategy. For a given investor, as long as risk aversion stays constant (e.g. risk appetite does not vary with wealth levels), the CAPM result will hold.

Relevance of the CAPM

A later section will delve into details about testing the CAPM and suggesting improvements, but, at the outset, there are other models that are supported by empirical data more than the CAPM. So, in a sense, the CAPM is "wrong" (but all models are likely wrong). Despite this, the CAPM remains useful, as it was the first (and remains the simplest) model of its kind; some newer models are more complicated and less intuitive (albeit arguably better performing), but are essentially extensions of the same framework. CAPM is used to evaluate portfolio managers (like Black Scholes' implied volatility, which we will discuss in the section on options, it sets a baseline for communication and comparison across investors), justify the success of index funds and serve as a starting point for estimating expected returns and for cost of capital computations (e.g. for valuing securities).

Interpreting the CAPM

Eq. 12.10 is often written as

$$E[r_i - r_f] = \beta_i E[r_{Mkt} - r_f] \quad \text{Eq. 12.11}$$

$$\text{where } \beta_i = \frac{\text{cov}[r_i, r_{Mkt}]}{\sigma^2_{Mkt}} \quad \text{Eq. 12.12}$$

This connects the expected returns of asset i to that of the overall market, with β capturing the sensitivity of asset's returns to the market. Plotted on the E[r] – β coordinate axes (Figure 12.8), the resulting line is called the *Security Market Line*; its slope indicates how much extra return an investor needs for a unit increase in market exposure (β). $E[r_{MKT} - r_f]$ shows the excess return of the market over the risk free rate, and is called the *Market Risk Premium*. The $cov[r_i, r_{MKT}]$ term in Eq. 12.12 summarizes to what extent the returns of this asset moves with the market; that is the component of the asset's return that cannot be hedged and needs to be compensated. The expected return of a stock is a linear function of its beta. The part of asset i's return that

---

[155] The term "equilibrium" is borrowed from physics. An equilibrium model is a model whose results are derived assuming every market participant tries to reach their goals, and prices adjust so that markets "clear" i.e. at the final prices, every economic agent is at their optimal point and has no reason to change allocations. Riskier assets need to have higher returns, for investors to hold them in equilibrium. Of course, in this framework, investors only care about non-diversifiable risk; if that were not true, the results would change.

Portfolio Theory, Asset Allocation and Factor Models

is unrelated to the overall market return can be hedged and, according to the CAPM, does not require compensation in terms of higher returns.

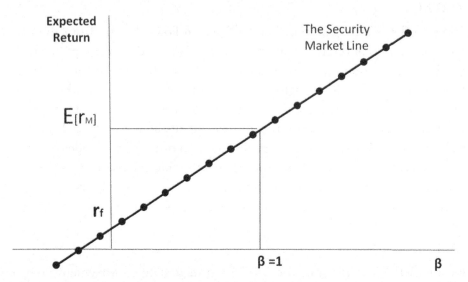

Figure 12.8 The Security Market Line

Example: Suppose the beta estimate for IBM and GD are 1.57 and 0.46 respectively. Assume the risk-free rate is 5%, the volatility of the market portfolio is 15.5% and average risk aversion is 3.47. An investor's portfolio comprises 50% IBM and 50% GD stock. What is the CAPM estimate of the expected returns of this portfolio?

Using Eq. 12.9, the market risk premium is $E[r_{MKT} - r_f] = A\, \sigma_{Mkt}^2 = 3.47 * (.155)^2 = 8.34\%$. If the expected market return were given to us, we could have used that instead. Using this result, and applying the CAPM (Eq. 12.11), the expected individual stock returns are 18.1% and 8.84% for IBM and GD respectively. The expected return for a 50-50 portfolio of these stocks is $0.5 * 0.181 + 0.5 * 0.0884 = 13.47\%$

Estimating Betas (and Alphas) in the CAPM

To formalize this idea further and understand how betas are computed, suppose we partition a security's risk into two orthogonal components - one that is correlated with the overall market movement (*systematic risk*), and another part that is completely unrelated to the overall market (*idiosyncratic or firm-specific risk*). One way to perform this decomposition is to run a regression (Annexure 3 covers regression basics) of the individual security's historical returns (excess returns over Treasuries, to be precise) on that of the market returns. Suppose the regression is represented as Eq. 12.11, and we have historical data for r_i, r_f and r_{Mkt}. We can create time series of excess returns (i.e. returns over the risk free rate)[156], for both the market and the stock, and run a regression of the security's excess returns on the market's excess returns (Eq. 12.13), and obtain estimates for the slope (*Beta*) and the intercept (we call this *Alpha*, or α)[157]. In security excess return – market excess return space, this regression line should pass through the origin (i.e. $\alpha = 0$), if the CAPM, on average, has estimated returns correctly over time. Figure 12.9Figure 12.9 shows an estimation exercise using a sample of

---

[156] Many popular academic papers have used monthly returns for 5 years (60 data points), but other frequencies (weekly/ daily) or time windows (shorter or longer periods) are also reasonable.

[157] Some people call this the Jensen Alpha.

data. The regression coefficient, beta, captures the co-movement between the market and the security (security's sensitivity to market movements), whereas the regression residual captures the idiosyncratic risk. The intercept (alpha) measures how well the model prices the security. A large alpha may either suggest mispricing (i.e. security is cheap if alpha is positive and vice versa) or an inappropriate model; it's a matter of judgement to decide which one it is.[158] Eq. 12.14 (obtained by taking variances of Eq. 12.13.) shows how the total variance (volatility squared) of a single stock can be split into (the square of) market risk and idiosyncratic risk. The idiosyncratic risk, which results from the volatility of the error term in the regression, cancels out for the aggregate portfolio. The CAPM ignores this risk[159], since, according to the theory, securities are expected to be held as part of well-diversified portfolios, so their idiosyncratic risk should cancel out and need not be compensated.

$$r_i - r_f = \beta_i(r_{Mkt} - r_f) + \varepsilon_i \qquad \text{Eq. 12.13}$$

$$\sigma_i^2 = \beta_i^2 \sigma_{Mkt}^2 + \overline{\sigma_{Idio}^2} \qquad \text{Eq. 12.14}$$

Figure 12.9 Estimating Beta and Alpha using the CAPM

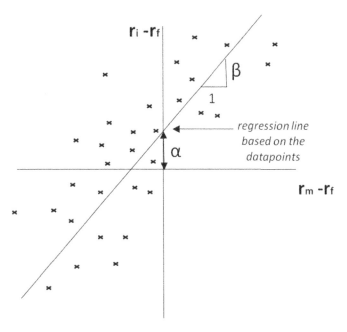

Even if an analyst believes that the future is going to resemble the past, using these ideas in practice is more different than it first appears. For example, the beta for a stock, calculated using weekly data can be very different (or even of opposite sign!) from the beta calculated with monthly data, over the same time interval. Betas computed over different time periods can also vary materially. This is essentially because of the quirks of regression as an estimation tool, or the noise in the data, especially in small samples. Various analytics systems deal with these issues differently, by smoothing estimates, considering subjective views with prior estimates (shrinkage estimators). Many analysts use industry betas (risk of the industry relative to the overall

---

[158] It is important to remember that the regression outputs are estimates of random variables; the issues of size and significance (discussed in Annexure 3) are important in deciding how heavily to rely on these statistical estimates.

[159] Subsequent empirical research has shown that returns vary with idiosyncratic risk, so this questions an important fundamental assumption of CAPM.

Portfolio Theory, Asset Allocation and Factor Models

market), which are easier to estimate, and then make an adjustment for whether this particular stock is more or less risky than the overall industry.

> ✓ Mean-variance theory predicts that all investors hold the market portfolio and mix it with the risk-free asset, in various proportions. This provides theoretical support for index funds.
> ✓ The Capital Asset Pricing Model (CAPM) follows from mean-variance theory and frictionless one-period investors. According to the CAPM, the expected return on stock is a linear function of its sensitivity to market movements (also called Beta). The stock's actual return above the CAPM-predicted return is called Alpha.
> ✓ In this framework, investors are only compensated for risk that is correlated with the market (captured by beta), and not for other residual risk that can be neutralized in a well-diversified portfolio. Systematic risk is priced by the market, whereas idiosyncratic risk is not.
> ✓ The CAPM, despite several drawbacks, can be used as a starting point for cost of capital computations and a baseline for evaluating investment managers.

INTRODUCTION TO FACTOR MODELS[160]

So far, we have discussed ideas grounded firmly in theoretical arguments, and investor behavior. However, the conclusions from this intellectual discourse have not stood up very well to empirical rigor. Also, the implementation details are tricky when it comes to replicating the theoretical ideas, despite having clear testable inferences. At the same time, Steve Ross' Arbitrage Pricing Theory (APT) developed in 1976, which postulated that a security's returns are a linear function of its sensitivity to various market indices or systematic "factors", was gaining ground. The CAPM, in fact, is a special case of a (one) factor model.

Arbitrage Pricing Theory Overview

It is worthwhile to quickly cover Arbitrage Pricing Theory (APT) since factor models are based on this idea; besides, the terminology takes a little getting used to. Security returns are assumed to follow a *factor structure* as in Eq. 12.15, i.e. the returns (r) on security i are a linear combination of k systematic factors (F) and a random error term. β_{ij} is the sensitivity of asset i's returns to the jth factor and is called the *factor loading* or the *factor sensitivity* or *factor exposure*. APT postulates (Eq. 12.16) that the expected returns of security i equals the sum of the risk free rate and the sum of the products of the corresponding factor loadings (from Eq. 12.15) and the factor *risk premiums* (RP_j) or *factor returns*, the excess return compensation for a unit exposure to that particular factor.

$$r_i = a_i + \sum_{j=1}^{k} \beta_{ij} F_j + \varepsilon_i \qquad \text{Eq. 12.15}$$

$$E(r_i) = r_f + \sum_{j=1}^{k} \beta_{ij} RP_j \qquad \text{Eq. 12.16}$$

---

[160] The section on Risk Models in Chapter 5 has a short discussion on the essentials of factor models; interested readers may want to read that before delving into the details here.

$$\text{var}(r_i) = \underbrace{\sum_{j=1}^{k} \beta_{ij}^2 \text{var}(F_j)}_{\text{Systematic Risk}} + \underbrace{\overline{\sigma_i^2}}_{\substack{\text{diversifiable} \\ \text{idiosyncratic risk}}} \qquad \text{Eq. 12.17}$$

Assumes factors are independent (otherwise the term also includes factor covariances)

Practically, to estimate the model, if the factors are returns on indices, then we can estimate the coefficients in Eq. 12.16 (i.e. the factor exposures) directly by computing excess returns for the security and the factors and running a time-series regression (similar to Eq. 12.13/ Fig. 12.9). If the factors are not returns, e.g. GDP growth, then we need to do this in two steps[161]. First, estimate β_{ij} (β, or factor exposure, of the ith security with respect to the jth factor) in Eq. 12.15 by running time series regressions, security by security, of historical security returns on the factors. Then, using the estimated β_{ij}, run cross-sectional regressions of r_i on β_{ij}, period by period, to estimate the risk premia, RP_j. Analysts can use the risk-free rate, risk premia and the betas to calculate future expected returns for any security, as predicted by the model. It can also be used to figure out which stocks have positive and negative alphas, to aid (quantitative) idea generation for stock picking.

CAPM as a Factor Model

CAPM can be visualized as a one-factor model, with the excess returns of the market over the risk free rate (*market risk premium*) as the single factor. The beta of any stock is that stock's loading to this market factor. Using this analogy, the stock's expected excess return is the product of the factor realization and the stock's loading to the factor, which turns out to be the CAPM model.

Multi-Factor Models

Since the CAPM's development in the mid 1960's, an "anomalies" strand of financial research continued for at least the next 20-25 years, pointing out the various dimensions in which CAPM was deficient. There were arguments about the true market portfolio (e.g. should it include human capital, since all investments should be included), as well as details regarding certain types of stocks outperforming others, systematically. The factor models framework provided a justification for researchers to extend the CAPM by including additional factors beyond the market factor, although this implied giving up the elegance of the equilibrium-based two-fund separation argument. Multi-factor models provide multiple sources of systematic risk; and are interpreted similarly to CAPM.

One of the most popular extensions of the CAPM into a multi-factor framework is the *Fama-French models*, which included two additional factors. Prior research had shown the deficiency of the CAPM in explaining the outperformance of small stocks over large stocks, even after controlling for possibly varying betas. Another anomaly related to "value" stocks (i.e. stocks with high Book Value/ Market Value) outperforming "growth" stocks. To improve the model's fit, factors related to these *Size* and *Value* anomalies need to be introduced.

One common way to construct factors is by creating *factor-mimicking portfolios*, and then use the historical returns of these portfolios as the factor returns[162]. To do this, sort the universe of stocks (e.g. S&P500) by the factor (e.g. size, measured by the logarithm of market capitalization) into deciles. For any period, the difference between the returns of the top decile and the bottom decile (i.e. returns of a portfolio that is long the top decile and short the bottom decile) is exposed primarily to the factor (the top decide has positions with very

---

[161] This two-step procedure is closely related to the Fama MacBeth regression procedure.

[162] In the previous section, we did not need to do this since we assumed that the factor returns were returns on published indices i.e. the index was the factor mimicking portfolio.

high exposure to the factor, and the bottom decile has companies with large negative exposure to the factor), and is a reasonable factor-mimicking portfolio. The risk is that, if factors are correlated, then this portfolio will have exposure to a combination of both factors. To fix this, researchers usually do a "double-sort" i.e. do a coarse "low-medium high" sort on the secondary correlated factor, and then within the low, medium and high buckets, sort on the factor of primary interest into deciles. Pick the highest and lowest (primary factor) decile names in each of the secondary low, medium and high buckets, to create the aggregate high-low portfolio. This version of factor returns tries to break the correlation between the two factors and create a return stream driven by the primary factor. Once we have these returns, we can run a time-series regression to obtain betas. Alternatively, for each security, we can use the value of each of these factors (size or value, as the case may be) as the factor loading, and run a cross-sectional regression to estimate factor risk premia.

Fama and French, through a series of academic papers in the early 1990s, showed that size and value explained security returns, and beta was no longer significant once these variables were included. Their model of stock returns is usually written in the form:

$$E[r_i - r_f] = \beta_i E[r_{Mkt} - r_f] + s_i E[SMB] + h_i E[HML] \qquad \text{Eq. 12.18}$$

where HML (*High Minus Low*), SMB (*Small Minus Big*) and $r_{Mkt} - r_f$ are returns of factor mimicking portfolios (i.e. factor risk premia), and β_i, s_i and h_i are the corresponding factor exposures of asset i., Some researchers subsequently criticized the model for econometric issues, lack of a theoretical foundation, not explaining other anomalies etc. One common addition to this model, based on Jegadeesh and Titman's research is to incorporate the effect of Momentum. This is done by constructing a factor mimicking portfolio WML (*Winners Minus Losers*), which is long the winners (top 30%) and short the losers (bottom 30%) of the past six months, created every month, and held for the next six months. Momentum has turned out to be one of the most persistent and robust anomalies, and is commonly explained using behavioral arguments (Over /Under-reaction, Disposition Effect, etc.). In 2014, Fama and French augmented their 3-factor model to include two more factors – Profitability and Investment[163] - and indicate that these factors may drive out the value factor. Around the same time (a little earlier), Hou, Xue and Zhang published the *q-factor* model, which uses market beta, size, investment and ROE factors to explain stock returns (ROE picks up some of the effect of momentum too, according to Novy-Marx).

It may appear, from this discussion, that the way to create better equity models is to keep thinking of factors and adding them on. This is not true. While the in-sample model fit will definitely improve if we add more factors (the r-squared of a regression will always improve if we add an additional variable, regardless of how relevant the variable is), but the precision of the coefficients will probably suffer; in such a situation, the model will perform poorly out-of-sample. The other issue is that the more factors we introduce, the more parameters we need to estimate. It's not only the regression coefficients that need to be estimated, but also the factor *covariance matrix*. The dimensionality grows exponentially, leading to (very) imprecise estimation. A few factors, sensibly chosen, is the ideal way to construct these models.

---

[163] They construct factor-mimicking portfolios by constructing return differences of diversified portfolios of companies with robust and weak profitability, and companies with low and high investment.

Capital Markets and Investments

- ✓ A stock's return can be represented as the product of the stock's sensitivity to a source of risk, and the expected return/ compensation for being exposed to one unit of that risk. This source of risk is called a risk factor; the stock's sensitivity is referred to as its factor exposure or loading. The compensation for being exposed to a unit of this risk is the factor return/ risk premium.
- ✓ The CAPM can be presented as a one-factor model, with the market as the (sole) factor, the stock's beta as the sensitivity, and $E(r_m) - r_f$ as the factor return or risk premium.
- ✓ Multi-factor models have been introduced, most notably by Fama and French, to improve the empirical performance of CAPM. Value, Size and Momentum are examples of popular factors.
- ✓ Introducing too many factors can lead to model estimation issues.

RISK MANAGEMENT IN EQUITY PORTFOLIOS[164]

Earlier, we used volatility to quantify risk, for single names as well as portfolios. We then decomposed risk into systematic and idiosyncratic risk, based on an assumed model specification. It is often useful to transform risk measures into boundaries on how much one could expect to lose, under certain outcomes. Depending on whether the portfolio performance is assumed to be purely random (a fair assumption for the short term) or based on how some broad economic variables (factors) perform (more suitable for a longer horizon), various risk metrics such as Value-at-Risk (or VaR) and Scenario Analysis Loss can be calculated.

Factor models often form the basis for most quantitative equity models. In this paradigm, as discussed above, a stock's return is assumed to be dependent on its exposure to several factors (market indices, for example), and how those factors perform in any period. Of course, factor performance is random, so each factor has an expected return (sometimes transformed to zero average by subtracting the mean return from every observation) and volatility. Different factors may be correlated; factor covariances capture this.

Since the factor returns have all been transformed to zero expected value (by subtracting the average), the expected return of any portfolio regardless of its factor exposures (the sum of the factor exposures of all the securities in the portfolio) is zero for any time period. However, this is simply the *expected* return; there is an uncertainty around this estimate. The systematic (i.e. market-related) uncertainty is represented by the portfolio variance and standard deviation (essentially a combination of the factor exposures of the portfolio, factor volatilities and covariances).

To elaborate, let us look at Eq. 12.17 again, where we express the variance of one security's return as a linear combination of factor variances, assuming the factors are uncorrelated. If the factors are correlated, the equation will also include additional terms containing factor covariances. We can think of a portfolio as one "composite security", and apply the same idea with an adjustment for idiosyncratic risk. It is important to note that the addition of a security into a portfolio is supposed to increase risk by less than the total risk of the security held in isolation, since the idiosyncratic risk is meant to be diversified away in a portfolio. Said differently, a security's marginal contribution to portfolio risk is usually lower than the total risk of that security.

Additional Information

---

[164] Like the previous section, most readers will benefit from reading the section on Risk Models in Chapter 5 before reading this section. All observations from that section apply here; some of them have not been repeated.

This framework is often expressed using *matrix notation*. While the formulae might appear visually obscure, the idea is exactly the same. First, from Eq. 12.15, the return (which is a random variable) on any security i (n securities), priced by factors j (taking values from 1 to k) is given by Eq. 12.19.

$$r_i = \alpha_i + \sum_{j=1}^{k} \beta_{ij} E(F_j) + \varepsilon_i$$

Eq. 12.19

For a portfolio of securities ($i = 1$ to n), each security having weight w_i the expected portfolio return is

$$E(R_p) = \sum_{i=1}^{n} w_i \left[\alpha_i + \sum_{j=1}^{k} \beta_{ij} E(F_j) \right]$$

Eq. 12.20

If W is a row vector ($w_1,\ldots,w_n$) of weights, β the n x k matrix of security betas to the k factors, and F the k x 1 column vector ($F_1,\ldots,F_k$) of factor returns, α and ε the n-dimensional vector containing all the security alphas and error terms, then portfolio expected returns can be written as:

$$E(R_p) = A + BF \text{ where } B = W'\beta, \text{ and } A = W'\alpha$$

Eq. 12.21

Portfolio variance is given by:

$$Var(R_p) = B\Omega_f B' + Var(E) \text{ where } E = W'\varepsilon$$

Eq. 12.22

$B\Omega B'$ is the systematic variance, and $Var(E)$ is the idiosyncratic variance.

A normal distribution is simple to understand and allows modelers to borrow standard statistical results to forecast future values. But, using normal distributions understates the likelihood of extreme outcomes relative to the actual historical returns; return distributions have *fat tails*. Risk managers need to be fully aware of this while using risk models and reading risk reports.

It is important to recognize that the estimation of risk, and the allocation of return to exposure to systematic risk (not great) or alpha (great!) is a direct result of the specification of the risk model, and the associated statistical quirks. A security's return in one period might show up as predominantly alpha using one risk model, and as mainly systematic risk compensation using another equally reasonable model. As such, it is important to interpret performance attribution and risk reports keeping this perspective in mind i.e. is the risk model appropriately specified and robustly estimated?

We now discuss a few common risk reports and metrics that institutions commonly use, applying this framework. *Scenario Analysis* is run by imagining a certain adverse scenario, representing it in terms of changes in various factors by certain amounts, and computing stock and portfolio returns as a result of these factor shocks. This provides an estimate of how much the portfolio is expected to lose under certain scenarios. While the factor changes can be chosen based on their volatilities and correlations (i.e. the covariance matrix), the Scenario Analysis exercise is based mainly on the factor exposures of the stock, and less on the volatilities and

Capital Markets and Investments

correlations. In practice, scenarios are chosen to resemble well-known historical shocks, such as the Lehman crisis or Technology bubble, and changes to factors during those episodes are replicated.

Value-at-Risk (VaR), on the other hand, is much more directly based on the factor volatilities and co-variances. Its answers the question: What is the lowest loss this portfolio is likely to incur, x% of the *time*? x is usually a small number, like 1% or 5%. The rest of the *time* (i.e. 99% or 95% in this example) the loss will be less than the VaR. *Time* is usually a short time period like one day, one week or one month. So, for example, market participants will typically refer to a 95% 1-day VaR (i.e. be explicit both about the likelihood and the time period). Once the portfolio variance is calculated (software programs do this easily) and scaled for the correct time period, we can construct a distribution (most analysis assumes normal distribution) of portfolio returns. This return distribution multiplied by the portfolio asset value is the loss/ gain distribution; the 5th percentile of that distribution is the 95% VaR.

Note, the 95% VaR essentially ignores how bad the worst 5% of the outcomes can get, so the extreme tail risk is not captured. Part of this also results from the fact that we have assumed a normal distribution; a distribution with fatter tails would have mechanically generated a higher VaR value. *Expected Shortfall*, which calculates the expected loss, assuming the VaR limit has been breached (i.e. expected loss in the worst 5% of outcomes in our example), measures this tail risk.

For benchmarked managers, keeping *Tracking Error (Volatility)* (see Chapter 5) within limits is an important dimension of risk management. This is earlier done by careful stratified sampling, but more recent techniques use optimizers to reduce the difference in factor exposures (especially the volatile factors) between the portfolio and the benchmark.

Equity portfolios are managed with limits on VaR, Tracking Error and Scenario Analysis losses. When these limits are breached, portfolio managers may be asked to sell positions to reduce risk, or pro-rata sales may automatically be triggered. Alternatively, the firm may decide that economic conditions are benign for markets and choose to run more risk. The exact details of how these reports are used to adjust portfolios depends on whether the fund is run in a centralized manner with one CIO, or if every portfolio manager enjoys high autonomy to implement trades, but has to strictly remain within risk bands.

- ✓ A portfolio, like a security, can be expressed as a linear combination of factors. So, systematic risk in a portfolio can also be expressed as a combination of factor variances and covariances, multiplied by factor loadings.
- ✓ Scenario Analysis measures portfolio losses because of well-specified shocks to the economy, detailed in terms of factor movements. x% VaR provides an upper bound for losses that will not be exceeded x% of the time. y% Expected Shortfall, a tail-risk measure, provides the average loss in the worst y% of outcomes. Managing Tracking Error is important for benchmarked managers.

PORTFOLIO CONSTRUCTION TECHNIQUES

While the problem (and the solution) as stated above is relatively straightforward, implementing the idea has been challenging. This is because some input parameters into the formulation above, mainly expected returns and correlation, are notoriously unstable and difficult to estimate (volatilities are easier), the model is tough to carefully test (distinguishing ex-ante expectations from ex-post realizations is tough, and risk is entirely an ex-ante concept). With this in mind, this section lists a few approaches to portfolio construction, building on the ideas above and then modifying them, to come up with more robust solutions.

Portfolio Theory, Asset Allocation and Factor Models

Markowitz Mean-Variance Optimization

This chapter has discussed mean-variance optimization in detail; here we introduce some practical considerations. Even without making any assumptions on investor preferences or the existence of a risk-free asset, if we know the mean and the standard deviation of each security's return distribution, and the correlation among these different securities, we can calculate which portfolio (i.e. the proportion held of each security) provides the maximum return for a given level of risk appetite (or conversely, which portfolio minimizes risk for a given target expected return level). Operationally, we fix the value for the standard deviation, choose portfolio weights to maximize the return, store the weights, maximum return and standard deviation and repeat the process for another value of portfolio risk. This iterative process traces out the Efficient Frontier, and we can pick any point (return and standard deviation) that we like. Usually, this optimization is run with several additional constraints such as limits on transaction costs, portfolio turnover, short sales, sector concentration, risk factor limits and liquidity constraints.

While standard deviations of securities are usually stable, it is very difficult to estimate correlations robustly (GARCH notwithstanding) as well as get an idea of expected future returns. Historical means of returns have not been usually very useful in predicting future returns. Small changes in these inputs can cause large changes in portfolio weights, limiting the use of the methodology. Nonetheless, it is simple to understand, so remains relevant in the practitioner's world. Robust optimization techniques, as highlighted by Grinold and Kahn, have also played an important role in making this framework useful for practitioners.

One important successful application of the Markowitz philosophy has been the *Yale Model*, an investment process popularized by the Yale endowment Chief Investment Officer David Swensen. The approach builds a portfolio following the Markowitz principle, by making sure that return streams of portfolio constituents have low correlation among them. Further, the framework emphasizes the benefits of a carefully selected portfolio of alternative investment managers like private equity and hedge funds, to access return streams that are not easily accessible by liquid market instruments. This supports the low correlation within portfolio constituents. These portfolios do not need regular income and instantaneous liquidity; and can participate in long gestation illiquid investments. If traditional market exposures fit the portfolio, they are easily obtained through low-cost index funds internally, than hiring expensive external managers.

The Yale Model has been very successful for some endowments, but many smaller endowments that have tried to replicate the process (spelt out in David Swensen's book) have had mixed experiences. This is because a key component of this approach is to be able to pick the best managers, more an art than a science. If the investment board is not very savvy at being able to sift through manager profiles and pick the ones with the most potential, chances are they will end up with the wrong managers, since most alternative managers underperform.

Black-Litterman Model

Since reliable estimates of expected returns are difficult to ascertain from historical data, Black and Litterman try to address portfolio construction by not having to base return expectations purely on historical realizations of returns; in fact, it also accommodates investors' subjective views about expected future returns. The model starts off by inferring security returns that are likely to hold in the base case; this may be from an equilibrium setting (e.g. CAPM), using from security covariances (which may depend on historical returns), risk aversion coefficient, market capitalization weights etc. It then takes the investor's views regarding expected future returns of securities, either absolute or relative to other securities, and also the uncertainty in those views to create a distribution of investor views. The initial equilibrium return distribution and the views distribution are combined to create a new returns distribution by a version of Bayesian updating, and the new portfolio weights are backed out. If an investor has no views, he will end up holding the initial portfolio, in line with market weights.

Risk Parity

The above methods all use an estimate of expected returns and risk (volatility) to come up with a suitable portfolio. But, estimates for expected returns turn out to be imprecise (ex-post); besides, the resulting portfolios are very sensitive to the estimates used. The risk parity methodology, first introduced by Bridgewater in constructing their All-Weather portfolio, does not use estimates of expected return. Risk-party implementations vary significantly across firms. Volatility is easier (and more reliable) to estimate, and is the central input into these portfolios. Some implementations use the inverse of the security's volatility estimate as its portfolio weight, and worry less about the correlation; many others assume static correlations based on how asset classes typically move in different phases of the business cycle. Risk parity portfolios also use leverage, to amplify the returns of low-risk assets to achieve overall return targets. For example, in a risk-parity based portfolio construction of stocks and Treasury bonds, the bond sub-portfolio may need to be levered significantly to match the risk level of the stock sub-portfolio. Alternative implementations make some assumptions about correlation, but rely more on the direction of return co-movement in different risk paradigms than the exact magnitudes.

> This section briefly discusses some common frameworks to construct portfolios. While the specifics of implementing these ideas varies from firm to firm, the broad themes are below:
>
> ✓ Markowitz mean-variance optimization is the most common technique, which we discussed in most of this chapter. The output is very sensitive to minor changes in input values; expected returns are especially difficult to figure out ahead of time.
>
> ✓ The Black Litterman model starts off with estimates of expected returns as an input from market data (e.g. CAPM model), but incorporates investor views and future uncertainty around those views to construct a portfolio.
>
> ✓ The Risk Parity method does not use market returns as an input, but only use asset class volatilities and correlations as inputs to crease a portfolio with low variance.

REFERENCES

Ang, Andrew (2014). *Asset Management: A Systematic Approach to Factor Investing*, Oxford University Press.

Bodie, Zvi, A. Kane, & A. Marcus. *Investments*. Mc-Graw Hill Higher Education

Idzorek, Thomas M. *A Step by Step Guide to the Black Litterman Model*. Morningstar/ Ibbotson

Swensen, David. *Pioneering Portfolio Management: An Unconventional Approach to Institutional Investment*. Free Press/ Simon & Schuster

Options Markets

13. Introduction to Options

We have talked about various asset classes and security types throughout out the book – fixed income and equities. We have also discussed futures contracts (delta-1 derivative), which the investor enters into today (without any cash payments) and will be mandatorily exchanged into the underlying (either physically or equivalent cash value i.e. cash-settled) on a pre-decided future expiration date, but at a price (the futures price) decided today (i.e. not the market price in future). The contracted parties have to transact on the expiration date (they have no choice) – one party gains and the other loses, depending on whether the underlying price on expiration date is higher or lower than the futures price when the contract is entered into.

WHAT IS AN OPTION? BASIC TERMINOLOGY

Let us extend this notion of a futures contract. In *"options"* contracts, one party (the "buyer") has the *right but not the obligation* (i.e. the choice but not the compulsion) to transact on the *"expiration date"* at a pre-decided *"strike"* price of an *underlying* security. The contract seller (sometimes called *"writer"*) just reacts to what the contract buyer wants to do on the expiration date. Clearly, this is more favorable to the buyer, so, unlike the futures contract, the buyer needs to pay the seller some money upfront (*premium*) to enter this contract, for the choice. In this case, the seller's gains are capped at the premium received, which gets eaten into (and may even turn into a net loss) if the buyer wants to *exercise the option* (i.e. transact) on the expiration date, since the buyer will do so only if he gains by transacting, when the option is *in-the-money* (ITM) (i.e. the strike price favors the contract buyer relative to the current underlying price). In other cases (option is *out-of-the money i.e. OTM*), the buyer may choose to let the option expire worthless, and loses the premium paid earlier.

At the simplest level, the option contract can either be a contract to buy the underlying at the strike price (a *call option*) or to sell the underlying at the strike price (a *put option*). Depending on the terms of the option contract, it can either be exercised only on the expiration date (*European option*, more common) or any time before expiration date (*American option*). The buyer of a European call option will exercise his right if the underlying stock is above the strike at expiration; the owner of a put will exercise if the underlying is below the strike. As the stock price goes up, the value of a call option increases (the underlying is more likely to end up meaningfully above the strike), and the value of a put option decreases. The opposite is true for declining stock prices. At any time, there are usually several dozen options trading for any underlying, of various strikes, maturities and types (call/ put).

Both options and futures (and swaps) are referred generically as *derivatives*, since their values are derived from the value of an underlying security. They are also referred to as *synthetic* instruments (as opposed to *cash* instruments), because they do not require a (large) cash investment to get economic exposure to the underlying. While we mainly discuss options with equities as underlying, options can be traded on most liquid instruments. Options on currencies and Treasury / Eurodollar / commodity futures are very popular too.

Introduction to Options

> - ✓ An option represents the right but not the obligation to buy (call option) or sell (put option) a certain number of securities at a pre-decided (strike) price of the underlying on (or before, for American options) the expiration date of the option.
> - ✓ Unlike futures, the option owner can choose not to complete the final transaction if the contract price is unfavorable relative to the underlying; for this choice, the option buyer pays a premium.
> - ✓ Options, along with futures and swaps, are referred to as derivatives because their value is derived from the value of an underlying security. They also represent a means to get exposed to market risk without putting down cash upfront.

SOME SIMPLE EXAMPLES – CALL AND PUT OPTIONS

Let us consider an IBM call option struck at $155, expiring on January 19, 2018. IBM's current price is 148. This option gives the option holder the right to buy IBM stock at 155 on January 19, 2018. This option will end up having value if IBM trades above 155 on that day (since it allows the option holder to buy cheaper than market price); otherwise it will be worthless. If IBM sells off below 148, the premium is lost, but no further losses are incurred. The option today is worth around $11. Despite being out of the money (by $7) today, this option is valuable today ($11, over 7% of spot) because there is a chance that the option can end up in the money at expiration. We will see later that the further out the expiration date, the more volatile the underlying stock (IBM in this example) and/or the closer the current price is to the strike price, the more valuable the option.

In general, the payoff (to the buyer) of a call option at expiration is given by the function $Max[S(T)-K,0]$, where K is the strike price and S(T) the price of the option at time T, expiration. The *moneyness* of an option (K/S) is determined by whether K/S is greater than, equal to or less than 1 (*in, at* or *out-of-the-money put*)[165]. Prior to maturity, if the call option premium is C, C-Max(S-K,0) is called the *time value*. S-K is the *intrinsic value* for in-the-money options. No-arbitrage considerations, discussed later, imply that the time value is always positive; the intrinsic value is zero (not negative, because of the Max function) for out-of-the-money options. The vast majority of options that are traded are out-of-the-money options. Graphically, the call option payoff looks like the left panel of Figure 13.1 below. In our example, if IBM stock ends up at 158, the call option payoff will be 3. At 166, the option will pay off $11, so the buyer will *break even* only if the option trades above 166 at expiration. To get the profit/ loss (P&L), we subtract the initial option premium from this payoff function.

---

[165] 110% moneyness *put* is in the money, 90% *put* is out of the money. 90% call is ITM; 90% put is OTM

Capital Markets and Investments

Figure 13.1 Payoff and Profit/ Loss diagrams for simple call and put options

a) Call Option Payoff = Max[S(T)-K,0]   b) Put Option Payoff = Max[K-S(T),0]

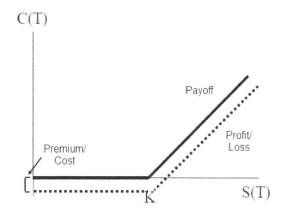 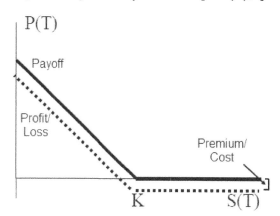

The right panel of Figure 13.1 shows the payoff of a *put* option. The IBM January 2018 put struck at 145 costs $18. This contract gives the option holder the right to *sell* IBM stock at 145, and will have value at expiration if IBM trades below 145 (since it allows the option holder to sell this at above-market price). The payoff function for put option is $Max[K-S(T),0]$. So, for this IBM put option to break even, the IBM stock has to trade below 127 at expiration.

- ✓ A call option's payoff at expiration is given by $Max[S(T)-K,0]$, where K is the strike price and S(T) is the price at expiration. A put option's payoff at expiration is $Max[K-S(T),0]$. The profit or loss from an option trade at expiration is the payoff minus the initial premium.

- ✓ The moneyness of the option at any time is given by K/S. If this value is greater than 100% (i.e. 1), it means that a put option will be exercised if the underlying price is at this level on option expiration date; it is the opposite for calls. A 110% put is in the money, a 110% call is out of the money.

OPTIONS TRADING - MECHANICS

As additional details, equity shares are actually exchanged when options on single-name stocks are exercised (physical settlement; index options are cash-settled. Monthly option expirations (third Friday of every month) are most common, but weekly and quarterly options are also popular. Each equity option contract is mapped to 100 underlying shares (*the multiplier is 100*), so one IBM Jan '18 145 put option actually costs $1800. If IBM trades at 143 at expiration, each contract will pay $200 i.e. $2 per stock times 100 (the multiplier).

Most options that we discuss here are quoted on exchanges or alternative trading venues, similar to equity stocks (and commodity/ Treasury futures). The decision to make options available is often solely decided by the exchange; the underlying issuer is rarely involved. In that sense, there is no real distinction between a primary and a secondary market; the exchange simply records the trade when two investors take opposite sides. Most of the trading here is also electronic, like stocks and futures. Some options are traded OTC, like swaptions (options on the swap rate), currency options or exotic options (discussed later in the chapter). For most underlyings with options, an investor can choose from several dozen options – type (calls/ put), expiration, strike, etc. and create complex trades by combining them.

Introduction to Options

- ✓ One most exchanges, one option contract represents the right to buy/ sell 100 shares (i.e. multiplier is 100) of the underlying.
- ✓ Options can be traded OTC or on an exchange. Fixed income options trade OTC.

USING OPTIONS IN TRADE CONSTRUCTION

Directional trades with Call and Put options

Let us consider the IBM Jan '18 155 Call option example above. That option begins to make money if IBM ends up above 155 at expiration. After deducting the premium, the option is valuable if the investor expects the stock to be above 166 at expiration. How does this compare to buying the stock?

A (meaningful) move up increases the value of both the option and the stock. For example, suppose we spend $11000 on the option (10 contracts) and on the stock (74 shares). Now, 10 option contracts maps to 1000 shares, so the option portfolio makes $1000 for every dollar the stock goes up, beyond the strike price. The stock portfolio, containing 74 shares, goes up by $74 for every dollar increase. At expiration, with IBM at 166, the stock portfolio has already earned $1332 (compared to current stock price at 148), whereas the option portfolio is flat. At any level between 148 and 166, the stock portfolio makes money, but the options portfolio is still losing money. For any increase in stock price below the strike price 155, the entire option premium is lost. After 155, the option portfolio begins to recoup its premium, at the rate $1000 per point move in IBM and eventually breaks even at 166. *The stock portfolio makes money at any level above the current price, but the option portfolio needs a meaningful increase in the stock price* (how much depends on the premium).

Continuing with this example, suppose IBM ended up at 168 at expiration, just two dollars above the break even. The stock portfolio is up $1480, but the options portfolio is up $2000, already beating the stock portfolio, which it was lagging by $1332 when IBM was at 166. For every dollar that IBM gains from 168, the options portfolio outperforms by $926. If IBM is at 175 at expiration, the options portfolio will have made $9000, whereas the stock portfolio will have made $1998. *For large stock moves, an <u>equal dollar investment</u> in options will often pay off much more.* This is why options are referred to as a source of leverage, because the investor needs to put down very little cash to control a large notional amount of shares. The next paragraph shows why this may not be prudent.

To elaborate on the risk, let us consider the situation when IBM sells off to $144. The option expires out of the money, and the options portfolio loses the entire premium of $11000, similar to any price below 155. The stock portfolio loses $296, and is still valued at $10704. This makes it clear that *from a risk perspective, it makes sense to deploy smaller amounts of capital to naked option trades, relative to stock trades.*

One way to size options trades is to look at the "delta", which we will do later. For the moment, taking a very conservative stance, let us assume we buy 100 shares and spend $14800 on stocks, or buy one options contract (to get exposure to 100 shares) and spend $1100 on the option. In this case, the options portfolio and the stock portfolio makes $100 for each dollar increase in IBM stock price beyond $155, and it needs to go above $166 to break even. But, the stock portfolio makes money from 148 to 155 too. So on the upside, the options portfolio will underperform the stock portfolio in a total P&L sense, but its returns may be higher, because it has a much lower investment (7% of the stock portfolio). On the downside, the options portfolio can lose only the premium ($1100). If the stock portfolio loses more than 7.5%, the stock portfolio will lose more than the option premium. For example, in a 15% sell-off, with IBM at 126, the stock portfolio will lose $2200. *The call option portfolio's loss is limited to the premium paid; a stock portfolio can lose more in large sell-offs.* But, if the stock does not move much, the option will lose its premium (whereas the stock will hold its value).

Capital Markets and Investments

Similar examples can be constructed with put options and comparing them to short positions on stocks; the takeaways are similar. Put options allow investors to express a bearish view on names, similar to shorts. Once the underlying trades below (opposite of calls) the strike price, the value of the put option increases very quickly, especially at/ close to expiration. If the stock ends up above the strike price at expiration, the put option is worthless, whereas the short stock portfolio (while possibly having lost money mark-to-market) still retains value; so it makes sense to limit naked options premium to be significantly smaller than notional exposure for short equity. Losses are capped at the premium paid.

An alternative trade construction using options to express directional long view is to put on a *risk reversal*. This involves buying a higher strike call and selling a lower strike put to finance the (partial/ full) cost of the call. Similarly, buying the lower strike put and selling the higher strike call is a bearish trade, and is called a *collar*. Like naked calls/ puts discussed above, these need to be sized suitably. . Investors also sometimes substitute deep-in-the-money call options for existing long stock positions to free up cash; these trades are called *stock replacement* trades.

So, options can be used both for rampant risk taking for highly convicted views and for prudent risk mitigation to improve risk-return profile. Essentially, the premium paid is like an insurance to protect the portfolio if the market moves against the investor. This premium also implies that you need a larger move (in the favorable direction) for the options portfolio to begin making money. The aim is to either try to minimize damage if the view is wrong, or to make a large sum by risking a small amount of cash if an outcome that the market currently views as unlikely ends up happening.

While we will discuss option pricing in detail in the next chapter, it is important to recognize that all financial security pricing can be visualized as some kind of (potentially complicated) NPV-type calculation. In this case, where the cash flows are not known, but contingent on the price of the underlying, the option premium captures the probability of receiving those cash flows. So, as the underlying gets closer to the strike (or is through it), or the expected future volatility of the underlying increases or the time to expiration gets longer, the option premium goes higher.

Volatility Trades with Straddles and Strangles

Above, we discussed how options can be used to express directional views. But, option prices also capture how volatile the stock is expected to be. One way to express views on the volatility of the underlying is to buy options and continually "delta-hedge" them; which we will discuss later. Alternatively, buying a call option and a put option (a *straddle*), both struck at the current underlying price, is another strategy to get long volatility. The payoff profile (as shown in Figure 13.2) looks like a "V", with a zero payoff if the stock stays at the strike price. The investor pays for both these options, so the P&L profile after accounting for option costs shifts the "V" down, through the x-axis. The cost of the straddle, captured by how much the tip of the V is below the x-axis, is a reflection of the market's assessment of the future expected volatility. If the stock moves more than that, the investor makes money (i.e. ends up above the x-axis, where the P&L is positive). So, it makes sense to get long this position if the investor believes that the market is assuming lower stock price movement than what will actually happen. If the straddle is expensive, the market is pricing in violent stock price moment; the investor would then choose to sell the straddle, collect the premium, and then hope that the stock ends up close to the strike price (often close to the current price) at expiration. Short-dates straddles are a good way to play "events" such as company earnings. A variant of a straddle (shown on the right panel in Figure 13.2, $K_1<K_2$) called *strangle*, comprises a long put and a call, but with the put's strike price lower than the call's strike. Owning this is cheaper than buying a straddle (both options are further out-of-the-money if the current underlying price is between the two strikes), but leads to a dead zone between the two strikes when the position does not make any money.

Introduction to Options

Figure 13.2 Payoff diagrams for Straddle and Strangle

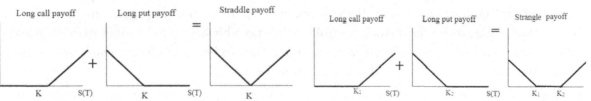

Covered call

A covered call strategy involves selling an out-of-the-money call option against a stock that the portfolio is already long. This is a yield-enhancing trade, because the investor earns the premium on the call, and is exposed to the economics (downside and upside) of the underlying stock until the strike price, after which any further increase in the stock price does not accrue to the gains. So, the investor is locking in the current (certain) premium in exchange for the (uncertain but potentially higher) upside beyond the strike price. It is often a good idea to sell a call close to the price target for the underlying stock, a level at which the investor would anyway be inclined to sell. The payoff is below in Figure 13.3.

Figure 13.3 Payoff diagrams for Covered Call

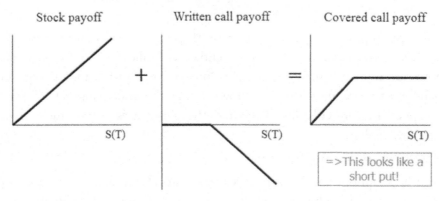

Protective Puts

An investor employs the protective put strategy to insure a long stock portfolio against a sell-off. This is achieved by owning out of the money puts in the underlying to complement the long stock holding. While the puts cost money, they insure the portfolio against any sell-off beyond the strike price, and function as insurance. The investor has full exposure to the upside. Figure 13.4 has the payoff diagram.

Figure 13.4: Payoff diagrams for Protective Put

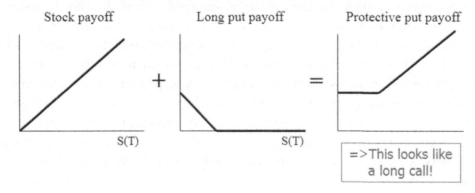

Capital Markets and Investments

Call spread, Put spread, Calendar spread

Investors in derivative securities often put on "*spread*" trades, where they buy one option and sell another simultaneously. For example, in buying a *call spread*, an investor buys a call option struck closer to the money and sells a further out-of-the-money call. This trade expresses similar long risk view as buying a call option, but the upside exposure that is far out is sold to cheapen the trade. So, this call spread makes money when the stock goes up (and ends up anywhere between the two strikes), but the upside is capped at the upper strike price. The maximum payout is the difference between the two strikes.

Similarly, a *put spread* is often a bearish trade or a defensive overlay (like a put); where the investor buys a put closer to the money and sells one further away from the money. This also makes the trade cheaper than the outright put, but caps the return on the trade at the lower put strike, whereas the outright put makes money all the way down.

A *calendar spread* involves buying and selling options with different expiration dates, but of the same type (call/put) and strike. This is often put on to express a precise view on the timing of an event, or the term structure of the volatility implied in option price (we will discuss this later).

Investors mix and match many of these building blocks to create complex trades. Regardless of the exact details, the general idea is that an option is sold to cheapen the trade or enhance yield, whereas an option is bought to either increase risk exposure, speculate or hedge against the downside.

> Investors use options in several ways:
> - ✓ In directional trades to express bullish or bearish views on the underlying.
> - ✓ To express views on the volatility of the underlying, using straddles or strangles.
> - ✓ As an overlay to a core underlying position – covered calls and protective puts.
> - ✓ As spread trades (call and put spreads) to reduce the initial premium of the option trade
> - ✓ To express views on specific dates/ events through calendar trades.

PUT-CALL PARITY

The price for call options, put options (of identical strike and maturity – any strike/ maturity combination but needs to be the same for the call and the put) and the underlying stock are tied together by no-arbitrage principles; this section discusses that relationship in more detail.

Let us look at Figure 13.4 again. The protective put payoff looks like that of a call option (Figure 13.1) shifted up by K units. Let us consider a portfolio of a call option struck at K and an asset that pays K for sure on the expiration date T (i.e. a zero coupon bond with face value K and maturity T). This portfolio of a call option and the bond will pay exactly the same amount as the protective put portfolio regardless of where the underlying (or any other security) trades at expiration. To develop this further, let us consider Figure 13.5 below:

Figure 13.5: Comparing Protective Put Payoffs to Call Option + Bond

Portfolio	Payoff Function	Payoff When $S_T \leq K$	Payoff When $S_T > K$
Protective Put	$Max[K-S_T,0] + S_T$	K	S_T
Call Option + \$K in bond	$Max[S_T-K,0] + K$	K	S_T

Since the Protective Put portfolio and the Call Option + Bond portfolio have the same payoff on the expiration date, regardless of underlying price, no arbitrage principles dictate that both portfolios have the same

Introduction to Options

value today. So, if P, C and S denote the prices of the put, call and stock respectively, r is the risk free rate, and suffixes 0 or T denote time periods (present or expiration, respectively), then:

$$P_0 + S_0 = C_0 + \frac{K}{(1+r)^T} \qquad \text{Eq. 13.1}$$

Eq. 13.1 is referred to as the put-call parity. It works for any call and put option with the same underlying S, strike K and maturity T. This result is very general; it holds for all asset classes and is independent of any option pricing model; only no-arbitrage assumptions are used.

> To elaborate, let us consider $S_0 = 100$, $K = \$120$, $T = 1$, $r = 8\%$, $P_0 = \$20$. The fair value of C_0, as given by put-call parity (substituting in Equation 1 above), is 8.89. Suppose, the market price of the call option is $10. In this situation, the investor can sell (write) the call at $10, and replicate it for 8.89, thus having $1.11 left over as a riskless arbitrage profit. Figure 6 lists the exact transactions.

Figure 13.6 Replicating the Call, applying Put-Call Parity

Trades	Cash flow at time 0	Cash Flow at time T	
		If S(T) <= 120	If S(T) > 120
Sell a 120 strike Call	10	0	-[S(T)-120]
Buy a 120 strike Put	-20	120 - S(T)	0
Buy a Stock	-100	S(T)	S(T)
Borrow face value of K (i.e. 120)	111.11	-120	-120
Net Cash Flows	1.11	0	0

Note, this relationship needs to be modified if the stock pays a dividend between the current time and expiration.

> ✓ The prices of a put option and call option of the same underlying with the same strike and maturity are related to the underlying price and the strike price through a no-arbitrage relationship. This result always holds, and is independent of any option pricing model.

EXOTIC OPTIONS

Apart from calls and puts (also called *vanilla* options), there are other less common option types. These options are collectively referred to as *Exotics*, and do not trade on the exchanges. These are OTC products, but fairly common, so we provide a few examples / structures below. These are often difficult to price using the pricing models that we will discuss next chapter, so they are often priced based on simulation.

Digital (or binary) options (they can be either puts or calls) are options that provide a fixed payout (often normalized to $1) if the strike is breached, and pay nothing if the underlying ends up below the strike. In contrast, the payoff to vanilla puts/ calls is proportional to how much the underlying breaches the strike by.

Barrier options are options that either *knock in* or *knock out* when a barrier is reached, e.g. a 95% S&P500 *PDO* (Put Down-and-Out), which knocks out when the S&P500 is 20% lower. In this case, the dealer is not selling the tail, and the option gets cheaper. They may make sense when they are much cheaper than the corresponding put spread.

Capital Markets and Investments

Contingent options usually refer to two underlyings, e.g. a 95% Put on the S&P500, provided the Euro (Currency) has depreciated at least 3% against the dollar. This cheapens the cost significantly, relative to a regular put, and allows investors to bet on specific scenarios. *Dual-digital* options, which combine digital options of two underlyings, are a special case of contingent options.

Bermudian options are similar to American options in the sense that they allow for early expiration, but only on pre-specified dates (not anytime)

Asian options are options whose final value is determined not by the value of the underlying (relative to the strike) on the expiration date, but by the average value of the underlying over a pre-specified number of days (often 1 month). This prevents the option value being influenced by possible manipulation of the underlying close to expiration.

> ✓ Call and put options with other conditions that modify the payoff function (from the vanilla put/call) or make the payoff contingent on certain conditions are called Exotic options. Examples include digital options, barrier options, contingent options, Bermudian options and Asian options.
>
> ✓ These options are analytically difficult to price, and are often priced based on simulation.

This chapter has provided some understanding of put and call options, their uses and their relationships with each other. In the next chapter, we will explore how these options are actually priced, on a stand-alone basis.

REFERENCES

Hull, John. *Options, Futures and Other Derivatives*. Pearson

Natenberg, Sheldon. *Option Volatility and Pricing*. McGraw Hill

14. Options Valuation

In the previous chapter, we developed some understanding and intuition about what options are, how they work, how investors use them and how different options are related to each other. In particular, put-call parity establishes a no-arbitrage relationship between the underlying price and the prices of puts and calls with the same strike. In this chapter, we explore how exactly to come up with the prices of the individual options, after making some assumptions about the behavior of the underlying price. We also discuss how to use volatility metrics to trade options.

OPTION PRICING OVERVIEW

After assumptions have been made to describe price movements (dynamics) of the underlying, options are usually valued using one of three techniques:

- Analytical / Formula: The assumptions on the underlying are formulated mathematically. The resulting equations are then solved to derive a formula for the price of the option. This is only possible in the simplest situations. But, once derived, it is trivial to repeat for other options.

- Trees: The dynamics of the underlying are represented using tree diagrams (such as the binomial models below). The underlying's price and the option's price are computed at each node of the tree, by progressively discounting the possible outcomes at the next step in the tree, arising from that node. This is often computationally intensive, but very useful for American options.

- Simulation: This technique is primarily used, usually for more complicated options, when the mathematical formulation describing the underlying's dynamics cannot be algebraically solved to a straightforward formula. The underlying's dynamics are simulated using random variables (by applying Monte Carlo techniques), often several thousand times (each of these a "path"), the option price calculated for every path by using the contractual payoff function and the underlying values. The option prices, one for each path, are then averaged. This is a "brute force" method, often used for exotic and path-dependent options.

> Options can be valued using:
> ✓ Analytical Formula
> ✓ Binomial/ Trinomial Tree frameworks
> ✓ Simulation

MODELING STOCK PRICES – A BINOMIAL MODEL

We start with a simple "binomial" model of stock prices, where the stock price, currently at S_0, can either go up to uS_0 $(u > 1)$ or down to dS_0 $(d < 1)$, (i.e. two future "states of the world") with probability p and $(1-p)$ respectively. Assuming $uS_0 > K$ *(i.e. option strike price)* $> dS_0$, the payoff of a call option in the "*up*" state is $uS_0 - K$, and *0* in the "*down*" state. Often, for modeling convenience, d is assumed to be equal to $1/u$. While all these assumptions seem restrictive (only two discrete states of the world next period, etc.), the model is actually pretty general. The time step can be shrunk, and many one-period models linked together to generate a rich set of outcomes at expiration. Figure 14.1 shows the tree diagram; C_0 is the option price, to be calculated.

Capital Markets and Investments

Figure 14.1 Security Payoffs in a binomial model

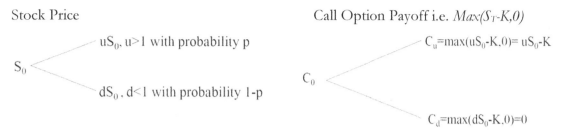

Call Option - Pricing mechanics

We will ideally try to adopt a no-arbitrage approach i.e. construct a portfolio of securities with known prices, which have the same payoff as the call option in every future state (i.e. both the portfolio and the option pay out equal amounts, in every (currently unknown/ uncertain) future realization of stock prices. If we can somehow come up with this *replicating portfolio*, the option price today has to be equal to this portfolio's current value, otherwise there will be an arbitrage opportunity.

In this particular case, we will try to construct the portfolio using the underlying (stock) and bank deposit. Let us assume that we have Δ (*delta*) units of stock, and B dollars in a bank deposit earning $r\%$ per period. This portfolio is currently valued at $\pi_0 = \Delta S_0 + B$. At expiration (time T), this portfolio is either worth $\Delta u S_0 + B(1+r)$ or $\Delta d S_0 + B(1+r)$, depending on whether the stock price goes up or down. Figure 14.2 shows the tree diagram.

Figure 14.2 Portfolio Payoffs in a binomial model

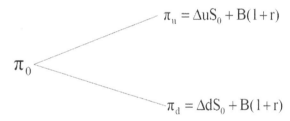

So, we want to find values of Δ and B, so that the portfolio payoff matches the option payoff in both states. To compute this, let us equate payoffs in both states i.e.

"Up" state   : $\pi_u = \Delta u S_0 + B(1+r) = u S_0 - K = C_u$

"Down" state : $\pi_d = \Delta d S_0 + B(1+r) = 0 \quad = C_d$

This is a system of two equations in two unknowns, Δ and B. We obtain the following solutions:

$$\Delta = \frac{u S_0 - K}{(u-d) S_0} \qquad \text{Eq. 14.1}$$

$$B = -\frac{1}{1+r} \frac{(u S_0 - K) d}{u - d} \qquad \text{Eq. 14.2}$$

From Eq. 14.1, *for a call option, Δ is between 0 and 1* (since $K > dS_0$). So, to replicate the call option, the investor need to buy stocks (but a smaller number of stocks than the number of options); this is intuitive because buying a call option and being long stocks both imply a bullish view on the underlying. A negative value of B in Eq. 14.2 implies that money needs to borrowed to finance this.

We now substitute these values to calculate π_0, which must be identical to C_0, the current option price, to prevent arbitrage. So,

Options Valuation

$$C_0 = \Delta S_0 + B = \frac{uS_0 - K}{u-d} - \frac{1}{1+r}\frac{(uS_0-K)d}{u-d} = \frac{1}{1+r}\left[\frac{1+r-d}{u-d}\right](uS_0 - K) \qquad \text{Eq. 14.3}$$

Eq. 14.3 indicates that the call price goes up when, everything else remaining the same, the underlying stock goes up, or the size of the up-move increases, or the strike price goes down, etc. This can be formally quantified by taking the partial derivative of the derivative price to each of these variables/parameters; these partial derivatives are loosely referred to as "*greeks*", because they are often represented by Greek symbols. Let us intuitively understand each of these. If the underlying stock price goes up, the option is more likely to end up meaningfully in the money at expiration. This would also happen if the strike price decreases. If the magnitude of the up-move gets larger, the option will now make more in the up-state, and is therefore more valuable. Note that the probabilities do not matter in determining the option's price; we will revisit this observation in detail later.

It is important to recognize that these option pricing results are independent of any model/framework and are robust to most reasonable assumptions. In our derivations above, we made very few modeling assumptions that influenced the results; it was more about laying out a general framework that we will continue to use. We made no assumptions about the return distribution and volatility of the underlying.

> *Example:* Consider a 1-period ABC call option struck at K=60. Suppose ABC's current price is $S_0 = 61$ and u = 1.1, d = 0.9 and r = 5%. To calculate the price of the call option, we can simply solve for Δ and B in the replicating portfolio, using Equations 1 and 2 (or use Equation 3 directly). Δ = 0.582 and B = -30.429. The option's price is $5.07.
>
> Let us confirm that the replication really works. We initially spend 0.582*61=35.50 to buy ABC shares. We borrow 30.43 (the value of *B*), so the cash outlay is 35.50 – 30.43 = 5.07, which is exactly the price of the option we calculated above. Next period, the loan payment amount is 30.43*1.05 = 31.95. If the stock price goes up, the stock will be worth 61*1.1=67.1, so our stock holdings will be worth 0.582*67.1=39.05. So, the net cash flow in the "up" state is 39.05-31.95 =7.10. In this state, the call option would pay 67.1- 60 = 7.10, exactly the same as the portfolio. In the "down" state, the stock would be worth 61*0.9 = 54.9, our stock holdings would be worth 0.582*54.9 = 31.95, which is exactly equal to the loan payment, making the portfolio payoff 0. The option expires worthless in the down state, so the payoffs are identical yet again. The replication works!
>
> Suppose instead, the option were trading at $6.00, an investor would sell the option and synthetically replicate it exactly as above (by buying stocks and borrowing money), with an outflow of $5.07, thereby netting a riskless 93 cent profit. The next period, the replicating portfolio payoff proceeds will pay for any potential liabilities from selling the option.

- ✓ We represent the future movement (from now until option expiry date) in the underlying stock price as either *up* or *down* states, and assume that the stock either moves up to uS_0 or down to dS_0:
- ✓ Calculate the option payoff in each of these states using the payoff function and the stock price.
- ✓ Replicate the option payoff in each state using a portfolio of stock and bond, weights decided today. Solve for the weights by equating payoffs.
- ✓ The portfolio's current value is known. This has to be identical to the option value, since the portfolio and the option generate identical cash flows, otherwise there will be an arbitrage opportunity.

Capital Markets and Investments

Further details

The simplicity of the framework we used raises a few questions, which we answer one by one in this section— Does it matter that we assumed that the call was worthless in the down-state, and in the money in the up-state? How does one pick sensible values for u and d? How sensitive are option prices to the underlying price movement? Why do the probabilities not show up in the option price?

Does it matter that we assumed that the call was worthless in the down-state, and in the money in the up-state?

While the exact option price depends on what payoffs we assume in the up and down state, *the methodology does not depend on the particular payoffs we chose*. To see this clearly, consider a general derivative that pays off Z_u in the up state and Z_d in the down state. This includes calls, puts and some exotic derivatives too. Figure 14.3 has the tree diagram.

Figure 14.3 Generalized Derivative: Payoffs in a Binomial model

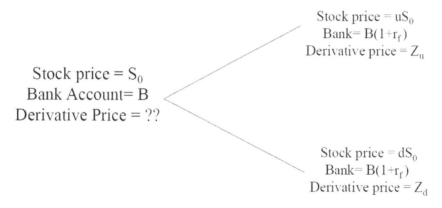

Using the same argument as above, we try to match portfolio payoffs with derivative payoffs, state by state, and set up equations to solve for portfolio weights. This leads to:

"Up" state : $\Delta u S_0 + B(1+r) = Z_u$

"Down" state : $\Delta d S_0 + B(1+r) = Z_d$

Solving these equations for Δ *and* B gives us:

$$\Delta = \frac{Z_u - Z_d}{(u-d)S_0} \qquad \text{Eq. 14.4}$$

$$B = -\frac{1}{1+r}\frac{uZ_d - dZ_u}{u-d} \qquad \text{Eq. 14.5}$$

And, the derivative price, by no arbitrage, is equal to:

$$Z_0 = \Delta S_0 + B = \frac{Z_u - Z_d}{u-d} + \frac{1}{1+r}\frac{uZ_d - dZ_u}{u-d} \qquad \text{Eq. 14.6}$$

By picking different values for Z_T, we can price different kinds of options. Examples include:

Call Options: $Z_T = \text{Max}(0, S_T - K)$

Put Options: $Z_T = \text{Max}(0, K - S_T)$

Double Digital Options: $Z_T = 1$ if $\{S_{Low} < S_T < S_{High}\}$, 0 otherwise

Options Valuation

How does one pick sensible values for u and d?

The magnitude of *u* and *d* capture how much the stock can move in the next period from its current level. Values close to 1 suggest low *stock volatility*. In practice, *u* and *d* are typically assumed equal to $u = exp^{(\sigma \sqrt{t})}$ and $d = 1/u$, where σ is the stock's annualized volatility and *t* is the time period (in number of years) in the binomial model. As we mentioned earlier, by shortening the time period, and representing the option in a multi-period binomial model, we can get a large number (not just two) of possible stock prices (and option payoffs) at expiration. In a binomial model with a large number of time steps, these values of u and d will generate option prices that converge to the option price from the Black –Scholes model (which we will discuss later) using the same volatility.

How sensitive is the option price to the underlying price?

The answer is, it depends. Options that are deep in-the-money move one-for-one with the underlying, options deep out-of-the-money move little with the underlying, and options struck at the current underlying price move approximately 50 cents for every dollar movement in the stock price. It also depends on how volatile the stock is, and how much time there is to option maturity.

To understand this better, we rearrange the first equality in Eq. 14.3 to obtain

$$C_0 - \Delta S_0 = B \qquad \text{Eq. 14.7}$$

So, if an investor is long the call option and short Δ units of stock, this long option short stock portfolio (or even the opposite) is "locally riskless" and can be replicated by a risk-free bond for small stock price movements. This is only possible if the call option price moves by delta dollars (remember, delta lies between zero and one) for every dollar movement in the underlying stock price. And, if not, there is an arbitrage opportunity. *Delta* (often denoted by δ, the lower-case version of Δ) is the partial derivative of the option price to the stock price. It is (arguably) the most important greek, and is also referred to as the "hedge ratio"; the portfolio is referred to as *delta-hedged*. For a put, $\Delta < 0$, so ΔS_0 is now a short stock position; to replicate a put, the investor needs to short stock. This intuitively makes sense, because a long put is a bearish position, similar to a short stock position. A delta-hedged portfolio (e.g. the long call- short stock portfolio in Eq. 14.7) has no sensitivity to small movements in the underlying (hence is equivalent to a risk-free bond). To see this, let's take the partial derivative of the portfolio value in Eq. 14.7 with respect to S_0. From Eq. 14.3, the partial derivative of the call price C0 with respect to S_0 is Δ, the partial derivative of the stock price S_0 with respect to S_0 is 1 (trivially). Assuming that Δ is independent of S_0 (bad assumption except for small "local" changes in S_0), we can treat it as a constant. Putting this together, the partial derivative of the delta-hedged long call short stock portfolio value with respect to the underlying stock is zero.

Why do the probabilities not show up in the option price?

Option prices do not depend on how often the stock goes up versus goes down, because the payoffs of the option and the replicating portfolio are identical in both the up and down state. The option price we solved for is the only (unique) price that prevents arbitrage. If the stock price is very likely to be high in the next period, this will cause today's stock price to be higher. The expectations for future stock prices is completely captured in the current price.

This works because of the way we described the world. The source of risk in the option is equity price volatility, which can be hedged perfectly (for small moves) by holding a suitable position in the stock. Since the number of sources of risk (one in this example) is fewer than the number of instruments bearing that risk (two – the stock and the option), risk has to be priced similarly across both these instruments. Since there are only two states of the world and three securities (stock, bond and option), it is possible to solve the system of

Capital Markets and Investments

two equations (the up-state and down-state payoff matching) to get a unique solution for the weights of the portfolio that replicates the third security; essentially the option is a *redundant security*.

Since the probabilities do not matter for option pricing, we can assume a different set of probabilities to make our lives easier. These special probabilities (*risk-neutral probabilities*) allow us to price options assuming that the investor is risk neutral, and expected cash flows (and not the uncertainty of these cash flows) are the only input. *The price of any security is its expected value using risk neutral probability, discounted by the risk-free rate.* To see this clearly, let's rewrite Eq. 14.3 as below:

$$C_0 = \frac{1}{1+r}\left[\frac{1+r-d}{u-d}\right](uS_0 - K) = \frac{1}{1+r}[\underbrace{C_u}_{uS_0-K} \overbrace{q}^{\frac{1+r-d}{u-d}} + \underbrace{C_d}_{0}(1-q)] = \frac{E^q(C_T)}{(1+r)} \qquad \text{Eq. 14.8}$$

Eq. 14.8 can be written as a NPV of expected future option cash flows (C_u and C_d respectively), using the risk-neutral probability (of up-state) q. So, although the cash flows are inherently risky, in this situation (because the source of risk in options is the same as that of the stock, and all possible payoffs can be achieved only by trading the stock and bond; the option is a *redundant* security), we can pretend that the cash flows are risk-free and discount it using the risk-free rate, provided we use the suitable risk-neutral probability q. Under certain conditions (all the time, for the purpose of this text), q is unique. Once we know q, we can simply use the option's (state-contingent) contractual cash flows to calculate its expected payoff (using q, the *risk-neutral measure*), and then discount this using the risk-free rate. So, we only need the q-probabilities for every state, the option's payoffs for each of those states and the risk free rate to price derivatives in one step. This is referred to as *risk-neutral pricing*.

Unlike earlier chapters where we took pains to figure out the correct discount rate to reflect the riskiness of cash flows, here we adjust probabilities instead, and discount the modified expected value by the risk free rate. These adjusted probabilities incorporate both the real-world probabilities, as well as risk-premia. We can price derivatives either by replication or by risk-neutral methods; both will give us the same answer.

> *Example:* Consider a derivative X that (trivially) pays off exactly the stock price in both the up and down state. Let us confirm that this derivative costs exactly the same as the current stock price. To apply the framework, let us calculate:
>
> $$X_0 = \frac{E^q(X_T)}{(1+r)} = \frac{1}{(1+r)}[q\,uS_0 + (1-q)\,dS_0] = \frac{1}{(1+r)}[\frac{1+r-d}{u-d}uS_0 + (1-\frac{1+r-d}{u-d})\,dS_0] = \frac{1}{(1+r)}[S_0(1+r)] = S_0$$
>
> So, the current price of this derivative is, indeed, equal to the stock price S0, as it should be.

Options Valuation

- ✓ This binomial pricing method is very general; it accommodates a range of option payoffs.
- ✓ How much the stock moves in the up and down state is usually calibrated to the stock's volatility; this is where the assumptions regarding stock price movements are embedded.
- ✓ The option price's sensitivity to underlying stock price movements is equal to how much stock is held in the replicating (stock-bond) portfolio.
- ✓ The probability of the up and down states do not matter in this framework. This is because we are working in a three security (stock, bond and option) and two state (up and down) world. Payoffs in the two states can be replicated using a portfolio of two securities; the third security can be priced in terms of the other two.
- ✓ Security prices can also be calculated as expected values using modified risk-neutral probabilities, discounted by the risk-free rate.

Multi-period models

In two-period models, the stock price can only take two possible values next period. While this may appear restrictive, multi-period models provide a convenient (albeit computationally intensive) workaround, by considering the earlier one period as the equivalent of multiple time periods in the current framework. The $d = 1/u$ assumption made earlier (i.e. $ud = 1$) causes multi-period trees to recombine, thus simplifying computational burden. Almost all real-world option pricing using binomial trees is done in a multi-period setting. Figure 14.4 illustrates this (note: number of time periods equals the number of possible final values.

Figure 14.4 Multi-period Recombining Binomial model

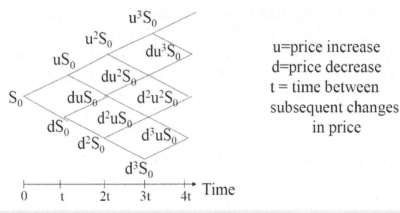

u = price increase
d = price decrease
t = time between subsequent changes in price

Example: Let's consider a stock ($S_0 = 100$) whose dynamics are described in Figure 14.5(a), with u = 1.05 and d = 0.95. We will calculate the price of an at-the-money European put, expiring at the end of period 2, with the risk-free rate at 0.05%. To price this put (at time 0), we break this up into three single-period sub-problems, one at each node, as shown in Figure 14.5(b).

Capital Markets and Investments

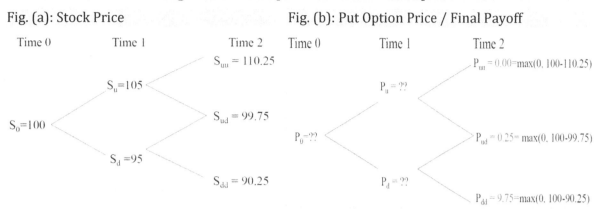

Figure 14.5 Two-period Binomial example

Let's first compute P_u (see Figure 14.5(b)). We will use the risk-neutral approach, so we first calculate the risk-neutral probability $q = (1+0.005-0.95)/(1.05-0.95) = 0.55$. We then compute discounted expected values using q i.e. $P_u = (0*0.55 + 0.25* 0.45)/1.005 = 0.112$. Repeating the same idea, we calculate $P_d = (0.25* 0.55 + 9.75*0.45)/1.005 = 4.5$. Then, using P_u and P_d as inputs, we solve the initial period sub-problem to obtain $P_0 = (0.112*0.55 + 4.5*0.45)/1.005 = 2.08$. This technique is formally referred to as *backward induction*.

Multi-period models are useful, because they allow for a richer and more realistic set of outcomes. They are also the primary technique used to price securities with embedded options, such as callable bonds[166]. So far, we discussed only the binomial model where the underlying has only two outcomes in the next period; extensions such as *trinomial models* (three branches out of every node) are also commonly used. The technique and the theory for pricing such options is straightforward; the detail is in the numerical implementation to speed up computation. Another detail for such models is the common use of *continuous compounding*, which we have not used here. This requires slight tweaks in the risk-neutral probability formula and the discounting formula discussed here, essentially replacing $(1+r)^t$ by e^{rt}, where r is the return per month/year, and t the number of months/years in a time-step. In our examples, r is the return per time-step, so t is trivially equal to 1.

.American Options

American options are another yet situation where binomial option pricing is very important. As a reminder, American options are options that can be exercised at any time before the expiration date (and not just at expiration, like European options). This makes American option valuation path-dependent (i.e. their value depends not just on the terminal value of the underlying, but also the path taken to get there), making the tree-based node-by-node technique (binomial or other) necessary. We will show later that an American call option on a non-dividend paying stock has the same price as a European option with similar terms, since it is sub-optimal to exercise an American call option before expiration. However, for put options and call options that pay a dividend, the distinction between American and European contracts matters.

> *Example:* To illustrate this, let us consider a put option as described in Figure 14.5, but which is American in nature. We will compute the same European option price tree as in Figure 14.5(b). But now, at each node (prior to maturity), we will compare the European option price to the payoff from exercising, and use the value which is higher (if this were a call option, the European option price would always exceed the payoff). We then discount cashflows in this modified payoff tree.

---

[166] Securities with path-dependent options (such as residential mortgages) are often priced by simulating (i.e. by Monte Carlo techniques) price histories, and computing an option price for each path.

Options Valuation

So, Figure 14.5(a) and Figure 14.5(b) are still relevant, as are the values of P_u, P_d, and P_0 in Figure 14.5(b) computed in the example above. Figure 14.6 below shows the payoff from exercising at every node. Comparing with the values in Figure 14.5(b), we see that the only node where the payoff from exercising is higher than the European option value is the lower node in Time 1 ($5 versus $4.5 earlier). So, if we get to the lower node, we will exercise the option, otherwise we will behave as if it were an European option. To get to the current option price (Time 0), we treat it as a one-period problem, with payoffs equal to 0.112 and 5.0 in the up-state and down-state respectively. So, P_0 = (0.112*0.55 + 5.0*0.45)/1.005 = 2.30; thus the American option trades at a 28 cent premium over the European option.

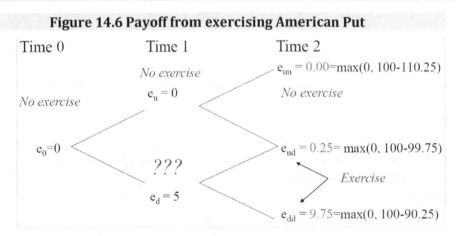

Figure 14.6 Payoff from exercising American Put

Boundaries on Option Prices

The discussion over the last two chapters has suggested several bounds (limits) on option prices, either in an absolute sense, or relative to other securities. For example, option prices are positive (trivially, since no chance of negative cash flows) and follow put-call parity. American options will never cost less than European options. Call options cost less than the underlying, because their value is always below that of the underlying. Similarly, put options will always cost less than the strike price of the underlying.

A call option pays either 0 or $S_T - K$ at expiration, depending on whether the underlying stock ends up above or below the strike. A portfolio comprising the stock S and a loan which pays K at maturity will pay $S_T - K$ at maturity, no matter what. When $S_T < K$, the payoff from this portfolio is negative. So, the payoff from the call option is more favorable, since the negative payoff is truncated at 0. The current price of the call option C_t, should therefore be greater than the current portfolio value, $S_t - PV(K)$, i.e. $C_t \geq S_t - PV(K)$.

Early Exercise of American Calls

If an investor were to exercise an American call option prior to maturity (at time t), he would get $S_t - K$. From the lower bound just derived, the call option price C_t is always greater than this payoff (*since* $PV(K) < K$), so *if an investor no longer wanted to hold the call option in the non-dividend paying stock, he would sell it in the open market (and earn Ct) rather than exercise it* (to receive the lower $S_t - K$).

The only time to potentially consider exercising an (in-the-money) American call option on a dividend paying stock is right before the stock pays a dividend, and if the dividend is more than the time value of the option. This is because the stock price is going to go down by the amount of the dividend, on the ex-dividend date, so the call option will trade down. A stock owner is indifferent because he receives the dividend to offset the lower stock price, but the option owner loses out. By exercising early, the call option owner prevents this loss[167]. If the time value of the option were greater than the dividend, then selling the option is best.

The example in **Figure 14.6** shows that there are times when it is indeed optimal to exercise a put early. With puts, the investor receives (in exchange for the stock) cash equal to the strike price early, and can invest the proceeds risk free. With calls, the investor pays the strike price early, foregoing the interest income.

> A common realistic extension to the binomial model includes extending it for multiple periods.
> - ✓ This allows for a range for terminal stock prices (instead of just two).
> - ✓ The tree recombines when d is assumed to be $1/u$, simplifying computation. The value of d is chosen based on assumptions regarding the underlying stock price dynamics.
> - ✓ This is the primary technique to price American options
>   - American options are never cheaper than European options.
>   - The current price of a call option is greater than the current value of a portfolio of one stock and bond with face value of K (maturing at option expiry).
>   - It is not optimal to exercise an American call on a non-dividend paying stock before maturity; it is better to sell the option if the investor no longer wants exposure. So, American call options on a non-dividend paying stock do not cost more than European options.

BLACK SCHOLES FORMULA

Stock prices generated by a binomial model (similar to the one above) with many time steps will lead to a probability distribution (stochastic process) of stock prices, which served as the foundation of continuous-time finance in general, and the Black Scholes formula in particular. This process is called *Geometric Brownian Motion (GBM)*, and is represented as: $\Delta S = \mu S_t \Delta t + \sigma S_t \Delta W_t$, where the Δ notation refers to "change" (very different from its meaning in the earlier sections on replicating portfolios), Δt is the change in time, ΔW refers to a random draw from the $N(0,1)$ distribution, and is formally called the Weiner process, μ being the average stock return and σ the stock volatility. So, stock price returns (stock price changes divided by the current price) are modelled as returning μ per period on average, with a volatility of σ. Values of u and d can be chosen so that the binomial process converges to this process, also referred to as a *random walk*. Stock returns are thus normally distributed in this framework; prices are log-normally distributed.

The Black-Scholes formula, which gives us the price of an option in terms of market variables, is derived from this general GBM (random walk) process (normally distributed returns/ lognormal prices), along with several other *assumptions* – continuous trading, constant volatility and interest rates, no transaction costs, easy short-selling, no dividends. Most of these assumptions can be relaxed. The relevant market variables on which the option price (C_t) is based are stock price (S), Time to maturity (T), exercise price (K), continuously compounded interest rate (r) and volatility (σ).

To derive the formula, Fischer Black and Myron Scholes applied the CAPM in their original paper, where they used the underlying as an analog for the market and the option as the single security to be priced. Robert

---

[167] This argument works for anything that makes the forward go down, like a very high borrow cost, or a drop in the interest rates. European options are priced off the forward, but American options also have the current intrinsic value as a floor.

Options Valuation

Merton contributed to the research soon after, coming up with replication-based and risk-neutral arguments. All these methods led to the same result (Eq. 14.9) for *call options*:

$$C(S_t, K, T, r, \sigma) = N(d_1)S_t - Ke^{-r(T-t)}N(d_2)$$ Eq. 14.9

where

$$d_1 = \frac{\ln(S_t/K) + (r + 0.5\sigma^2)(T-t)}{\sigma\sqrt{T-t}}$$

$$d_2 = d_1 - \sigma\sqrt{T-t}$$

$N(y)$ is the probability that a $N(0,1)$ random process is less than y

σ is the stock volatility

Examining this formula through the replication lens $C_t = \Delta S_0 + B$ (comparing to Eq. 14.3 above), $N(d_1)$ is analogous to the hedge ratio Δ and gives the number of shares to neutralize effects of small stock price movements, and $-Ke^{-r(T-t)}N(d_2)$ is similar to the bond holdings B. Since *Black Scholes prices satisfy put-call parity (all models do, since it is a no-arbitrage condition without strict assumptions), we can figure out the price of put options by substituting the call price result*:

$$P(S_t, K, T, r, \sigma) = C(S_t, K, T, r, \sigma) + Ke^{-r(T-t)} - S_t = Ke^{-r(T-t)}N(-d_2) - S_t N(-d_1)$$ Eq. 14.10

- ✓ The Black Scholes formula connects option prices to price of underlying security, strike price, expected volatility of the stock, time to maturity, and financing (interest) rates.
- ✓ This formula relies on Black-Scholes assumptions, which are assumptions on how stock prices behave, and assumptions about information flow, trading costs, etc.
- ✓ Mathematical techniques are applied to the assumptions above to get to the Black Scholes result. Several different methods, such as CAPM application, replicating portfolios and risk neutrality can be used to get to the same result. The Black Scholes result matches with the result from a binomial model, if the binomial tree is calibrated consistently with the Black Scholes assumptions.

Graph of Call Option Prices before Expiration – some more Greeks[168]

Most variables in the above formula are unambiguous and can be substituted to derive the Black Scholes prices (strike and maturity are contractual, underlying price and risk free rate are observable), but how does one choose the correct value of *volatility*? Analysts can look at the historical standard deviation of the underlying for context, but finally have to make a judgment call regarding a suitable level of volatility going forward. Putting in a reasonable value of volatility in equation (say 35%), we can plot the value of a call option at different values of the underlying. A higher volatility assumption leads to a higher call price, before maturity. Figure 14.7 shows this, assuming r = 0.044, T=0.5, X=160, S=140.

---

[168] While these pre-expiration prices and Greeks can be computed in several ways, using a formula is easiest because we simply substitute different values of inputs, to get prices at different times, Greeks, etc.

Capital Markets and Investments

Figure 14.7 Graph of Call Option Price before Expiration Date

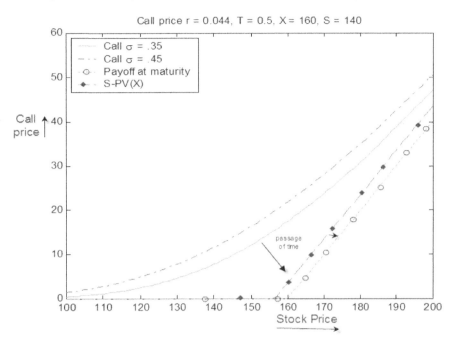

The line to the right (dotted line with circle) is the payoff at maturity. That is simply $Max(0, S_T - K)$ and does not depend on volatility assumptions. The curved lines towards the left are call option prices before maturity (6 months in the graph); the higher curve has a larger volatility assumption (45% versus 35%); the price sensitivity to volatility is called *vega*, and is highest for at-the-money options with long time to maturity. In the formula, volatility is multiplied by the square root of time, so volatility assumption changes in near-dated options matter less. The tangent to these curves at any point (i.e. stock price) is the *delta* at that price, and represents the hedge ratio. These lines are *convex*, i.e. the *delta* decreases as the underlying sells off, and increases as the underlying increases; the rate of change in delta as the underlying changes is called *gamma*. They are also asymptotic to the line (with the black diamond) showing $S_T - PV(K)$. With the passage of time, all these lines pull towards the kinked maturity payoff line i.e. all else remaining the same, option prices go down as the time to maturity decreases, the effect being especially large for near-the-money options. This *time decay* is referred to as *theta*.

The volatility of the underlying stock and the time to maturity leads to the possibility that the stock can end up through the strike price even if it is currently out of the money. The longer the time to maturity and the higher the assumed stock volatility, the greater the chance of this option ending up in-the-money and exercised. This is called the option's *time value*, and goes to zero at maturity. It is distinct from the option's *intrinsic value*, which captures how much the option would pay if the underlying's price at expiration were equal to its current price. It is the higher of zero, and the difference between the strike price and the current underlying price, i.e. the option's final payoff. The total option price (which could be the price obtained by Black Scholes, or the other models discussed above, or the traded market price) is the sum of the time value and the intrinsic value of the option. The intrinsic value is unambiguous and can be calculated directly; the time value is the difference between the total price and the intrinsic value (i.e. it is model-dependent).

Options Valuation

- ✓ The price of an option before maturity is higher than the payoff at maturity, for any stock price. On a price graph, it is a curved line that sits above the broken line denoting the maturity payoff
- ✓ This is because the volatility of the underlying stock ensures that the stock can end up through the strike price even if it is currently out of the money. The longer the time to maturity and the higher the assumed stock volatility, the greater this value (often called the option's time value). This is calculated as the difference between the option's price and intrinsic value.
- ✓ The delta of a call option is its sensitivity to the underlying's price. It increases as the option gets more in-the-money. This increase in delta as the underlying moves (in the "favorable" direction) is called gamma or convexity, and benefits the option owner.
- ✓ Other important "Greeks" include vega, or the option price sensitivity to changes in volatility and theta, or the option's price sensitivity to the decrease in time to maturity (i.e. the passage of time).

Implied Volatility and Realized Volatility

We discussed above, that most inputs in the pricing formula are unambiguous, with the exception of volatility. Since there is a one-to-one relation between volatility and option price (through the formula), the volatility assumption pretty much decides the price. If two investors disagree on the option price (and both believe the Black Scholes model), this is because they disagree on option volatility. Alternatively, we can flip the pricing formula, use the option market price as an input (along with other observables), and back out what volatility the price is implying. This *implied volatility* now becomes an alternative metric to quote and compare option prices (higher prices and implied volatilities go hand in hand), and makes comparisons across different strikes, maturities, issuers (and comparisons over time) easier.

What happens if the implied volatility is very different from the historical volatility? Well, historical volatility is relevant, only as far as it provides an estimate for volatility going forward. If the expected future volatility is very different from the historical stock price behavior (e.g. imminent product launch, earnings or lawsuit hearing), then the history is less of a guide. But, if the implied volatility of the option is very different from the expected future volatility, then the option price in the market may not accurately reflect this volatility expectation. Let us assume that the implied volatility of a call option is too low (the argument works in reverse if it is too high instead). That's similar to saying that the option price is too low, so the investor should buy the option. But, since the option price depends on several other variables besides volatility, the investor is exposed to other risks too. While many of these are either predictable (e.g. time decay) or not huge (e.g. changes in the risk free rate), the big uncertainty is the price of the underlying stock. If the investor does not have a view on the stock price (but has a view on its volatility), he should *delta-hedge* that risk by going short Δ (i.e. $N(d_1)$) units of stock. Now, if the stock ends up being more volatile (as the investor expected) and goes up, the call will make more money (unless implied volatility goes down) than the short stock portfolio will lose (since option delta will have increased with the underlying increase, but the hedge is according to the old lower delta. Now, the investor needs to re-balance the hedge, in this case shorting more shares. If the stock price subsequently decreases (the expected high volatility continues), the short portfolio makes more money on the way down than the call option loses. This technique (delta-hedge and rebalance) can help monetize the difference between implied volatility and subsequent realized volatility, assuming transaction costs are very low. The lucrativeness of this strategy depends on how much the delta moves with the underlying (referred to as *gamma*, the rate of change of delta with underlying price). The options with the highest gamma are at-the-money near term options. The transaction costs are typically lowest for the brokers, so they often put on

Capital Markets and Investments

the gamma trades. Further, this makes money only when the stock is volatile (i.e. goes up and down by large amounts); large moves in one direction does not necessarily help. Gamma is also referred to as *Convexity*; convexity here captures the rate at which delta changes, in fixed income, it is the rate of change of duration.

Drawbacks of Black-Scholes - Modifications

The Black-Scholes model drawbacks arise from its many simplifying assumptions (while many of them can be relaxed, the exact result changes), or weakness in empirical validation. The no-arbitrage relationship worked neatly in a two-period two-state (up-down) setting in an earlier example (right after Equation 3). In a multi-period setting, where the stock price can move all over, if the option is mispriced, this arbitrage is not that easy to detect (because of uncertainty in volatility outlook) or implement (because of transaction costs, frequent trading, etc.). Delta-hedging / gamma trading is one way to keep it within reasonable limits. Also, the stock returns in reality may not follow an exact GBM or random walk; the volatility (even if correct) may not adequately capture the potential future dynamics of the stock price.

Further, if the Black-Scholes model were exactly right, the option prices for all the various strikes and maturities for a single issuer or index would imply the exact same implied volatility. While this was somewhat true before October 1987, the Black Monday crash changed how investors viewed options; they were now willing to pay up for the lower strike puts, as insurance for bad market outcomes. A few extra pennies for a far OTM put can lead to an implied volatility several points higher; causing implied volatilities of lower strike options to be higher than at-the-money options. On an implied volatility- strike price graph as in Figure 14.8, this looks like a "smirk" and is referred to as *skew*; in cases when the upside is also bid, it resembles a "smile". It is difficult to arbitrage this implied volatility difference, for the reasons discussed above. Since OTM options are more liquid than ITM options, implied volatility for lower strikes (relative to spot price) are usually inferred from puts, and higher strikes from calls. However, for liquid puts and calls of the same strike (one of them has to be ITM and the other OTM, or both ATM) and maturity, the implied volatility is usually very close, since the put call parity relationship does not require rebalancing, etc. it's a static replication and much easier to arbitrage.

Figure 14.8 Implied Volatility Skew is because of non-Lognormal underlying Price Distribution

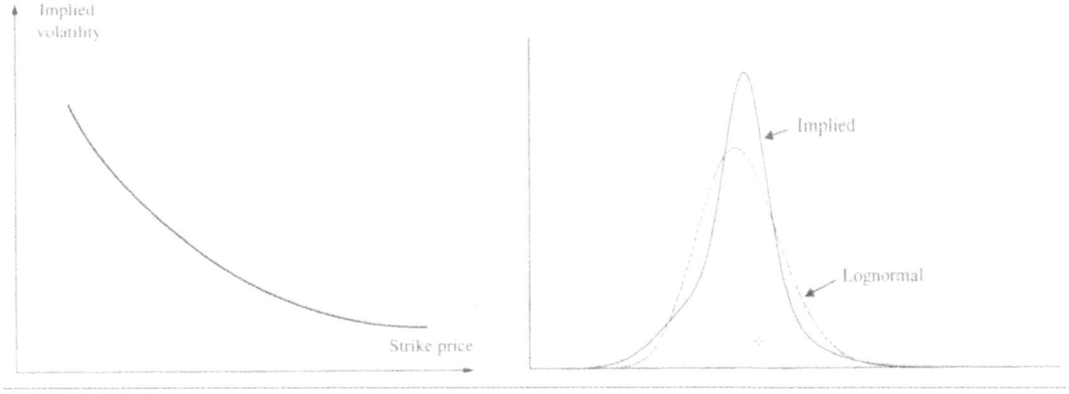

Source: Hull, John. *Option, Futures and other Derivatives*

Stochastic Volatility and Jump Process adjustments

One mechanism to generate this implied volatility pattern is by modifying the GBM assumptions related to stock price dynamics. The most effective adjustments have been related to introducing stochastic volatility (Heston) and jump processes (Merton), or using them together. *Stochastic volatility* involves not assuming stock price volatility to be a constant but having its own stochastic process (e.g. GBM). The random processes (W) in the two GBMSs (related to stock price and volatility) are connected through a correlation assumption. A

Options Valuation

Jump process, which is added to the stock price GBM, is an essentially Poisson (arrival) process, which causes the stock price to "jump" down significantly, at random infrequent intervals. If the true stock price process is not a simple GBM, delta-hedging no longer makes the hedged portfolio riskless. This increases option premium for the downside. To be clear, while it may be easy to come up with innovative stochastic processes, the big challenge is in coming up with realistic processes that are easy to solve mathematically, to reduce to a formula.

Relevance of the Imperfect Black Scholes Formula

While Black Scholes model is imperfect (and no one really believes it), it continues to serve as the benchmark in option pricing. Investors may price options using proprietary sophisticated models (or not), but option prices are always quoted in terms of Black Scholes implied volatilities (by inverting the Black Scholes pricing function). These implied volatilities also allow investors to easily compare options – across strikes (i.e. moneyness), maturities and issuers, or over time for the same issuer/ strike (moneyness)/ time-to-maturity.

- ✓ There is a one-to-one relationship between the option price and the assumed value of stock volatility in the Black Scholes model. All other inputs except volatility are directly observable and unambiguous.

- ✓ Option prices are often quoted in volatility terms rather than in dollars and cents; it is easy to go from one to the other by inverting the Black Scholes formula. The volatility obtained through the Black Scholes formula by using option prices as an input is called implied volatility.

- ✓ Black-Scholes model suggests that the implied volatility calculated using any strike or maturity should be the same, for any particular issuer. The implied volatility for any option represents the same physical idea –the volatility of the underlying's price. But, that is not validated by option prices ("smiles" and "smirks" are common, as out-of-the-money puts are more expensive), providing an empirical criticism for the model.

- ✓ Implied volatility makes it easy to compare option prices across strikes and maturities, as well as to compare option prices across issuers.

- ✓ Comparing implied volatilities to the volatility of the underlying using historical price data (realized volatility) gives an idea of how expensive options are.

VOLATILITY-BASED OPTION TRADES

Option investors often use options either to put on event-driven trades or hedges, as described in the previous chapter. They may also put on implied volatility related trades, such as gamma trading. In many cases they form their views based on the historical difference between implied volatility (say, ATM 3m option) and realized (historical) volatility, and will *buy or sell implied volatility depending on how far it is from realized volatility, relative to historical differences*. Usually, the current difference is expressed as a percentile, relative to the last year (or the last similar regime). For example, an analyst may conclude that implied volatility is expensive because it is trading 1.5 times 60-day realized volatility, which is in the 95th percentile over the past year. Or, while comparable stock implied volatilities are typically at the 60th percentile (relative to realized) currently, this stock's volatility is at the 95th percentile. Similar statements can also be made regarding the *skew*, where investors use the implied volatility difference between the 110% moneyness (i.e. K/S = 1.1) and 90% moneyness (K/S

Capital Markets and Investments

=0.9) as a metric of skew steepness. *Term structure of implied volatility* also provides interesting trading opportunities. Skew and term structure positions are entered into by buying one option and selling another, with different strikes, to gain exposure to the difference in implied volatilities. Some investors also consider implied correlation trades, where they try to get exposure to difference in the implied volatility of a basket of securities (e.g. an index or ETF) and its major constituents, by taking opposite positions in the index option and the single-name options.

We discussed put spreads and call spreads in the last chapter. A variant of this is a 1x2 spread (*1-by-2 put/call spread*), where the investor takes opposite positions in the closer to the money strike and the further out of money strike (like a call or put spread), but trades two of the further OTM option. This is often done (especially on the put side) when the skew is steep, where the buyer of the 1x2 put spread is fine getting long the market at the lower strike, and also gets near-the-money protection for a low cost by monetizing the steep skew. Similarly, a 1x2 call spread allows for cheap upside, with a commitment to get short if the stock rips (a risk). This is less likely because the call that is being sold often does not pay much, because of the smirk in the implied volatility curve.

The risk with the 1x2 spreads is, of course, that the underlying can move violently beyond the strike of the option that has been sold. To risk-manage this, investors often put on *fly trades*, where they also buy a way out of the money option, in addition to the 1x2 spread (so, it is a 1x2x1 trade), to avoid naked exposure to massive market moves. So, after a very large move, the investor is neutral since he is long and short two in the money options. The payoff diagram looks like a butterfly, if the three strikes are equally spaced out, hence this is called a fly trade. The loss is never more than the initial premium, if the strikes are equally spaced. , and set up well if the skew is steep. However, the mark-to-market characteristics of both 1x2 and fly trades are not great. Even if the market starts moving in the investor's direction, the options that have been sold often gain value quickly (and there are two of them), not generating enough P&L. The trade starts making money if the move happens close enough to expiry, when the (two) options that have been sold are far enough out of the money to be very unlikely to end up in the money, but the option strike nearer to the money (which the investor owns) is in play.

An alternative instrument to express views on current implied volatility (versus future realized volatility) is through *variance swaps*, where (realized) variance (i.e. volatility-squared) is the underlying. Like other swaps (see Chapter 9 for interest rate swaps and Chapter 5 for index swaps), a variance swap does not require an upfront payment to enter into, and leads to either a cash inflow or outflow on the settlement date, based on whether the trade worked in the investor's favor or not[169] i.e. if the realized variance between trade inception and settlement is above or below a pre-decided reference variance, called the strike (similar to the swap rate in interest rate swaps). Specifically, the payoff at settlement is *Notional * (Realized Variance – Variance Strike)*. Importantly, to calculate variance for this instrument, the convention is often to assume zero average return, so the variance is just the square of the daily returns, added and annualized. The fair (i.e. no-arbitrage price in an ideal world) price for the swap (i.e. the fair Variance Strike) is a weighted average of the implied volatilities of the options for the same maturity at various strikes, with a higher weight for lower strikes[170]. . Volatility swaps, a similar product with volatility (instead of variance) as the underlying, are also traded.

VIX

Other important volatility-related instruments are the VIX futures, and options on these futures. The *VIX* is an index published by CBOE that is essentially a weighted average of 30-day implied volatility of S&P500

---

[169] This is unlike options, which have an initial premium, and only pays off if the underlying trades in a direction so that the option is in-the-money.

[170] This portfolio of options replicates the payoff of a variance swap.

Options Valuation

options. Far out of the money puts have more weight than at the money options (or, out of the money calls). Also, since the S&P options are usually not exactly 30 days away, this is a weighted average of the implied volatility of the options expiring in the first two months. When investors are fearful of market conditions, the cost (i.e. implied volatility) of OTM puts goes up, raising the value of VIX. The VIX is very reactive to market conditions[171]..

It is impossible to trade the spot VIX, which is published real-time based on option prices. The tradable instrument is *VIX futures*, which cash-settles to the VIX value once every month, 30 days before the expiry of the corresponding S&P options (i.e. on a Wednesday at the open). So, VIX futures exist for various maturities and reflects the current expectation of the value of VIX on the expiration date. If investors expect a current bout of volatility to quickly subside, the VIX futures (which tracks a forward value of VIX) may not follow the spot and disappoint; the front month VIX future is usually the most responsive to spot VIX. *Options on VIX futures* are also heavily traded; their value also depends on the implied volatility of VIX, or the *vol-of-vol*. To be clear, *calls* (not puts) on VIX futures provide downside protection. ETFs that hold a formulaic amount of VIX futures to provide exposure to market volatility have also become fairly common. In fact, much of the movement in VIX during market close happens because rebalancing by these ETFs, especially the levered ETFs.

Investors exposed to VIX futures (using any of the instruments) need to be cognizant of the term structure of the futures. With an upward-sloping term structure (called *contango* in the futures markets)[172], if nothing changes in the markets, a long position in futures expiring further out in time will lose money, since it will "pull" to the lower near-dated value. This is another version of negative carry, and affects commodity futures as well.

- ✓ Time series of the history of implied volatility are used to generate option ideas:
    - Implied volatility-to-realized volatility ratios
    - Difference between implied volatilities of out-of-the-money puts and calls (volatility skew)
    - Implied volatility of 1-month versus 3-month options (volatility term structure)
- ✓ 1x2 put spreads (and fly trades) set up well when the skew is steep; calendar spreads set up well when the term structure is steep.
- ✓ The VIX index is an index of the implied volatility of 30-day S&P500 options, with out-of-the-money puts being heavily weighted. The VIX rises during difficult market conditions, as puts are bid up.
- ✓ Spot VIX is not tradeable; the VIX futures, which settle to the VIX every month, are the primary mechanism to get exposure to (forward) implied volatility. Options on the VIX futures are also common; VIX calls are the hedge instrument against adverse market moves.
- ✓ A long position in futures contracts with a steep upward sloping term structure (contango) is a negative carry position, as the forward price rolls down to the lower spot price if market conditions remain unchanged.

---

[171] So, the (zero expected value/ fair) strike for a 30-day variance swap is the VIX (squared).

[172] A downward sloping futures curve is called a *backwardated* curve; the phenomenon is called *Backwardation*.

Capital Markets and Investments

SUMMARY

In this chapter, especially in the sections on pricing, we delved into a lot of detail. To quickly summarize, options can be priced using formulae (easiest to understand, low computation burden, easy to run scenarios/sensitivities, but rigid assumptions and difficult to come up with initially), trees (less of a black box, very important for American options, but computationally tedious) or simulation. Both replication and risk-neutral methods can be used in most cases. In a few situations though (e.g. some exotic options), this approach will not be possible. In those cases, we can simulate a few thousand runs of underlying stock prices at expiration (based on an assumed distribution of the underlying stock returns), figure out the option value in that situation using the payoff function, and then average across all possible outcomes. Simulation is a brute-force technique for figuring out a reasonable option price for even the most complex options.

Finally, while we have focused the discussion on single-name equities while discussing options, the majority of equity options are actually traded on equity indices. With the growth of ETFs over the last decade, investors also routinely trade options on ETFs to express thematic views. Interest rate, commodity and currency option markets are all huge, in many cases bigger than the equity derivatives market.

REFERENCES

Hull, John. *Options, Futures and Other Derivatives*. Pearson

Natenberg, Sheldon. *Option Volatility and Pricing*. McGraw Hill

Whaley, Robert. *Understanding VIX*. SSRN

Annexures

I. Return - Concepts and Calculations

This Annexure discusses some basic return concepts used throughout finance.

TYPES OF RETURN – SIMPLE, COMPOUND

In this section we discuss briefly the different ways to calculate returns. Conceptually, returns capture how much the investment made (or lost) as a proportion of the original investment. This number is unit-free, and often expressed as a percentage. The most straightforward calculation expresses return as *Total Returns*,

$$R = \frac{Cash\ Flows\ (e.g.\ dividends\ or\ interest\ received, position\ sold) - Investment\ Price}{Investment\ Price}$$

Assuming positions can be sold at any time (i.e. secondary market prices are available), and that there are no intermediate cash flows (dividends/ coupon), returns equal the *Price Return*,

$$R = \frac{P_{End} - P_{Begin}}{P_{Begin}} = \frac{P_{End}}{P_{Begin}} - 1$$

By definition, R above (price return or total return) is a *holding period return;* the values are computed when the investment is entered into and exited. Since different investments have different *investment horizons*, returns are often expressed on an *annualized* basis. Exactly how this annualization is implemented is an important detail. For example, if I hold an investment for 6 months and earn R, the annual return can be expressed as 2R i.e. simply multiplying by a time factor representing the ratio of the investment horizon to one year. If R was earned over a two-year period, the annualized return following this method would be R/2. This is called a *simple* average return.

In general, returns to an investment can accrue from either price changes over the holding period, or from intermediate cash flows (coupons, dividend, etc.). Returns from price changes are called *capital gains*, whereas the returns from intermediate cash flows are called *current yield* (or *coupon yield*), *dividend yield*, etc.

Compounding single period returns

The return calculation is intuitive and straightforward but, if calculated over multiple periods, it does not recognize the fact that returns earned in the first time period are effectively part of the principal outlay to earn returns in the second time period. For example, if I invest $100 in a bank CD and earn $5 in year one and $5 in year two, the simple return as calculated above would be 10% i.e. (10/100) over the investment horizon (or 5% per annum) but this would not recognize that I actually had $105 ($100 of the initial investment and $5 from the return to invest in the second year). Recognizing this would suggest that $10 over two years is less than a 5% return, since the second year's return is below 5%. The formal method to reflect this precision is to use the principle of *compounding*, discussed below. If the magnitudes of the returns are small and we are only considering a few time periods, then the difference between these methods will be small.

If R_1 is the return earned in period 1 and R_2 is the return earned in period 2, simple return calculations will suggest that two-period return is $R_1 + R_2$. As we mentioned above, this is not totally accurate. If we had a dollar at the beginning of period 1, this would grow to $(1+R_1)$ dollars at the beginning of period 2. Over period 2, the entire amount of $(1+R_1)$ will grow at the rate R_2. So, over two periods, 1 dollar would grow to $(1+R_1)*(1+R_2) = 1+R_1+R_2+R_1R_2$, or the return is $R_1+R_2+R_1R_2$. For small values of R_1 and R_2, R_1R_2 is a tiny number, so the simple return calculation is adequate, but not perfect. In general, the *compounded return* (or *geometric return*) over *n* periods is given by:

Relevant Return Concepts

$$R_{1 to n} = (1+R_1)(1+R_2)\ldots(1+R_n) - 1 = \prod_{t=1}^{n}(1+R_t) - 1$$

Note, this is not an annualized return, but a cumulative return over *n* periods. To annualize this return (assuming each period is a year), we need to solve for R is the equation,

$(1+R)^n = 1+R_{1ton}$

Said another way, if F is the final value of a n period investment, and P the initial value, the compounded return over the period is the value R that solves the equation $F = P(1+R)^n$, whereas the value R_s in $F = P + R_s*n$ gives the simple return. If F>P (i.e. the investment made money), $R_s > R$ for the same F and P. Said yet another way, a lower compound return will generate the same final payout as a higher simple return. Alternatively, 5% compounded return will generate a higher final payout than a 5% simple return.

Log-normal prices and normal returns

In many models, prices are assumed to be distributed log normally (since they are non-negative), then log (1+R) is distributed normally. This is because

$$1 + R = \frac{P_{End}}{P_{Begin}} = e^{\log(\frac{P_{End}}{P_{Begin}})}$$

Also, for small values of R, $\log(1+R) \approx R$, so R is approximately normally distributed. The "small R" assumption is valid for short time intervals (holding periods) such as daily, and less suitable for longer horizons such as a year.

TIME VALUE OF MONEY

We compounded single period returns in the previous section (instead of simply adding them together) because the interest earned in the earlier period can also earn interest in the next period, which simply adding returns does not capture. So, getting the same amount of cash earlier is better than getting that exact same amount later, because the money received earlier could have been invested to earn interest[173]. Said differently, an investor would be indifferent between a higher amount in a later period and a lower amount earlier, i.e. money has time value. Specifically, if *P* is the amount in the earlier period and *r* is the rate of interest per period (also referred to as the *cost of capital*), the investor is indifferent between receiving *P* in the earlier period and *P(1+r)* in the next period. In general, the investor is indifferent between *P* today and $P(1+r)^N$ N periods later.

In the example above, $P(1+r)^T$ is referred to as *Future Value* of *P* dollars in *T* periods, if the relevant interest rate is *r*. Alternatively, if an investor is entitled to *X* dollars *T* periods from now, the *Present Value* of the *X* dollars *T* periods later is $\frac{X}{(1+r)^T}$. This is a direct implication of the equation in the earlier section: $P(1+r)^N = F$ i.e. *P* grows to *F* in *N* periods at the rate *r*.

Cash flows occurring at different points in time are not equivalent and should not be added together, until they are converted into equivalent dollars in the same time period. So, directly comparing *P* to *X* in the example above is wrong, since they are available at different times. Comparing $P(1+r)^T$ to *X* is correct, because they are both *T* period (equivalent) cash flows. Alternatively, comparing *P* to $\frac{X}{(1+r)^T}$ also makes sense, because they are both current period value. Investors usually work with either current period or terminal period cash flows, but principally

---

[173] This, of course, assumes that the interest rate is positive, which has not been true in the institutional market in Europe for the past few years.

Capital Markets and Investments

one could work with any period cash flows, as long as all cash flows are converted to equivalent values for that period, using the compounding formula.

So far, we have assumed that all these cash flows are certain (there is no doubt that they will be paid/ received), so a bank interest rate (close to a risk-free rate) that the investor can access is a fair rate to discount the cash flows. But, if the cash flows are risky, then a (higher) discount rate that appropriately reflects the risk of the cash flow needs to be used. The discount rate (or cost of capital) should represent the return the investor can earn in an alternative investment, bearing a similar level of risk.

Another implicit assumption in this framework is that the investor can easily borrow or lend any amount of money for any length of time at the applicable interest rate; borrowing and lending rates are the same.

NET PRESENT VALUE

The idea of Time Value of Money leads directly to Net Present Value (NPV), a project evaluation tool in its simplest form, but widely used in financial analysis to value securities. Suppose a project pays C_i (with certainty) in period i (i takes on values from 1 to N, representing N successive periods), and the market interest rate is r% (and is unlikely to change). What is the fair value an investor should pay today (time 0), to get access to the projects future cash flows?

Adding up all the N values of C_i to come up with the fair value of the project is incorrect because, as explained above, they occur at different points in time and are not equivalent. All these cash flows need to be converted (*discounted*) to the same time period before they can be added; let us convert all these cash flows to the equivalent cash flow today (we could choose any period). C_i in period i is equivalent to $C_i/(1+r)^i$ in today's terms, because if the investor were given $C_i/(1+r)^i$ today, that would grow at the rate r% to C_i in i periods. So, discounting all (future) project cash flows to the present, the value of the project in today's terms i.e. the *Present Value* (PV) of the project is[174] $\sum_{i=1}^{N} \frac{C_i}{(1+r)^i}$. If the investor is offered this project today at price P, the *Net Present Value* (NPV) is $\sum_{i=1}^{N} \frac{C_i}{(1+r)^i} - P$ (often written as $\sum_{i=0}^{N} \frac{C_i}{(1+r)^i}$, i.e. $P = C_0$). Note, P is in today's terms and does not need to get discounted (i.e. $(1+r)^0 = 1$). A positive NPV implies that the project should be undertaken, a negative NPV suggests that the project should be ignored (or potentially shorted in a frictionless world). If the cash flows are risky (i.e. uncertain), then the discount rate should be higher than the market interest rate, to reflect this. For a given set of cash flows, the NPV decreases as the discount rate increases. Different projects have different investment profiles and magnitudes, so analysts need to be careful comparing NPV across projects. Figure I.1 discusses a simple illustration to calculate NPV.

---

[174] The *summation* (Σ) notation is a convenient shorthand for writing expressions without repeating similar terms which are to be added to each other. For example, $\frac{C}{(1+r)} + \frac{C}{(1+r)^2}$ is identical to $\sum_{i=1}^{2} \frac{C}{(1+r)^i}$. In Eq. 7.1, for example, we would have to write out nine similar terms, if we did not want to use Σ.

Relevant Return Concepts

Figure I.1 NPV and IRR Calculation Example

NPV and IRR Calculation of a project that requires initial investment of $100, pays $5 each of the first four years, and then pays $105 in the 5th and final year						
Discount Rate (r)	4%					
Time Period (i)	0	1	2	3	4	5
Cash Flows (C)	-100	5	5	5	5	105
Present Value or PV (i.e. equivalent to today's dollars) of Each Cash Flow	-100	4.81	4.62	4.44	4.27	86.30
Net Present Value (NPV) of Investment	$4.45					
Internal Rate of Return (IRR) of Investment	5%					

The figure above lays out a project that costs $100 in initial investment, and pays $5 for each of the next four years (of course, these numbers can all be different). Further, at the end of the fifth year, the project returns $105 as a final payment. Alternatively, the investor can invest the initial investment to earn 4%, by taking on a similar level of risk, so 4% is a suitable discount rate.

We have now made all necessary cash flow and discounting assumptions to calculate NPV. Using the Present Value formula $\frac{C}{(1+r)^i}$ from the previous section, we calculate the value of each of these cash flows (which occur at different times) in terms of today's dollars. Adding each of these PV values leads to the NPV. A positive NPV (4.45 in this example) implies that we should proceed with the investment.

The NPV formula (e.g. in Microsoft Excel or a financial calculator) gives us the NPV directly without having to lay out each cash flow, but the cash flows have to have a specific pattern – an initial investment, a constant periodic payment, and a final payment. If we calculate each PV value ourselves, we can calculate the NPV of any investment, as long as we can specify the cash flows and the discount rate.

The general NPV formula discussed above can be simplified (i.e. not written as a sum of several terms) by making further assumptions about the pattern of cash flows. For example, if we assume that the project pays a fixed cash flow C every period in future (i.e. for ever, without a terminal date), such a cash flow stream is called a *perpetuity* and the formula reduces to $\frac{C}{r}$, where r is the discount rate[175]. Instead of the payment continuing to perpetuity, if the payment stops after a fixed number of periods (say, T), then such a stream is referred to as an *annuity*. The formula changes to $\frac{C}{r}\left[1 - \frac{1}{(1+r)^T}\right]$, Alternatively, if the cash flow is *growing at the constant rate g* per period and continues forever (i.e. $C_i = C_{i-1}(1+g)$, and $C_1=C$), the NPV formula changes to $\frac{C}{r-g}$. We discuss some of these formulae in detail when we discuss equity valuation in Chapter 11.

INTERNAL RATE OF RETURN (IRR)

The Internal Rate of Return (IRR) is a similar concept to the NPV, but works a little differently. Instead of solving for the Present Value using market interest rates (or a risk-adjusted discount rate), the IRR instead solves for the discount rate required to equate the PV to the current price, i.e. find the discount rate that

---

[175] These formulae follow from the properties of geometric series.

Capital Markets and Investments

makes this a zero NPV transaction. The IRR is then compared to the relevant market rate of return for investments of similar risk. Assuming a similar setup as the example in the NPV section above, the IRR is the solution to the equation below:

$$\sum_{i=1}^{N} \frac{C_i}{(1+IRR)^i} - P = 0$$

The equation above has higher order terms and is not easy to solve analytically for large number of periods. So, numerical methods involving iterative steps are used; this is usually done using a computer or a financial calculator. To continue with our example in Figure I.1, the IRR (i.e. the discount rate that sets the NPV to zero) turns out to be 5%. Since this is greater than our assumed discount rate (or cost of capital) of 4%, the project is lucrative and should be pursued.[176]

More details on the IRR methodology

It is possible that the IRR equation will have multiple solutions for IRR (the number of solutions are related to the number of changes in sign in the cash flows); one sign flip in the cash flow guarantees only one solution. When multiple solutions arise, there is no precise recommendation regarding which IRR to pick.

Will the IRR be the actual return that the project earns, if the stated cash flows remain the same? Not necessarily. The IRR methodology assumes that all the intermediate cash flows (i.e. the $5 inflows in period 1, 2, 3 and 4) are reinvested at the same rate as the IRR until the terminal project cash flow. If market conditions change over time, and the intermediate cash flows end up being reinvested at a different rate, the actual return of the project will be different from the IRR.

IRR, being a rate of return, is easier to compare across projects. Reinvestments are assumed to be at the IRR; if that does not end up happening, the IRR will be different from the ex-post realized rate of return. An investment opportunity should be accepted if the IRR is greater than an appropriate discount rate for that project; in these circumstances, NPV (calculated with that discount rate and cash flows) will also turn out to be positive. NPV is a more unambiguous method than IRR, since it does not ever have multiple solutions, but IRR is more intuitive in cases with only one solution, or when the investor is comparing several investments with similar risk.

---

[176] To be clear, you do not need a discount rate to calculate the IRR. After calculating the IRR, you need to compare the IRR to a suitable discount rate.

II. Introduction to Financial Statements – Concept of Capital Structure

The purpose of this Annexure is to introduce, to readers with no background in finance or accounting, the absolute basics of the financial statements that companies use to communicate with the investing public. The sole intention is for readers to be able to follow along the content in the rest of the book, especially the section on equity valuation (and possibly structured products). This short summary does not even scratch the surface adequately; anyone remotely interested in using financial statements should consult more advanced material.

By their very nature, these financial statements are "backward-looking", as they only capture what has happened and present the current (i.e. not future) picture, but serve as a basis for analysts to forecast what the future might look like for the company. In addition to these statements, fundamental analysts rely on management guidance and outlook for future performance, often discussed at quarterly calls or at investor meetings.

Most listed firms release results quarterly, and file forms with the Securities and Exchange Commission (SEC) that detail performance. They file forms 10-Q (Quarterly Report), 10-K (potentially more detailed Annual Report), and 8-K (form to disclose current material corporate events to shareholders).

As background, almost all transactions that a company participates in (e.g. buying or selling something) get captured on one (or more than one) financial statement. There are three main financial statements – the Balance Sheet, the Income Statement and the Cash Flow Statement. These are all prepared following strict accounting standards (Generally Accepted Accounting Principles or GAAP in the USA) and are then audited by accounting firms, to certify that the reports have complied with the standards. Principles such as *accrual* (when the revenue is "actually" earned versus when cash is received), *matching* (aligning the timing of the revenues and the corresponding costs), *conservatism* (taking a conservative stand on subjective decisions, such as when and how much provisions to allocate for losses from its debtors, etc.)

BALANCE SHEET

The Balance Sheet of a company is prepared *as of a specific date*, and provides a snapshot of the company's finances as of that day. The balance sheet has two "sides" (i.e. columns), though these sides are often presented one below the other instead of side by side.

One side (the left side in the USA) lists the *Assets* i.e. what the company owns (or is owed by some counterparty). An alternative interpretation of the Assets side is that it records the *Uses of Funds*. Broadly, assets are categorized into *Current Assets* and *Fixed* (or *Non-Current Assets*). Standard examples of items that show up on the Assets side include Cash, Pre-paid Expenses, Property Plant & Equipment (PP&E), Accounts Receivable, Investments, Intangible Assets (e.g. Goodwill, usually a by-product of Mergers/ Acquisitions).

The other "side" of the balance sheet reflects what the firm owes stakeholders, and is referred to as the *Liabilities* side. This also captures the various *Sources of Funds*. This is broadly divided into *Liabilities* (what the firm owes external stakeholders, e.g. creditors) and *Owners Equity* (the residual interest that the owners i.e. shareholders hold in the firm). Liabilities include operating liabilities such as Accounts Payable, Provisions for Warranties, Deferred Tax Liabilities (i.e. taxes not yet paid because the IRS only charges taxes based on realized incomes), Advance Payments, and financial liabilities such as lines of credit, loans, corporate bonds or other borrowings by the firm. The difference between assets and liabilities is referred to as Net Assets. The Equity (or Capital), mechanically, is the difference of all the assets that the firm owns, less the liabilities that it needs to pay back (the *Book Value* of Equity). So, the totals on both sides of the balance sheet always match, i.e. the balance sheet always balances. Any financial activity by the company shows up as an effect on both sides of the balance sheet (or in some cases, on the same side with opposite signs), so the balance sheet stays balanced at any point in time.

There are a few line items that show up on the "wrong" side, with the opposite sign; these are called *contra* assets or liabilities, as the case may be. Examples include *Accumulated Depreciation* (a contra-asset), which shows up on the Assets side, but as a deduction from the PP&E value. Assets and Liabilities that are likely to be extinguished in one year or less are called *Current Assets/ Liabilities;* longer-term Assets and Liabilities are referred to as *Non-Current* (sometimes *Fixed* in the case of assets).

Accounting for *shareholding* in subsidiaries depends on the percentage holding. According to GAAP, holdings greater than 50% of the subsidiary require line-by-line consolidation (listing the minority holding in net assets before calculating the book value of Equity), whereas minority holdings are shown only in the Equity section.

Capital Structure

The financial liabilities and the equity capital is often referred to the *Capital Structure* (How is the company financially funded). Instead of the book value of equity (from the balance sheet), the market capitalization of equity (product of market price of a share and the number of shares outstanding). In this context, the focus is on the various types of financing and their relative size and seniority. A related concept, *Enterprise Value* (i.e. what is the value of the firm?) is the sum of the various components of the capital structure. The company's management and Chief Financial Officer's Office spends significant time thinking about whether Enterprise Value can be changed by modifying the capital structure, especially when debt can be raised cheap (raise debt to buy back equity) or equity markets are overvalued (issue equity to pay down debt). The conceptual basis for this (or the lack of it, as the case may be) is discussed in the chapter on Equity Valuation.

This idea of a Capital Structure is pervasive, and the concept is used when discussing the financing of any pool of assets. Specifically, when discussing Special Purpose Vehicle (SPV)-based structured products (CLO, CDO, CMBS, REIT, MLP, etc.) which pool a portfolio of assets, and finance them by issuing debt and equity, the leverage is calculated similar to that of a company.

Annexure: Introduction to Financial Statements – Capital Structure

Figure II.1: Balance Sheet Template

```
Consolidated Statement of Finance Position of XYZ, Ltd.
As of 31 December 2015


ASSETS
  Non-Current Assets (Fixed Assets)
    Property, Plant and Equipment (PPE)
      Less : Accumulated Depreciation
    Goodwill
    Intangible Assets (Patent, Copyright, Trademark, etc.)
      Less : Accumulated Amortization
    Investments in Financial assets due after one year
    Investments in Associates and Joint Ventures
    Other Non-Current Assets, e.g. Deferred Tax Assets, Lease Receivable and Receivables due after one year

  Current Assets
    Inventories
    Prepaid Expenses
    Investments in Financial assets due within one year
    Non-Current and Current Assets Held for sale
    Accounts Receivable (Debtors) due within one year
      Less : Allowances for Doubtful debts
    Cash and Cash Equivalents


TOTAL ASSETS (this will match/balance the total for Liabilities and Equity below)


LIABILITIES and EQUITY
  Current Liabilities (Creditors: amounts falling due within one year)
    Accounts Payable
    Current Income Tax Payable
    Current portion of Loans Payable
    Short-term Provisions
    Other Current Liabilities, e.g. Deferred income, Security deposits

  Non-Current Liabilities (Creditors: amounts falling due after more than one year)
    Loans Payable
    Issued Debt Securities, e.g. Notes/Bonds Payable
    Deferred Tax Liabilities
    Provisions, e.g. Pension Obligations
    Other Non-Current Liabilities, e.g. Lease Obligations

  EQUITY
    Paid-in Capital
      Share Capital (Ordinary Shares, Preference Shares)
      Share Premium
        Less: Treasury Shares
    Retained Earnings
    Revaluation Reserve
    Other Accumulated Reserves
    Accumulated Other Comprehensive Income

    Non-Controlling Interest


TOTAL LIABILITIES and EQUITY (this will match/balance the total for Assets above)
```

Source: Wikipedia

INCOME STATEMENT

The *Income Statement* (*Profit & Loss Account*, in UK) shows the revenues and expenses (calculated following GAAP rules) for the company over a specific interval of time (often a quarter or a year, ending on a specified date). It helps investors understand the relationships between the revenues, costs and net income (i.e. profit) and assess the profitability of the business. This provides analysts an idea of how much the firm is selling (*Sales*), what costs it is incurring (both direct costs to produce and sell the product/ service (*Cost of Goods Sold*) as well as overheads or *Selling, General & Administrative (SG&A) expenses*), *Operating Margins*, *Earnings Before Interest, Taxes, Depreciation & Amortization (EBITDA)*, *R&D costs*, *Interest Expense*, income tax expenses, income from investments, irregular or one-time costs (e.g. discontinued operations) as well as non-cash costs such as *Depreciation/ Amortization*.

The *Net Income* (Sales Revenue less all costs) is split into a *Dividend* payment, and *Retained Earnings*, which flows through to the Equity section of the balance sheet and adds to the Equity book value. This is how the two statements are connected; profit or loss-making transactions affect the income statement, which affects Equity in the balance sheet.

Figure II.2: Income Statement Template

```
Income Statement

Period Ending
Total Revenue
Cost of Revenue
Gross Profit
    Operating Expenses
    Research Development
    Selling General and Administrative
    Non Recurring
    Others
    Total Operating Expenses
Operating Income or Loss
    Income from Continuing Operations
    Total Other Income/Expenses Net
    Earnings Before Interest And Taxes
    Interest Expense
    Income Before Tax
    Income Tax Expense
    Minority Interest
    Net Income From Continuing Ops
    Non-recurring Events
    Discontinued Operations
    Extraordinary Items
    Effect Of Accounting Changes
    Other Items
Net Income
Preferred Stock And Other Adjustments
Net Income Applicable To Common Shares
```

Source: Wikipedia

CASH FLOW STATEMENT

The two statements discussed above are produced using GAAP rules based on *accrual* concepts, and allow firms some leeway in deciding on how to report revenues, costs, assets and liabilities (e.g. when to book revenues, when to recognize losses, etc.). In contrast, the *Cash Flow Statement* reconciles the period beginning and ending cash balance on the balance sheet by showing the inflows and outflows of cash, and is far less subjective.

Cash Flow Statements are usually broken up into three sections – Cash from Operations, Investments and Financing. The statements start with the Net Income, add back Depreciation and other non-cash charges, add increases in Current Liabilities/ decreases in Current Assets, subtract decreases in Current Liabilities/ increases in Current Assets, adjust for non-operating (e.g. investments) gains or losses, etc. (interest expense is not adjusted under US GAAP, considered operating cash flow) to get to *Cash Flows from Operations*.

Cash Flow from Investing includes Capital Expenditure (i.e. change in Fixed Assets, excluding the effect of Depreciation), Investments, Interest or Dividend Receipts, etc.

Cash Flow from Financing includes Dividend payments, Sale or Repurchase of stock, increase or decrease in Debt, and other financing activities.

Figure II.3: Cash Flow Statement Template

Net income
Operating activities, cash flows provided by or used in:
Depreciation and amortization
Adjustments to net income
Decrease (increase) in accounts receivable
Increase (decrease) in liabilities (A/P, taxes payable)
Decrease (increase) in inventories
Increase (decrease) in other operating activities
Net cash flow from operating activities
Investing activities, cash flows provided by or used in:
Capital expenditures
Investments
Other cash flows from investing activities
Net cash flows from investing activities
Financing activities, cash flows provided by or used in:
Dividends paid
Sale (repurchase) of stock
Increase (decrease) in debt
Other cash flows from financing activities
Net cash flows from financing activities
Effect of exchange rate changes
Net increase (decrease) in cash and cash equivalents

Source: Wikipedia

FOOTNOTES AND DISCLOSURES

The above statements (obviously) include many numbers, and most of them allow some flexibility in reporting. These numbers often have footnotes, which are explanatory and supplemental notes. These are an integral part of the financial statements, and are as important as the statements themselves.

These footnotes discuss accounting policies and changes, contingent liabilities (e.g. guarantees) which do not show up explicitly on the balance sheet because they haven't crystallized, related-party transactions, and more detail on the important numbers in the statements (business combination, debt coupon/ maturity details, investment portfolio constituents, ageing schedule of receivables, pension obligations, business segment-level data, revenue recognition policies, loss provision norms) and other details or assumptions related to the statements. They often dominate the report, in volume and detail, and contain rich information. Companies and their accountants sometimes come up with creative assumptions which imply favorable numbers in the statements (*window dressing*); the investment professional needs to read the footnotes in detail to uncover these deviations to allow for an apples-to-apples comparison across similar companies. *Earnings Quality* refers to the reliability of the statement values without having to adjust them materially, as well as the drivers of earnings.

The 10-Q or the 10-K have various sections detailing the statements and explanations. One useful section is *Management Discussion and Analysis (MD&A)*, which discusses the main drivers of the business. While much of the content is boiler-plate and rarely changes quarter to quarter, it's a useful starting point to get some idea about how the business works. Management is also required to be accurate, so they will often change the language subtly to reflect their outlook.

Capital Markets and Investments

USING THE INFORMATION IN THE FINANCIAL STATEMENTS

Financial statements are the most objective and factual communication from a company to its investors. The statements report how a company has performed over the past quarter/ year, and the current financial state of the business, allowing investors to compare that with their expectations. Financial statements makes comparisons over time and across companies easier, providing analysts with tangible evidence if the management is getting closer to expected targets.

Metrics

The most direct information from the financial statements is the tangible information that they provide. Examples of such questions are:

> What were the revenues, how much did they grow? How profitable was the new business? Did the management meet its cost-cutting target? Did the company collect on their pending receivables? What is the liquidity situation of the company? How much did it pay out as dividends?

Modeling, Forecasting

Much of the analytical work related to assessing a business is done through the lens of a financial model. These models typically try to project key line items in the financial statements several quarters/ years out based on past trends, management guidance and the analyst's view of business conditions. Mechanically, analysts try to lay out past income statements on a spreadsheet (each year in a different column) and try to predict the statements in future years. They also try to estimate the other key non-income statement variables (e.g. capex) to get to an estimate of the cash balance in future. Depending on the analyst's perspective, he could either try to discount these cash flows, or try to value the company on a forward multiple based on these pro-forma estimates. This is discussed in more detail in the chapter on Equity Valuation.

Ratio Analysis

A succinct technique to examine these numbers is to compute ratios. This allows analysts to compare a company over time, as well as against other peers, and is an important input into valuation.

For example, Debt/ EBIDTA is a quick way to figure out how levered the company is. Of course, the details of the capital structure and the debt maturity profile matters, but the ratio is a useful starting point. Similarly, EBITDA/ Interest Expense gives an idea of how large the profits are in relation to the interest expense. To assess operating performance and cost management, investors may look at SG&A Expenses as a proportion of Sales, for companies in the same industry. The financial market often values and trades firms by applying a multiple to (forecasted i.e. forward-looking values of) key ratios and metrics. The Du Pont Analysis framework helps decompose a firm's financial metrics into a set a relevant ratios, to facilitate comparison with company peers.

Management views

While most of the management guidance is revealed through quarterly calls, investor presentations and occasional 8-K or press releases, investors also analyze the discussion accompanying the financial statements and the assumptions used to generate the reports.

III. Macroeconomics Primer

WHAT IS MACROECONOMICS?

Macroeconomics (in contrast to microeconomics) deals with economic issues affecting a region as a whole – is the region *growing* at a suitable pace, are *employment* levels high, are *prices* under control, etc. Government policies (especially related to taxes, government spending, exchange rate management and tariffs, money supply and interest rates) influence these macroeconomic variables significantly, so market participants try to predict macroeconomic data (and watch macroeconomic data releases with interest), to form an opinion on how policymakers are going to react next. They also analyze government policies and try to predict the effect of policy on these macro variables.

Macroeconomic analysis (including the analytical frameworks) is often top-down, clubbing disparate economic agents and looking through the lens of aggregate economic data. Macroeconomists try to assess the economic situation looking at these aggregates and recommend suitable policy responses, and also estimate what happens to important economic variables when faced with these economic and policy changes. This analysis is important in formulating government policy decisions, but political considerations also play a very important role.

The most important economic variables that macroeconomists are often most vocal about are:

Output Growth – The output an economy produces (during a specified time e.g. year/ quarter) is the most important macroeconomic variable that economists track. In a regime with a stable population, a higher value of output suggests that the constituents of the economy have been productive. A related issue is the distribution of this growth across the different economic agents, but that is an income inequality issue, under the purview of development economics.

Employment – The proportion of the labor force that is unemployed (some unemployment will always exist for structural reasons, or as people transition between jobs) relates to both the slack in the usage of economic resources as well as the social aspects of individuals being unable to earn a living. Low unemployment usually goes hand-in-hand with high growth (formalized through Okun's Law); it would be strange if the economy were growing rapidly without using up a lot of labor. If the economy is at or near *full-employment*, then this will create pressure on prices if demand increases further.

Inflation - Stable prices (rising very slowly) are an important determinant of economic health, and some governments consider this to be an explicit goal. Rapid price increases either suggest bottlenecks/ shortages in the production process (cost push inflation) or sudden surges in demand, relative to the current production capacity (Demand-pull inflation). The *Phillips Curve* is a stylized representation of inflation-unemployment tradeoffs.

The International Sector – Exports, imports (i.e. the current account), capital flows, foreign currency reserves (i.e. the capital account), all components of the *Balance of Payments Accounts*, are important determinants of the exchange rate. In an open economy with a flexible exchange rate regime, policymakers need to monitor these variables and react to any weaknesses. We discuss currencies in a later section.

Of course, the composition of these macroeconomic variables matters. For example, a government's spending on infrastructure, food stamps and primary education subsidies have very different implications.

Capital Markets and Investments

MEASURING OUTPUT (GDP) GROWTH

Since (growth in) economic output is arguably the most important macroeconomic variable, we now discuss how it is quantified and measured. Economic output is measured in terms of *Gross Domestic Product* (*GDP*), which measures the total output that has been produced over that period. The output can be measured using current market prices (*nominal*) or using a base year's price (*real*) to negate the effect of a higher GDP because of rising prices; relative changes in GDP are used as the primary measure of growth. However, US GDP data gets released infrequently (every quarter), is available with a (one-month) lag and is iteratively revised the next two months. The GDP details are also referred to as *national accounts*.

GDP is calculated through a bottom-up accounting process; we discuss a few approaches:

The *Expenditure Approach*, the most common method of calculating GDP looks at the demand side, and tracks what the economy spends; it comprises Consumption (C), Investments (I), Government Spending (G), Exports (X), Imports (M); the National Income Identity is GDP = C + I + G + (X-M). To understand the drivers of GDP growth, we need to understand how each of these variables evolve and what they depend on.

Other methods of calculating GDP are the *Income Approach*, which focuses on what each *factor of production* (i.e. labor, , land, capital, entrepreneurship) is paid i.e. Wages (W), Rent (R), Interest (Int) and Profit (P); the total of these four components is called *National Income*. To get to GDP, Depreciation, Net Foreign Factor Income[177], Sales Taxes are added to National Income; Subsidies are subtracted. The *Output/ Production Approach* or the *Gross Value Added Approach*, a third method, adds the value of sales of all final goods and services, and subtracts the value of intermediate goods consumed to make those final goods. While all these approaches should give the identical result, they are often different because of measurement errors (statistical discrepancies).

The Expenditure Approach to GDP– Drivers of Aggregate Demand

The Expenditure Approach is the most common framework to discuss GDP and its constituents, and serves as a framework to understand aggregate demand[178] of the economy, so we will now spend more time to understand its ingredients.

Consumption

This refers aggregate demand for goods and services by individual households (it excludes house purchases, which shows up as a part of investment below). The different kinds of goods and services are all valued at market prices and added up, so nuances are ignored. However, some details are available in the GDP release.

Conceptually, consumption is driven primarily by disposable income (income net of taxes); interest rates may also play a role in the consumption-saving decision (income is either saved or consumed or paid out in taxes). Moreover, consumer age (i.e. life stage of consumer), historical consumption habits (i.e. permanent income) also affect consumption. These ideas play a role while modeling consumption demand.

Investment

Investment primarily comprises capital expenditure by firms, and increases the capital stock. This depends mainly on how well the firm is doing (related to income/ profits), but also on the availability of credit and the interest rate. Of course, the future outlook for the business (growth capex) and the age of the capital stock

---

[177] The difference between payments made to foreigners for US output and payments made to US residents for foreign output

[178] A subtle difference between aggregate demand and GDP is that GDP is an *ex-post* (after-the-fact) number based on *realized* values, whereas aggregate demand is *planned* expenditure, based on current values of relevant variables. For planned expenditure to be equal to realized output, the system needs to have ample capacity i.e. there are no supply bottlenecks. This is why inflation and employment are also important variables to watch for.

Annexure: Macroeconomics Primer

(maintenance / replacement capex) are all important. While examining aggregate numbers, items such as inventory accumulation and drawdowns need to be treated carefully.

Government Spending

This is the total money the government spends on projects, subsidies, etc. For the most part, it is a politically determined number. Models usually treat this as exogenously given. Government expenditure is either financed through raising taxes, selling government bonds or printing money.

Exports

This depends mainly on the exchange rate, and government incentives to the export sector, apart from global demand for the country's goods and services.

Imports

This also depends on how well the country is doing; imports rise (like most other variables) in countries as GDP increases.

Drawbacks of GDP as a Measure of Economic Activity

GDP misses some important elements of economic activity. There may be significant chunks of economically productive activities which do not result in formal pricing and transfer of money (i.e. the *non-marketed sector*). Examples include two people helping each other, people helping out at home (versus hiring household help, which, ideally, shows up in GDP), volunteer work, etc. Another segment of economic activity that gets excluded in GDP accounting is the *underground economy*, which mainly includes illegal activities which are typically paid using means that are difficult to track. Even if the measurement were perfect, GDP reports only the total amount of economic activity; it does not point to *how the gains from these activities are distributed* across the citizens. If the distribution of GDP across the population were skewed, it would suggest an unequal society. This is why development economists supplement GDP with additional metrics.

MACROECONOMIC THEORY AND MODELS[179]

Basic Premises of Economic Modeling

Macroeconomists use "models" or analytical frameworks which attempt to simplify (after making lots of assumptions) but capture the essential features of the real world to explain how different economic variables are connected and determine economic outcomes if one or more of these variables change. Models start by detailing which variables are deemed to be *exogenous* (i.e. determined outside the model and move because of "shocks" not explicitly explained by the model), which economic factors are considered by the model (and how they are driven by model variables), and which variables are *endogenous* (determined within the model based on how the economic factors react to exogenous shocks). In the real world and the most general models, every variable is endogenous and affects every other variable, and everything is jointly determined, but smaller piecemeal (*reduced-form*) models are sometimes more insightful, tractable and easier to work with. Most models work on the principle of *equilibrium*; each economic factor in the model is a "force", potentially pulling the endogenous variables in different directions. Based on the (given) values of the exogenous variables, the endogenous variables eventually get set at levels that balance these forces[180], and the model is then said to be in equilibrium. In the simpler models, the path to equilibrium is reduced to a single period, and every adjustment takes place instantly in a precise predictable manner, thus generating a clear forecast. Good models simplify the details but retains the essence, a difficult (if not impossible) tradeoff in a complex world. These models

---

[179] This section essentially discusses the IS-LM model (originally by J.R. Hicks, 1937 and A. H. Hansen, 1953) with a few tweaks and extension

[180] These "forces" are determined by the exogenous and the endogenous variables, so there is a strong feedback loop from the (changes in) endogenous variables to these forces, which dampens these forces.

need to generate equilibrium values that exist and are ideally unique (and preferably not too many), and the equilibrium is stable.

We will work through a few examples next, and explain these terms more tangibly. Also, any model (that we discuss or otherwise) is a reflection of economic theories (a surmise of how the world works); they may or may not hold in practice. We first begin by describing some building blocks.

The Production Function – Factor Market Equilibrium

For a modeling exercise, the modeler starts by deciding which variables we take as (externally) given, and how these variables affect relevant economic decisions/ choices, and how all these decisions aggregate to determine a set of endogenous macroeconomic variables.

A *production function* captures the relationship between multiple inputs and the final output. Of course, the exact relationship depends on which product we have in mind, since the inputs are very different if the final output is a car from the inputs if the final output is a loaf of bread; every business (and firm) will have its own version of a production function. But, as macroeconomists, these differences are not of first order importance. We are trying to model the GDP of a country, top down, and want to capture the relationships between the fundamental ingredients (factors of production) required to create the GDP in very broad terms.

It is often assumed that Labor (N) and Capital (K) are the fundamental *factors of production*[181] required to generate GDP (Y). Empirical studies (that examine historical data) have established that, for the US economy, such a relation between GDP and its constituent inputs (i.e. factors) can be represented as[182]:

$$Y = AK^{0.3}N^{0.7}$$

The coefficient A reflects how efficiently labor are being deployed to create output, and is referred to as *total factor productivity* (or simply productivity)[183]. It is a surrogate for the role of technology, organizational skill, institutions and infrastructure, etc. The production function for a country does not remain fixed for ever; economists frequently refer to a change in the production function as a supply shock or a productivity shock, which is often expressed mathematically as a change in the value of A.

Every (profit maximizing) firm will continue to employ additional amounts of labor and capital only so long as these factors create more value than the cost to employ them. The value of employing an additional unit of labor or capital (i.e. *Value of Marginal Product*) is calculated by multiplying the product's price and the *Marginal Product of that Factor* (i.e. the incremental output produced by an extra unit of that factor, all else remaining same). The marginal product of any factor is usually positive but diminishing (i.e. marginal product of each successive unit goes down), so profit is maximized when the cost of employing an additional unit of the factor (i.e. wage for labor) is equal to the value of its marginal product. The amount of labor employed by using a version of this concept, aggregated across all firms, determines the labor demand from firms at different wage rates.

Labor Market Equilibrium – Full Employment

The people who supply labor, in their minds, weigh the benefit of an additional hour of leisure versus the wage they could earn if they worked the extra hour, for every hour of work that they consider putting in. This, aggregated across all individuals, generates the amount of labor supplied at each wage level, or the labor supply

---

[181] Some economists, depending on the context, may want to include Land and Entrepreneurship/ Organization as additional factors

[182] Such a functional form is often referred to as a Cobb-Douglas production function. The exponents indicate the share of income that each factor receives (and sum up to one).

[183] While A is not directly observable, if we know the actual values of Y, N and K (from the national accounts) and accept that the functional form above is the true representation, we can back out the value of A in any given year.

Annexure: Macroeconomics Primer

curve. The labor market is in equilibrium when, at the current wage, the labor supplied equals the labor demand[184]. This equilibrium amount of labor (let's call it $\underline{N}$) is referred to as the *full-employment labor*[185]. Given the capital stock (K) of the economy (the exogenous variable in this example), the corresponding level of output (i.e. GDP) (can be calculated using the production function) i.e. $\underline{Y} = AK^{0.3}\underline{N}^{0.7}$ is called the *full-employment output* or *potential output*. This is the maximum GDP that the economy can produce in a sustained manner at current (factor and output) prices.

Unemployment

In the set-up described above, there is no room for involuntary unemployment of labor. If less labor is demanded than is willing to be supplied at current prices, the wage is supposed to adjust downwards (so that less labor is supplied and more labor is demanded) leading to equilibrium. In the real world, wages are observed to be sticky (union contracts, etc.) in the short term; the rigidity of wage contracts leads to unemployment.

This is a major philosophical difference between Keynesian and Classical schools of economic thought; Classical economists believe in frictionless markets in which prices and quantities adjust instantly, whereas Keynesians believe in a world with frictions and rigidities, which leads to off-equilibrium markets in the short term. This also leads to different prescriptions for government policy; Classical economists suggest doing nothing, whereas Keynesians want the government to help the economy along, since markets do not work perfectly. We will return to this later.

We have also taken the price of the final output as given (for example in the value of marginal product calculations). In reality, this is determined by the demand for a product (in the case of one isolated product in the economy), in addition to the factor costs of the producer. In the aggregate economy in the context of GDP, the *price level of the economy* (i.e. prices of a standardized basket of goods in current dollars) is the relevant price, largely driven by factor costs and producer profit margins.

A Simple Aggregate Demand-based Macroeconomic Model of the Goods Market[186]

To discuss a far more complicated model that the one above, let us imagine an economy where there is no supply constraint, i.e. there is ample slack in the economic capacity to produce whatever is required without moving prices materially (i.e. output is way below full-employment)[187]. So, the elements of aggregate demand that we discussed earlier become key, and they collectively determine the output (GDP, the endogenous variable denoted by Y) of the economy. Keeping the ideas very simple (since this is just an illustrative example), we assume that aggregate consumption demand depends on aggregate income (Y), as does investment (business profits). Algebraically, using the notation from the previous section on GDP, we can represent this as:

- Consumption demand i.e. $C = a + cY(1-t)$ [188]
- Investment demand i.e. $I = b + iY$ (suppose firms decide investments independent of taxes)
- Government spending i.e. $G = \underline{G}$
- Exports $X = \underline{X}$ (depends on incomes of other countries), and

---

[184] Similarly, the market for capital is in equilibrium when the value of the marginal product of capital equals the interest cost.

[185] Note, full employment labor (or output) depends on the prevailing wage rate.

[186] This is a simplified description of a standard macro model in an introductory macroeconomics class. It is not meant to be realistic (models rarely are), but aims to show how models are theorized and the macroeconomic linkages involved.

[187] Based on what we just mentioned above, this economic slack cannot exist in a pure Classical world i.e. we are discussing a Keynesian paradigm here and exists because of sticky prices/ wages.

[188] *c* is called the *marginal propensity to consume*; it's the amount by which consumption changes for a unit increase in income.

Capital Markets and Investments

- Import demand M = mY

(i.e. G and X have fixed exogenous values $\underline{G}$ and $\underline{X}$; constants a, b, c, i, t and m are also exogenously given and have positive values, additionally, c, I, t and m are less than one). Putting this together in the form of an equation representing the market equilibrium, we solve for the level of output Y^* that satisfies the demand, so

$$Y = C + I + G + (X - M)$$

Subsitituting, $Y^* = a + cY^*(1-t) + b + iY^* + \underline{G} + (\underline{X} - mY^*)$

Now, suppose firms decide to invest more (say, b goes up by Δb), Y increases right away by Δb (since I goes up by that amount immediately, but this initial increase in Y "trickles down" to further increases in Y (consumer and business incomes go up, causing consumption demand C to increase by cΔY(1-t) i.e. cΔb(1-t), I to further increase by iΔb, which causes an additional increase in Y (the increase in M by mΔb offsets part of this). This again shows up in higher incomes, and the story (formally, the *transmission mechanism*) keeps repeating. Each incremental increase is smaller[189], so the increase eventually dies out, but output and incomes are now higher by more than the initial incremental investment Δb. This effect is called the *multiplier effect* of an increase in investment (exogenous changes in consumption or government spending, etc. also have their respective multipliers)[190].

We can also solve the equation above; it has only 1 unknown Y, which can be solved for easily. Let Y* be the solution[191]:

$$Y^* = \frac{a + b + \underline{G} + \underline{X}}{1 - [c(1-t) + i - m]}$$

A 1 unit increase in either of the autonomous (or non-income sensitive) components of consumption, investment, exports or government spending, would lead to a change of 1/[1-(c(1-t)+i-m] in the above framework. This is greater than 1 (since the denominator is less than one), a direct consequence of the multiplier effect.

Model Applications

Apart from the GDP itself, the national accounts (of which the GDP is a part) also reveal details about several facets of the economy, though the various components of GDP. For instance; the size of the *fiscal deficit* (the difference between government expenditures and revenues) as a % of GDP and how this deficit is financed (increasing taxes, issuing bonds, etc.) affects economic outcomes (and also defines political debates).

More generally, government policies (e.g. taxes and government spending) that affect the goods market and the government budget directly are called *fiscal policies*. The above framework can be used to understand various fiscal policy alternatives. For example, an increase in government spending coupled with increasing taxes by an equal amount (i.e. not affecting the fiscal deficit) is expansionary, since the tax increase reduces incremental

---

[189] The reason for smaller (but positive) incremental increases is because *c(1-t)+i-m* is assumed to be less than 1, but greater than zero. This is the amount by which demand increases for a dollar increase in income/output. If demand increased by more than one dollar for a dollar increase in income, the model would be *unstable* and *explode*; instead, this assumption leads to *convergence*.

[190] Now, for this to work out nicely in the model, the ripple effects in C, I, etc. can be large, but not too large (if the incremental next round demand created by the initial Δb increase in demand is greater than Δb, demand will grow too fast, and output will never be able to catch up.

[191] For the above model to make sense, we need to assume that *c(1-t)+i-m < 1*, which intuitively means that if Y increases by 1 unit (e.g. if demand outstrips initial supply by one unit i.e. excess demand is one unit), that leads to an incremental excess demand of less than one unit, so the excess demand keeps shrinking, until for the next increase in Y, the excess demand is zero, and the model is back in equilibrium. This is a *stability condition*.

Annexure: Macroeconomics Primer

demand only partially (because the resulting decline in income gets distributed across both consumption demand and saving), but the government spending affects demand more strongly (since all of it increases demand directly). Said another way, the multiplier for government spending is stronger than the multiplier for tax. Similarly, the relative magnitudes of the tax and the government spending can help answer questions on the effectiveness of alternative fiscal policies, such as raising taxes versus reducing spending.

Adding Interest Rates, Money and Financial Assets to this model[192][193]

An important detail that we left out of the previous model is that investment demand (as well as consumption/ savings in some versions) depends heavily on the prevailing interest rates. Companies invest in more projects if the interest rates are lower (more projects have positive NPV), pushing up demand.

Rewriting the above aggregate demand equation, it now takes the form

$$Y = a + cY(1-t) + b + i_y Y - i_r r + \underline{G} + \underline{(X - mY)}$$

This model now has two endogenous variables, Y (GDP) and r ([194]real interest rate, which is the difference between the nominal interest rates and inflation expectation). i_y and i_r capture the sensitivity of investment to income and interest rates. Earlier, we could solve the model (uniquely) for Y, but now, we can only solve for an equilibrium level of Y for a given level of r (since there are now two variables and only one equation, we need to fix one of the variables to solve for the other). Economically, from an initial equilibrium, an increase in the interest rates will cause investment demand to go down (getting the market off equilibrium). In the current version of the model, this will lead to a decline in Y though the multiplier mechanism that we discussed above, helping the market back closer to equilibrium. Thus, several combinations of Y and r values are consistent with goods market equilibrium (the earlier model had a unique solution); the equilibrium values of Y and r are inversely related to one another.

One standard extension to the above framework involves introducing the concept of *money*. Let us assume, simplistically, that individuals can hold their financial wealth/ savings either in the form of cash (money) or in the form of a bond (asset). People hold money (instead of returns-generating assets) to fulfil transactions and purchases, and also to speculate (i.e. buy the bond in future when its price drops, which happens when interest rates go up). Every individual's (different) expectations of future interest rates, relative to the current market rate, drives this decision; if many people expect rates to go up, more cash will be held and vice versa. We assume that, following the *Quantity Theory of Money*, the *transaction demand* for money is a constant proportion of real income (e.g. KY)[195]. Additionally, following an idea introduced by Keynes, the *speculative demand* for money is an inverse function of interest rates (-Lr), with zero demand at a very high rate (r_{max}) since everyone is holding their entire non-transaction balance in bonds, and very high demand at a very low interest rate (r_{min}), since everyone wants to hold all cash and no bonds. So, the money demand (M_d) can be written as:

---

[192] In this section we continue to assume that there is slack in the economy, and demand drives output.

[193] To make incremental headway, modelers try to extend models. In doing this, they keep in mind the dimensions of economic reality that the current model is skipping, as well as variables that we would like the model to help us predict/ understand.

[194] Macroeconomic variables can be stated in nominal (i.e. in current currency units) terms or in real terms (i.e. in terms of the currency value (i.e. the price level) of a prior period, essentially adjusting for the effect of realized and expected inflation. The nominal interest rate is approximately the sum of real interest rates and inflation expectation. We use real values in this chapter unless explicitly stated.

[195] According to the Quantity Theory of Money, K is interpreted as $1/v$, where *v is the (constant) velocity of circulation of money*. v is the ratio of money supply and nominal GDP, and denotes how many times the money "turns over" in a period.

Capital Markets and Investments

$M_d \equiv KY - Lr$, when $L > 0$ and r lies between two bounds r_{min} and r_{max}

$M_d \equiv KY$, if $r \geq r_{max}$

$M_d \equiv \overline{\overline{M}}$ if $r = r_{min}$ $\overline{\overline{M}}$ is a huge number, as speculative demand is massive

The supply of nominal (i.e. in dollar terms) money (M_s), for the purposes of this model, is determined exogenously (say, M*), for example by central bank policy. Given a price level P in the economy, the real money supply is M*/P. In equilibrium[196], Y and r have values such that $M_d = M_s$. If $r_{min} < r < r_{max}$, this translates to:

$$\frac{M^*}{P} = KY - Lr, \quad \text{where P is the price level of the economy}$$

Suppose the economy's money market is initially in equilibrium. An increase in Y leads to an increase in transaction demand for money. Since money supply doesn't change, less money is available for speculative balances. For speculative demand to go down, interest rate has to go up, bringing the money market back in equilibrium. Another way to think about this is that individuals need to free up cash for transactions, since incomes are higher, so they sell bonds, which leads to the interest rate going up. In this model, the combinations of Y and r that keep the money market in equilibrium are positively related.

There are a couple of exceptions (to this positive relationship between Y and r), which we briefly alluded to earlier. If the entire stock of money is absorbed in transaction balances, the national income is high and the current real money stock cannot support any further increase in income (since additional transactions cannot be completed with current money stock. If markets are in equilibrium at these levels, speculative demand has to reduce to zero, i.e. $r >= r_{max}$. Said differently, for a fixed money supply, Y=M*/PK for any $r \geq r_{max}$. So, fiscal policy will not help and will only raise the price level; a positive productivity shock or monetary policy are the ways out. At the other extreme, when the interest rate is at the floor r_{min}, there is massive demand for speculative balances, so an increase in income will not lead to any changes in the interest rate. In this case, the economy is said to be in a *liquidity trap*, and monetary policy is ineffective.

So, in this current set-up, we have two markets – a goods market and money/asset market, and two endogenous variables Y and r. So, equilibrium in this setup (i.e. equilibrium in both these markets) occurs for a unique (Y, r) pair, unlike when we only discussed the goods market equilibrium for various (Y, r) combinations. Mathematically, it involves solving the goods market and money market equilibrium equations simultaneously, for Y* and r*.

$$Y = a + cY(1-t) + b + i_y Y - i_r r + \underline{G} + (\underline{X} - mY)$$

$$\frac{M^*}{P} = KY - Lr \quad \text{if } r_{min} < r < r_{max}$$

So, changes in Y or r caused by changes in exogenous variables in one market will affect the other market as well. For example, suppose the government wants to increase expenditure ($\underline{G}$). This increase in $\underline{G}$ will cause Y to increase through the multiplier, but this increase in Y will lead to an increase in transaction money demand. Given the fixed money supply M*, speculative demand has to go down (i.e. people buy bonds to free up cash usage in the economy) leading to an increase in the interest rate r. This increase in r *reduces* Y (because I goes down), but this reduction in Y is less than the effect of the initial rise in $\underline{G}$, so Y goes up overall., but less than a system where I does not depend on r. This reduction in private investment because of increased government spending is referred to as *crowding out*.

---

[196] In this framework, the bond (i.e. asset market) is a mirror image of the money market (since these are the only two choices), so money market equilibrium implies asset market equilibrium and vice versa.

Annexure: Macroeconomics Primer

General Equilibrium, Full-Employment and Price Level Adjustments

So far, we have discussed a demand-driven economy where production can be increased easily without affecting prices. In an economy with such slack, it is only logical that one would expect the product prices to go down and stimulate more demand. But, as discussed in the section on the production function and the labor market, this may not be easy to accomplish, over the short term, because prices may be sticky and difficult to change, either in the factor market (labor unions) or product market.

We can formulate a richer version of the above demand-based model to recognize that the productive capacity in the economy can respond to prices, by going back to our initial discussion of the production function and labor market. For the economy to be in general equilibrium, all markets need to be in equilibrium. This implies that, for the economy to be in equilibrium, the labor market would be in equilibrium, the economy running at full-employment, and the output would be the full-employment output (at the current prices).

Any joint equilibrium of the goods and money markets does not ensure full-employment output, since the labor market may be off-equilibrium. The output (Y^*) in that equilibrium is unique, and is at the (Y^*,r^*) combination above. If this value of Y is less than the full-employment output, over time, the economy's price level would go down as producers lower prices, causing the real money supply to increase (nominal money supply remaining the same). This would lower interest rates (more money available for speculative balances, bidding up bonds), and spur investment demand, leading to an increase in output through the multiplier, until it reaches full-employment. Alternatively, if the initial equilibrium output is higher than full-employment output, this indicates that producers and factors of production are being over-utilized, and will hike prices soon. The higher price level will shrink real money supply, causing rates to rise (as bonds need to be sold to generate cash, since there is less money to go around), constraining investment and output through the multiplier.

The Role of Money and the Banking System

During our discussion of the money market above, we assumed that the money supply is fixed and is determined by policy. In reality, that is largely true, but the behavior/ actions of individual economic agents can influence the effective amount of money that is circulating in the economy.

Money supply (somewhat strangely) has many definitions, labelled M1, M2, M3, etc. M1, the narrowest measure, includes the currency in circulation, and generally also includes time deposits/ current account balances, which can be withdrawn instantly. *Broad*er concepts, such as M2, also include savings deposits. M3 includes institutional time deposits, repos and institutional money market funds (i.e. liquid cash-equivalent instruments). The currency in circulation, bank cash in vaults and the bank deposits with the country's Central Bank (e.g. the Federal Reserve in the US, bank of England in UK) is collectively called the *monetary base* (i.e. the money that has been physically printed). These values are regularly published in central bank reports.

The *fractional reserve banking system* (which all countries follow), allow banks to lend out a large proportion of the money (but not all of it; banks have to hold back *required reserves*) that people deposit, so the same physical currency can be re-deposited and re-lent multiple times (and counted several times in the definition of money supply). Individuals decide how much of every incremental dollar they need to hold in the form of currency for spending needs (and deposit the rest in a bank), based on the payment infrastructure for transaction processing, etc.; this is reflected in the *currency-deposit ratio*. The *required reserve-deposit ratio*, mandated by the Central Bank, regulates how much of the deposit can be re-lent, and effectively controls the money supply by curbing the propagation of the lending cycle. Assuming banks are lending as much as they can under applicable laws (i.e. there is high demand for loans), one can use the values of the currency-deposit ratio and the reserve-deposit ratio to figure out how much effective money supply a certain monetary base can generate. The ratio of the monetary base and the eventual money supply is called the *money multiplier*. Essentially,

Capital Markets and Investments

$$Money\ Supply = Money\ Multiplier * Monetary\ Base,$$

$$where\ Money\ Multiplier = \frac{1 + Currency/Deposit}{Currency/Deposit + Reserves/Deposit}$$

$$and\ Monetary\ Base = Currency + Reserves$$

Many analysts, instead of calculating the money multiplier using the above ratios, use the ratio of M2/Monetary base as an empirical proxy for the money multiplier.

The Central Bank of a country can also affect the monetary base directly, through its policies. These include *open market operations* (buying and selling bonds of the national government, effectively releasing or taking away cash from the system), *discount window lending* (lending to banks for their daily operations), providing credit against collateral of financial securities (i.e. *repo operations*), and more recently, quantitative easing, etc. Government policies that affect the money supply and the financial liquidity are referred to as *monetary policy*. In many countries, the central banks often communicate monetary policy through target overnight inter-bank rates (and conduct open market operations to keep the rates there); these are considered monetary policy since their primary effect is to influence financial market liquidity. The impact of changing these short-end overnight rates on the longer term rates is questionable. Central Banks traditionally did not control the longer term interest rates until recently, when they have engaged in *quantitative easing* by buying up bonds of their government. These policies can be reflected in the model discussed earlier, by changing the money supply. Of course, monetary and fiscal policies can be linked, for example, if the government decides to print money (increase money supply) to finance increases in government spending.

Incorporating the idea of a dynamic money supply based on loan /investment demand (i.e. the currency deposit ratio and reserve deposit ratio) adds more layers to the model we discussed above.

Modeling Summary

This section has breezed through some basic macroeconomic models[197], but has sometimes delved into agonizing detail, presumably leaving the reader perplexed. The main purpose was to illustrate the ideas behind macroeconomic modeling and highlight its complexity, its level of abstraction and resulting imprecision. We highlighted the rudimentary drivers behind economic activity in several markets (labor, goods and money), and how these markets interact in the economy, through some variables (interest rates, employment) that affect outcomes in several markets. The model helped us understand the role of policy variables (government spending, taxes, money supply) in influencing different components of economic output, and how transmission mechanisms across various markets are relevant in connecting all the parts of the economic landscape. For example, the interest rate and income sensitivity of investment, the role of private consumption and government spending in affecting demand, the labor market dynamics and how producers respond to it, the monetary policy of the government, and the demand for money for transactions and speculation are all woven together to construct a theory of how the economy functions.

That said, such models rely on restrictive but simplifying assumptions, many of which may have important implications for results. In this framework, we assume instantaneous adjustments in the money and goods markets, but rely on labor market rigidities to generate underemployment equilibria. This can be distilled to assumptions regarding how quickly markets respond to stimuli; which turns into a discussion on beliefs and philosophies about how markets and economic agents behave. Even in a framework as simple as the one discussed here, we needed to impose additional restrictions on the speed of adjustment to generate meaningful

---

[197] While these frameworks may appear complicated, most of these ideas were in place by the 1930s.

Annexure: Macroeconomics Primer

results. For example, economists who lean towards the Keynesian ideas of market frictions and slow adjustments will prefer government intervention, but a free-market Classical economist will believe that a positive supply shock through the production function is the only way to stimulate growth. A firm believer in free-markets will expect the benefits of growth to automatically trickle down to the disadvantaged sections of society; whereas a market skeptic will advocate for redistributive government policies and overlook the adverse effect for individuals to game the system and not put in an honest effort. Finally, model results depend directly on the assumptions, which in turn depend closely on beliefs and views; tweaking these slightly can generate very different results.

Over the last several decades, macroeconomists have tried to close these gaps. Economists from different camps, instead of debating their philosophical differences, have tried to build on their common ground and portray the other ideas as special cases of their own philosophy. To augment the models, they have tried to introduce dynamic models (instead of the static analysis we discussed earlier) and micro-foundations of macroeconomic aggregates. At the same time, progress in empirical research and the acceptance of reduced-form models (instead of full-blown theoretical constructs) have encouraged the application of time-series econometric techniques to try to fit the data with loosely specified models.

Beyond the Static Macro Models

While most basic analysis is *static* in nature and encapsulates only a single time period, the more relevant question is how today's economy and policies shape tomorrow's financial markets. By introducing multiple time periods and allowing variables the flexibility to react to economic updates with lags, questions that appear straightforward in the single-period instantaneous change static world now appear more nuanced and uncertain; hence economists often diverge in how they believe current shocks affect the future economy. Also, by explicitly considering multi-period frameworks, economists are forced to pay attention to the short run, and how the economy transitions between two long-run equilibrium states.

Economists in the 1950s-70s tried to come up with models to explain the macroeconomic aggregates from a bottom-up perspective. This included models of consumption incorporating human behavior such as Modigliani's Life Cycle Income, Duesenberry's Relative Consumption Expenditure and Friedman's Permanent Income Hypothesis, wealth effects, etc. Labor economists studied labor-leisure choices to model labor supply. The Lucas critique supported such models by pointing out that aggregate macroeconomic functions are all policy-dependent (individuals will change their behavior when government policies change) and micro-founded models will perform better; aggregate functions estimated with historical data should not be used for analyzing potential policy actions.

Macro theorists now commonly work with Dynamic Stochastic General Equilibrium (DSGE) Models[198], which assume households maximizing their "utility" based on consumption and leisure time, firms maximizing profits in a rational expectations setting (agents perfectly anticipate the future and act accordingly). Households are constrained by their budgets (which are affected by their factor income), firms are constrained by the production function and factor availability/costs. Markets work efficiently in most setups. Most shocks to the system are generated from the supply side (productivity). Some models refine this to introduce heterogeneous agents, sticky prices driven by market structure, frictional unemployment, etc. These models aspire to be logically consistent, introduce several moving parts, making them difficult to solve and interpret. While these models are used by financial institutions such as Central banks, they have been large black boxes, for

---

[198] Kydland and Prescott first introduced this idea in 1982. The models with flexible prices, frictionless markets, fully rational agents are also called Real Business Cycle (RBC) models.

Capital Markets and Investments

the most part, and inferences have not been that different from traditional models. Calibrating these models to historical data have not provided intuitive/ precise structural parameters.

Alternatively, some empirical macroeconomics[199], instead of calibrating equilibrium models, choose to estimate reduced-form macroeconomic models with few restrictions using time-series econometric techniques, considering all variables to be endogenous. The models set up a system of Vector Auto-Regressions (VARs), with variables expressed in terms of their (and other variables') lagged values (i.e. lagged values of the dependent variables are the independent variables). Steps involve deciding on the optimal lag length, checking model stability (if magnitudes of the estimated regression coefficients are too large, the model will not converge after an exogenous shock and Vector Error Correction and Co-integration models are more suitable), analyzing impulse-response functions to check the response of a dependent variable after an exogenous shock, other variables remaining constant. These models are empirically motivated and worry less about theoretical foundation.

Models have definitely evolved to become more detailed and realistic. This has introduced more assumptions and moving parts; there are, indeed, more model features now than can potentially go wrong. At the same time, details such as the term structure of interest rates, lags, regime switches, externalities, incentives and information asymmetry, intertemporal issues such as intergenerational national debt and Ricardian Equivalence, gradual updating of expectations (instead of a pure rational expectations), policy variables overshooting model targets, etc. have found their way into macroeconomic discussions. While it is possible to incorporate any of these effects into most models, as a special case, specific assumptions need to be made regarding their exact nature. These nuances complicate the model further, solutions may not be unique, and incorrect assumptions may aggravate the problem.

When analyzing a dynamic economic system, maintaining the right level of granularity in the analytical framework is often critical, since the same economic "shock" can get transmitted differently depending on the details of exactly how different economic agents react to the shock. Both static and dynamic macro models (including the reduced-form empirical models) have so many unrealistic and restrictive assumptions, yet so many moving parts, that it is doubtful that these models will consistently generate accurate predictions.

The Bridgewater (Ray Dalio) Approach to Macroeconomics

Over the past few years, Bridgewater founder Ray Dalio has discussed his bottom-up "transactions-based approach" of analyzing the economy. Instead of looking at both demand and supply in terms of quantity demanded or supplied, the idea is to look at the demand side in terms of dollars available to buy, and the supply side in terms of quantity offered for sale. The premise is that most fluctuations happen from the demand side, and is heavily influenced by the credit available in the economy. Spending can happen either through (non-borrowed) money or credit. To spend more non-borrowed money, the buyer has to do something productive to earn that money, but to spend using credit, all that is required is a contract with a seller, who is willing to rely on the buyer's promise to pay in future to make a sale (and profits) that would otherwise not occur. As part of a business cycle, when spending growth (maybe because of easy credit) outpaces the growth in productive capacity, prices rise (i.e. inflation occurs), leading the central bank to curtail credit and money, causing a slump in spending. This causes a recession. Recessions end with the central bank lowering interest rates and easing credit, as this stimulates demand for goods and services by reducing debt servicing costs and also inflates prices of financial assets, causing a wealth effect. Over the longer-term, debt can rise faster than income. This cannot continue because debt servicing costs become excessive, despite interest rates

---

[199] Chris Sims pioneered this thought process.

being lowered to their floor. This has to be fixed by reducing debt burdens through debt restructuring, austerity, debt monetization and wealth redistribution. This can cause a depression, and monetary policy cannot stimulate credit growth.

Unlike a "hard" science with well-defined physical laws, macroeconomic analysis is unlikely to lead to the precisely correct forecast, but it definitely provides some idea (educated guess) about what is more likely to happen, at least qualitatively. These models also force economists to think through the important input variables, the relevant transmission mechanisms, the adjustment speeds of different markets, the final outcome of exogenous changes, and the path taken to get there.

CURRENCY MARKETS

This is predominantly an institutional off-exchange over-the-counter (OTC) market, run by the large dealers, though several ETFs also provide exposure to the currency market. Forwards are the most common instrument, where (like a futures) parties enter into a contract to buy/ sell one currency for another on a specific date in the future at a pre-decided exchange rate. , which is different from todays' *spot* exchange rate. As an example, by convention, EURUSD of 1.05 denotes the price of 1 USD in terms of EUR i.e. an investor need to give up 1.05 USD to get back 1 EUR[200].

Unlike the NPV-based frameworks that can be applied to most asset classes, most investors try to form an views on future currency movements based on historical reference points and balance of trade/ capital account flows of a country. The amount of foreign reserves a country has, how much it is likely to earn through exports (net of imports), and how much capital inflows it is likely to receive, all point to an estimate of whether the currency of one country is likely to appreciate or depreciate, relative to others.

The main theory about currency pricing is *covered interest parity*, which is essentially a no-arbitrage condition related to investing in safe assets in different geographies. In a world with free capital flows, a US domiciled investor is indifferent between investing USD 1.05 in a US bank for one year, versus converting USD1.05 to EUR1 at the current spot rate, investing EUR 1 in an European bank for a year, and converting the EUR proceeds back to USD at the end of one year, if both strategies return the same. The EURUSD exchange rate a year ahead is unknown today, but investors can lock in a currency conversion rate at the current one-year forward rate, if they do not want to deal with the uncertainty of the exchange rate in future. Once locked into the currency forward, the investment in USD should yield the same as converting to EUR, investing in Europe and converting back at today's forward rate, otherwise there would be an arbitrage opportunity. This no-arbitrage condition decides the forward rate. Eq. **III.1** shows the relationship that determines the forward exchange rate.

$$EURUSD_{Spot} \times x\ year\ Interest\ Rate_{US} = 1 \times x\ year\ Interest\ Rate_{Europe} \times \frac{1}{EURUSD_{x\ year\ forward}}$$

Eq. III.1

The relation holds for interest rates of any maturity (*x* years) and the currency forward of the corresponding expiration (and countries, of course). Now, if the interest rates move, the forward exchange rates will also move, so positions expressed in the currency markets are often an expression of views on interest rates.

---

[200] Of course, EUR and USD can be replaced by any other currency pair; the convention remains the same.

Capital Markets and Investments

PRACTICAL MACROECONOMIC CONSIDERATIONS FOR FINANCE PROFESSIONALS

It is very difficult for even the best macroeconomists to get their forecasts consistently right (compared to a top stock picker managing a portfolio, for example), for the various reasons discussed earlier. So, for the user of macroeconomic research, getting hung up on model forecasts is futile. But, it is critical to understand the transmission mechanisms for government policies and external shocks to the broader economy and markets. Much of the water-cooler macroeconomics discussions still continue to be based on simple traditional models, so understanding those linkages (and where they might break) is useful. Most finance professionals will have ready access to the views of various camps; being able to contrast these disparate views against one another and synthesize the opinions is valuable. Once the professional takes a view, knowing how that view might turn out to be wrong (and spotting the early warning signs of the miscalculation and correcting course) is key.

For financial analysis, forming a view on where macro variables are headed in future is very important; the values of macro variables today useful to the extent they inform this view (except for forecasting policy announcements, where current macro variables are the most important input). It is important to check in with this view and update it on a regular basis. For this, following the macro data that is continually released on different parts of the economy, assessing how it stacks up against expectations and what it means for the initial view is essential. As discussed in Chapter 6, new forms of "big" data may play an important role in forming quick estimates of macro variables.

For example, investors have a good sense of the relative shares of consumption, investment, government spending, etc. (also, goods versus services) in GDP. They assess whether ongoing macroeconomic releases shed new light on their views on the economy as whole, or these components in particular i.e. are the macroeconomic data releases likely to be leading, lagging or coincident macroeconomic indicators of broader economic activity[201]. They also try to guess how policymakers will respond to the current economic outlook, and which parts of the economy will be especially affected by changes in policy, through various transmission mechanisms. On the supply side, they follow the role of regulation, technology, etc. in either easing on making difficult the conditions for business owners and workers, and forming an opinion on how that affects the cost and supply of labor to these firms, the output produced by these firms (cost and quantity, etc.). For longer horizons, investors need to appreciate big structural shifts that are taking place, be it the composition of the workforce, the evolving distribution of wealth and income, the demographic shifts, and what that implies for macro variables and the economy as whole.

Economic cycles have historically lasted for varying periods of time, so simply being in a certain stage of the business cycle does not tell us what will happen next. Changes in policy rates (lower), inflation trends (decreases) and strength in some key sectors such as housing usually help support a growth cycle. As conditions tighten (usually because of the Fed raising rates or inflation rising e.g. oil prices going higher), the economy slows down. Since the financial markets themselves are a leading indicator of the economy (i.e. investors' view of the future outlook are incorporated in today's security prices), if investors are trying to predict future stock (or bond) prices, they need to go beyond developing a sense of the future economic outlook. Rather, the issue is often about deciphering what future conditions are priced into the market today, and whether the analyst's opinion of the future macro outlook is different from that. Analysts track global central bank behavior, interest rates, relative performance between early-stage cyclical stocks (e.g. housing, consumer discretionary) and late-stage cyclicals (e.g. energy, materials) to sense where the leading economic indicators are headed[202]. They track leading economic indicators (survey data such as PMI is a common one, as is housing starts/ permits/ prices),

---

[201] Financial markets themselves are (very imperfect) leading indicators of (expected) future economic activity, so finding indicators that lead the financial markets is especially difficult.

[202] Choosing the appropriate lags while trying to decide which variables lead markets (and by how long) is important, albeit imprecise.

Annexure: Macroeconomics Primer

which are usually co-incident with the stock market, to look for divergence between the future economic activity indicated by this data and what is being indicated by current security prices. At the same time, they are mindful of secular/structural trends (i.e. retail moving online, ageing demographics, etc.) and whether these forces have gathered enough momentum to overwhelm shorter term cyclical effects, or if cyclical effects will dominate.

This big-picture thought process eventually gets granular by getting mapped to various industries and sectors, the effect on demand and supply in those industries, and the overall industry outlook. Analysts also speculate on which firms are best poised to benefit from these changes; this becomes an important input into analyzing and forecasting prices of stocks, commodities, etc. Fixed income and currency investors use macroeconomic insights to draw inference for future interest rate, inflation and growth paths. Like most forecasting, it is arguably easier to form an opinion on *what* pivotal economic outcome is eventually likely to occur, than get specific about *when* this is likely to happen.

MAJOR US MACROECONOMIC DATA SERIES

We end this annexure by discussing some important US macroeconomic data releases in this section[203]. Most data series report hard facts, whereas some capture sentiment and opinion polls. Some datasets are collated using surveys, while others are obtained from records as a normal course of economic activity. For most important data series, *consensus forecasts*, which reflect the aggregation of views of several prominent economists (and are a proxy for expected values), are often available before the actual release. Comparing the actual release to the consensus estimate allows a casual data observer to gauge whether the data was better or worse than expectations. Economic data is often *revised* (sometimes multiple times) after it is released, and these revisions often significantly deviate from the initial estimates. Data series may be *seasonally adjusted (SA)* or *not (NSA)*, using statistical techniques, to adjust for the fact that certain months are naturally more active than others (e.g. Thanksgiving to Christmas for retail sales), and allow for sensible month-over-month comparisons by eliminating natural and expected movements in the data, rather than raising flags about economic changes. These adjustments are however not perfect, and often instead end up introducing more noise in the data. Data series also fluctuate because of changes in the business cycle, which are longer term movements; these fluctuations (which show up in the data) are meaningful and may reflect fundamental changes in economic outlook. Depending on the data series, it may be presented in real (i.e. inflation adjusted) or nominal dollars. As mentioned above, almost all data series have an initial release, and are then revised multiple times.

Data on Overall Economy – Employment and GDP

Employment status reports are important because they directly provide data to address unemployment-wage inflation issues, and also provide information on how fast the economy is growing (and indicates how consumption is likely to grow in future, based on current wages and employment), and how much below full capacity the economy currently is. Further, the employment reports are among the most current macroeconomic releases, with short lags.

- The most important employment report is the *Employment Situation* or the *Non-Farm Payrolls* report, released by the Bureau of Labor Statistics in the U.S. Department of Labor on the first Friday following the reporting month. It is probably the macro data point that affects financial markets the most, despite being prone to large monthly revisions. This report is detailed and has two broad components

---

[203] Most other countries have similar data series, so the same ideas are relevant, with some modifications.

Capital Markets and Investments

– the Household survey and the Establishment survey. The Household survey contacts 60000 households to determine how many people are employed, working full-time or part-time, actively looking for work, to determine various employment statistics, including the unemployment rate[204]. The Establishment survey polls 400000 firms, covering 45% of the non-farm labor force, and provides industry-level information on how many jobs were added or lost that month, how long people worked on average, etc.

- The Non-Farms Payroll report is so important that *ADP* (a payroll processing company), in collaboration with Moody's Analytics, has made a business out of predicting key statistics from the Payroll report, two days before the Payroll report is released. ADP uses a sample of 20 million (non-farm) paychecks it processes covering 350,000 companies and, with Moody's Analytics, statistically analyses that data (along with the Philadelphia Federal Reserve's Aruoba-Diebold-Scotti Business Conditions Index) to predict important variables, like the addition to Non-Farm Payrolls.

- The Department of Labor also releases information on *Weekly Jobless (Unemployment Insurance) Claims*, every Thursday, for the previous week. While this data is noisy, it is very current. Analysts often use a four-week moving average of this data series.

- *GDP* data is initially released by the Bureau of Economic Analysis in the US Commerce Department at 8:30am on the last Friday of January, April, July and October (i.e. 4 weeks after the end of the quarter). This is referred to as the advance release, and is normally revised twice (preliminary and final reports), each a month apart. GDP is broken up into four major components – personal consumption expenditures, gross private domestic investment, net exports and government spending, which are further broken down, offering a granular organized view of the economy. However, the data often has (only) moderate impact on financial markets, since it is considered "old news, yet imperfect", released four weeks after the quarter has passed and susceptible to large revisions.

- The Conference Board, a private research house, publishes the *Leading Economic Indicators (LEI)* Index, using a weighted average of manufacturing, housing and financial data published in other reports, which may be leading the broad economic cycle. While this is sometimes discussed, it rarely impacts financial markets significantly.

Consumer Data

Since consumption constitutes 70% of the US economy, the monthly *Retail Sales* report (released by the Census Bureau, Commerce Department) is especially important in highlighting promptly (2 weeks after the end of the month) how active the consumer has been. The report, prepared by surveying large and small retailers, includes expenditure on goods and food services, but excludes the rest of the service industry (about two-thirds of personal expenditure). The data is subject to significant revisions at the end of the month.

- The *Personal Income and Spending* report, published by the BEA with a month's lag, is another consumer-focused report, with the data collected from payrolls and retail sales, but also includes spending on services, unlike retail sales.

- Two popular consumer sentiment-based monthly indicators are the *Consumer Confidence Index* (by the Conference Board) and the *Survey of Consumer Sentiment* (by the University of Michigan). These are both survey-based indicators, with the Conference Board focusing on consumer reactions to the labor market and business conditions, whereas the University of Michigan focuses on personal finances and income. The entire sample is new in the Conference Board survey, whereas 40% of the Michigan survey constitutes repeat participants. U. of Michigan polls 500 people; the Conference Board polls 5000.

---

[204] Importantly, potential employees who are discouraged and not looking for work are not counted in the unemployment rate statistic.

Annexure: Macroeconomics Primer

These numbers have not been strong predictors of consumer spending, but the U. of Michigan survey is considered a better leading indicator, since it polls people about attitudes.

Manufacturing/ Services Data

- The *Institute of Supply Management (ISM)* publishes monthly surveys by purchase managers in the manufacturing and non-manufacturing (i.e. service) sectors every month. Results of the *Manufacturing survey* are released on the first business day of the next month, and affect market movements significantly, since it is available before any other major macro release for the month. It is computed using questionnaires to 400 companies across 20 industries, asking them if activity is rising, falling or unchanged in several areas such as new orders, production, employment, supplier delivery, inventories, etc. A weighted average of these numbers is presented as a *diffusion index* – a value above 50 represents growth; below 50 represents a slowdown. The Non-Manufacturing Survey index is calculated similarly, and released on the third business day of each month.

- The *(Advance) Durable Goods Orders* report, released three to four weeks after the reporting month by the Census Bureau in the Commerce Department, polls over 4000 manufacturers from 89 industries (hard products). Analysts often strip out Defense and Aircraft orders, because they are lumpy and volatile and may mask underlying trends. Because this report tracks orders (and not production that has already occurred), it affects financial markets significantly, despite having almost a month's lag.

- The *Factory Orders* report, which is released a week later, also includes non-durable goods (food, clothing, fuel, etc.), but the durables goods report is more eagerly awaited because it has more predictive power for economic health (since it represents discretionary purchases).

- *Industrial Production and Capital Utilization*, published mid-month (for the prior month) by the Federal Reserve Board, measures the volume of industrial output (prices are ignored) and the slack in manufacturing capacity. While manufacturing is a relatively small component of GDP, it is more volatile and reactive to changes in policy. Capacity Utilization gives an indication of how easily manufacturers can produce more without significant investments, so can serve as a good indicator of future investment spending and inflationary pressures.

Housing Data

Like the Durable Goods Report (or even more), analysts believe that housing is a robust predictor for the future direction of the economy.

- The Census Bureau sends out mailers to builders in 19,000 localities asking about *Housing Starts* (i.e. excavation for foundation) and *Building Permits* filed. The report is available mid-month, and covers single-family homes, townhouses/ condos and apartment complexes.

- The National Association of Realtors reports *Existing Home Sales* every month (with a four-to-five week lag); only transactions that have finally closed (i.e. several months after contract signed) are counted. They also publish indices of Pending Home Sales and Home Affordability.

- *New Home Sales*, published monthly by the Census Bureau, counts transactions when the contract is signed. The data is published four months after the reporting period. New Home Sales are considered a better barometer than Existing Home Sales, because it captures new economic activity and has stronger multiplier effects.

- The Mortgage Bankers Association publishes the *Mortgage Application Survey* every week.

- The *Case-Shiller Index* tracks single-family home prices in 20 metropolitan areas, and publishes composite indices capturing home price movements.

Capital Markets and Investments

Federal Reserve Reports

- The FOMC puts out a *statement* (press release) right after it concludes each of its eight meetings announcing its target for Fed Funds rate and other policy measures, along with a commentary on how it sees the economy and policy variables evolve. Some FOMC meetings also have a press conference. These are very important market-moving announcements, especially when monetary policy holds center stage. Minutes of the FOMC meetings are released three weeks after the meeting, but by that time it is old news for the markets.

- The *regional Federal Reserve Banks publish manufacturing reports* – New York Fed's Empire Manufacturing report is published two weeks into the month it covers, the Philadelphia survey follows a week later on the third Thursday, Richmond on the last Tuesday of the month. These reports serve as a preview to the ISM manufacturing report for the month released in the following week. The Chicago Fed releases a *National Activity Index* (four to five weeks after the month it covers), which is a weighted average of 85 economic indicators.

- The *Beige Book*, published by the Federal Reserve Board two weeks before FOMC meetings, compiles anecdotal information about business conditions in each of the 12 Districts.

- The Federal Reserve conducts a *Senior Loan Officer Survey*, asking up to eighty large domestic banks and twenty-four U.S. branches and agencies of foreign banks questions on changes in the standards and terms of the banks' lending and the state of business and household demand for loans. The Federal Reserve generally conducts the survey quarterly, so that the results are available in time for the corresponding FOMC meeting.

- Federal Reserve *Flow of Funds Report* is a quarterly report that includes detail on the assets and liabilities of households, businesses, governments, and financial institutions, and how they have changed over time, offering insights into where capital is flowing in and out of in the economy.

Inflation

Most inflation indices reflect the ratio of prices on a basket of goods and services at two points in time. An unexpected increase in the inflation rate leads to an increase in bond yields.

The *Consumer Price Index (CPI)* is published monthly by the Bureau of Labor Statistics two to three weeks after month-end. Housing represents over 40% of the basket, with Food and Transportation being other important components. The data is collected by visiting stores and conducting telephone interviews with retail stores. A subset of the CPI basket, called core-CPI, excludes food and energy (about 25% of the basket), since those prices often fluctuate because of transient factors, less relevant to policy makers thinking longer term.

The *Producer Price Index (PPI)* also published by the Bureau of Labor Statistics, is usually announced the day before the CPI release. PPI measures price movements at the wholesale level, and excludes services (whereas services, including housing, constitute over half the CPI). PPI is published for crude goods (raw materials), intermediate goods and finished goods. Core-PPI excludes food and energy, a 40% share of finished goods PPI.

The Personal Consumption Expenditure (PCE) Price Index, released monthly by the Bureau of Economic Analysis, is announced on the last day of the month for the prior month. While it is more delayed (by about two weeks) than the other monthly inflation measures, it covers the broadest basket. The Federal Reserve Board pays close attention to this when deciding on monetary policy.

The GDP Deflator is published along with GDP. While the basket underlying this measure is very broad, it is published only every quarter.

REFERENCES

Abel, Andrew & Ben Bernanke. *Macroeconomics*. Pearson

Baumol, Bernard. *The Secrets of Economic Indicators*. Pearson

Dalio, Ray. *How the Economic Machine Works*. Bridgewater

IV. Basic Statistics and Data Analysis

Like other Annexures in this book, the purpose here is to familiarize readers without a quantitative background on the basics of statistics. It's not a substitute for taking a class in introductory statistics, or studying the subject in any detail. Anyone who will spend time with data will benefit from some knowledge in statistics.

Broadly, data can either be *time series* (different values capture different points in time e.g. stock price history of Facebook) or *cross-sectional* (different values represent different entities e.g. last month's returns of 500 stocks in the S&P500, or the grades of 25 students). The standard framework to view data is through the lens of a *random variable*, which *realizes* (i.e. takes on) different numerical values in different iterative *draws* (similar to a lottery machine spitting out numbers). The entire dataset is visualized as multiple iterations of this "lottery machine". There is an underlying *data generating process* (i.e. *distribution*) that governs what values the random variable (i.e. output of the lottery machine) takes on. That process can potentially have predictable as well as unpredictable random components. The purpose of the statistical tools is to isolate the stable parts of the process, and provide some direction in "guessing" what values are more (or less) likely in the data.

At one level, even if we are describing how the historical data evolved, we want to have some confidence that it will evolve similarly in future. Since some data patterns are easier to model than others, in a few cases, transforming the variable makes it easy to apply structure to the process.

Example:

Table IV-1 below shows two random variables x and y, and their realizations in 12 draws (i.e. 12 observations each of x and y).

Table IV-1: 12 Observations of random variables x and y

x	y
-1	6
2	15
5	21
3	14
4	25
15	58
3	13
5	19
2	10
-4	-1
-8	-17
-6	-10

One way to graphically represent the dataset is a *frequency chart (or frequency distribution)*, which has the value of the variable on the x-axis and the number of times it occurs (i.e. its frequency) on the y-axis. By studying this chart, analysts can get an idea of how often the different values of the variables occurred. The frequency can

Annexure: Basic Statistics and Data Analysis

also be normalized to a percentage by dividing the frequency by total number of observations; this is referred to as *relative frequency* or *probability distribution* and indicates the relative likelihood of realizing one value versus another.

> *Example:* Table IV-2 below shows x and its frequency, based on the raw data in
>
> Table IV-1. Observations appearing multiple times in
>
> Table IV-1 show up only once here, and the frequency column records how often the observation shows up.
>
> Using another example, in a dataset of 1000 coin tosses, the raw dataset (
>
> Table IV-1) will have 1000 rows, but the equivalent of Table IV-2 will have only two rows.

Table IV-2: Relative Frequencies Based on Table 1

x	freq(x)	Rel. Freq (x)
-8	1	0.08
-6	1	0.08
-4	1	0.08
-1	1	0.08
2	2	0.17
3	2	0.17
4	1	0.08
5	2	0.17
15	1	0.08

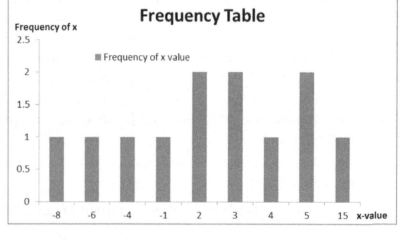

SUMMARIZING DATA

The first ideas we will discuss deal with summarizing data. In this section, we deal with only one variable at a time.

Central Tendency – Mean, Median and Mode

The most basic way to summarize the data (test scores of 25 students in an exam, or the history of Facebook stock price, or stock returns) is to compute an average. This average, which adds up all the values and dividers by the number of observations, is referred to as the *arithmetic mean* (or simply the mean, or Expected Value). For a random variable x, the Expected Value $E(x)$ or mean μ is denoted by:

$$\mu(x) = E(x) = \frac{1}{n}\sum_{i=1}^{n} x_i$$

The mean captures, on average, what value the data set is centered around, and is a measure of *central tendency*. Every value is given equal importance. The measure is heavily influenced by outliers (extreme values), and the mean value may not actually belong to the dataset.

> *Example:* Using the dataset in Table IV-1, the mean of x is 1.67 (i.e. 20 ÷ 12). Note, 1.67 does not belong to the dataset. Also, this number is heavily influenced by extreme values; if we exclude the value 15, the mean drops to 0.45.

Capital Markets and Investments

Above, we calculated a "simple" average, where each observation was considered equally important. While this works fine for a raw dataset, it is not directly applicable if the data is presented in the format in Table IV-2. In this situation, we introduce the concept of *weighted average*, where the average is calculated by multiplying each observation by its weight (i.e. how important the observation is, in this case its frequency), adding these products together, and then dividing this sum by the sum of weights.

$$\mu(x) = E(x) = \frac{\sum_{i=1}^{n} w_i x_i}{\sum_{i=1}^{n} w_i}$$

> *Example:* From Table IV-2, using the frequency as the weight, the mean of x is 1.67 (as it should be, since it is the same dataset as Table IV-1. The simple average calculation above is, trivially, an equally weighted average, with every observation having the weight 1.

Alternative measures of central tendency include the median and the mode. The *median* is the value that divides the data into two equal halves i.e. if the data were sorted by size, the median would lie in the middle of the dataset. It is also referred to the 50th *percentile*, since 50% of the dataset lies below it (the 99th percentile is the value that separates the top 1% of the data). The *mode* of the data set is the value that occurs most often.

> *Example:* The median of the dataset in Table IV-1 (or Table IV-2) is 2.5. It is the average of the 6th and 7th largest observation, since the dataset has 12 observations. The dataset has three modes – 2, 3 and 5 all occur twice in the dataset.

Dispersion – Standard Deviation

The measures of central tendency give us a good idea of where the frequency distribution of the data is centered. Measures of *Dispersion* capture how much the distribution is "spread" around the central tendency. So, dispersion measures give the analyst some confidence on how "precise" the central tendency measure is likely to be; a large dispersion value indicates that the distribution is widely spread out and the central tendency is not very representative.

There are several measures of dispersion; *range* is the difference between the minimum and maximum observed values, the *interquartile range* (or $Q_3 - Q_1$) is the difference between the 75th percentile and the 25th percentile values. But, by far, the most popular and important measure is *standard deviation* (σ), or root-mean-squared deviation (computed by calculating the square root of the average of the square of the deviations from the mean); its square (σ^2) is called *variance*.

$$\sigma(x) = Standard\ Deviation(x) = \sqrt{\frac{1}{n} \sum_{i=1}^{n} (x_i - \mu)^2}$$

When discussing stock returns, the standard deviation of historical stock returns is referred to as *realized volatility*. Standard deviation or volatility is always positive.

> *Example:* Using our dataset, the range is 23 (i.e. 15- (-8)), the interquartile range is 6 (i.e. 4.25-1.75), and the standard deviation is 6.03525.

Some useful properties of these summary statistics:

1. Mean and standard deviation both have the same units as the original data, i.e. if the data is in percentage points, the mean and the standard deviation are in percentage points.
2. If we add or subtract a constant number to each value in the dataset, the mean changes by that amount but the standard deviation does not. i.e.

$$\mu(x + k) = \mu(x) + k, but\ \sigma(x + k) = \sigma(x), where\ k\ is\ a\ constant$$

Annexure: Basic Statistics and Data Analysis

3. If we multiply a constant number to each value in the dataset, both the mean and the standard deviation get multiplied by that number. i.e.

$$\mu(x.k) = k.\mu(x); \; \sigma(x.k) = k.\sigma(x), where \; k \; is \; a \; constant$$

4. There is a conceptual and minor formulaic difference while calculating statistics for a sample versus a population; we are ignoring this detail, for the most part.

These summary statistics are essential; we will discuss more measures later.

PROBABILITY – DISTRIBUTION TYPES

The *Probability of x_1* i.e. $P(x=x_1)$ is the chance or the likelihood that the random variable x takes the value x_1. While this suffices for discrete variables (i.e. x can on take specific values), for continuous random variables, $P(x_1 < x < x_2)$ i.e. the probability that x lies between x_1 and x_2 is a more suitable characterization.

This likelihood is governed by the data generating process / distribution mentioned earlier. For any random variable x, the *probability distribution* (or *Probability Density Function*) plots $P(x)$ for all possible values of x (x plotted on the horizontal axis, $P(x)$ on the vertical axis). The *Cumulative Distribution $D(x)$* tracks the area under the probability distribution $P(x)$ curve for all values of x less than or equal to a specific value i.e. $D(x_1) = P(x \leq x_1) = \sum_{x=-\infty}^{x_1} P(x)$.

Essentially, we are adding up all probabilities for x taking on any value less than or equal to x_1. For continuous variables, the discrete summation is replaced by integrals. For any value of x_1, the area under the density curve to the left of x_1 denotes the probability of the random variable taking on a value less than x_1. This is the cumulative distribution value at x_1. The probability distribution and cumulative distribution functions are closely related; we can move from one to the other.

Probability distributions cannot take on negative values or values greater than 1, and the sum of all the probabilities (for all possible values of x) add up to 1. Figure IV.1 below shows the density and distribution functions for a commonly used distribution – the *normal distribution*.

Figure IV.1 Probability Density and corresponding Cumulative Distribution

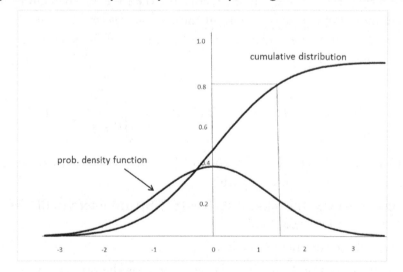

Any function is characterized by its *functional form* (i.e. $y = a + bx$ is a linear (affine) function of y on x) and the *value of the parameters* in the function (i.e. $y = 2 + 3x$ is a different function from $y = 5 + 4x$; the parameters a and b take on different values). So, if we have some idea of these two aspects – the functional form and the parameter values, we can characterize the distribution.

Capital Markets and Investments

There are several well-known probability distributions (functional forms); any function that follows the properties above qualifies as a probability distribution. But, there are few that analysts use often; the *Normal Distribution* is the most common, but the *Poisson* and *Binomial* distributions (or *processes*) are also seen. A plot of the data often helps choose which distribution to calibrate to. Calculating the moments helps back out suitable parameters. The density function is effectively an estimate of the function that has generated that relative frequency table. Of course, there can be probability distributions that follow the rules above (non-negative, and add up to one), but their density functions are difficult (or impossible) to specify using a formula. This is not a problem, as long as there is a relative frequency distribution table to work with (such as Table IV-2). Instead of using a formula to determine the likelihood of a particular x value, we simply reference the table to find out. Such distributions are referred to as *Empirical Distributions*.

It's often a good idea to use the Normal distribution, absent other information. Aside from being well-understood and easy to use, theoretical arguments such as the *Central Limit Theorem* says that, under fairly general conditions (independent and identically distributed variables), means estimated from a random sample of values will converge to a Normal distribution, *regardless of the underlying distribution from which these values are drawn*. So, even if the data generating process for these values in the sample is non-normal, their mean converges to a Normal Distribution.

Normal Distribution

The *Normal* (or *Gaussian*) *Distribution* $N(\mu,\sigma)$ is fully characterized by its mean and standard deviation, which can be estimated from the data. The probability density of the normal distribution is given by

$$P(x) = \frac{1}{\sigma\sqrt{2\pi}} e^{-\frac{1}{2}(\frac{x-\mu}{\sigma})^2}$$

This density function will sum to 1, across the full range (negative infinity to positive infinity) of x values. It also takes only positive values. Looking at the density graph, we see that most of the values are clustered around the mean; the standard deviation determines how much the values spread around the mean. The distribution is *unimodal* (only one peak), *symmetric* (distribution of x values greater than the mean is identical to the distribution less than the mean; it can be "folded" along a vertical line passing through the mean, and overlap completely on both sides) and *asymptotic* (x can take on any value from $-\infty$ to $+\infty$). The normal distribution with mean $=0$ and standard deviation $=1$ is called the *standard normal distribution*. There are many useful results documented for standard normal distributions, so analysts often convert normal distributions with different means and standard deviations to the standard form (so that they can apply the documented results easily). For any value x, drawn from a Normal distribution with mean μ and standard deviation σ (i.e. X ~ $N(\mu,\sigma)$), $z = (x-\mu)/\sigma$ is the transformed standard normal value i.e. Z ~ $N(0,1)$ (look closely at the density function formula above to see why this works).

Annexure: Basic Statistics and Data Analysis

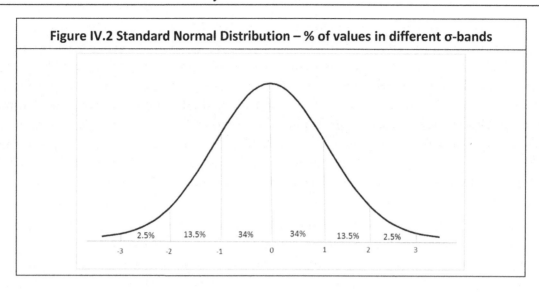

Figure IV.2 Standard Normal Distribution – % of values in different σ-bands

68% of the values of any data drawn from a normal distribution lie between ± 1 standard deviation of the mean, 95% lies within 2 standard deviations and 99.75% lies within 3 standard deviations. Figure IV.2 shows this. Putting it differently, *the 95% confidence interval for a Normal distribution is μ ± 1σ*, and so on. The distribution is symmetric, so values on either side of the mean are equally likely - the mean, median and mode are the same value. So, if a value of x lies far in the tails of a specific normal distribution, it is unlikely to have been generated by that distribution.

When we relate a data point's distance from the mean (in units of standard deviations) to its likelihood of occurrence, we often *assume* that the data is being generated by a normal distribution. There are some well-known distributions which resemble a normal distribution but have fatter tails (e.g. t-distribution; although, for a large number of observations, the t-distribution converges to Normal). So, a value that appear to be an outlier and very unlikely in the Normal distribution world may not be that unlikely if we were to assume that a different distribution accurately described the true state of the world. We need to always keep this reality in mind while drawing inferences. To be specific, using normal distributions understates the likelihood of extreme outcomes relative to the actual historical returns; return distributions have *fat tails*. Risk managers need to be fully aware of this while using risk models and reading risk reports.

Drawing inferences about the population from sample statistics

We said that we would not obsess over the difference between sample and population, and that has been true so far. But, we need to get into this detail to make one final point. The big picture philosophy is that data that we observe (no matter how much data, for how long) is a sample drawn from a population. We can calculate the sample statistics, but we actually care about the population statistics and its distribution (because that's where the next data point will come from), and try to infer that from the sample(s). As the sample gets larger, our estimates regarding the population get more precise. The sample mean is an unbiased estimate of the population mean. However, the distribution of the population mean inferred from the sample has a lower standard deviation than the sample standard deviation; it is referred to as the *standard error* and is calculated as $\sigma/\sqrt{n}$, where n is the number of observations in the sample (if the sample is very large, the standard error is tiny, and the population mean is almost a point estimate equal to the sample mean). So, in some situations when we are discussing the population mean's distribution, $\mu \pm 1\sigma/\sqrt{n}$ is the correct 95% confidence interval.

A *Binomial distribution* has only two outcomes (i.e. two values of $x - x_1$ and x_2). The common example is a coin tossing sequence, with either *Heads* or *Tails* (each with probability 0.5). Alternatively, it could be a laboratory

Capital Markets and Investments

test, with either *Success* or *Failure*, where the $P(Failure) = 1 - P(Success)$. This follows the rules of a density function mentioned above (each value is positive, and collectively sums to one). Typical applications can be generalized into assessing the likelihood of k successes in n trials (each trial generates one value of x), or the sequence of those successes. Importantly, if a success scores a 1 and a failure scores 0, the expected value (mean) of a binomial distribution is np, where n is the number of trials and $P(Success) = p$, and the standard deviation is $\sqrt{[np(1-p)]}$. For a large number of trials (n >25), the binomial distribution can be approximated by a normal distribution with these parameters, so we can apply the ideas discussed above.

The *Poisson distribution* is a discrete distribution often used as a counting process to model arrival rates/ times and service times in queueing theory. i.e. when does one expect to see the next event, or how many times does one expect to see the event in a certain time window. This is used to model jumps in option pricing.

SOME MORE SUMMARY STATISTICS

The following statistics provide additional details about the distribution the dataset is drawn from, and can be calculated from the data.

Skewness: This shows the symmetry (or the lack of it) in the distribution (e.g. the mean, median and mode are not equal). These distributions have "tails" pulled more to one side than other. .

Figure IV.3: Different Levels of Skewness in distributions

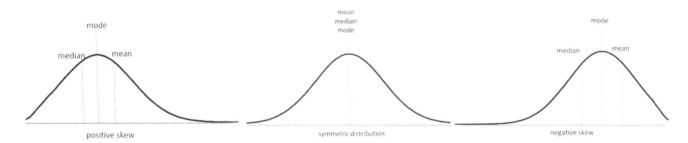

Kurtosis: This statistic, as shown in Figure IV.4 indicates how "peaked" the distribution is. A normal distribution has a kurtosis of 3, so a measure of "excess kurtosis", which subtracts 3 from the actual kurtosis value, is commonly used. Leptokurtic distributions, often relevant in finance, have a higher peak and fatter tails than a normal distribution.

Figure IV.4 Different levels of Kurtosis in Distributions

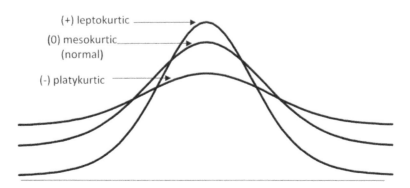

There are many other kinds of asymmetric distributions (Weibull distribution, Beta distribution, where these measures matter more; in finance we use these more as references to the non-normality of the underlying

Annexure: Basic Statistics and Data Analysis

distribution. Some distributions like the normal distribution can be completely described by the mean and standard deviations, whereas (in addition to mean and standard deviation) skewness and kurtosis are important characteristics other distributions. Of course, the density or the distribution functions describe the data fully; but characteristics such as mean (and median/ mode), standard deviation, skewness, kurtosis etc. (also called *moments*) are a convenient way to summarize what the distribution looks like.

Since the data distributions in finance are skewed, but it is easier to work with normal distributions, advanced financial analysis (e.g. derivative pricing) often requires superimposing different kinds of distributions together, to generate similar data patterns.

FURTHER COMMENTS ON DESCRIBING DATA

We can think of any variable as a random variable (e.g. stock prices), and can try to summarize it. Suppose we are looking at one year's data (i.e. 250 observations, since there are 250 trading days). But, if the price has moved up in a straight line the entire time, the average isn't very informative of the average value of the stock during that time. In such a situation, it may make sense to supplement the average price with the average of the daily price *change*, i.e. returns. In fact, it's far easier to work with the return estimates (and add them to existing prices if we need price estimates), since each day's return can be thought of as random, whereas tomorrow's price will definitely depend on today's price (i.e. likely close to it). The predictable part of tomorrow's price is today's price; the return is the random component added to the predictable part (i.e. today's price) to arrive at tomorrow's price. In formal terms, this issue is referred to as *non-stationarity*. Also, once the return is realized, it is known with certainty for that day (i.e. it may be a random variable, but the realization is certain; tomorrow's realization is likely to be different).

Summarizing the data (e.g. by calculating the mean) gives the analyst some idea of how the data has been in the past, and also gives the analyst a basis to predict future data, by specifying parameters in a model. The aim is not to exactly nail the future outcome, but have some context of the ballpark. Some variables exhibit statistical patterns that are more difficult to deal with (e.g. rising price), whereas others may be easier. Also, when analysts use historical data to predict future values solely based on the data (and a model), there is an implicit assumption that the future is likely to be similar to the past, overall. If there are structural reasons why the future is likely to be different from the past, the analyst needs to incorporate this separately, either explicitly in the model or by manually modifying the estimate.

MULTI-VARIATE ANALYSIS

So far, we have been examining a *univariate* setting, where we cared about only one random variable, and what values it is likely to take on in future. In many forms of statistical analysis, we care about bi-variate and multi-variate environments, where we care about the association and co-movement of different variables i.e. how does one variable move with another?

The most obvious bivariate analysis is to plot two variables on the horizontal and vertical axis and eye-ball it. That gives us an idea about how they are associated – do they go up or down together, is there an inverse relation, or is there none at all. A useful statistic to compute is the *covariance*, which captures the level of co-movement. Formally,

$$Cov(X, Y) \equiv E(XY) - E(X)E(Y) \equiv \sum_{i=1}^{n}(x_i - \mu_x)(y_i - \mu_y)$$

A negative covariance indicates a negative (i.e. inverse) relationship and vice versa. However, the magnitude of the covariance depends on the magnitude of these variables (i.e. the scale). So, if variable X is expressed in kilometers instead of meters (variable Y remaining the same), Cov(X,Y) will change by a factor of 1000. This

Capital Markets and Investments

makes it difficult to assess the strength of the relationship. So, an alternative is to calculate the *correlation coefficient (ρ)*, which is essentially a scaled version of covariance which lies between -1 and +1. Formally,

$$0 \leq Correlation \equiv \rho(X,Y) \equiv \frac{Cov(X,Y)}{\sigma_x \sigma_y} \leq 1$$

Example: Using the data in Table 1, the correlation between X and Y is 0.98. The covariance is 103.33.

We will emphasize that a high covariance or correlation (or even regression statistics, discussed below) does not prove that movements in one of these variables lead to changes in the other; no causation is implied. It merely suggests co-movement or the lack of it. More often than not, the patterns suggested are *spurious*; analysts need to carefully decide which results are reliable, without cherry-picking the ones that help support their hypothesis.

Covariances and correlations can also be presented for more than two variables, although they are always calculated using pairs of variables. So, in a multivariate setting, these correlations are presented in a matrix/table, with the diagonal elements (i.e. correlation of a variable with itself) equal to one.

Regressions

The next step in analyzing multivariate data is to run *regressions*. It is another tool to measure the association between variables; in a sense it extends the idea of covariance (or correlation).

How do regressions work?

Regression "fits" a line through the data i.e. finds values of *parameters/ coefficients a (intercept)* and *b (slope)* in the equation y = a + bx (say, a' and b') so that the difference (or *error*) between the actual y (from the data) and the estimated y (from the model y = a' + b'x) is "low" in the data. If there are only two data points, suitable choice of a' and b' can reduce the difference to zero, for each of the two observations. Of course, having only two observations suggests that the model is unlikely to represent the population well; you need large datasets (relative to the number of parameters being estimated) to get a good idea of the population characteristics. But, if the dataset is large, no values of *a* and *b* can get the difference between the actual and estimated y to be zero <u>for every observation</u> in the data (unless y and x are related by an exact linear relationship). In this (common) situation, the regression tool chooses a' and b' which *minimize* the *sum of squared "errors"* (i.e. the sum of the squared differences between the estimated and actual y values); this method is also called *Ordinary Least Squares (OLS)*. One of the big advantages of regression is that it can easily be extended to a setup with more than two variables; the same technology and concepts can estimate *a, $b_1, b_2, \ldots b_n$*, for a model y = a + $\sum b_i x_i$. Many text books continue to use the y = a+bx notation to discuss multivariate regressions, but a, b, y and x are vectors and matrices in this framework. Basic data tools, from Microsoft Excel to statistical software packages (R, S-Plus, Stata, MatLab) to scientific libraries all have built-in routines for regressions.

For both bivariate and multivariate settings, the analyst has to tell the model which variable(s) is/ are *x* i.e. the independent variable, and which one is the dependent variable. Obviously, there can only be one dependent variable in this set-up, but multiple independent variables. In the two-variable case, if we swap the dependent and independent variables, the new values of *a* and *b* will not be inverses of the old values. The OLS method, because it squares the errors, penalizes large errors a lot and tries to reduce their magnitude by a suitable choice of a' and b'. One large error will likely have a larger effect on the sum of squared errors than many small errors, so extreme values in the data significantly affect the choice of a' and b'. This is why some analysts *winsorize* datasets (i.e. ignore a small proportion of "outliers") before running regressions.

Example: Let us try running a regression with the dataset in Table IV-1. We assume that y is the dependent variable, and x the independent variable. The regression output is below:

Annexure: Basic Statistics and Data Analysis

Figure IV.5 Regression Example – Excel Output

SUMMARY OUTPUT

Regression Statistics	
Multiple R	0.98
R Square	0.97
Adjusted R Square	0.97
Standard Error	3.44
Observations	12

ANOVA

	df	SS	MS	F	Significance F
Regression	1	3837.60	3837.60	323.45	6.0457E-09
Residual	10	118.65	11.86		
Total	11	3956.25			

	Coefficients	Standard Error	t Stat	P-value	Lower 95%	Upper 95%	Lower 95.0%	Upper 95.0%
Intercept	7.59	1.03	7.34	2.5E-05	5.29	9.90	5.29	9.90
X Variable 1	3.09	0.17	17.98	6E-09	2.71	3.48	2.71	3.48

The value of *a* i.e. the *Intercept* is 7.59; and the value of *b* (regression coefficient of the independent variable i.e. *X Variable 1*) is 3.09. In multiple regressions, the output will contain one coefficient value for each independent variable.

Interpreting regression results

The main question while analyzing regression outputs is to what extent the independent variable(s) affect the values of the dependent variable. The regression output contains the values *a'* and *b'*. Since these values are estimates using a sample drawn from a population (i.e. they are statistics like mean and correlation, but more complicated), their standard errors are also reported. A positive value of *b'* implies that there is a positive relation between the *y* and *x* variables (positive slope in graph); a positive *a'* indicates that the regression line has a positive y-intercept, i.e. estimated y is positive when x equals zero. The regression line, by construction, always passes through the (sample) means of *x* and *y* in the dataset. In a multiple regression, the coefficient of a dependent variable captures the effect of a unity change in this variable on the dependent variable, *assuming all other independent variables stay the same* (i.e. the *partial* effect of this independent variable on the dependent variable)

Two concepts – *size* and *significance* – drive the strength of these relationships, as measured by these regression parameters. *Size* captures how large the magnitude of the estimated coefficient is. This obviously depends on the scale (i.e. units) in which the variables are measured, so needs to be viewed in that context. The standard thought experiment questions to assess size are, "How much would y move if x moved by 1 unit? Is that amount meaningful or tiny?"

The other concept, *significance*, looks at the magnitude of the standard error relative to the magnitude of the estimate. As both a' and b' are estimates, their standard error tells the analyst how precise these regression estimates are. A high standard error implies high variability (imprecision) of the estimate, and if the value of the estimate is small, the analyst cannot be confident even if the sign of the relationship is reliable. The *t-statistic*, which is the estimated coefficient value divided by the respective standard error, shows how many standard errors the estimate is away from zero. So, using the standard normal distribution percentiles from earlier, this directly allows the analyst to conclude how probable it is that the true value in the population lies above or below zero, as the case may be (i.e. how likely is it that there is a positive (or inverse) relationship between the dependent and independent variables). The *p-value*, answers a very similar question in probability units (how likely is it that the true sign is opposite to the estimated sign?). High t-statistics (greater than 2) and small p-value imply that the coefficient is likely to be different from zero (i.e. t-stat greater than two (less than minus two) implies that the coefficient is greater (less) than zero with 95% confidence.

> *Example:* Continuing with the example above, although we have not discussed the units of x and y or provided any physical/economic interpretation, based on the regression output, we can say that we'd expect a 1 unit increase in the x variable to imply a 3.09 unit change in y. The standard error of this estimate is 0.17, leading to a t-statistic value of 17.98, which means that the estimate is almost 18 standard errors away from zero. The analyst will have a high degree of confidence in this estimate. Similarly, the intercept is estimated precisely, because the t-statistic is 7.34. As a thumb rule, t-stats above 2 are considered significant, although analysts sometimes accept lower values if the dataset is small, or *there are too few degrees of freedom (df column captures this; the 10:1 ratio is high).*

While the above t-test is useful to check the significance of predictor variables one at a time, a *F-test* (not discussed in this book) can be used to test the joint hypothesis that these coefficients are not all zero. Another important regression diagnostic is the *R-squared* statistics, which (imperfectly) measures how well the regression model "explains" the dataset. The R-squared statistic is the ratio of the *Explained Sum of Squares* (i.e. sum of square of differences between model y and the mean of y) and the *Total Sum of Squares* (i.e. sum of squares of differences between model y and the mean of y). Alternatively, it can be expressed as 1 minus the ratio of Sum of Squared Errors and Total Sum of Squares. The R-squared statistic takes values between 0 and 1; higher R-squared values suggest a better fit. Now, a higher r-squared may suggest a spurious relationship; in fact it is common to see reasonably high R-squared with no significant coefficients. In fact, if we increase the number of independent variables (i.e. multivariate), the r-squared mechanically increases, even if the new variable has no incremental explanatory power. So, analysts often look at the *adjusted r-squared*, which makes an adjustment to the r-squared value for the number of explanatory variables. But, adjusted r-squares can be negative.

> *Example*: In the above example, the r-squared value is 0.98 and the adjusted r-squared is 0.97.

> Beyond this point, interpreting regression results becomes more an art than a science. Data sets are often not as large or as clean as analysts would like. They may contain different regimes. The choice of which variables to include, and exactly how to include them matters (i.e. the model *specification* - should they be squared? Should two variables be multiplied? etc.). The models need to be parsimonious (i.e. estimate few parameters relative to observations). T-statistics are likely to be low for small datasets. Deciding on model specification, acceptable t-statistics and r-squared values given the economic reality are qualitative decisions that the modeler needs to take.

Issues with Regressions

Regression estimates may suffer from some common issues, discussed briefly below. These may or may not be concerns, depending on the context and the exact question we ask of the data. The first issue affects the magnitude of the estimates; the last two affect the standard errors and the significance.

- *Omitted Variable Bias*: The coefficient of an independent variable may be biased (i.e. wrong, even in large samples), if, in a multivariate regression, an independent variable (i.e. x-variable) ends up being correlated with the error term. This ends up happening if the model has omitted a relevant independent variable, but one of the included variables happens to be correlated with the missing variable. In that case, the coefficient of the included variable gets affected by the effect of the missing variable. This is a problem, if we are trying to interpret the coefficient of the independent variable, in terms of size and significance. It can be fixed by considering "instrumental variables" or "proxy" variables, which are correlated with the omitted variable, but not too correlated with the included variables.
- *Multicollinearity*: This problem occurs because the various independent variables may be correlated among themselves, so the coefficients for any one variable are not estimated precisely. There is no

Annexure: Basic Statistics and Data Analysis

bias in estimation. The standard errors are high. It often shows up through high r-squared values, but few (if any) significant variables. This can be fixed by choosing variables judiciously, getting larger volumes of data, demeaning variables, etc.

- *Serial Correlation/ Heteroskedasticity*: Regressions assume the error terms of successive observations to be independently and identically distributed; deviations from that assumption lead to these situations. Two classic examples are serial correlation (error terms are correlated with one-another, e.g. low errors follow each other or vice versa) and heteroscedasticity (the volatility of the distribution for the error term is not same for all observations). One way to fix this is by using modified standard errors (White or Newey-West standard errors); another alternative is to estimate more sophisticated models (e.g. GARCH).

V. Introduction to the Bloomberg Software/ Terminal

The next few pages offer a whirlwind introduction to Bloomberg terminals. It is not meant to be comprehensive, but simply provides the motivated reader some basic perspectives to start using the tool.

BASIC ORIENTATION

The Bloomberg software has been ubiquitous in the financial services front office. In the last few years, it has enhanced its compliance, risk and regulation offerings, and invested in more sophisticated models, thereby covering more divisions of the business. Bloomberg portrays itself as a *one-stop* shop for finance professionals, from real-time news dissemination, economic releases, a data repository that is easy to access and compare, tick-by-tick market monitoring, organizing workflow (setting alerts), communication and messaging, trade execution and order management, portfolio analysis, risk management, modeling and pricing OTC securities, sensitivity analysis and several other tasks. While there are niche service providers for every business line, many finance professionals need to access Bloomberg for some task or another. Beginning to use Bloomberg may be daunting, because of its unusual interface and myriad of functions.

A Bloomberg terminal is *subscription-based*, but many school libraries may have a subscription that students can use. Many finance firms also have shared terminals that employees can use. And some people may have a dedicated terminal too. From a terminal, it is possible to create a username/ password profile, similar to an email service. The sales representative for the terminal often gets involved to verify credentials, so it takes a few hours/ days to get set up. The terminal monitor(s) are identical to regular monitors, but the keyboards are special, with the function keys having special functions. It is also possible to get a sticker sheet/ key from Bloomberg which maps the function keys on a regular keyboard to the special Bloomberg functions, allowing users to use a regular keyboard if for some reason (e.g. remote access) the terminal does not have a Bloomberg keyboard.

Once the user logs in, four Bloomberg panels (windows) launch. They are identical in function, almost like separate instances of a software. This allows the user to perform multiple tasks at the same time. Bloomberg tasks are done interactively, so every click or command results in an output, which can sometimes be expanded further. All instructions are entered either using the mouse (clicking on a word like a website) or typing functions in the command bar at the top of the panel. The autocomplete feature is excellent, so it's almost like using the command bar as a Google search bar, if you don't remember the function.

Broadly, there are two kinds of functions in Bloomberg – some functions need context (e.g. a "security" to be "loaded" i.e. last viewed on the terminal) since the function makes sense only once the context is specified. For example, the *HP (Historical Prices)* function in Bloomberg needs a security (which may be an index, single stock, mutual fund, ETF, bond, etc.). Of course, instead of performing this in two steps (loading the security e.g. *IBM US Equity*) and then typing *HP*, *IBM US Equity HP* typed at the same time will also show historical prices for IBM, as the panel instantly changes. Some functions work for certain security types/ asset classes and not others e.g. *YA* (yield analysis) works only for fixed income securities and not equities (though recently it was adopted for fixed income ETFs). The other type of function doesn't need any context or a security to be loaded e.g. *WEI (World Equity Indices)* provides prices and returns for the world's major indices, with the same output regardless of what was viewed just before that. The output can be interactively changed to show different date ranges, etc. by using various menus, check boxes or drop-down boxes on the panel. So, unlike a webpage, you can actually type instructions to get specific information, and you can also click around to get

Annexure: Introduction to Bloomberg Terminal

other relevant information or to drill down into details. But every small step changes the screen output right away, unlike some software applications where you "submit" a request and wait.

GETTING STARTED

The easiest way to get live help from the terminal is by hitting the *Help (F1)* key twice, which pops up a chat window with a live agent. They can remotely access your terminal and follow your keystrokes and see exactly what you see. In many cases, live help may be unnecessary or inefficient. For those situations, help documentation on a particular function is available by clicking the "?" sign on the top right, near the command line, which directly takes the user to help documentation regarding that particular function.

The *BPS (Bloomberg Professional Service)* function is the most organized way to get started. It has a navigation bar classifying its resources into asset classes, community functions, industry verticals, monitors, infrastructure-related details, etc. each with its own cheat sheets, tutorials, functions, etc. Cheat sheets contain a list of all relevant functions for a certain task, so are very useful. There are several thousand Bloomberg functions, so going through the cheat sheets in the relevant asset class is a starting point to get to know what functions are available. If the function doesn't exactly do what the analyst needs, the help desk may have a work-around. The other place to start is the Menu button, which lists the major markets from where one can drill down.

Most people learn the tool by playing around. The easiest way to try this is by loading a security. To do this, type *<Security Ticker> <Country Code> <Asset Class>*. For example, to load the IBM stock, one would type *IBM US Equity (or F8)*. The autocomplete is very helpful. To load the IBM bond, one would enter *IBM US Corp (or F3)*, which would list all the bonds that IBM has outstanding; the user can pick one. Once the security is loaded, the main menu page has all the commonly listed functions related to that security/ asset class. There are several other functions that are not shown, so it is a good idea to glance through all the cheat sheets for the asset class. There are also function that help compare this security to other "similar" ones, helping relative value discussions.

Another prominent feature of Bloomberg is its Launchpad, which is a set of screens which contain news, market monitors, contact lists for instant messaging communication, etc. These can be highly customized to display exactly what is of interest, by selecting tickers, news keywords, alerts, or uploading client portfolios, etc. The Launchpad is launched with the *BLP* function, stays on as long as the user is logged on, and can be minimized to save screen space. It can have several tabs, potentially containing a lot of information. A good Launchpad can serve as a quick starting point.

FUNCTIONS

There are some functions that do not require a security to be loaded. Many of these are asset class specific. For example, overview functions like *WEI* is for global equities, *BTMM* is for government bonds, *WB* is for global bond market overview, *USSW* is for swaps, *SWPM* models swaps and swaptions, *EQS* helps filter equities with certain criteria, *FSRC* screens for bonds, *FXIP* is the foreign exchange information portal, *OVME* models options on equities and rates, *OVML* models currency and commodity options etc. There are also functions like *BIO* to look for people, and *TOP* for the most popular news stories. *FIRS* is another useful news function, which filters news relevant for different asset classes and also provides a concise summary of overnight market activity in other geographies. *PRTU* helps create custom portfolios, *PORT* is a portfolio management tool, etc. *CIX* allows users to create *custom indices*, by combining other securities that Bloomberg publishes prices for. But many of the functions are related to a specific security, which needs to be loaded first, as explained above.

Capital Markets and Investments

Below, we discuss a few functions for securities across major asset classes. It is futile to cover a lot of ground, because functions are very context specific, the information is readily available and these functions change frequently. So, the discussion below is illustrative and not remotely comprehensive.

Before diving into asset class details, we list some basic security-specific functions that work for securities in all asset classes: *GP* (Graph Prices), *HP* (Historical Prices), *DES* (Description), *QR* (Trade and Quote Recap), *CN* (Company News), *CF* (Company Filing), *TRA* (Total return Analysis, assuming reinvestment of interim cash flows). *HS* helps analyze the spread over time between two similar securities.

- Equities: *FA* is the Financial Analysis screen, which contains balance sheet data, *ERN* has earnings data and projections, *RV* and *EQRV* are relative value tools to compare valuations across competitors, *BRC* lists all the sell-side research, *OMON* launches the options trading on this security, *CN* shows news related to the company, etc. There are functions to monitor quotes, trades, market depth, track company events, and much more. Some functions like *HDS* (Holders), *NAV* (Net Asset Value) and *MEMB* (Constituents) work only for mutual funds, ETFs and Indices, which are also treated similar to equities in the Bloomberg system.
- Government Bonds/ Corporates: The Ticker (obviously) and the asset class (Govt/ Corp) depends on whether it is a government bond or corporate, but functions are largely similar. *YAS* is a useful yield and spread calculator, and can be used for basic sensitivity analysis, by changing value of yield, etc. *FIHZ* is a useful horizon analysis tool, which calculates total estimated return from a fixed income security, considering coupon and reinvestment rate. *FIRV* and *COMB* help compare bonds. *FSRC* helps search bonds.
- Currencies: *FXFA* is a convenient screen to monitor the relation between spot exchange rates, forwards and interest rates. Currencies are primarily traded through forwards, which settle to the spot on the expiry date. The forward curve (i.e. forward price plotted against expiry date), which essentially reflects interest rate differentials between the two countries (follows from no-arbitrage) can also be seen in *FXFR* and *FRD*. *FXFM* shows an estimate of the probability distribution of future exchange rate values.
- Commodities: Commodities are primarily traded on exchanges through futures, which settle to the spot price upon expiration. The term structure of the futures is relevant for future expectations for commodity prices and storage costs, and can be viewed using the *CT* function. While CT shows the current curve, *CCRV* allows the user to plot curves for multiple historical dates.

EXCEL INTEGRATION – FLDS, BDP, BDH, BDS, OVERRIDES, XLTP

An important security level function is FLDS, which lists all the fields that Bloomberg calculates for that security and their current values. Some of these fields (e.g. prices) have history, others do not. The Bloomberg Excel Add-in allows users to download this data from the terminal through Microsoft Excel. While a specific field can be viewed on the terminal by running that exact function, it can be easily pulled into Excel, so fields from different securities and functions can be viewed alongside each other.

Bloomberg has three main functions to extract data – *BDP()*, *BDH()* and *BDS()*. *BDP()* provides the current value, BDH() provides historical data from a specified time range and BDS outputs lists of data, like an array function. While the syntax below uses values, we can reference cells like other Excel formulae.

For BDP, the syntax is *BDP ("<Security Ticker>", "<Field>")*, where Security Ticker identifies the security and field is the field (from the long list in FLDS) that we want the data for. For example, for IBM's price, we would enter *BDP("IBM US EQUITY","PX_LAST")*.

BDH gives us historical data, so we should make sure that the relevant field has historical data saved in Bloomberg, which a flag on the FLDS page next to the field indicates. So, to get historical data, we would

Annexure: Introduction to Bloomberg Terminal

enter *BDH("IBM US EQUITY", "PX_LAST", "20151231", "20160430")*, to get daily data from December 31, 2015 to April 30, 2016. There are other optional arguments in *BDH* that allow the user to get data at different frequencies, suppress dates, etc. Some data fields have default parameters inbuilt (e.g. *EQY_BETA* is relative to a benchmark); an advanced user can override the benchmark that the data field normally uses and customize it.

BDS outputs a list of data. The syntax of the function doesn't change; it's the field that has the list embedded. For example, *BDS("IBM US EQUITY","INSIDER_HOLDING")* provides insider holding data from Form 4.

Another excellent resource within Bloomberg is *XLTP*, an overall (non-security specific) function, which takes users to a library of spreadsheets built in Excel, with clever implementation of these functions and graphs to provide useful information and analysis. Users can download these sheets, and customize them to analyze ideas, refine models or get more insight into relative valuation.

Bloomberg is currently launching the BQUANT environment, which will unify these quantitative functions into a common framework.

Index

1

1-by-2 put/ call spread, 241

A

Accrued Interest, 101
Activism, 175
Agency Bonds, 32
Agency brokerage, 37
Agency Theory, 23
Allocator, 50
Alpha, 69, 73, 206
Alternative Investments, 54
Alternative Trading Systems (ATS), 44
American option, 217, 234
Arbitrage Pricing Theory, 208
Asset Allocation, 73
Asset Backed Securities (ABS), 167
Asset class, 30
Asset manager, 50
Asset-Liability Mismatch (ALM), 114
Asymmetric Information, 23

B

Backward induction - Option, 232
Backwardation, 242
Balance Sheet
    Current Assets/ Liabilities, Owners' Equity, Fixed Assets, Accumulated Depreciation, Book Value, 250
Bearish/ Bullish, 20
Behavioral Finance, 24
Benchmark indices, 65
Beta, 69, 73, 206
Bid price, 37
Bid-Cover Ratio, 94
Bids wanted in competition (BWIC), 46
Binomial Distribution, 281
Binomial Model, 226
Bitcoin, 85
Black Scholes Model, 235
Black-Litterman Model, 214
Blockchaining, 84
Bloomberg terminal, 287
Bonds, 27, 90
Bootstrapping, 100
Bottom-up investment, 52
Breakeven - Inflation, 129

Business Cycle, 121
Buyer's curse, 94
Buy-side, 17, 50

C

Calendar Spread, 223
Call option, 217
Call Spread, 223
Capital Allocation Line (CAL), 199
Capital Asset Pricing Model (CAPM), 203
Capital Introductions Group, 40
Capital Market Line (CML), 202
Capital Markets Division, 37
Capital Structure, 26, 173, 251
Carry Trades, 125
Cash Flow Statement
    Cash Flow from Operations, Investments, Financing, 253
Central Bank, 77, 120
Central Tendency
    Mean, Median, Mode, 276
Clean Price, 101
Clearing, 37
Clearing and settlement, 40
Clearing house, 40
Closed-end fund, 53
Collar, 221
Collateralized Loan Obligations (CLO), 168
Collateralized Mortgage Obligations (CMO), 165
Commercial bank, 36
Commercial Mortgage Backed Securities (CMBS), 167
Commingled fund, 56
Commodities, 34
Company Filings
    10Q, 10K, 8K, 250
Compliance Division, 42
Consultants, 50, 60
Contango, 242
Conversion Factor, 127
Convertible Bond Arbitrage, 159
Convertible bonds, 28
Corporate bonds, 32
Corporate Credit
    Analytics, 156
    Bankruptcy, 148
    Bonds, 151
    Capital Structure, 146
    Credit Default Swaps, 154
    Default Risk, 148

Index

    Electronic Trading, 156
    Fundamental Analysis, 149
    Liquidity, 155
    Loans, 152
    Quantitative Models, 158
    Recovery Rate, 148
Corporate Governance, 175
Corporate treasury departments, 59
Covariance, 283
Covered call, 222
Credit Default Swaps (CDS), 154
Credit Rating Agencies, 149
Cross Sectional Data, 275
Crowdfunding, 84
Cryptocurrencies, 85
Currencies, 34, 268
Current Yield, 107
CUSIP, 27
Custody, 41

D

Dark pool, 44, 190
Data Analysis Tools, 275
Day Count Convention, 95, 102
Delivery Option
    Cheapest To Deliver (CTD), 127
Delta - Option, 230
Derivatives, 28
Desk strategist, 38
Dirty Price, 101
Discount Factor, 100
Discount Rate, 98, 175
Discounted Cash Flow
    DCF, 176
Disintermediation, 16
Dispersion, 277
Diversification, 195
Dividend Discount Model, 177
Duration, 110
Duration-based Hedging, 118
DV01, 111

E

Economic data, 121
Efficient Market Hypothesis, 22
Electronic Communications Network (ECN), 44
Emerging Markets, 35, 121
Empirical Distribution, 279
Endowments, 58
Enterprise Value, 172
Environment, Social and Governance (ESG), 76
Equities, 27, 172
Equity Multiples
    P/E, EV/EBITDA, 179
Eurodollar Futures, 131
European option, 217
Excess return, 72
Exchange Traded Funds (ETF), 54, 134
Exchange traded market, 43
Exotic option
    Digital, Barrier, Contingent, Bermudian, Asian, 224
Expectations Hypothesis, 123
Expected Return on Equity, 175
Expected Shortfall, 70, 213
Expiration Date, 29

F

Factor covariance matrix, 211
Factor Mimicking Portfolio, 209
Factor model
    factor structure, factor exposure, factor loading, factor sensitivity, factor returns, 208
Fama-French Model, 209
Family office, 58
Fed Funds, 120
Fiduciary standard, 58
Financial Statement Footnotes
    Earnings Quality, 254
Financial Statements, 250
FinTech, 80
Fisher Equation, 122
Fixed Income, 31
Flattener, 125
Flight to Quality, 125
fly trade - option, 241
Forward curve
    Forward Rate Agreement (FRA), 103
Forward rate, 127
Forwards, 29
Foundations, 58
Frequency Distribution, 276
Fund of funds, 59
Fundamental Investing, 52, 181
Futures, 29, 127

G

Gaussian Distribution, 279
General Collateral (GC), 96
Geometric Brownian Motion, 235
Gordon Growth Formula
    Dividend Discount Model with Growth, 178
Government Bonds, 31
Graham-Dodd Valuation, 177
Greeks – options
    Delta, Gamma (Convexity), Vega, Theta, 237
Gross Basis, 128

Capital Markets and Investments

Guidelines, 51

H

Haircut, 96
Hedge funds, 55
Heteroskedasticity, 286
High Frequency Trading, 57, 97, 190
Hybrid instruments, 28

I

IEX, 191
Immunization, 115, 116
Implied volatility, 238
Income Statement
    Cost of Goods Sold, SG&A, EBITDA, Depreciation, Interest Expense, Net Income, 252
Index, 63
Index Rebalancing, 64
Index Rules, 63, 67
Index swaps, 57
Index Value
    Total Return Index Value, 66
Indifference Curve, 194
Inflation, 122, 129
Information Technology Division, 42
Insurance companies, 59
Inter dealer broker, 38, 97
Interest Rate Risk, 109
Interest Rate Swaps, 31, 131
Internal Rate of Return (IRR), 92
Investment bank, 36
Investment Banking Division, 36
ISIN, 27

J

Jump Process – Option pricing, 240

K

Key-Rate Duration, 116
Kurtosis, 281

L

Leverage, 41, 125, 173
LIBOR, 130
Limited liability, 27
Limits to Arbitrage, 23
Liquid alts, 56
Liquidity, 97
Lit market, 44
Long, 20
Long-only fund, 20, 53
Long-short fund, 53

M

Macaulay Duration, 111
Macro Investing, 182
maker/taker model, 45
Margin investment, 41
Market maker, 37
Market microstructure, 43, 75, 97, 189
Market portfolio, 201
Marketplace Lending, 84
Mean-Variance Efficient (MVE) Portfolio, 200
Mean-Variance Efficient Frontier, 200
Mean-variance Optimization, 198
MiFID II, 79
Minimum variance portfolio, 196
Model Robustness, 183
Modified Duration, 111
Modigliani-Miller, 174
Mortgages, 32
    MBS, 139
    OAS, 143
    Prepayment Risk, 140
    TBA, 141
Multicollinearity, 286
Multilateral Trading Facility (MTF), 189
Municipal bonds, 32
Municipal Bonds, 144
Mutual fund, 53

N

NBBO, 189
Net Basis, 128
Net Present Value (NPV), 92
No-Arbitrage, 20
Nominal interest rates, 122
Normal Distribution, 278

O

Offer price, 37
Off-The-Run, 95
Omitted Variable Bias, 286
On-the-Run, 95
Open Interest, 128
Open-end fund, 53
Option
    Strike, Underlying, Expiration, Writer, Premium, Exercise, In/Out-of-the-money, Moneyness, Intrinsic Value, Time Value, Multiplier, 217
Options, 29
Order management system (OMS), 45
Outsourced CIO (OCIO), 61
Overconfidence, 24
Over-the-counter (OTC), 45

Index

P

Paid-in Kind (PIK), 90
Partial Duration, 116
Passive management, 52
Pension plans, 58
Pension Plans
    Funding Status, 115
Performance Attribution, 73
    Brinson-Fachler, 73
Performance Evaluation, 71
Physical Settlement, 127
Poisson Distribution, 281
Preferred Habitat Theory, 122
Preferred stock, 28
Price-Yield Relation, 106
Primary Dealer, 97
Primary market, 17
Prime Brokerage, 40
Principal-Agent Problem, 24
private equity, 55
Private Wealth Management, 57
Probability
    Distribution, Density, Cumulative Distribution, 278
Proprietary trading, 38, 60
Protective Put, 222
Pull-to-par, 103
Put option, 217
Put Spread, 223
Put-Call Parity, 223

Q

Quantitative Easing, 121
Quantitative Investing, 51, 83, 182

R

Rating Agencies, 17
Rational Expectations, 123
Real interest rates, 122
Realized volatility, 238
Registered Investment Advisor (RIA), 58
Regression, 209, 283
Reinvestment Risk, 108
Replicating Portfolio - Option, 227
Repo, 95
Residual value, 28
Returns
    Total, Price, Annualized, Holding Period, Simple, Compounded, Log, 245
Reverse Repo, 96
Risk factor, 69
Risk management - Equity, 211
Risk management – sell side, 40
Risk model, 69
Risk Neutrality
    Probability, Pricing, 231
Risk Parity, 215
Risk Premium, 197
Risk Reversal, 221
Risk-adjusted returns, 21
Robo-Advisor, 51, 57, 84
Rolldown, 104

S

Sales & Trading, 37
Scenario Analysis, 71, 211
Secondary market, 18
Securities lending, 20, 41
Securitization, 161
    ABS, 167
    CDX, CDO, 169
    CLO, 168
    CMBS/ CMBX, 167
    CMO, 164
    Risk Retention, 170
Securitized Products, 33
Security Market Line, 205
Security Selection, 73
Sell-side, 17
Separately Managed Account, 56
Sequential pay, 33
Serial Correlation, 286
Settlement
    Physical and Cash, 29
Settlement date, 47
Sharpe Ratio, 72, 191, 198, 201, 203
Short, 20, 41
SIP, 189
Skew - option, 241
Skewness, 281
Smart-beta, 51, 69
Socially Responsible Investing (SRI), 76
Spot Rate, 100
Standard Deviation, 277
Standard Error, 280
Standard Normal Distribution, 279
Statistics, 275
Steepener, 126
Stochastic Volatility – Option pricing, 240
Stock Replacement, 221
Stocks, 27
Stop-out Yield, 94
Straddle, 222
Strangle, 222
Strategy Index
    Custom Index, 65
Stratified Sampling, 65

Stress Tests, 78
STRIPS, 99
Structured credit, 33
Structuring, 39
Style drift, 50
Swaps, 29
Swaptions, 31, 135, 219, 288
Synthetic Credit Indices (CDX), 169

T

Tax shield of Debt, 174
T-Bills, 95
TED Spreads, 131
Term Structure of Interest Rates, 98, 123
Term structure of option volatility, 241
TEV
    Tracking Error Volatility, 65, 73
Time Series Data, 275
Time Value of Money, 19
TIPS, 129
Top-down investment, 52
Total Return Swaps (TRS), 66
Trade date, 47
Tranche, 33
Treasuries, 31
Treasury Auction, 94
Treasury Bonds, 89
Trinomial model, 233
Two-fund separation, 65, 201, 209

U

Underlying, 28
Utility Function, 194

V

Value Investing, 183
Vanilla option, 224
VaR, 70, 211, 212
Variance swap, 242
venture capital, 55
VIX
    VIX futures, Options on VIX futures, 242
Volatility, 277
Vol-of-vol, 242

W

Weighted Average Cost of Capital (WACC), 176
When-issued market, 94

Y

Yale Model, 59
Yield Curve, 98
Yield to Maturity (YTM), 93

Z

Zero Coupon Bonds, 99
Zero Interest Rate, 77
Zero Interest Rate Policy (ZIRP), 77, 121

Made in United States
North Haven, CT
07 January 2024